CW01206733

PRAISE FOR NATURE BOY

'Seán's passion for the natural world spills over on every page of this fantastic book. A stunning testament to the wonders of nature'
Pádraic Fogarty

'With disarming honesty, eloquence and humour, Seán Ronayne recounts how he took possession of a childhood taunt and made it his adult mission. Whether it's the humble magpie in your back garden, the poignant song of the last male ring ouzel in Ireland, or a close call with a gravity-challenged rhino in Nepal, his stories will reinvigorate a love of nature, at home and much further afield'
Magnus Robb

'Seeing the world through Seán's eyes is like getting a big, delightful hug. Informative, inspiring and insightful, this book is a heartfelt and enthralling personal journey of a life ensconced in nature'
Anja Murray

'Through Seán's beautifully sincere exploration of how nature has so deeply shaped and defined his life and has given him solace and refuge during challenging times, he brings home just how vital the natural world is to all of us, whether we know it or not, as well as how tragically divorced so many of us have become from it ... Please read this book, now!'
Niall Hatch, BirdWatch Ireland

'A gorgeously personal and deeply moving account of living a life fully immersed in the fantastic wonderland that is nature. This book opens a door to the alternate, enchanting universe that still surrounds us, but is being erased fast. Sublime'
Eoghan Daltun

'Seán is a man who reveals wonder from within the ordinary. Trapped in a Barcelona apartment during lockdown, he chose to look up to the skies, and through a microphone and curious mind revealed a nightly treasure of passing migrant birds that had been invisible to the rest of the city'
Ken O'Sullivan

Seán Ronayne is a Cork-born ornithologist and naturalist who has spent his life immersed in nature. Following a childhood spent exploring the fields and woods of his hometown, Seán went on to study zoology at University College Cork (UCC), as well as a master's in marine biology, also at UCC. After graduating, he worked at a seabird sanctuary in the UK, and then returned to Ireland to enroll in a master's in ecological impact assessment, specialising in ornithology.

He secured his first professional ornithologist job in 2017, and in 2018 he moved to Barcelona with his partner Alba, a Catalan native, where he began recording birds and wildlife in earnest. Following their return to Ireland in 2020, he embarked on his project to sound-record all of Ireland's regularly occurring birds, taking him all over the country in search of rare and elusive species, some of which were on the cusp of extinction. He has now just three species left to record, out of almost 200, and has amassed a collection of over 12,000 recordings of Irish birds and other wildlife.

In spring 2024, *Birdsong*, a documentary about Seán's recording project, was released to great acclaim. *Birdsong* is directed by Kathleen Harris and produced by Ross Whitaker and Aideen O'Sullivan for True Films.

Wild Silence, an album of Irish wild soundscapes, recorded by Seán in a variety of habitats, is available at https://irishwildlifesounds.bandcamp.com/album/wild-silence

Seán lives near Cobh, County Cork, with Alba and their dog Toby. *Nature Boy* is his first book.

https://soundcloud.com/irishwildlifesounds

NATURE BOY

SEÁN RONAYNE

A JOURNEY OF BIRDSONG & BELONGING

HACHETTE
BOOKS
IRELAND

Copyright © 2024 Seán Ronayne

The right of Seán Ronayne to be identified as the author of the work has been asserted by him in accordance with the Copyright, Designs and Patents Act 1988.

First published in Ireland in 2024 by HACHETTE BOOKS IRELAND

1

All rights reserved. No part of this publication may be reproduced, stored in a retrieval system, or transmitted, in any form or by any means without the prior written permission of the publisher, nor be otherwise circulated in any form of binding or cover other than that in which it is published and without a similar condition being imposed on the subsequent purchaser.

A CIP catalogue record for this title is available from the British Library.

ISBN 9781399738156

Typeset in Epigraph by Bookends Publishing Services, Dublin
Printed and bound in Great Britain by Clays Ltd, Elcograf S.p.A.

Hachette Books Ireland policy is to use papers that are natural, renewable and recyclable products and made from wood grown in sustainable forests. The logging and manufacturing processes are expected to conform to the environmental regulations of the country of origin.

Hachette Books Ireland
8 Castlecourt Centre
Castleknock
Dublin 15, Ireland

A division of Hachette UK Ltd
Carmelite House, 50 Victoria Embankment, London EC4Y 0DZ

www.hachettebooksireland.ie

Contents

Prologue ix

Chapter 1 1

Chapter 2 25

Chapter 3 59

Chapter 4 89

Chapter 5 125

Chapter 6 153

Chapter 7 177

Chapter 8 205

Chapter 9 253

Chapter 10 277

Chapter 11 295

Chapter 12 327

Conclusion 373

Endnotes	381
Appendix	383
Resources	386
Irish Bird Sounds	388
Acknowledgments	404
Index	409

To Laia.

I've loved you from the day you were little more than a seed in your mother's womb. News of your arrival was the best thing that's ever happened to us. Know that you owe me nothing in life, but I do have just one wish. All that I ask from you is that, one day, you fly the flag for nature and love it as it so deserves. To stand up for it and give it the voice that it needs. This book is for you, my little one. You bring us both untold hope and happiness and we are counting down the days to meet you.

Ens veiem aviat petita meva.

The illustrations within this book are by Robert Vaughan
www.robertvaughanillustrations.com

Prologue

IT WAS SEPTEMBER 2019 AND I HAD BEEN LIVING IN CATALUNYA for over a year, having moved there from Ireland the previous summer. I rummaged in the kitchen of the apartment in Barcelona that I shared with my partner, Alba, banging pots and pans, opening and closing cupboard doors, until I emerged with the new tools of my trade.

I had just come home from an interesting talk by Magnus Robb, the wildlife sound-recordist and composer, at the Ebro Delta Birding Festival. His scheduled talk about the autonomous capturing of birds calling in the dark of night as they pass overhead on their nocturnal migrations had captivated my imagination. Magnus had described in almost mystical detail how he captured the sounds of masses of incredible birds in the dead of night, passing over his home in Portugal, while he himself slept soundly in his bed. He described documenting habitat-specific birds – birds he'd never expect to encounter in the region by day, which were flying and vocalising at close range at all hours of the night. The concept that it was possible to encounter any bird from any place or habitat blew my mind.

And so a few days later, with my second-hand Olympus LS-12 sound-recorder that I had purchased on eBay in one hand, and in the other a Pyrex measuring jug, I went out to the balcony, placed the recorder inside the jug, hit record, and sealed the jug with some cling film stretched over the top. This recorder can run for up to 48 hours, and the cling film would protect it in the rare event of any wind and rain that might occur in sunny Catalunya. I'd been using my Olympus recorder to capture the sounds of the new and unknown species I was encountering since purchasing it in May 2018, but until now I had only been using it handheld.

The balcony itself was not a place I ever spent time as it was quite claustrophobic. It looked out to a series of high-rise flats across the narrow street – above us was the bottom of the balcony above, and to the left and right were solid brick walls. You could only see a sliver of sky, and it all felt very urban. I tended not to open the doors or windows, not only for the mosquitoes, but for the noise, too. It was a never-ending cacophony of sirens, ratcheting air-con units and shouting that seeped its way into the apartment. Upstairs, the footsteps of my neighbours sounded like those of elephants. Next door, the repetitive bass of my neighbour's reggaeton rattled through my head. In bed, I wore earplugs to sleep. But even that usually wasn't enough to drown out the wall of anthropogenic noise that dominated the soundscape and forced its way into my brain, unannounced and unwelcome.

I was never an indoors person; I always longed to be out there. My mother recalls me constantly digging in the dirt in our back garden in Cobh, County Cork, taking in 'creepy crawlies' to show to her in overzealous delight. My clothes would wear out from evenings spent climbing trees and wading through brambles. I was a wild child, and I never changed.

While I loved living in Catalunya, the chaotic aural environments of Barcelona's streets were a riot for my brain. The groans of engines, the startling beeping horns, the sea of voices. They all collided into a sonic overload that raged in my head like forgotten pocket keys bashing and clanging around in a washing machine. To take my swollen, throbbing mind elsewhere, I'd often look up as I walked about during the day, between teaching English classes. Later on, on my days off from bird surveying, I'd wonder what passes over this chaotic spot in the comparative calm of the night. Now my new project was to intercept the nocturnal calls of birds as they migrated south to spend their winters in Africa, passing right over our small balcony as we slept soundly. At the time, I did not see this little boxed-in space as a place to encounter the wonders of nature. Oh, how that would change.

The morning after Magnus' talk, having set out my recorder for the night, I jumped out of the bed and ran out to retrieve it from the balcony. I felt like a kid at Christmas, awakening to see what presents had been delivered during the night. The recorder was still running – great! The next step was to begin the analysis.

Each bird species has a unique shape or series of shapes that represent their calls. I downloaded sound-editing software called Audacity onto my laptop and taught myself how to identify the shapes of bird calls by looking at spectrograms. So, instead of sitting and listening to ten hours of audio – an impossible task – I scanned the sounds visually, which is a much more time-efficient process. At first every shape was new to me – I was stopping to play barking dogs, beeping horns, slamming doors, motorised window shutters, and all other manner of unwanted noise – sonic bycatch, if you will.

After I had sifted through a few hours' worth of recordings, I began to develop a familiarity with the visuals of these unwanted sounds, and so I skimmed past them. I learned to know what to avoid, what not to waste my time on. Up until that point, I'd only ever encountered a handful of species from our balcony: feral pigeons, non-native monk parakeets – escaped pets that have formed a self-sustaining raucous population throughout the urban landscape of Catalunya – and yellow-legged gulls, the Mediterranean equivalent of our own herring gull.

Then a new shape appeared on my laptop screen – it looked somewhat like the shape of a small barking dog, but different. I played it. I'd never heard a call like it. It was quite a dog-like explosive 'kwark'! This was the moment I began to look at the world around me in a very different way. No urban streetscape would ever look the same to me again.

At 4 a.m. on 22 September 2019, I had logged over 40 calls from at least two black-crowned night herons as they navigated over the urban sprawl of El Prat de Llobregat on their migratory journey south to spend the winter in the wetlands of tropical West and Central Africa, before their northward return to Europe in the spring. I screamed the news to Alba. My obsessions with topics run deep and I'm relentless in chasing details. Alba knew I needed to take things to the limit, so when I had these exciting moments of discovery, at least to me, she'd be the first person I'd tell.

From this moment on, I recorded every single night of the year.

I upgraded my equipment and bought a Dodotronic parabolic reflector – parabola for short. Parabolas look like little satellite dishes and are the audio equivalent of a photographer's zoom lens. This enabled me to reach further up into the night sky, and thus it brought the 'voices' of even more nocturnal migrants to my attention.

So many out-of-context species flew directly over our flat, right in the heart of the city – from the high-pitched, guttural-cronking calls of groups of flamingoes, breaking through the sirens and barking dogs, and far removed from their typical shallow, saltwater foraging habitats to the sweet fluttering 'prrioop' calls from flocks of European bee-eaters so great in number that their sounds took up to eight minutes to pass over my microphones, as they shared the skies with echolocating bats. European bee-eaters are typically thought of as a diurnal species, migrating by day, stopping occasionally to feed on their favourite prey item of, you guessed it, bees! But here they were, flying in great numbers down the Catalan coast in active migratory flight in the dead of night.

For as long as I can remember, my mind has been swirling with the vocalisations of birds, and now I was able to look at their visual representation using the editing software. I could see the sound via spectrogram analysis. This was a game-changer for me, and I began to hear and interpret bird sound in a different way. Intricate details – subtle calls, dialects and mimicry – that I had previously missed were now slapping me in the face.

At first, I was the only one recording in Catalunya in this manner. I'd send on sounds to a few Catalan friends, and I think they really surprised them. These friends began to forward the results and it triggered several others to start dabbling in this strange method, too.

Several of us had been inspired by Magnus Robb's talk, and seeing my initial successes, we set up a WhatsApp group by the name of 'Nocmig Catalunya'. 'Nocmig' is the designated term for the study of nocturnal migration of birds.

At this point in my life, I had qualified with a master's in ecological impact assessment from University College Cork in Ireland, and secured a job doing ornithological surveys on potential wind-farm sites back in my home country, but I had left all of that behind to move with Alba to her hometown of El Prat de Llobregat. I hadn't been able to secure a job working in ornithology in Catalunya – the fact that my Spanish was poor and my Catalan worse being the main barriers – so it was great to have this connection to a group of fellow birders with whom I could talk shop while finding my feet in a new country. I'd been teaching English for some time, but it wasn't for me. I was longing to fall back to my true calling – a career in ornithology.

This group became a hub of excitement and discovery as, each morning, we all reported the bizarre and unexpected birds that had revealed themselves over our roofs the previous night. Soon, distinct and undeniable patterns began to emerge: those who lived in well-lit, built-up areas or those in geographical bottlenecks – narrow physical passes – scored the most birds, but sometimes in an incomparable manner. And, after some research, we soon discovered why. Birds are attracted down to the artificial light of our city spaces that can disorientate them and cause them to call to one another in a state of confusion. In extreme cases, as can be seen in the US, birds can collide with towering skyscrapers that thoughtlessly fail to turn off their aesthetic, non-essential lights after hours, sometimes resulting in tens or even hundreds of casualties a night during peak bird-migration periods. Thus, those of us in the group who lived in Barcelona often registered a far higher number of birds than those who recorded in more rural, less artificially lit areas.

I recorded every night without fail until the unexpected happened. In March 2020, Covid arrived and turned the world upside down. To find myself locked in the confines of a one-bedroom apartment surrounded by concrete was a devastating blow.

Nature has been the one true constant in my life from the very beginning. From when I was soaking it all up as a babbling toddler in a pram, all the way through my teens and into adulthood, my world revolved around it and it supported me like another parent. Even in the darkest of moments, nature was there to hold me up and help me limp through.

And so, even when I couldn't leave my shoebox apartment under Barcelona's strict lockdown rules, when I couldn't find a way to nature, it found its way to me – through the fascinating and unexpected nocturnal bird calls I captured from my balcony every night.

The one thing that's been a constant, which had already given me so much, took on a new dimension. It enabled my mind to escape the concrete prison of our flat and to float out there with nature, like it always had, but it also led me to pursue a project around a topic that would change my life in countless ways – sound-recording and sharing the sounds of our wonderful birds with the world.

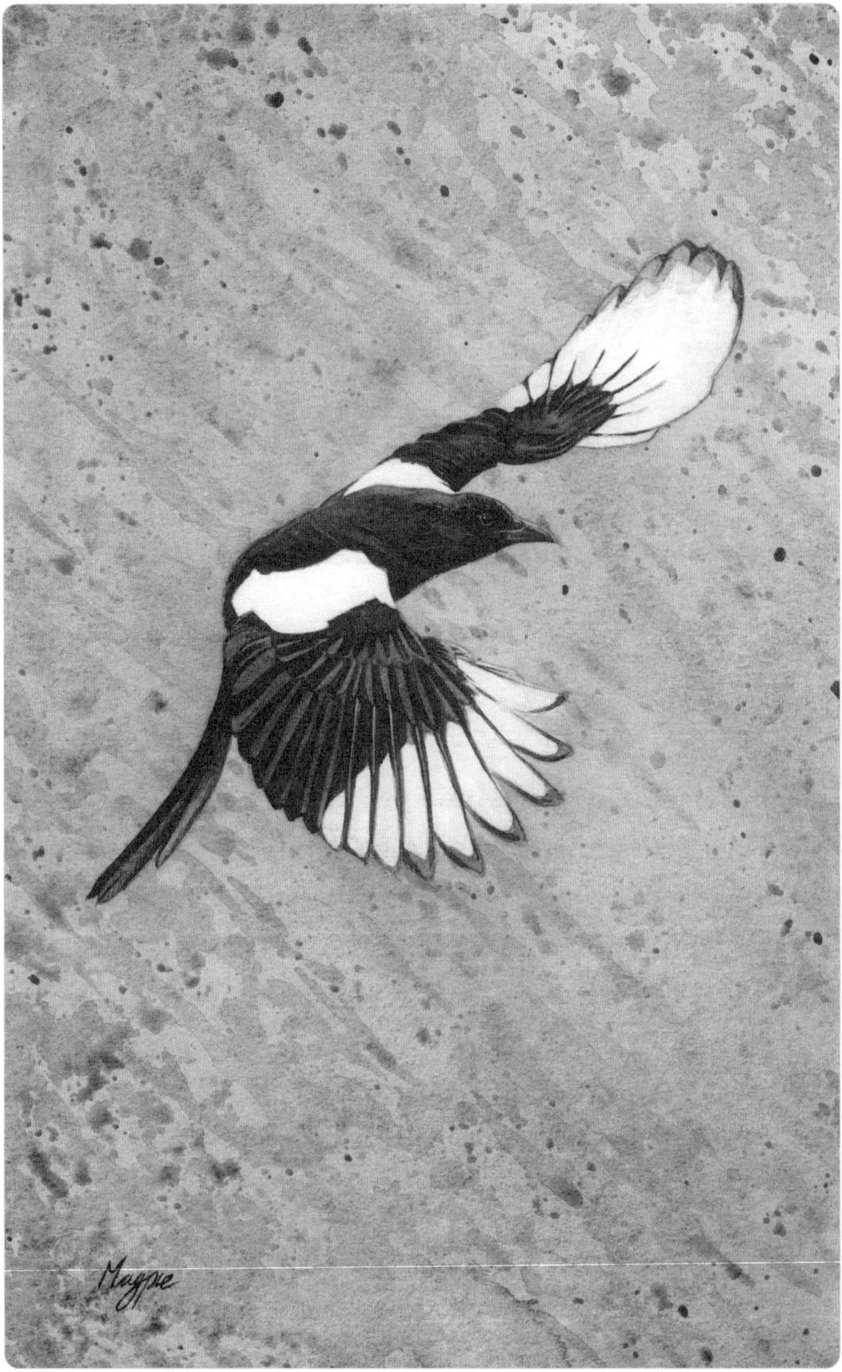
Magpie

Chapter 1

I REMEMBER IT LIKE IT WAS YESTERDAY. MY FATHER TERRY AND Granny Betty were in the front seats, I was sitting in the back with my grandfather, Pops. I'm not sure why we called him Pops – I think it's an American term, but it's what stuck, one way or another. Maybe it's because it was an easy word to roll off my tongue, with me being just a little bruiser. Every Sunday, we would go for a spin around Great Island in my parents' beige Ford Escort. Great Island is the largest of several islands nestled in the safety of Cork Harbour, including Tota Island, which houses a wildlife park, and Spike Island, a former prison island known as 'Ireland's Alcatraz'. Cork Harbour is one of the largest natural harbours in the world, some say second only to Sydney, and has been a working port and a strategic defensive location on the south coast of Ireland for hundreds of years.

We all lived in Cobh, the largest town on Great Island and just a 30-minute drive from Cork city, connected to the mainland by a bridge, a ferry and a railway line. Cobh was the last port of call for the RMS *Titanic* before she set out across the Atlantic on her doomed maiden voyage, and the town has a strong naval history. My father worked most of his life as a mechanic for the Irish navy, making sure the boats were ready to go out on fisheries and drugs patrol. But, to me, it was just home. Our house was nestled at the top of a steep hill, as are many houses in Cobh. It was a detached home with a front garden, backed up against several mature trees, and overlooking Cork Harbour. Here I lived with my mam, my dad and my younger brother, Conor. It was even higher than my grandparents' house, a kilometre away near the seafront in Cobh – the house where my dad grew up. Pops and Granny Betty didn't drive and this spin around Great Island was a weekly treat for them. A break from the monotony of town life, and a chance for us all to soak up some nature. I loved it too, of course. In fact, there was nowhere I loved more.

One balmy summer afternoon, after we'd all just finished our Sunday lunch, we chose the island's coastal route for our weekend pilgrimage. This was our favourite route, as the others passed through agricultural lands and were much less nature-filled. I specifically remember rounding a sharp bend, trees in full leaf arching in a canopy over the roadway. The midsummer sun fractured through the deciduous foliage and threw a wonderful display of green hues interspersed with beams of golden light onto the roadway in front of us. As we cruised along, windows ajar, allowing the fresh summer breeze to flow through the car, Pops threw his eye up to the canopy above. A glint of excitement took over his demeanour. He turned to me and asked: 'Have you ever seen a magpie, Seán?'

'No,' I replied. 'What's a magpie?'

My response made him smile even more.

At the time, this pile-on of excitement was insignificant in its meaning to me, but I understand it now. Pops spent his whole life in Cobh. He worked as an operator for Irish Steel during the week, but on weekends he loved nothing more than taking long walks through the woods and fields in the more rural parts of the Island. I feel such a sense of pride and love for Pops. He was a good man, who sought out the beauty in the world and saw the creatures we share this planet with for what they are – our brilliant, wondrous comrades in life. Not conveniences, pests or things we should control or be wary of. Just brothers and sisters eking out a successful existence on this planet, with their own challenges and burdens to bear, and peaks to climb. Their own families to raise, and their own happiness to seek. Pops was a simple man who didn't ask for much in life and appreciated just being, and all of this rubbed off on my father, too. Both my dad and Pops loved nature and sought it out in all its glory. I think it was a chance for them to bond doing what they loved, where they felt most at home.

Dad told me about how himself and Pops would bring back injured animals to the house when he was a kid. The two of them would do everything they could to nurse them back to health and, eventually, release them back to nature. They were always out there when my dad was younger, but when he grew up and had a family of his own, these weekend outings were their chance to get back out into nature together. Although Granny Betty didn't directly seek out nature, she appreciated it. She loved getting out there and would always look forward to those trips.

Dad stopped the car at the side of the road and we stepped out as quietly as possible, not wanting to startle the prize that sat in the branches above. This was my first lesson in fieldcraft: we spoke in hushed tones and crept around the side of the car, hardly daring to move, slowly inching into position with crouched gaits. I copied Pops and Dad. Granny sat still and watched from inside with Mam. Pops' eyes were transfixed on the treetops as he pointed up. 'Do you see it?'

My eyes shifted from watching my foot placement in the green shade of the towering trees, fearful of stepping on a twig, to scanning the leafy behemoths that loomed above my little self. My neck hung back, my mouth open as if catching flies. My eyes flickered from left to right, and then across to Pops and Dad. Pops looked at me with eyes wide open, smiling and nodding his head in a beckoning manner. I looked back again and saw some movement further up in the tallest tree. I didn't really know what I was looking for, but then I saw it ... I just knew that this was the magpie! I'd never seen such a regal-looking bird before.

It sat there at the top of a large ash tree, visible through a gap in the dense green crowns of sycamores, hawthorns and other ashes. Pops explained to me that the magpie is a member of the crow family, but that it didn't look like a crow. And he was right – it was beautiful: its striking black and white colour with long tail gave it an exotic look. It was unlike anything I had ever seen in my short life. But then it got even better: it moved position, hopping to another branch, where it was even more exposed to one of the rays of sunlight breaking through the canopy. Now all of the black feathers began to shimmer with greens and purples, almost like magic. 'Wowwww!' I giggled with surprise and looked up at Pops. I was hypnotised by the raw beauty of this bird. I stood there with my jaw agape, reminding myself to breathe at times. Then, the magpie turned its head and began to call – presumably in response to another magpie, somewhere out of sight. It was a new sound to me and one that struck me. I could see its beak open and close as it gave this loud crackling series of calls – almost like a series of exploding bangers. It certainly wasn't shy in making itself heard. Pops and Dad admired the bird, too, but they were more taken by something else. They were in awe at my wonderment, for in that moment they both knew the family tradition of a love for nature had been firmly passed on to another generation.

Magpies have an unfair reputation in Ireland and many other countries. I have heard them referred to as an alien or non-native species. Invasive alien species are those species that are not only *introduced* by humans to an area outside of their natural range but that then go on to spread and thrive to the point that they begin to have negative impacts on native flora, fauna, habitats, economy and more.

Despite an unfounded belief among some that ruthlessly killing birds with rifles or inhumanely trapping them will benefit them financially, this is certainly not true of the magpie. Although there is no smoke without fire. It is believed that magpies are somewhat recent colonists to Ireland, with the first flock said to have crossed the Irish Sea in 1676, leaving from Wales and arriving in Wexford.[1] To refer to these birds as alien or non-native reveals a misunderstanding of the terms. In the case of birds that extend their range as a result of population expansion, for example, we can refer to them as natural pioneers or colonists. This could be considered especially true of birds that make the crossing to the nearest neighbouring land mass, as was the case here in Ireland with magpies. Birds can willingly extend their range for a number of reasons, including in response to large-scale habitat destruction, habitat restoration, climate change or simply as a result of seeking out new resources because of population growth/saturation in a given region. Whilst you could argue that the first two points, or even the third, refer to human-made scenarios, these scenarios still push the birds to make a decision of their own volition. They are not physically relocated by humans.

In recent years, there have been a number of such colonisation events. The most famous of these was the arrival of great spotted woodpeckers to Irish shores, where today the unmistakable, explosive tree-drumming display can be heard throughout the country. The first birds began to appear in 2007 and 2008, as stragglers along the east coast, and as singles on Cape Clear Island in Cork and Great Saltee Island in County Wexford. At the time it was widely thought that these birds were coming from the UK, which was later proven through DNA analysis of feathers.

There are just eight bird species listed as invasive to Ireland: red-vented bulbul, Indian house crow, ruddy duck, Canada goose, Egyptian goose, sacred ibis, common myna and rose-ringed parakeet.[2] All of those listed occur in Europe (some have not made it to Ireland but are flagged because of the possibility) through human introduction, mostly in the last century, and all species have a track record of having notable negative impacts when introduced outside of their natural ranges – and magpie is not one of them.

It is also thought that magpies have no natural predators in Ireland. But of course they do: foxes, pine martens, buzzards, sparrowhawks and more are all natural predators of magpies. And, of course, one of our own true non-native species is a ferocious predator of birds: the domestic cat.

Sparrowhawk *(Accipiter nisus)*
Family *Accipitridae (hawks, eagles, kites, harriers and old world vultures)*
Conservation status *Green-listed (BoCCI, 2020–2026)*[3]
Vocalisations *The most frequently encountered call is a high-pitched, repetitive, chattering 'kih-kih-kih-kih-kih', usually given in the breeding season.*

Outside the scientific community, some people have a long-held belief that magpies are attracted to and steal shiny objects, including expensive jewellery. Another strike against this 'troublesome' bird. And guess what? It's also not true. There was a study published in 2014 debunking this myth.[4] Rather than magpies being master jewel thieves, humans tend to notice when they occasionally pick up shiny objects but pay no heed when they pick up non-shiny, non-valuable objects. So the myth has come from the observation bias of humans.

Why do we vilify nature? Why call wildflowers 'weeds' or refer to certain species as 'pests'? This is all undeserved language, and a clear indication of our anthropocentrism – that humans alone possess intrinsic value in this world. Why do we fear the randomness and chaotic beauty of nature, when we too are a part of this beautiful mess? Why do we pretend to be above it all? Because we're not. Magpies are wonderful creatures in their own right, with complex lives and a plethora of emotions. Just like us.

Magpies and other members of the crow family (corvids) have been observed attending 'funerals', in which they appear to mourn the death of a conspecific (member of the same species). At least, this was the initial view from our human perspective. However, it has been suggested that such death rituals in corvids are not what they seem, and that they might use these 'funeral' events to learn about danger – they inspect the body of the deceased in an attempt to understand what has happened.[5] It was also found that decreased foraging occurred in the vicinity of an observed death of a conspecific, with birds avoiding food in these danger zones for the following three days. Thus corvids, including magpies, have a society in which they observe, react and learn, just like we do.

Magpie (Pica pica)
Family Corvidae (crows)
Conservation status Green-listed (BoCCI, 2020–2026)
Vocalisation The most commonly encountered vocalisation is the harsh chak-chak-chak-chak. This is utilised for a variety of purposes, from alarm call to contact call, depending on its volume, speed and intensity. Magpies are beautiful songsters, with an unusual warbling song interspersed with clicks, and sounds not too dissimilar to laser beams from a sci-fi movie, but because their song is very quiet, humans rarely hear it.

Corvids are typically known for their raucous, atonal calls, and it is thought that they do not sing. The characteristic call of our magpie is a series of husky, strident notes, given in quick succession, almost like the rattling of a Gatling gun. But this is only what *we* hear. Magpies have several types of vocalisation, several of which we never get to experience in life, either because we genuinely do not hear them or because we do *hear* them, but we aren't *listening* to them. Sometimes, we listen for what we expect to hear, and we miss anything novel or unexpected. For instance, for many years science assumed that only male birds sang. Of course, this is not at all the case.

Whilst most cases of female song have been detected in tropical regions, it has also been discovered closer to home. Take the familiar barn swallow. This is a species most Irish people will be familiar with as the cheery harbinger of summer. A beacon of light that pulls us out of the damp, grey grips of winter. Their cheerful, melodic song, interspersed with high-pitched, fluid notes, connected with a variety of clicks, brightens up our skies every year.

It was widely thought that our very own swallows were only represented by male singers. However, song in female swallows was described and qualified for the first time in 2020,[6] despite them being a common and widely studied passerine songbird, with over a thousand scientific papers published in their name! Females were noted as being ten times less likely to sing, and typically singing earlier in the breeding season – perhaps she is more occupied with tending to her young later on. Female song in barn swallow sounds similar to that of the males, but are slightly less complex. Whilst studies are still ongoing, it is believed that females sing to compete with rival females in both attracting a male and guarding that male. It is also thought to be a pair-bonding exercise.

Barn Swallow *(Hirundo rustica)*
Family *Hirundinidae (swallows, martins and saw-wings)*
Conservation status *Amber-listed (BoCCI, 2020–2026)*
Vocalisations *The most typically heard vocalisation is the simple 'whit-whit', given in flight and when stationary. When excited, their disyllabic 'tsu-whit, tsu-whit' often alerts human ears to an approaching bird of prey. Song is an uplifting melodic series of fluttering notes, interspersed with a variety of clicks.*

Magpies have three well-documented song types: babble song, soft song and, my personal favourite, whisper song. Of these three scarcely heard songs, babble song is the most frequently encountered, though it is still a very rare thing for us humans to encounter. Babble song is described as 'a series of soft warbling sounds interspersed with higher-pitched units'.[7] It's very quiet, and most often sung by the male, although the female can also sing it. It's typically sung in the courtship phase, before the true breeding season commences – like a pair-bonding or partner-attracting exercise. Babble song is often sung in harmony between a pair after a bout of mutual preening. Soft song is similar in function to babble song, and is again sung by both sexes, only it is more uniform in sound and lower-pitched. Whisper song, as the name suggests, is extremely quiet, and is sung by both sexes during the process of nest-building. This to me is so beautiful, and makes me think of a loving, tender moment shared between a couple who are building their future family home. I might be anthropomorphising, but I strongly believe that we share such characteristics. After all, who are we to think or claim we are the *only* species who experience love, tenderness, passion, joy and fun?

Standing there as a small child, free from the biases we pick up as adults, I could only see the shifting iridescent colours of the magpie's feathers, and was content to share this experience with the people I loved and looked up to, especially Pops. Every weekday, I would go to spend the day with him and Granny Betty at their home on the seafront in Cobh. I was too young to go to playschool at this point in my life. They both adored me – I was their first grandchild (my brother Conor wouldn't arrive for another few years). I adored them too, and loved every minute of my time there. My parents would drop me down to their house each morning before they went to work. My grandparents were early risers and would be up and ready for my chaotic energy and cheeky smile. I can still picture the house and even remember its smell. To my little self, its towering three storeys seemed all the more impressive. The house was bookended by similarly tall houses, which climbed the hill of Harbour View leading up to the great cathedral of Cobh. The house was like a time capsule, full of trinkets, antiques and memories.

Although my father had long moved out of the house, lots of his stuff was still there. He showed me the old wine-brewing vats in his childhood bedroom, complete with fireplace. Back then, all the rooms had fireplaces, because there was no central heating, and the winters weren't as forgiving as they are today. Health and safety also wasn't a thing, and the thoughts of embers flickering onto the wooden floor or woollen rugs, while everyone slept soundly, didn't worry people as it would today. My dad told tales of how himself and his two brothers shared the room and got up to all kinds of bother in there, as is to be expected from a roomful of young, boisterous boys.

The old floorboards in the room creaked underfoot as I made my way to one of the two big sea-facing windows. I could see right out over the expanses of Cork Harbour. Here, my dad spent many hours gazing out to sea, watching the comings and goings of boats, birds, dolphins and even the daily movements of the prisoners of Spike Island, of which he also had a bird's-eye view.

I spent my days here with my grandparents while my parents were at work. Of the two, my granny was definitely the dominant character: a strong woman both physically and mentally. Originally from Kerry farming stock, she had a strong frame, with a big booming voice to match. She didn't mince her words and didn't suffer fools gladly. You didn't mess with Granny. But all of that aside, she was very loving, caring and quite funny – often in her directness, in an unintentional way. She filled the voids of the old house with her frequent singing of old Irish ballads as she went about her business, always keeping herself busy. She was a great cook, and her meringues were to die for: snowy white, sweet, crunchy on the outside and chewy on the inside – literal sugar pies. I blame her for my meringue addiction. Despite having tasted meringues all over the country, in some of the fanciest restaurants you can imagine, none have ever compared to hers.

Pops was the quieter of the two, by a long stretch. He was a hard worker who kept his head down, and he had a really gentle manner. He was softly spoken, a man of few words who liked to avoid confrontation. He had long flowing white hair, but was bald as a coot in the centre. To cover this up, he grew his hair out and combed it over the top, keeping it in place with hair wax. I can still remember it whipping up and flowing through the air on windy days, like white sheets on a washing line. He'd scramble to put it back in place, to cover up the bald patch. My mother always referred to him as a dote, and I think it was a very apt description. He certainly doted on me, and did everything in his power to make me happy when I was there, as did my granny. I'd regularly mount his back and he'd pretend he was a horse and I a cowboy. He'd make his best neighing sounds and trot around the hallway cumbersomely, with me laughing in hysterics on top. This is the definition of a love for a grandchild. Making a pure fool of yourself just to make them laugh.

Every week, they'd bring me on the train to Cork city – which was a big adventure. Despite taking this journey with them for two years, I still loved each one as if it were the first. We'd start our adventure with a short wait at the platform at the station in Cobh, again with a view to the inner harbour right in front of us. The tracks were separated from the deep-water quay by a set of old green railings. Beyond this is a small stretch of water, approximately 700 metres out. Then you have another small island, Haulbowline, which is only about a kilometre in length. This is the home of the Irish navy, where my father worked as a mechanic. Next to it was Irish Steel, where my grandfather worked as an operator before his retirement. The water only stretched a kilometre or so to our right before meeting the rocky shoreline of Whitepoint but, to our left, it stretched for several kilometres spanning not only Cobh, but Whitegate and Aghada on the shoreline opposite us. The view out to the mouth of the harbour is impeded by the several islands nestled in the harbour's centre.

We'd sit on the wooden benches that flanked the platform and we'd watch the gulls coursing along the quay. During periods of bad weather, trawlers would come into the harbour and berth alongside for shelter, and even more gulls would congregate, feeding on the scraps the men would fling overboard as they cleaned their boats and did all the little jobs they were too busy to do while on the high seas. As a child, I was like a sponge, always looking, learning and questioning. I watched everyone and everything, as I tried my best to understand the hectic but fascinating world around me.

When the train came, I'd dash on and try to get to my favourite seats – the ones with a seaward view and a big table between two couches. We'd all sit down and gaze out the window as we made the short journey to the city. We'd pass through the upper reaches of the harbour and work our way up past the muddy estuarine parts, and eventually to the lower reaches of the River Lee. The gulls of the platform would swap places for mud-probing black-tailed godwits, redshanks, greenshanks and dunlin.

All of these waders overwinter in significant numbers in Cork Harbour, which is designated as a Special Protection Area, under the European Union Directive on the Conservation of Wild Birds. This means these sites are safeguarded under EU law, in order to preserve the habitats of migratory birds, as well as rare and threatened species. Cork Harbour is an internationally important wetland that holds significant numbers of wintering and breeding waterfowl. It is designated for an amazing 23 species, of which two occur in internationally important numbers, namely black-tailed godwit, with its long knitting-needle-like bill, and redshank with its bright-red legs and apt nickname: the sentinel of the marsh. Redshanks are the meerkats of the bird world, always on the lookout for danger and, when they see it, they let out an ear-piercing string of high-pitched 'tsee-tsee-tsee-tsee-tsee' calls.

We were spoiled for choice and, as our train zoomed by the estuaries, we'd scan the mud ahead of us and pick them all out. Birdwatching at speed!

As our train slowed on the approach to Kent Station in Cork city, we would look at the cormorants sitting on big old wooden pier supports, wings outstretched and drying in the sun. Some days a man would sit on a small wooden platform positioned directly above the river, overlooking the water below – always with a peak cap and sunglasses. He was looking for salmon that would swim upriver and become entangled in a draft net outstretched from the river wall near an old wooden punt. It was held at the surface via a series of floats, and weighted at the bottom so it would stay open in the water table. One man would row the boat so that the net formed a loop and they would both haul it ashore in the hope of a catch. The watcher gave the added bonus of knowing when and where to strike. There was plenty to see as long as our eyes were open to it, and I always had Pops as my knowledgeable guide.

As much as I loved our trips to the city, Pops and Granny had plenty of ways to keep me occupied when we spent the day at home. Pops had a great skill for making paper aeroplanes, and I would ask him to make one every day. I'd watch him in astonishment as he made all of the intricate folds by hand. I practically danced as we went through the front door to launch it. Stepping outside, we would cross a small road to reach the rusty metal railings that stretched the entirety of the street. Behind the railings was a steep drop of about 80 feet that led down to Harbour Row, and we had a clear view of Cork Harbour for many kilometres. There was a real sense of openness about it – the perfect place to launch our planes. From here, we could see all of the little islands dotted in the centre of the harbour, and we could see navy and cargo ships coming in from the mouth, way out at Roche's Point. A pilot boat would motor out to the larger boats so a local navigator could temporarily take the helm and avoid the hidden sand banks and rocky outcrops. We had a bird's-eye view of it all.

I was too small to reach over the top of the railings, so Pops would lift me up and I'd sit on his shoulders. I was the pilot and Pops was both the aeronautical engineer and co-pilot. A man of many talents! Before launching, I'd take in the sweeping views with butterflies in my stomach. I felt like I was on top of the world – almost like a bird. I looked down at the drop below and the blues of the harbour out in front of me. We'd do a countdown from ten and, as soon as it left my fingertips, I became that plane. I imagined I was a bird soaring to the spectacular backdrop of Cork Harbour. In that moment I was a herring gull, patrolling over my marine kingdom, gliding on updrafts and looking out for my next fish supper. It was so liberating and it's a memory that's so clear in my mind's eye despite me being so young then, and three decades having passed since.

Other days, I'd go 'downtown' with Granny Betty to seek out lemon meringue. Downtown is the main hub of the town, where it's mostly flat. A famous row of brightly coloured houses, known as the 'Deck of Cards', is built in a step-like fashion along one of the steepest hills that leads residents and tourists alike down to the seafront. We went to a very specific place, where the meringue was to die for (but not as good as Granny's, of course): Vicky Barry's café, where my father served his time as an apprentice mechanic back in the day when the building had been a car-repair garage.

My days down with Pops and Granny Betty are forever etched in my memory. They were innocent, joyful times.

At weekends, I'd often visit my mother's parents – Granda Dave and Granny Cahill. They lived in a more rural part of the town – a 15-minute walk from our house. I loved going to their place – they had a lot of land out the back where I'd roam and look at the various butterflies and birds. Granny Cahill didn't know much about nature – instead she knew about taking care of people. My mother has four siblings, so Granny Cahill had her work cut out. She never stopped. Any time I called there, she'd have tea and biscuits out and I'd tell her all about my wildlife adventures. And although she didn't know all of the creatures I spoke about, she always listened to me and beckoned me on with a smile. Granda Dave, on the other hand, enjoyed nature quite a lot. He grew up on a rural farm in County Limerick, some two hours northwest of Cobh. He often told me how he was kept awake at night by the incessant crexing calls of late-night corncrakes, and how quails used to flush from the long grasses and wildflowers as they walked through the fields – both are now long gone from Limerick. You see, in those days meadows were cut by hand at the end of the year. Ground-nesting birds were much better off back then, before we industrialised our farming systems.

Granda Dave was quite the character. He loved to socialise, and he would develop the accent of whoever it was he was chatting to. They say that this is a character of highly sociable people, that they do this to try to find common ground with whomever they speak.

Nature Boy

Despite his outgoing manner and love for mixing with anyone who came his way, he also had a knack of getting himself into some highly awkward situations. I can remember one Christmas he was gifted a pair of binoculars by a cousin of mine. He couldn't wait to try them out and so he began scanning from the kitchen window into the garden behind. He mustn't have noticed his half-naked neighbour glaring back at him from the window across from his gaze, assuming he was looking at them. He did eventually though and flushed red with embarrassment, he snapped the binoculars down from his face and took a dive for the couch. I think he found it quite hard to look them in the eye for some time, but I have to say, somewhat apologetically, that everyone else found it hysterical.

When I turned three, I was old enough to start playschool. It was the best thing for everyone, because I was a very active child and it wouldn't have been fair on my grandparents to keep on minding me. But it was great! There weren't a lot of kids my age on my street so I didn't really get a chance to meet many until playschool. But boy was my teacher in for a rude awakening! I entered the building like a storm. I was capable of saying or doing anything; I had no filter at all. On my first day there, I looked around, grimaced, waved my hand over my nose and exclaimed, 'Poooooh – there's a weird smell in here.' My mother's face flushed a deep red and she hushed me quiet. 'Seán – stop it, please. You can't say things like that. Sorry – he's only joking.'

'No, I'm not, Mam!' I replied.

Typically, one of my aunties would collect me after class, and they dreaded it – afraid of what my teacher had to say about my behaviour. Even at that young age, I remember frequently getting into trouble. I didn't mean to, I just said and did things the other kids knew not to. I'd call my classmates names, take their stuff and generally said things that were out of line. But I didn't know they were out of line.

I spent a lot of time in the 'bold corner' – a corner of the room we had to stand in with our back to the class when we misbehaved. Not for long, just to teach us a little lesson. I spent more time there than anyone else. I remember one time being asked to stand there and telling my teacher to 'let me go immediately or I'll call the guards'. She tried to hold back her amusement, rolled her eyes and told me to sit down, but to behave. I was off the hook.

At the front of the playschool was a small grassy area with a slide. On sunny days, towards the end of the day, we'd finish up out here as we waited to be collected. I remember waiting impatiently on the ladder for a nervous classmate to go. He must have taken too long for my liking – I pushed him off the top, and slid down like nothing happened. He wasn't hurt but he started to cry. Off to the bold corner again. My aunt arrived not long after and knew by the look on the teacher's face that I'd done it again. Although I didn't feel like I had differences to the other kids, looking back, I definitely did. I had no patience, I always interrupted or did silly things, I spoke out of line. I didn't really flow like the others did in group games. I was an 'unruly' misfit of a kid. Was I, though? Looking back, I don't think so at all. I was just different and my schooling needed to be approached in a different manner. I understood animals and nature far better than my peers. I didn't get into trouble with nature; I was a part of it. I was at peace there. I didn't step out of line or fidget. I listened intently to what nature had to say. We understood one another. I knew this and so did my parents. But in school back then, things were seen differently.

At home after school or on weekends, I longed to be out in nature. It wasn't possible for me to sit still in the house. Although I had some toys, I wasn't really into them. I much preferred to be outside, digging in the dirt, climbing trees, and exploring and learning about everything I could find out there. We had a small back garden with a lawn, but nature still found a way in. If I discovered a new creature in the garden, I'd pick it up and bring it inside to show my parents, much to my mother's delight. I spent the majority of my free time out there – it was my *real* classroom. I didn't quite belong in the school classroom but, here, even though it was a suburban garden, I belonged. In the mornings, we'd wake up to a beautiful dawn chorus. We were lucky that we were surrounded by many elms, ashes and sycamores.

This was before Dutch elm disease became widespread in Ireland, when ash dieback disease was unheard of. Dutch elm disease is a fungal disease specific to elms and is spread by the elm bark beetle. Although it originated in Asia, it reached Europe through tree imports, and was first recorded in Ireland in 1958, from which time it took a devastating toll on the Irish wych elm population, wiping out thousands of mature trees across the country. Ash dieback disease is yet another fungal infection that was imported to Ireland, having been first detected here in 2012. It seems we never learn from our mistakes, as we now have a new imported disease: fireblight – a bacterial disease that affects hawthorn in particular. Hawthorn is a very important tree here in Ireland, being a staple species of our hedgerows and treelines, which dot the innumerable, otherwise intensively and often unsympathetically managed cow fields that blanket the majority of our land.

Because we had such a verdant border of mature trees at our house, the dawn chorus was diverse and well populated with blackbirds, robins, dunnocks, wrens, great tits, song thrushes, woodpigeons and more. It was as varied and melodic as could be in a leafy suburb.

Each morning, I heard a slightly different rendition, and each was better than the previous one. Each species occupies a different frequency so as not to step on one another's toes. At the lowest end of the scale were the woodpigeons, with their bass-heavy cooing tune. The rich and fluty melody of the blackbird was a step up – they brought some technical flare to the chorus. Right up at the other end of the scale were the tiny goldcrests – Ireland's smallest birds. Their songs sounded higher than anything else, a sweet series of see-saw-like phrases that ended in a wonderful flurry.

Every spring and early summer morning, I vividly remember waking up to the resident blackbird. Blackbirds are one of the first birds to sing at dawn. Their song is one of the most beautiful we have. It's such an eloquent tapestry of warm, rich notes, joined together in perfect harmony and flow, like cursive writing in song form. Their beautiful tunes are also woven with mimicry – sounds they've learned in their lifetimes around the neighbourhood. One example from its repertoire in particular always made me laugh as a kid – it used to mimic the stereotypical ringtone of an old landline phone 'rriiing-rriiing, rriiing-rriiing'. Several studies have found that increased eye size in birds enables them to gather more light than birds with smaller eyes. This means that these larger-eyed birds, like the blackbird, can sing earlier, as they already have the benefit of seeing any predators that would be alerted to their presence. Smaller-eyed birds need to wait a while longer, until it gets a bit brighter, for their own safety. You don't want to get snapped up by a barn owl in the twilight, when you can't see it coming.

The view of the harbour from our house was slightly obscured by a large grey-blue convent directly in front of our house. In the grounds of the convent are several gargantuan conifers. I don't know what species they are, but they certainly aren't native. We have three native conifer species here in Ireland – Scots pine, juniper and yew. These looked very different to any of those. Firstly, they dwarfed all of those species and, secondly, they had distinctive pine cones I had seen nowhere else. They've been there a long time, though, and every year a pair of hooded crows nested on the top of the tallest. I'd watch them from my window, repairing and adding to their generational stick nest each spring. I'd see the female sitting tight incubating the eggs and the male bringing her food. The occasional bad storm would hit in early spring and I'd watch her in the tree hunkered down, swaying in the violent gusts. I hoped with all I had that she wouldn't get blown out. She never did. She'd stay on top of her precious cargo no matter what, only occasionally popping up her head to assess the situation.

These were my neighbours, I really felt that. Just like the foxes that bred in a den up the road and visited each night or the hedgehogs that lived under one of the wilder garden boundaries. I didn't think of my neighbourhood in a human context, because I didn't really interact with my neighbours that much, at least not as much as I did with my animal neighbours.

Thanks to Pops' early lesson that Sunday, I would also enjoy magpies in and around the garden. In fact, they too bred in some of the trees opposite my bedroom. I am forever indebted to Pops.

He gave me the gift of nature – somewhere I could retreat to and recharge throughout my whole life. Though nature is fleeting, and I learned a harsh lesson very early on in my journey through this world. Pops died suddenly of a brain aneurism ... I was just four. I didn't get to spend a lot of time with Pops, but the sight of the magpie with him is the first thing that comes to mind when I think of him, and of my early childhood in general, and I am very grateful for that.

You never know what moment in your life may be significant to your future self. Little did I know that watching that magpie with Pops would be a memory that would live in me forever. It's a reminder to cherish every moment with family, and not to get lost in the stresses and challenges of life. But also to focus on the now and appreciate the simple things. Live in the moment and be happy.

Nature is so endlessly beautiful, and it can lift the spirits of us all no matter what the day has brought. But to share its beauty with others – to share this excitement with others – elevates this feeling to another level. To be able to show something as beautiful, simple and pure as a common magpie to someone who has never seen one before is a special treat. This beauty is everywhere. We all too often forget the beauty in the every day. We only need to take the time to look at and listen to what is right in front of us, and you never need to look too far. Stop searching for the big show – there's no need. Open up your mind and let it come to you.

Whitethroat

Chapter 2

I HAVE TWO STANDOUT MEMORIES FROM MY EARLY LIFE. ONE was Pop's introduction to the magpie and the second comes from my regular visits to Cuskinny Marsh Nature Reserve with Dad. Cuskinny is a reserve of varied habitats, including brackish lagoon, marsh, woodland and rocky shoreline, just east of Cobh, and it boasts a kaleidoscope of wildlife in a relatively compact 12 hectares, owned by the Bird and Ronan families and managed by BirdWatch Ireland. Like Pops, my father had a great affinity for the outdoors, and he was very generous with his time and knowledge. It was like passing a torch – from Pops to Dad to me.

I remember clearly being pushed in the pram along the Tay Road, a long rural road that stretches the length of the reserve. Dad would wheel the pram the two and a half kilometres from our home near St Coleman's Cathedral, up Bishop's Street hill, passing my schools-to-be, eventually dropping down through the leafier Cuskinny Hill. This was our gateway to nature. Here, Dad would teach me all that he knew of the local flora and fauna. Everything that Pops had originally pointed out to him when he was a child. This same place provided me with an education in nature all throughout my childhood, and still does. Despite having travelled far and wide in life, Cuskinny will always hold a special place in my heart.

These Dad-powered visits took place in the early 1990s, and back then the roads were quieter; there were fewer cars down around the reserve in particular. Having passed through the many housing estates of the town, when we began the descent of the hill, a noticeable change occurred. First, the footpath disappeared, stopping abruptly at the last house – the last one for quite some distance. More visible was the sudden appearance of trees, and lots of them. Great big elms, ashes, sycamores, oaks and chestnut trees. They grew tall and proud and created an inviting tunnel-effect over the small road, tempting us to continue down to our nature-filled refuge, nestled in the peaceful outskirts of town. Both sides were bound by old stone walls, from which grew a rich covering of native plants: ivy, navelwort, honeysuckle, bramble and a great variety of ferns, of which the prehistoric maidenhair spleenwort was most abundant. As we took the first sharp bend and entered this new world, the maelstrom of intrusive sounds of the town were replaced by a gentle babbling stream, which flowed along the left-hand boundary wall. It rose suddenly from a spring, the water icy cool and with exceptional clarity. My father later told me how he would stop and drink from this when he was young, on his regular visits down to the fields behind Cuskinny. He'd take his two collies, Charlie and Garrett, there for long walks. Sadly, like many of our roadside streams, it has since been covered over – 'tidied away'. I don't know who by, but it's a big loss. No wildlife may avail of it nor can we drink from it. It's a pity these little details are so commonly erased from our landscape, often unnoticed and unquestioned.

To the right, behind the other wall, was a large estate, several hectares in size, owned by the lovely Mrs Wanda Ronan. In there were red squirrels, foxes, hedgehogs, a great variety of birds and a wonderful mixed woodland. She very kindly allowed us to enter during my teenage years, and it was an extra special treat to get to know this hidden site. Mrs Ronan owned most of the lands that made up the reserve that is open to the public. She kindly allowed some local conservationists to manage it under the guidance of BirdWatch Ireland, in the best interests of the eclectic flora and fauna that call it home.

Continuing down the hill, some cow fields appeared on the left, with an old cottage sitting amidst an overgrown hedgerow. My father had known the occupants, who had long since moved on. To the left of that cottage was a huge oak, rumoured to be the oldest on Great Island. Its great big, gnarled trunk and numerous thick, irregular branches seemed to confirm this. It's surely several hundred years old and still stands at the time of writing.

At the bottom of the hill, we would reach a crossroads and have three choices: turn right into the private grounds of Mrs Ronan, go straight on over the humpback bridge to get to the seaward side of the reserve or turn left along the Tay Road, which skirts the western boundary of the marsh and runs back towards the town in a loop if you take a left at Cow's Cross and go up the big hill at Ticknock.

The 'marsh' at Cuskinny refers to a brackish lake surrounded by a reedbed on all sides bar the south, where a mosaic of grassland, gorse and blackthorn scrub, and even fragments of saltmarsh, occur. Walking north along the Tay Road, a small gap in the rustic stone wall provides an entrance to view the lake. We spent countless hours there, watching the mute swans, mallards, shelduck, moorhens and other residents going about their daily lives. The ducks and swans here were accustomed to people feeding them bread so they automatically came close whenever anyone appeared. This meant we had wonderful views of them.

Of course, in recent years people know better than to throw bread into the lake, as it has little to no nutritional value for the birds and can result in a reduction in water quality – with the uneaten bread contributing to algal blooms and having the potential to increase disease risk as a result of heightened bacteria in the water column. Algal blooms like this are caused by excess nutrients entering the water. It comes as a result of many sources aside from bread-feeding, the most common of which is nutrient runoff from slurry spreading, particularly when it is spread not long before, or even during, periods of heavy rainfall. This seems to happen a lot in Ireland, despite being prohibited by regulations. I jokingly, somewhat darkly, predict and tell Alba of incoming rainfall based on the sudden appearance of tractor-driven slurry-spreaders on rural roads.

The excess nutrients in the water from events such as these can lead to an explosion of algal growth. When this algae dies and decomposes, a sharp drop in oxygen levels in the water occurs and can result in a serious dying-off of fish and aquatic invertebrates.

Certain algal blooms are toxic and can even be harmful to birds and mammals, including ourselves. I recall at times seeing a mound of discarded bread at the marsh, peaking a foot or two above the meniscus – certainly enough to trigger a eutrophic response considering the small size of the marsh, as well as the frequency of the dumping events. Clearly it was a result of commercial dumping, presumably from a local bakery. Of course, this wasn't all eaten, and some days later it would begin to mould, decompose and discolour the water. Thankfully bread-throwing is now a rare sight at the lake, and people either bring vegetable scraps or simply come to observe and take a breath.

In spring and autumn, Dad and I would witness spectacular numbers of swallows, house martins, sand martins and swifts, often in their hundreds, circling over the marsh. The sound of it all was mesmerising – the swallows with their merry little tweets, the house martins and sand martins with their contrasting clicking and grating calls, and the swifts screaming high above. These birds were so numerous that they'd swoop all around us, the sound of their wings flickering and their bodies whooshing as they flew past. Occasional splashes could be heard as birds gracefully skimmed the water at speed for a drink. They would fly high and low, catching flies to fatten up between their great migrations between Europe and Africa.

Early each year, the resident pair of mute swans would work together to make a nest in the reedbed. We'd watch as they built their jumbo-sized nest of sticks and stringy green vegetation with great care. We'd wait with bated breath over the following weeks for the cygnets to appear. The male would still come to say hello when we popped by, but we'd only see glimpses of the female's pearly white plumage through little gaps in the reeds, as she sat tight on her clutch of eggs. Some weeks later, the first hints of life came in the form of the hoarse but cutely squeaky contact calls of the young – given to stick together and to stay within earshot of their parents. Each year, we'd count the fluffy grey cygnets as they'd emerge from their nest, bobbing up and down like corks on the water. Ripples hit like waves – they had a lot of growing up to do. They kicked their little legs at the speed of light, as they frantically tried to keep up with the strident sweeps of their mother's hulking black-webbed feet, like great big paddles.

They were wise to do so because, sadly, their numbers always dropped in this early stage of life. Over the years, we witnessed grey herons and hooded crows flying low over the water, plucking the helpless cygnets from the surface. It was tough to see, but my father explained to me that this was part of nature, and it's true. Birds have to fight for each meal. They don't have the luxury of popping down to the local shop, so to disturb a bird who is seeking out a meal, regardless of how cute and fluffy that meal is, is not okay. One year, however, we watched as the tables turned. A great black-backed gull, the largest gull in the world with a wingspan of 1.5 to 1.7 metres, decided it would try its luck with plucking one of the cygnets for lunch. This proved to be a fatal mistake, as the male swan chased it down and drowned it by repeatedly standing on its head and back, flapping with vigour to push it under. The struggle eventually finished, and the swan swam off as if nothing had happened, the limp body of the huge gull left floating, wings outstretched.

***Mute Swan** (Cygnus olor)*
***Family** Anatidae (ducks, geese and swans)*
***Conservation status** Amber-listed (BoCCI, 2020–2026)*
***Vocalisations** Mute swans are not at all mute. In fact they have a number of vocalisations and other sounds. The most typical vocalisation is a very unique grunting or rumbling, often followed with a hoarse whistling sound. They also hiss aggressively when agitated or alarmed. In terms of non-vocalisations, they display and defend their territory by slapping their wings off the water surface, eventually building enough speed to become airborne, where their feathers whistle in flight – the display is finished by a drawn-out splash landing.*

In winter, kingfishers would come to the reserve to feed on the sticklebacks and young mullet that take shelter in the calm waters there. Kingfishers don't breed at Cuskinny so they disappear during the summer months, presumably because of a lack of a stable earthen bank above flooding level that they need in order to excavate their nesting burrows. In winter, Dad and I had a kingfisher ritual. We would stop and wait at the viewing area and we'd listen. Their unmistakable calls announced their presence – a sharp 'tsip-tsoooo' – and next there would be an electric flash of cobalt blue as they darted past, low over the water. They'd then settle out of sight on a low-hanging tree branch from which they'd stalk fish. Most of the time, this was all you'd get, but on occasion one would land closer and we'd get to take in their true beauty.

Seeing a kingfisher up close was always a moment we cherished, because it didn't happen often, and there is, in my opinion, no Irish bird with such exquisite colours that can compare to it. Not even close. The first thing that hits you is the general pattern of intensely saturated blues and oranges, but when you look more closely, the origins of the electric flash we see in flight becomes apparent. Running down their back is a strip of blue that's hard to put into words. It reminds me of a perfect Floridian summer sky, which I was fortunate enough to experience on a trip in 2008. It exudes warmth, character and just pure joy. It brightens up the grey skies of an Irish winter, it thaws the soul. The wings and head are more of a royal blue, but are flecked in that same Floridian blue at the ends, like frosty tips. Generous white splotches behind the cheek and around the 'chin' complement the vivid blues, like fluffy clouds floating by. Under the eye and throughout the breast is a rich mandarin-orange, like the sun shining through. When you see them up *really* close, you can even tell males and females apart. The beak of a bird is made up of two opening parts: the upper and lower mandibles. In kingfishers, the upper mandible is always black, regardless of the sex. But in females, the lower mandible has varying amounts of orange pigmentation. To remember this rule of sexing, I was told that it looks like the female wears some lipstick, hence the orangey-red gloss.

When I was here with Dad, I was calm – a different person to the wild child I was at home. I would take it all in and I wanted to understand everything. I raced through life at a hundred questions per hour. My favourite game was 'guess the sound'. Dad would mimic the sounds of various birds and mammals that we frequently encountered and ask me to guess the species. I thought it was hilarious and we would also reverse the roles, although I preferred to be the guesser. Dad would ask me, 'What does the curlew say?' and I'd reply with an enthusiastic 'Currr-LEW!' He'd continue to my favourite: 'What does the frog say?' I'd reply with a great big 'RIBBIT-RIBBIT', and we'd erupt into a fit of laughter. My dad was teaching me the natural sounds of the landscape and making it fun. This is a memory that will be etched in my mind until the day I die. So innocent, so pure and a cornerstone for who I was to become in later years.

As we mimicked the species around us, we would continue past the viewing area and along the Tay Road, where we'd admire the willows and reeds to our right. Water rails squealed their pig-like sharmings from deep within, but very seldom did they show face, only teasing their presence with their bellows and the shuffling of reeds marking out their passage below. Flashes of pink, white and black followed by a distinctive duo of hollow clicks and three-note whistles indicated that a volary of long-tailed tits was working their way through the dense, tall stands, feeding and calling in tandem. Even when I was young, it was their calls that first drew my attention. This was thanks to Dad. Some years, if we were lucky, we'd find one of their nests. Dad had a particular eye for picking them out, having had a fascination with finding nests from a young age. He had a great eye for their subtle differences and could easily tell what species called a nest home. This really impressed me and still does – I don't know how he does it. We would wait, hiding a safe distance from the nest, as the species he named would always turn up. The nest of a long-tailed tit was like no other: a beautiful green dome made of mosses and lichens, skilfully held together by spiderweb. A real artisan home. Delicate and special, a fitting snug for such a dainty little bird.

An old overgrown track in there, just beyond the bounding stone wall of the Tay Road itself, was a reminder of life gone by. My father remembers when it was in use, but now nature has reclaimed it. This route would eventually lead us to 'the laneway', which was a driveway that cuts off to the right of the Tay Road and skirts the northwestern boundary of the marsh. It led to two residences, both of which previously made up what is locally known as the Old Fever Hospital. Here, sailors with fever bound for Cork city were isolated to prevent the spread of whatever infectious disease they may have had. Local rumour has it that a large mound on the seaward end of the marsh is a mass grave, where the unlucky ones were buried.

To the left of the laneway, the Ballyleary stream runs along the Tay Road and feeds into the lake. This area is a distinctly wet woodland that looks like something out of the Florida swamps. Alder, ash and various species of willow reach up from the flooded ground, bordering the stream. In parts, there are open pools. Elsewhere, the damp, muddy soil plays host to a vibrant neighbourhood of damp-loving plant species: meadowsweet with its generous white flecking of flowers and distinctive marzipan aroma; opposite-leaved golden saxifrage, an ancient woodland indicator species with a dark green base and contrasting yellow-green tips, which forms carpets scattered throughout; and water mint announcing its presence with its globular pink flowers and toothpaste-like aroma.

If we took ourselves back to the crossroads, but this time continued straight, we would work our way to the seaward side of the reserve. A small car park on the right opened out the view to

Cork Harbour. Directly below our feet was a rocky shoreline. Here, we would watch brent geese grazing on seaweeds and algae in winter, and sit and watch the glimmer of the harbour on a summer's day. Leaving the car park, you cross a small humpback bridge. This is where the Ballyleary stream, having travelled down along the Tay Road and through the lake, enters the sea. This bridge was another spot for us to look for kingfisher. We would always stop and peek our heads over, waiting for one another and looking together you only had a split second. Kingfishers are very wary and move like little blue rockets. During the winter and early in the morning was best. They would often sit on an overhanging branch right under the bridge. We'd pop our heads over, see a flash of lightning blue, and be left with a smile and a still-bouncing but empty fishing branch.

Down below is where I'd fish for crabs as a kid. The stream flows under the shadows of the old stone arch and there's more of a saline influence to the waters. The ground is sunken slightly below sea level, and the road and bridge sit several feet above us. Dad would keep any scraps of meat from home – fatty rasher rinds, steak grizzle, chicken bones, and so on. We'd bring those along with some twine, and we'd find a broken twig to act as a little fishing rod. The twine would be attached to the end of the stick, and 2 feet down, the meat was tied off at the end. The bank of the stream overhung a foot or two above the water and I'd sit in the grass and dangle my little legs over the edge. Dad would kneel by my side. We'd slowly lower the meat over the edge until we saw it sit on the stony bottom. Everything was visible. You'd see the crabs slowly emerging from all around and shuffling sideways through the seaweed towards the tempting prize. Bigger specimens would ward off the smaller elfins that would gather in numbers. Our aim was to catch the biggest and most impressive of the group. The larger crabs were often battle-scarred, sometimes with just one beefy pincer – but one was more than enough to fight off the smaller competition. When a big one took hold of the meat, we'd slowly haul it to the surface. They'd be so adamant in eating their prize that, more often than not, they wouldn't let go. We had to be careful not to get nipped ourselves, so we'd gently hold the carapace of the crab behind the pincers, which meant they couldn't reach back and get us. I'd look at each one in awe and take in all the details: the independently moving stalked eyes, their eight spider-like legs and their formidable pincers, with tooth-like nodules for smashing and pulverising. I'd not look long, because I knew they needed to go back, so with that I'd plop them back into the stream unharmed. At the end of our session, we'd leave them the scraps as a thank you.

As this section of the marsh was a few feet below sea level, the wall bounding the road above was a favourite of mine to meander across. I'd amble along, arms outstretched like a tightrope walker, Cuskinny Bay to my right and the saltmarsh a few feet below to my left. One evening, I was carefully tip-toeing along the top, navigating my way through the old rounded stones and vegetative cover of the wall top. I was talking to my dad who was next to me on the road when all of a sudden there was a pop and I dropped down to the marsh below. I found myself in darkness, with only green-dappled light making it through above. I'd walked on top of a hollow in the wall that was covered by just a few strands of ivy. It was essentially a human pitfall trap. I fell right down and into the mass of vegetation below. Dad was still chatting to me for a few seconds before he realised what had happened, by which time I was crawling out, spitting leaves out of my mouth and pulling spiderwebs and twigs out of my hair in a tantrum. I stood there back on top with my hands on my hips and gave my dad the glare. I was always a dramatic kid. I think I enjoyed trying to make people laugh, really. I screamed for him to help me down from the wall, for fear of falling back in. I was unscathed bar a few light scratches ... and a dented ego. I could see my dad struggling to hold back the laughter, with my hair pointing in all directions, leaves sticking out from my collar, hair and pockets, like an angry little troll emerging from below ground. A woman passing by on horseback looked at me in bewilderment and asked if I was okay, probably drawn by my dramatic outburst.

Dad interjected in a jovial tone, 'He's fine, don't worry!'

To which I replied, 'I'm not fine, *act*-ually!'

I was. Every time myself and Dad pass this wall, we burst out laughing. Not a word needs to be said.

When I wasn't out in nature, I was thinking about it or studying my bird book. My parents gifted me my first book when I was five or six and it became an extension of my body. It had simple drawings of various ages and sexes of the most common species. It was pocket-sized and had a plastic cover which meant I could bring it outside. I drilled over every species on repeat, day in, day out. Many species were familiar to me, but many I only knew through the book. But when I did encounter a new species for the first time, I already knew what I was looking at thanks to my obsession with this little guide. I put a little pencil tick next to each species I'd seen and longed to add new birds to my list. The corners were rounded with use, and the edges of the pages were browned with mud and thumb-flicking.

My mother, although not a nature person in the same sense that Dad or I were, knew how much it all meant to me, and she would always gift me with new books and encourage me to explore. Each Christmas, she would surprise me with all of the latest guidebooks, and I gradually added general Irish nature guides, bee guides, slug and snail guides, mammal guides, mushroom guides, tree guides, and any other nature-based identification guides you can imagine. I'd devour each guide as it came, but would always fall back to my bird guide. It came to the toilet with me, I brought it to bed and I brought it to the dinner table. Every day. My parents would try to encourage me to leave it be so we could have a chat, but I'd side-eye the open pages as I pretended to pay attention.

At nighttime, from the age of around eight, I'd go out in the garden with a headlight. My mother gave me a small digital camera one Christmas and I'd use this to document my garden safaris. The garden was a different place under the cover of darkness. The slugs and snails came out, as did the spiders, moths and woodlice. New species that were waiting to reveal themselves were out there, and I wanted to find them. I'd ask my parents to turn on the outside wall light. This attracted the moths. I'd see all manner of Irish moths, of which there are approximately 1,500 species. Lemon-yellow brimstone moths with their rusty brown wing patches were a common sight at the wall light and were a real favourite. But they were only one of many species that frequented the garden. Elephant hawkmoth was another, a real vivid pink and green brute – like a fighter jet of the Irish moth world. The 'elephant' part of the name comes from the caterpillar's likeness to an elephant's trunk. Adults often feed on honeysuckle, and the caterpillars often feed on rosebay willowherb and bedstraw, both of which were common in the immediate vicinity. Each time I encountered a new species, I'd read up on them and learn all about them. My education was a very organic process in that sense. I learned on the job, and that's still very much the case. For me, there is no better way.

Other nights, I'd try my hand at sugaring for moths. This involved boiling up a concoction of sugar, bruised fruits that were past their prime, and wine, to make a sweet syrup into which I'd dip strands of cloth. I'd hang them around the garden and do rounds with my torch. This recipe was irresistible to so many species of moths, who'd stop to drink this enriching treat. I'd watch under the headlamp as various species landed and unfurled their proboscises, using this long tubular appendage to lap up the syrup.

When I fancied something different, I'd go on a slug search, trying to find and identify as many species as I could. My favourite by far was the leopard slug. These are really impressive with a rich brown body with striking black spots, just like a leopard. They're also big – up to eight inches long. Their Latin name, *Limax maximus*, alludes to this, literally translating as 'biggest slug'.

I'd get lost out there in the world I loved more than any other, with my headlamp, book and little camera. My parents would have to call me in to go to bed.

When I was old enough to go to school, I had to cut down on my days of exploration in Cuskinny and adapt to a new, far less free-range learning environment. My restlessness followed me into the classroom, so, though my memories from school are mostly pleasant, I tended to get myself into trouble somewhat frequently. I somehow had to spend six or more hours stuck inside the same room, on the same seat, at the same desk – something I would never dream of doing if I had the choice. I'm a natural wanderer, both physically and mentally, and to tie me down to one spot for this length of time and have me operate in a repetitive, orderly manner was like trying to fit a square peg into a round hole. I made it work, but not without some fireworks. During subjects I didn't have a *grá* for, I'd be disruptive. I didn't quite fit in with the others, and I was very much aware of this. So to compensate and to entertain myself, I would try to make the class laugh however and whenever possible. This also combated my boredom. I was always looking for ways to make silly jokes or funny noises to get a reaction. When I was done with that or if I was told off, I'd knock it on the head, but I'd disengage and enter my own world. Anything to escape from the monotony.

My mind was always drifting off, thinking about nature. I'd look out the window and watch birds come and go, dreaming about my next adventure in the countryside. I was never too far from a window in school, and I had great views through the old single-paned glass. We didn't have many trees outside but there was always something to tempt my eye away from the tedium of the blackboard. Song thrushes would crack snails off their favoured stone anvils, teasing out the fleshy molluscs from within. Blackbirds would tilt their heads, listening for worms in the 'neatly' trimmed lawn. They always reminded me of a pet dog cocking its head to the side as it interprets a familiar command. Rooks and jackdaws were ubiquitous and frequently passed by in flight, fluttering unitedly as they sought out opportunistic feeding in the suburbs. Occasionally, I'd be treated to a flock of oystercatchers commuting past at height, their pied patterns zipping by with paced intent. Although these are typically birds of coastal habitats, they do also feed inland at times, often probing soft grassy fields for earthworms with their long but narrow, carrot-like beaks. It was on these inland forays that they'd fly past my line of sight, as I longed to be out of the classroom. My body was inside but my mind was not, no matter how much my teachers tried to draw me back in. This power was mine, and it couldn't be taken away by anyone.

Oystercatcher *(Haematopus ostralegus)*
Family *Haematopodidae (oystercatchers)*
Conservation status *Red-listed (BoCCI, 2020–2026)*
Vocalisations *The most typical call is a characteristic disyllabic 'chu-cheep'. Alarms are a fast and repeated 'pik-pik-pik-pik'.*

Despite my intermittent mental presence in class, I still had a grasp of what was happening and I got good grades, even in the classes I loathed. My favourite subject was nature, and I guess I was a bit of a show-off during this class. I knew all the answers and even had the nerve to correct the teacher when the opportunity arose. Probably not the best idea, as I was already walking a fine line. Some of our teachers had a nature table and I adored this. It was my favourite space in the room. It was just a large table or worktop at the side of the class dedicated to nature. It was empty at the start of the year, and we'd all fill it together. We were encouraged to bring in items from the countryside, and it was then our responsibility to teach our classmates about the item. We'd bring in all sorts – shells, eggs, skulls, antlers, interesting rocks, pressed leaves or flowers – anything we could find that was wild and interesting, but not living. Our teacher once rescued some frogspawn from a desiccating puddle. Without his intervention they had no future, so he put them in a basin with some algae and water and we watched them slowly transform into little froglets. It instilled a sense of awe and wonder in us all. It made us really care about those little frogs-to-be.

This direct connection to nature is something I feel many of us lack nowadays. Any schools I have visited to give talks to the students haven't had a nature table. In fact, on a recent visit, I asked the kids, 'Do you all know what the dawn chorus is?' I was met with silence and a crowd of shrugging shoulders and raised eyebrows. This shocked me to my core. It's no secret that nature in Ireland is on its knees like never before, with 63 per cent of our birds at risk of extinction (either red- or amber-listed). This is largely due to our capitalist, resource-draining society that has covered Ireland with industrialised farms, drained our bogs, overgrazed and burned virtually all of our uplands, and blanketed the rest in swathes of non-native conifer crops.

But I also strongly believe it's because of a widespread loss of connection to nature. People do enjoy and appreciate nature; I see it all the time. Just recently, I saw people rejoicing at the surprise appearance of a pod of common dolphins, foraging and frolicking close to the shore in Cobh. But people don't know how to interact with nature. These same people were clapping, screaming and whistling to the dolphins as if calling a dog. They've forgotten how to love nature, how to enjoy it and how to interact with respect

... or how *not* to interact, *out of* respect. Teachers are key here. Why not bring back the nature table? Governments are also key. Maths, geography and history are mandatory, so why not make an education in nature, the very core foundation of continued life on this planet, a mandatory subject? And let's not stop at kids. Why not educate the very adults who strip away nature on a daily basis in the name of vanity? Many do so because of a lack of awareness of the consquences of their actions. Education won't solve all, but it will make an enormous difference.

A teacher who stands out in my mind as someone who did an exemplary job of teaching his students to love and respect nature was Mr McSweeney ... but I was never assigned to his class. Now, don't get me wrong, my teachers were great, but Mr McSweeney's class was meant to be for me. He was a hands-on nature enthusiast, but his class consisted of the best-behaved, most studious pupils, and I only ticked one of those boxes. I clearly remember walking past his classroom in the hall and peeping in. I was blown away by all the bird posters on the walls and the big nature table full of treasures. The large window in the classroom looked out on a collection of well-stocked bird feeders. Oh my God, how I yearned to be a student in Mr McSweeney's class. I do remember having to sit into his class once when our teacher was sick and it was another world. The kids in it had so much nature in their day and I was so jealous. To top it off, every year, RTÉ Radio 1 hosted (and still do) a live-aired dawn chorus event from Cuskinny Nature Reserve. Despite being able to count my years on my fingers, I knew the reserve place like the back of my hand. So it was incredibly galling that two students were selected from Mr McSweeney's class to represent our school for a part of this event with RTÉ. I never did make it down there, but there is time yet. I still think back to this at times, and I really wished I had been put into this class. To know that there was a teacher who actively engaged with nature in class, that it was a class I could not access was a real shame.

When I say I was different to the others, I mean this in almost every sense of the word. I didn't like sports in general, and I outright detested football – a core of young male socialisation and conversation. I tried every sport under the sun and I was terrible at them all. I broke my thumb playing basketball after I managed to stand on the ball before it bounced back up. I had legitimate whiplash after a game of football in PE class in school when I kicked the ball hard at the very same time as a member of the opposing team. He kicked the ball that little bit harder and my leg shot back. The force of the kick ran up through my body like a Mexican wave, causing my neck to whip backwards.

Sports clearly weren't for me, instead I found all of my fun in nature. It kept me fit and active. It quenched my thirst for knowledge and maintained my curiosity in life. It made me feel calm when I had a tough day. It gave me everything I needed to feel whole.

In school, there were always trends that everyone strived to follow. I guess this is part of human nature: to fit in and be a part of a clan. To belong. But I just didn't feel part of *their* clan and I didn't have the desire to be a part of it, either. I had nothing against them, I just didn't 'get' them. I already had my clan and that was nature and all of its components. In school, Nike runners were cool; I wore green Doc Martens. I distinctly remember sitting in the outdoor toilet in the school yard (these toilets were a throwback to the 1960s when outhouse 'jacks' were common). I hated needing to go out there because they were full of cellar spiders. Although I love and respect all of nature's creatures, spiders have always given me the heebie-jeebies. They make the hairs on my arms stand on end and send a shiver through my body. Cellar spiders particularly so, probably because of their long, dangly, alien-like limbs. They occupy dark, damp, undisturbed spaces, and outdoor toilets are a favourite. They're spider hunters, actually. I'd sit there with my eyes fixed on the closest culprit, making sure it didn't advance while I did my business. I must have been taking my time this particular day, because someone waiting at the door became impatient and banged loudly, telling me to get a move on. I sat in silence in the hope they'd move on, but they peeked under the door at my dark green Docs: 'Oh that's Seán Ronayne, anyway. Hurry up, Nature Boy! I need to pee.'

Short or shaved hair was also cool in school; I sported a fine mop of curls. Other trends were WWF Wrestling and collecting Premier League football cards. I preferred to spend my free time roaming the fields and woods, collecting shells, feathers and animal skulls. The fields behind Cuskinny were my favourite. They climbed over the back of the reserve and opened up to a sprawling view over the lake and beyond to Cork Harbour. I felt like I was on top of the world up there.

When the longer summer days allowed, I'd wander up to these fields after school with Dad, taking in the flora and fauna en route. When we reached the fields, we'd sit back in the meadow, surrounded by long grass dotted generously with beautiful yellow buttercups, stunning purple knapweed and striking white oxeye daisies. Often, we'd find other flattened spots in the grass where the local fox had done the very same. We'd lie on our backs and close our eyes. The warm summer breeze would envelop us and we'd allow ourselves to dissolve into the land. All manner of butterflies, bees and hoverflies would drift from flower to flower, filling the air with a vibrant buzz as they pottered along, feeding from nature's sweet, life-giving nectar. Grasshoppers stridulated from the tips of larger grass blades, adding to the diverse soundscape of a thriving ecosystem. A row of old oaks and sycamores lined the field's lower end, separating it from the marsh. From here, came another element of welcome sound, and in the warm glow of the evening sun we'd be serenaded by the local songbirds: chaffinches, chiffchaffs, robins, blackbirds and more.

To me, these simple but honest scenes were life. I flourished on them, and they gave me the energy I needed to get by in the 'other world'.

The term 'songbird' refers to a specific suborder of birds. Firstly, all songbirds are those that are capable of perching on branches or similar due to their unique grasping capabilities as a result of their toe arrangement. Perching birds are assigned to the order known as 'passerines', but not all passerines sing. Passerines are further divided into three suborders, the largest of that is *Passeri*. This suborder is also known as oscines or, to the lay person, songbirds! It is this collection of birds that are known for the melodic tunes we all love so dearly.

Chiffchaff *(Phylloscopus collybita)*
Family *Phylloscopidae (leaf warblers)*
Conservation status *Green-listed (BoCCI, 2020–2026)*
Vocalisations *The most familiar vocalisation is the song, which is an onomatopoeic 'chiff-chaff-chiff-chiff-chaff'.*

It should come as no surprise that I earned myself the nickname 'Nature Boy' from some of my classmates. I wore it with hesitant pride. I knew it was said in a jeering manner but, to me, it was a cool badge to wear despite that. I guess it kind of hurt because I knew I didn't really fit in, but I loved nature, and to have that recognised by others made me proud. I was a nature boy, and I still am!

I remember occasionally meeting classmates walking along the Tay Road and I felt a little embarrassed passing with my binoculars around my neck because I knew they'd bring it up in class the next day. Whatever. I'd put my red-flushed head down, give them a nod if I had to, and go back to my world. I tried to share nature with my class as much as I could but it often didn't resonate in the way I expected it to.

I once brought in my prized Venus flytrap. It usually lived in my room and would catch any fly that dared enter. I think my classmates thought it was quite cool at first, but one day when I came back from lunch, I noticed that every trap was shut, which was unusual. On close inspection, I saw that each one had been triggered by and had enveloped little balls of tinfoil. A few days later, the plant died. This was one of the first times in my life that I realised not everyone respected nature in the way that Dad, Pops and I did. The person who did if found it really funny, which baffled me. How could people be so cruel? I knew that nature would never treat me or others in this way; this malevolent streak is a human trait.

When I couldn't get out in nature, I would often watch UK-based nature documentaries and dream of seeing some of the exotic species that were missing from my Irish bird book. A great revelation came one evening when I chanced upon an Irish nature documentary, in the Irish language but with English subtitles, by the great Éamon de Buitléar. Although a new discovery to me at the time, Mr de Buitléar was a groundbreaking natural history filmmaker whose wildlife series *Amuigh Faoin Spéir* (*Out Under the Sky*) was a truly beautiful work of art, featuring the best of wild Ireland told in our native tongue with such touching traditional music. It really was a perfect homage to the Irish natural world and its raw enchantment.

It was in an episode of this wonderful series that I came across a bird that was not in my book. At first, I couldn't understand how this could be – after all, my dog-eared companion was the bible. But on the telly in front of me, I could see with fine-feather detail a common whitethroat singing with pride atop a sun-yellow gorse bush. The song was unfamiliar to me, although it reminded me of a dunnock. It sang a repeated and predictable fast, scratchy, gravelly verse of notes. It almost sounded like it was a human blurting something out as quickly as possible, as a last say in a heated argument it didn't want to lose and before the other got a chance to reply. A pause of a few seconds was followed by the next verse. My curiosity soon turned to a sense of adventure, and I persuaded my father to go in search of this new gem. To my amazement, within an hour, we had tracked down our very own at Roche's Point, a nearby gorse-lined coastal headland. It was a true moment of epiphany in my budding ornithological journey. Just like the bird on the telly, it was sitting in a windswept gorse bush at the edge of a cliff on the point. I memorised its features from the show: the main things to look for were the grey head, rusty brown wings, and the striking white throat, from which it gets its name. Its song was very distinctive, too: a fast, gravelly collection of notes given in a short, repeated verse. When excited, it would rise into the air and sing another type of song that was more varied in tone and delivery, and much longer. This song flight in whitethroats is packed full of mimicry of other species: birds it had heard here in Ireland, in Iberia as it passed through, even from its African wintering grounds. Little did I know that this bird would reappear later in my life and would remould my understanding of Irish birds.

Common Whitethroat *(Sylvia communis)*
Family *Sylviidae ('typical warblers' and a number of babblers)*
Conservation status *Green-listed (BoCCI, 2020–2026)*
Vocalisations *Whitethroats are most easily detected by their songs, of which there are two primary forms. When relaxed, they give a series of short gravelly, repetitive bursts, typically from a perch atop a gorse bush, a tree or similar. When excited, as a result of a rival male or by the presence of a female they want to impress upon, they fly into the air and sing a highly mimetic version of their previously described song. Their mimetic song can be anywhere up to 90 per cent composed of the imitations of other species the bird has heard in its life. And because they are lifelong learners (some birds have a critical learning window, often a few months, after which their song is set), Whitethroats can continue learning all the way from Ireland to Senegal, and back.*

From here on in, everything was about birds. I wanted to know and see them all. I outgrew my little bird book and upgraded to the *Collins Bird Guide*,[8] the modern-day bible of bird identification for Europe. I devoured it. In fact, I ordered a second copy. I kept one in the bathroom while the other would accompany me in the bedroom or at the kitchen table.

I must have opened the pages a hundred times a day, every day. Sometimes, I would open at random and read about the bird I landed upon. I learned all about the different types of feathers, which I'd never been exposed to before. Primary projections, tertial steps, undertail coverts – it was all there. These fine details helped me hone my skills and enabled me to make sense of closely related, similar-looking species. For example, willow warbler and chiffchaff look very similar. Willow warblers tend to be brighter green and yellow toned, compared to the browner, olive-toned chiffchaffs. Also, chiffchaffs typically have dark legs and willow warblers usually have pale orangey legs. But these features aren't reliable. They can vary from bird to bird in both species. But the *Collins Guide* told me that primary projection is a solid feature to separate these two. Primary projection refers to how far the primary flight feathers (the largest feathers on the wing and those essential for flight) pass beyond the tertial feathers (those that protect the primary and secondary flight feathers) when the wings are at rest. In chiffchaffs, the primary projection is about half the full length of its tertials. However, in willow warbler, the primary projection is equal to the full length of the tertials. They also sound similar but different – this took more practice. The calls of each are a variation of a disyllabic 'hu-eet'. However, the chiffchaff always sounds like it's in a rush, and the separation between syllables is much less pronounced, sounding more like a fast, rising 'hweet'. Willow warbler is much slower, with the syllables clearly pronounced, 'huu-eeet'. It almost sounds like a slowed-down water droplet.

I'd soak up the wonderful illustrations by famed Irish bird illustrator Killian Mullarney, and I'd pore over the text, which offered a surgical breakdown of identification features for all plumage variations. This was proper nerdy stuff and I loved it. Other times, I would think of a bird I had some hesitations on, and I'd drill the details until my hesitations were no more. My goal was to have the ability to identify any Irish bird species with ease. Some very closely related species took some work to be able to identify in the field with ease.

This devotion to the *Collins Bird Guide* was, of course, heavily supplemented by daily visits to nature, often with my father. Cuskinny was a mainstay, but we occasionally branched out to places further afield. Galley Head in west Cork was a big adventure we'd go on now and then. My brother Conor, six years my junior, was old enough to join us at this point. Conor also had an affinity for nature but didn't necessarily 'live' it like I did.

Galley Head is, as the name suggests, a coastal headland. At its tip is a lighthouse, which was open to the public when I was a child. The biggest draw of this site was the great view to the open Atlantic and the wildlife that it offered. In my early teens, I saved my Christmas, birthday and pocket money for a few years and bought a telescope for bird- and whale-watching. Galley Head is famed for its whale-watching as well as the spectacular movements of migrating seabirds in spring and autumn. In winter, we'd go here with the telescope on calm days and scan the seas for any signs of cetaceans (whales, dolphins and porpoises). Calm days were best because the blow of a whale was visible for many kilometres and it wasn't broken up by the wind. A surfacing fin was also much easier to spot.

One day in early spring, we had incredible views of two fin whales feeding just a kilometre or two offshore – a stone's throw through the telescope. The fin whale is Ireland's largest mammal (after the blue whale, but that is rarely seen) and grows to an amazing length of up to 25 metres. Common dolphins played in the waves that washed from either side of the whales' heads as they cruised through the surface waters. They looked like flies buzzing around the heads of a cow. That very same day, we heard some rustling in grass by our side, and out popped a pygmy shrew, Ireland's *smallest* mammal, weighing just 4 grammes. These exploratory trips outside of Cuskinny opened my eyes to a whole other world of nature just waiting to be explored, but Dad and I always returned to our home turf.

One winter's evening another big change came. It was a Sunday, so with no school on the agenda, I was free to do what I loved and take a trip to Cuskinny. My father was tired as he had been working overtime that week. The last thing he needed was me parading him around on a never-ending quest for birds. We were about to take the final hill down to the reserve when a flock of birds in a berry-laden tree caught my eye. 'WAXWINGS!' I exclaimed. My father nearly took the car off the road with the fright of my outburst. Waxwings are a unique-looking bird from Scandinavia that rarely venture south, usually only doing so in winters in which the berry crop up there fails. This would make it a rare migrant or even a vagrant to Irish shores, and this concept did not yet exist in our understanding of birds in Ireland. We didn't know that 'rarities' could occur, and that a whole sub-niche of birding was built around so-called 'twitchers' following up these rarities. A bit like storm-chasers, they sought out the adrenaline of seeing far-flung, out-of-context rarities in their home country.

My father thought I was mistaken and said, 'Seán, cop on, those are starlings.'

'No! I'm telling you, they were waxwings,' I insisted.

Exhausted, my father gave me an ultimatum: 'Seán, I don't have the energy for this today. I can't be driving all around the island for the day chasing things down. If I turn around and they're starlings, I'm going home. Do you want to turn around or will we continue to Cuskinny?'

I replied without hesitation: 'Turn around, quick!'

I could see my dad's 'I told you so' face creeping up, only for it to flicker to a face of excited disbelief when we found them. For the first time in my life, I had taught my dad a lesson, and we both smiled – me partly in smugness, my dad knowing that I was reaching a new level in my knowledge and understanding of the natural world around us. We stopped the car at the side of the road and rolled down the windows. There they were – a flock of waxwings devouring the berries in the garden we'd just passed. Neither of us could believe it. They were much bigger than we'd both envisaged. We'd thought they were robin-sized but these were more starling-sized, although they looked nothing like starlings.

The first thing that jumps out about a waxwing is its big sleeked-back crest, almost like a punk rocker's mohican. Then, there are the ultra-yellow tail and wing feathers that look too bright to be real. The cherry on top is the wax-like red feathers halfway up – they literally look like wax seals, hence the name 'waxwing'.

They were in our bird book but they shouldn't be here! What was happening?

As it turned out, there were particularly damp conditions in the berry-forming period in Scandinavia that year. This meant that the berry crop largely failed and the waxwing population fled south in search of food. I discovered this after finding an online forum where local bird news was shared. It was mainly a UK-based website, but there was a small section for Irish bird news and it was here I learned of their presence, and also where I met another Cork-based birder, Harry Hussey, who would later become an invaluable friend. This was my introduction to the world of avian vagrancy – something that would play a major role in my continually expanding ornithological life.

Waxwing *(Bombycilla garrulus)*
Family *Bombycillidae (waxwings)*
Conservation status: *Amber-listed (BoCCI, 2020–2026)*
Vocalisations *A rapid high-pitched liquid 'sirrrrrr' trill*

The thrill of finding these waxwings faded when I went back to class the next day, because I had nobody to share it with. I knew the news of their presence in Ireland would fall flat, despite it being huge to me. Everyone else spoke about who was dating whom or the results of the previous night's game, and no matter how much I tried to care about these things, I just couldn't. I had no experience with girls and I was terrified of speaking to them, so that chat was out. I did try to force myself to watch football for a period in the hope that I could 'normalise' myself, in a sense. After all, if the common whitethroat could mimic others, why couldn't I? My forced foray into the world of football spectatorship didn't last long. It was such a weird process and confirmed that it most certainly was not for me. How did people decide what team to follow? Did they pick one at random? Did they pick the team with a history of wins? What the hell is the offside rule about? Watching football to me was just *so* boring. In my eyes, it boiled down to watching a group of millionaires kicking a ball up and down a field for 90 minutes.

Sure, that's an oversimplified view and I knew that there must be something to it, because millions of people around the world watched it, but to me it was utterly meaningless. But I still wanted to be accepted. Nobody wants to be an outcast, and I increasingly felt that I was.

So, at the age of 13, I went through a year-long period where I pretended I didn't like nature. This was the peak of my awkward teenager phase. I was moody and very sensitive to what others thought about me, and so I wanted to act like part of the 'cool' crowd, or at least who I perceived to be the cool crowd. This period of denial just so happened to coincide with the arrival of a pod of orcas into Cork Harbour. It was a family pod consisting of a male, female and calf. These spectacular pied cetaceans graced the harbour for a few weeks, and everybody saw them. Everybody except me because I was doing everything in my power not to look at or interact with nature, because it wasn't cool!

Some weeks after the orcas first turned up, the female of the group was found dead, floating near the mouth of the harbour. It was the talk of the town. They seemed fine and healthy and so her death had people wondering if she had been struck by a boat. After some time, UCC conducted a post-mortem and they discovered she had a severe abscess in her jaw which caused blood poisoning. Although I never saw her, my heart sank for her and her family. Perhaps they knew. Is it possible they sensed her death was near and they came inshore to calmer waters to ease her passing, away from the risk of predation in her weakened state? I did some reading and pondered even further. It is known that some orcas can have a diet that focuses heavily on the shark family. The teeth of such shark-eaters can become abraded due to the sandpaper-like texture of shark skin, because of their armour of V-shaped scales, known as dermal denticles. Could she have been a shark-eater, whose teeth wore down to the point of infection? Even in my rebellion against nature, it was still there, and I eventually came to my senses. Who was I fooling? Nature had always been there for me, and going against it felt so wrong. Just like the whitethroat, I tried to mimic everyone around me. But by trying so hard to fit in, the only thing I ended up doing was losing myself and missing out on the things that made me happy.

Holding back my urge to be in nature was like trying to hold a balloon underwater – it just wanted to rise back to the surface with all its might. Nature never judged me for my long hair or my green Doc Martens. It was always there to pick me up when I was down. I realised I'd made a big mistake in turning my back on nature and, of course, it welcomed me back with open arms.

Gull-billed Tern

Chapter 3

I TURNED 18 ON 20 APRIL 2006. THIS IS THE BIRTHDAY THAT we typically associate with entering adulthood. Life becomes real. If I could travel back in time, I'd take myself by both shoulders, look myself in the eye, and tell myself to be strong, to hold on tight and to get ready for a fight. I'd give myself a hug and tell myself not to be scared. If only I could have had all of that.

I'd just finished my first year of exams in my BSc in environmental and earth system sciences in UCC. This was the gateway to zoology, but it meant I first had to study a lot of subjects I had no interest in: mainly chemistry, physics and geology. The former two I found extremely tough and boring. I was there to pursue a more formal education in nature, and this is what drove me through the other not-so-fun subjects. I knew I'd drop them like a hot pancake as soon as I could. For now, I just wanted to get the grades I needed to pass.

College for me involved a lot of self-imposed pressure. I'd never failed an exam in my life and I'd always strived to do my very best at school. The exam format was nothing like what I'd become accustomed to in secondary school. University exams were much more complex and required a more flexible way of thinking. Run-of-the-mill answering just didn't cut the mustard.

Throughout my first year of college, I felt a little left out. At 17, I was the youngest in my year. I'd come to class each week and hear of the tales of student nights out from all of my peers. They'd talk about what clubs they went to, who made a fool of themselves, who hooked up with whom. But I couldn't join in because I was underage. In a sense, I felt like this stopped me from making connections with my classmates. I only knew them through class itself because socialising revolved around nightlife – we were young adults discovering ourselves and having our first taste of freedom. Most of my classmates also lived in student accommodation in Cork city, but I still lived at home with my parents. College was just a short train journey for me, so there was no need to spend what little money I earned in my part-time job working in a houseware store on accommodation.

The looser boundaries of college compared to secondary school suited me. It also helped that I was actually interested in the subjects being taught, or at least most of them. But I still struggled socially with my classmates. Even though everyone there had some interest in nature, I still felt ... different. I avoided small talk at all costs, and clung dearly to my two childhood friends, Gary and Olly. If I had to have a conversation I steered it towards classwork or my birding adventures – nature was always my lifebuoy, even when it came to chit-chat.

Not being old enough to go out and socialise only added to my feelings of being a bit of an outcast. I didn't turn 18 until our study month in April, which was set aside to prepare for the end-of-year exams. There was no way I was going to party during that month, so I knuckled down and studied day and night.

Before exams, students would gather outside the allocated buildings and chat about what they'd prepared for and what topics they thought would come up. I just couldn't – my stomach was in knots – so I'd find somewhere to hide. I'd sit there, head in my hands, and drill over my notes again and again, breathing rapidly. I always felt like I wasn't quite ready, despite having pored over the notes obsessively during study month. In a sense, the process mirrored my studying of my bird book, only the feeling was very different. I studied the bird book out of passion, a burning desire to learn as much as I could about a subject I loved deeply – the feathered friends who were by my side from my first days in the pram exploring with Dad. Although I tackled my exam notes with the same intensity, it was fuelled just as much by a fear of failure as it was by a drive to embark on a career that would enable me to study what I loved.

I always knew that pursuing a career in nature would never bring me great riches, but I didn't care. I never had a love for flashy things, bar good equipment related to nature-watching – cameras, binoculars, telescopes, etc. We spend the majority of our lives sleeping and working, and sleeping is a breeze – I've got that one under control – but working is another matter. Being stuck at a desk in a corporate setting would be hell on earth for me. So, to carve out a career working with nature was a dream beyond dreams. I wouldn't be paid as well as a banker or solicitor, but I'd get enough to have what I needed and

I'd be happy. So, failure in my studies was never an option, even if it meant drowning in chemistry and physics books. I had to force-feed myself those subjects, but biology went down easy.

When exam time came, I was still nervous as hell. The thing that always calmed me was nature. There was one place above all I'd go to bring me back to a state of equilibrium: Roche's Point. All my life I worried about exams. This was totally self-imposed. I needed to get as high a grade as possible, and to do this I studied hard. But I would always get distracted by the very thing that calmed me – nature. It was either directly outside my window or in my racing mind. Even then, in the midst of my pre-exam jitters, nature would still break through and rise above it all. But I couldn't allow it to be there when I was focusing on my exam notes, so I developed a system whereby every 30 minutes to an hour, I would either look out my window at the birds or I'd physically go out there and look at whatever nature appeared at my feet. And at the end of the day, I promised myself I would immerse myself fully at one of my favourite nature-filled locations – most often Roche's Point. I had this to look forward to; it fuelled me through the monotony of the heavy study I imposed upon myself to achieve the good grades I wanted.

Roche's Point is the easterly jaw that opens the calms of Cork Harbour to the wilds of the Atlantic Ocean. At its tip sits a gleaming white lighthouse whose foghorn resonated through my bedroom on foggy winter mornings, a soothing sound that also told me I'd need to wrap up warm for the day ahead. On the highest points of Great Island, including from Pops' and Granny Betty's home, I could see all the way out to Roche's Point. But it was blocked from view by the convent in front of our home. Roche's Point was farther away from our familiar Cuskinny, having to circumvent the harbour to get there – about a 30-minute drive. If I were a bird, though, I could have flown directly across the harbour from Cobh to Roche's Point in no time, and when I looked out at it from the hills of Cobh, I'd often imagine doing just that: soaring high over the various islands and the lighthouse – next stop: France! We visited a lot when I was a teenager, and it was another place in Cork that I came to know like the back of my hand – the birdlife, the flora, the smells and the sounds. I made a map of all of it in my head.

On visits in my free time from college, Dad and I would park up just below the lighthouse with a view back through the harbour to Cobh. Behind are a series of fields where we'd stroll, binoculars around our necks, inhaling the refreshing salty air. The sound of the waves crashing against the rocky point filled the air, and the honking of the raven was never far, with a pair nesting in an oversized stick nest on the cliffs. To our right was the iconic lighthouse, which guides ships safely into Cork Harbour, reminding them to keep clear of the jagged rocks that frame its entrance.

On these very rocks, a plethora of coastal birds roosted. Cormorants perching high with their wings held wide to dry off between fishing expeditions. Gulls roosting on one leg with their heads tucked under a wing, taking an opportunistic nap. Oystercatchers foraging for mussels and other tasty morsels that clung to the rocks and were laid visible at low tide. The sound of the powerful Atlantic waves crashing against the rocks set the tone here. Herring gulls wailed overhead and commuting oystercatchers pipped in announcement as they flew from one exposed rock to another. Now and then, the goat-like sounds of the cormorants could be heard echoing from the rocks

– they'd bicker and jostle for position when new birds landed to roost and dry off. Sometimes, we'd see dolphins playing offshore. Anything was possible, and every visit was different. We were free here and happily drenched in nature, away from the madness of the town.

Cormorant *(Phalacrocorax carbo)*
Family *Phalacrocoracidae (cormorants and shags)*
Conservation status *Amber-listed (BoCCI, 2020–2026)*
Vocalisations *Seldom heard, except when on the nest or at roost. The most typical vocalisation is a fast guttural 'gurr-gurr-gurr'.*

Under the towering shadow of the lighthouse there is a dark protrusion of jagged rocks, upon which birds abound and waves crash. Below the surface of those waves are all manner of fish, crustaceans, seals and other sea life. Each trip there taught me something new. A feeling of pure happiness and belonging enveloped me like a warm blanket on every visit. I cherished every moment I spent there.

Whenever I found myself stuck inside the library, preparing for exams, I'd take myself there in my mind's eye. I knew this place so intimately that I could see every nook and cranny when I closed my eyes. I'd smell the distinctive sea air, which I was led to believe was ozone back then. I learned that in school way back, but our knowledge of the world is constantly updating. We now know that this smell is, in fact, dimethyl sulphide (DMS), a trace gas produced by bacteria as they consume phytoplankton, a form of microscopic marine algae. So, DMS is a chemical, and in high concentrations it smells horrendous, but in trace form it's rather pleasant. It's the signature smell of sea air.

In my mind, I could also hear the family parties of choughs, screeching at height, tumbling and rotating for fun in the wind. Choughs are a rare and mainly coastal species of crow. They have a special lipstick-red curved beak that they use to pluck invertebrates from the soil, and thus they seek out grasslands with a sward of just a few centimetres or less. In winter, they congregate in large flocks, including at Roche's Point. To see these airborne show-offs gather in numbers is a special sight. They laugh in the face of a strong Atlantic gale. In fact, they dance with it, making it look like it's nothing but a play thing. In Europe, choughs are protected under Annex I of the EU Birds Directive, which requires member states to designate Special Areas of Protection (SPAs) where important feeding or breeding sites occur. This species of acrobatic crow is declining in Europe and has a highly fragmented range. Seeing these choughs at Roche's Point was always a highlight. They were the crown of the site and we always sought them out. So having these soaring graciously through my mind brought me a sense of tranquillity when I was feeling jittery in the library.

Chough *(Pyrrhocorax pyrrhocorax)*
Family *Corvidae (crows)*
Conservation status *Annex I (EU Birds Directive), Amber-listed (BoCCI, 2020–2026)*
Vocalisations *Typical call is a shrill, high-pitched 'shree-oww'.*

On exam day, with a hurricane in my stomach, I'd sit down and brace myself for the paper to arrive. I'd manically scan the sheets for reassurance. Did my topics come up? Of course they did, Seán. I'd over-prepared to no end and they were all there. I'd never felt such a feeling of relief. College isn't so bad after all. I *can* do this.

After such a stressful slog, it was time to celebrate and now that I was 18, I could finally party with my friends. I was so excited to go out that night – I'd heard so many stories about the fun people had in An Bróg, The Thirsty Scholar and Freakscene. We all met in a classmate's house before we headed into town and partied all night. Throughout the year, I never really made any connections with my classmates, bar a few people I already knew from home, as well as the friends they'd made themselves. It's not that I didn't want to make friends, I just wasn't good at it. I watched how my friends from home so effortlessly ebbed and flowed with chit-chat. There was rarely an awkwardness in their body language or conversation. But when I tried to talk to new people, everything about it felt forced. I didn't want to look them in the eye and this made them feel weird. I knew that – I could see it in their reactions. I didn't know where to put my hands and I didn't know what to say. I'd blurt things out that didn't make sense and that would make people feel even more uncomfortable. I really wanted them to know I wasn't weird, I just didn't know how.

I thought, *Maybe I am weird?* This whole process of trying to fit in almost always played out in the same way, and so I tended not to bother with it. Small talk was just such a strange concept to me. What was the point of it? What do I care what they did for the weekend?

Do I need to ask them if they have any holiday plans? Do people care about these things? I found it easier to blend into the background. I could just be quiet, observe, and avoid this awkward process – a process that brought me nowhere anyway.

But on exam night, I could finally have a drink with people, and maybe that would cut out my awkwardness and fears of socialising. I sipped on a can of lager and with each mouthful I swallowed my inhibitions. I felt more and more at ease as I neared the end of the can. I wasn't focusing on where to look or where to put my arms, and I found a voice I never had. This socially confident person, whom I didn't know, really impressed me. I was happy to let others take the wheel. It felt liberating, really. I made connections with people like never before and, for the first time in my life, I actually enjoyed approaching people and making conversation. We had a great time and I felt so free after the intensive month of reclusion, anxiety and focus. But this is not the way, not at all. Using alcohol to feel normal is not a way to live. Although I was just trying to fit in, my peers didn't need a crutch to socialise – for me, it only served to mask my social fears. I wasn't addressing the cause because I didn't know what that cause was.

I definitely overdid it, so I woke up in my friend's house the next morning feeling unwell. We all felt the same way. But when others were starting to feel better, I still didn't feel great at all. I took some paracetamol and I felt a *little* better, but still not right. I shrugged it off and told the guys I was going home. I took the train as always, and that sensation was still there: a strong headache and an intense feeling of nausea and abdominal cramping. Everything ached. *God,*

I shouldn't have drunk so much, I thought. I opened the back door at home and my mam greeted me with an undeniable 'I told you so' look.

I smiled at her and just came out with it. 'I don't feel too good, Mam. I'm going to go to bed.'

She gave me the look again, but also couldn't help but worry. 'Okay, Seán, take it easy. I'm going to the shops, do you need anything?'

'No,' I replied, 'I'm just going to lie down.'

I was lying in bed and things weren't getting any better. I began to feel worse and worse. My temperature was rising, my head was pounding, and I was just feeling generally unwell. I never really tended to get headaches, and this was unlike anything I'd ever experienced. I felt like my head was going to explode with the pressure. But it wasn't just that, my whole body was aching. It was as if the pain in my head was pulsating throughout my body. I knew now that it wasn't just a hangover. My mam soon came home from the shops and came in to see how I was. I told her I was coming down with something, and she told me to stay in bed, that I was in the best place for me. I needed to take it easy and recover. I felt horrendous and I didn't budge from the bed. And then everything escalated ...

I had an urgent and intense feeling of nausea. I jumped up from the bed, having been there for a few hours, and ran to the bathroom, which was just opposite my bedroom. This was the first time I'd stood up since coming home. The first thing that hit me was dizziness, weakness and the extreme cold that trembled over my body. Kneeling down on the cold tiles of the bathroom, I vomited violently and lay there shivering, teeth chattering. I was very unwell. I didn't want to disturb anyone though, so I made my way back to bed, my vision notably blurred.

The second I lay down, I started to spin; in fact, the whole room was whirling around me. I immediately wanted to vomit again. I sat up in bed and it stopped, though I was so exhausted that sitting up was the last thing I wanted to do. I lay down again and the room spun violently. I held my breath and hoped that either the nausea would pass or that I would pass *out*. I nodded off, but it wasn't long before I woke up and had to dash to the toilet again. I nearly fell over. This time, I added explosive diarrhoea to my rapidly growing list of ailments. I just sat there on the toilet, miserable, cold, aching and defeated. I was feeling weaker by the minute. I didn't have the energy to get back to bed and didn't want to face the nausea, so I sat there shivering, confusion starting to creep in.

My mam had gone to collect my father from work, and on arriving home they both went to my room to find it empty. I was slumped over on the toilet seat, head and arms dangling, gravity feeling too much for my body. I was still just about compos mentis when I awoke. The door boomed, knock, knock, knock. 'Seán, are you in there?'

I replied, my voice barely audible. 'Yeah, I'm here.'

'Are you okay?'

'No, I feel really sick.' I buttoned myself up and struggled to the door. My mam looked shocked. I was pale, sweating and generally looked dreadful. They both helped me to my bed. Our GP was away on holidays and it was too late of a Friday evening for any other clinic, so my mother called an out-of-hours doctor.

At this point, the pain really began to surge. It was coursing through my veins like fire. The doctor on call came to the house and, after examining me, she said I had a severe case of gastroenteritis, and that I needed to drink plenty of fluids and rest well. I looked at her and said, 'Oh, hi Jennifer! I had no idea you were a doctor. Congratulations!' My mother gave my father a confused and equally concerned look. Jennifer is my aunt and is not a medical professional. My mother shrugged it off as some strange misunderstanding. I took some medication, drank some water and went to bed. I had my phone on the bedside locker and my parents told me to ring if I needed anything, and said they'd be checking on me regularly regardless. My father needed to eat his dinner after working overtime and so himself and my mother went about catching up in the living room.

The pain was really building now and the sensation of nausea was indescribable. I just had to go to the toilet. I dragged myself out of bed feeling extremely weak and extremely hot, but feeling icy cold at the same time. I was shivering uncontrollably and each step forward was like trying to walk in a straight line after stepping out of a washing machine on full spin.

Then, there is a gap in my recollection. I was crawling from my bed to the bathroom for fear of passing out. I must have stood up to sit on the toilet because the next thing I remember is waking up on the floor. My face slowly unstuck from the tiles as I came to and lifted my head. I *must* have passed out. There was the nausea again. How could I vomit any more? I was so thirsty. I leaned my head over the bowl and dry-retched. Nothing was coming up yet the nausea would not leave me. I passed out again and later woke to my parents calling my name.

They carried me to the room and brought me a bucket so I didn't have to go to the bathroom again. They were really concerned at this point. I hung out of the bed with the bucket underneath, occasionally retching to life between the intense bouts of full-body quivering. I was writhing with pain and moaned audibly between spasms. Then nothing. I must have fallen asleep. My parents, exhausted with worry, retired to bed to regain some energy. They took turns checking up on me.

I woke in the middle of the night, in a moment between the regularly spaced visits from my parents and went into autopilot. I jumped up to go to the bathroom and just about made it in the door when all 6 foot 2 of me came crashing down like a falling tree. I landed face-first on the tiles of the bathroom. I knocked a tooth out, loosened several more, and my lips split. Blood and saliva splattered the floor. The crash woke my parents, and they found me unconscious and in a contorted heap. My mam screamed and started to cry. This woke me and I asked her if I'd hurt anybody. She stopped and asked me what I meant. I'd become quite delirious. 'Did I hurt anyone in the car crash? Is everyone okay?' I didn't drive, I didn't even have a theory test to my name.

Panic set in for my parents. They knew something was *seriously* wrong with me, but it was four in the morning – there was nobody we could call for help. My parents didn't go to bed again. When I insisted on going to the toilet, they took an arm each and essentially dragged me into position, propping me in place. They knew I was very private, and so they turned their backs while I did what I needed to do. Nothing was helping now. I didn't know pain this intense was even possible.

When I was a young child, playing in the yard at school, I distinctly remember my hands feeling numb in the cold winter air. Sometimes,

I'd fall and slap my cold-numbed fingers on the icy ground. The pain was so bad I'd take a big gasp of air and hold my breath and fingers, dancing around and not daring to breathe until the worst of the sharp pain had subsided. This pain felt a bit like that, but *much* stronger ... and constant. It pulsated throughout my body in relentless agony. At 9 a.m., having watched every minute pass waiting for medical help to become available, my parents called Peter Morehan, a well-respected doctor in the town.

My mother explained everything, telling him that they had been up with me all night and that I'd been passing out, with my condition continually worsening. I was in excruciating pain and talking gibberish.

'I'm coming straight up,' Dr Morehan replied. This was despite having a full waiting room. He clearly knew something our non-medical minds didn't.

Dr Morehan was at the front door within five minutes. My mother directed him straight to my room where I was huddled in bed in the darkness. He asked for the curtains to be opened and I saw a look of shock come over his eyes. The sudden light was agony. I had a stabbing pain that seemed to go from eye to brain, and I asked for the light to be dimmed. They kept the curtain open but closed the blind. Although I had been drifting in and out of myself, the real Seán was here now. Not the Seán who'd just been in a car crash or the Seán who was congratulating his aunt on becoming a doctor.

I was asked several questions about my symptoms and Dr Morehan took my pulse and did a number of other physical tests. I could sense something. There was an urgency in his eyes. The way he observed me, and then the look that he unintentionally flashed across to my parents said something. He stepped outside and made a phone call to Cobh Hospital. Within five minutes, an oxygen tank and mask arrived at the front door by taxi, and Dr Morehan had me connected to a drip and began administering all kinds of medicines. The empty containers were just dropped on the spot, scattered all around the room. He was acting fast – not a moment was wasted. He stepped outside again and called Cork University Hospital. He was preparing them in advance for my arrival, listing off my symptoms and the medication he had administered. Another local doctor, Harry Kelleher, had arrived for backup in the meantime. They both worked together preparing me for the ambulance.

I started to ask questions: 'What's going on?'

They looked at one another and then Dr Morehan turned to me with a smile and said, 'You need to go to hospital to be rehydrated, Seán. It's nothing serious. It's just that you've lost a lot of fluids, and the only way we can rectify this is with a quick hospital admission. Everything is fine.'

Of course, it wasn't fine, but I was too delirious to think about it.

It wasn't long before the ambulance was at the front door. My mother thanked Dr Morehan for his quick action, and he grabbed her hand and looked her in the eye: 'Sylvia, you have to understand that Seán is in *serious* danger. You need to know that.' He also told her that all of my vital organs were shutting down. Nobody knew what was wrong but my vital support system was hardly functioning and things were quickly getting worse. My heart was hardly beating and my blood pressure was at rock bottom. I didn't hear this in person, thankfully, but this is why I had been passing out every time I stood up.

I was awake for everything. My dad came with me in the ambulance whilst my mother followed behind by car with my aunt Vivian, her sister. I remember lying there but being able to see a sliver of the blue sky and streetlights melting past in a blur. I was *begging* for pain relief, which they administered, but it hardly dulled the pain. The ambulance was moving *so* quickly. The sirens were on constantly and I could feel us swerving in and out of traffic, the driver beeping with urgency. I remember thinking, *This is serious, there's something more than just dehydration going on here.*

Although I was very much awake, everything was moving in a strange way, like flashes of reality interspersed with some other strange world. I looked at my dad, who was holding back tears. He held my hand tightly but was looking out the window with worried red eyes. Then the pain would grip me again. I wouldn't wish this agony on my worst enemy. It was gruelling.

When we arrived at A&E, there were two teams on standby – medical and surgical. Nobody really knew what was going on with me, so they had to be prepared. I was wheeled into resuscitation as medical staff hurriedly exchanged notes. After some initial tests, the surgical team were stood down and the medical team took control. The first thing I remember was how chaotically busy it was. This is where all of the critical cases are brought so every practitioner was in the zone, focusing on saving the lives of the people in each curtained partition.

I briefly took in my surroundings and then the reality hit me once again. The pain coursed through every inch of my body and I begged for morphine. They told me I was already at capacity. I was gasping with thirst and pleaded for water. They couldn't give me any but they did dampen some cotton and allowed me to moisten my mouth with that. I had tubes and needles inserted all over and they all peered over me. Nobody knew what was wrong. They conducted so many tests, and face after face appeared. Then my body couldn't take any more. My heart stopped. Medical staff rushed around me and began chest compressions, and I came back. I woke up and knew nothing of it, although the dull pain in my ribcage told the tale.

Upon waking, I looked at the nurse to my right and asked her if she'd give me a spin across to Womanagh Bridge in east Cork to see the gull-billed tern. She looked at me, bewildered. 'Sorry, what do you mean?'

'It's a rarity!' I replied.

Even at death's door, I was still thinking about nature. Before my admission, this bird had turned up not far from where I lived and I really wanted to see it.

The gull-billed tern is a species of migratory tern which breeds in mainland Europe and migrates south to winter in Africa. In the spring, when they return to the likes of Spain and France, they sometimes fly too far north when the winds are southerly and the weather is particularly sunny and warm here. The weather lulls them into a journey too far up the coast. When the weather settles back to its cold, wet normality, and they realise they're the only one of their kind here, they turn back and head down to Spain or France.

Perhaps I was doing what I always did to escape reality. Just like I thought about the choughs of Roche's Point when I was stuck studying, here I was fighting for my life but thinking of this exotic bird – far brighter than my current situation. Nature was guiding me through the darkness. The nurse smiled and told me that we could go when we were done here. I was on another planet.

***

Gull-billed Tern *(Gelochelidon nilotica)*
Family *Laridae (gulls, terns, noddies, skimmers and kittiwakes)*
Conservation status *Least Concern (IUCN Red List). Does not occur on the Irish BoCCI list, as it is a rare vagrant.*
Vocalisations *A rather comical-sounding, almost toy-like 'kah-wek'*

***

All this time, my parents were sitting with a social worker in the hallway. He'd come to prepare them for my death. He didn't tell them this directly, but they knew it. And, in a way, they rejected him, for accepting him would mean accepting a fate that was unfathomable. One of the doctors exploded from the two swinging doors that connected the resuscitation room to the waiting room. He looked at my parents and said it outright. 'I'm sorry. Although we're trying everything, we cannot find what's wrong with your son. I'm afraid he's not going to survive.'

My mam looked at him in shock. '*What?* There must be a mistake, he's too young. It can't be right.'

He told her to call all of my close family right away; they needed to come and say goodbye. I had septicaemia and I was going into a state of shock. At the rate my organs were failing, I didn't have long and there was no sign of a diagnosis despite their very best efforts. My brother was called out of class, my uncles and aunts left work, and my grandparents were collected from their homes. They all came to say their last goodbyes. To me ... an 18-year-old who had just been out celebrating finishing his exams with his friends. All of my hopes and dreams – to live a life studying, protecting, and sharing the wonders and beauty of nature – were about to be taken from me.

All of my loved ones gathered in the hallway in silence, the stillness only cut by the sniffles and gulps of those closest to me, trying to understand what was happening, trying to find the strength to be there for my parents and brother. Nobody knew where to look or what to say. How can you prepare for a situation like this? Granda Dave looked at my mam and told her, 'He'll pull through, he's strong.' But, deep down, my mam knew that nobody is invincible and there is only so much hardship the human body can withstand.

Behind the doors, I knew myself that I was dying. I lay there on the bed, delirious, broken and just about clinging on. That feeling of sleepiness that was constantly trying to force itself upon me wasn't what it seemed. I knew now that if I gave into it, I would never leave this hospital. I'd never again listen to the cries of the curlew echo through the creeks of Cork Harbour, never again would I pick blackberries on a glistening autumn morning with Dad, and never again would I listen to the whitethroat sing from the tops of its beloved golden gorse. All of it would end right here on a cold metal hospital bed. I never thought I'd be in this situation so young and I knew there and then I wouldn't let it happen. I had to sit up and fight. Lying down took some of the pain away but it meant I was also occasionally slipping away.

I asked to elevate the bed so I could straighten up and not let the sleepy feeling win. I'd rather be writhing in agony than drift away. Soon my thoughts were confirmed. My parents and brother came to see me, and I could see them pause for a moment. I heard my mother telling Conor, 'Be strong for Seán. Don't let him see you with tears in your eyes.' Despite their best intentions, I heard all of this. I was far more lucid than my droopy-eyed, slumping appearance suggested.

I *knew* they were coming to say goodbye and so I mustered every last ounce of strength I had in me to put on a front of reassurance.

They stood around my bed and Conor said to me in a quivering voice. 'Seán, you know I love you, don't you?'

I replied: 'I know, Conor, I love you too!' in as upbeat a tone as I could manage.

My father was too sad to speak, he knew he'd break down, so he looked at me and smiled, his face radiating love and support. Then my mother grabbed my hand and said, 'Seán, you have to fight this, you're too young to go.'

This was the first time she'd let the mask slip. And that was the final call to arms I needed. Despite the agony and the growing sensation of exhaustion, I knew I was going to resist with all I had in me. I looked at my mam and smiled. 'Mam, I'm not going anywhere, don't worry.'

What I wasn't aware of was that the woman who was about to save my life had been called in on her day off. Professor Mary Horgan, an infectious disease specialist, had been working on my bloods upstairs all this time, trying to find the cause of my illness. She worked tirelessly for hours on end and it paid off. A new face rushed into the room and told my parents. 'He has meningitis!'

I overheard and blurted out, *'Meningitis?'*

Professor Mary Horgan had cracked it. I really didn't have much time left. I was struggling to stay conscious and we all knew what that meant. It was death, not sleep that I was trying to fight.

It was midnight at that stage and they started administering everything they could to stabilise me and reverse the most life-threatening effects of the meningitis. My heart slowly started to come back and my blood pressure started to creep up. My parents were told I was still very much in the danger zone. They sat outside and asked everyone to kindly go home. Not that they didn't appreciate their love and support, but they just couldn't cope. They could hardly live with their own thoughts. They didn't hear anything for a while but they thought that this was a good thing. No news is good news.

Then, after some time, I started to stabilise and they moved me out of the resuscitation unit. My parents followed me, teary eyed with relief. I was brought to a recovery ward within a recovery ward. My room was boxed in behind a glass wall, where I could see out and people could see in, but I couldn't infect people. I was so exhausted and the agony had finally begun to subside. I really didn't mind where they brought me as long as I could just lie there and catch my breath. The doctors all wore what looked like hazmat suits and they began to insert several tubes into my body to drain wastes and to siphon out the septicaemic fluid that had almost brought me to my end. I saw it leave my body through the tube. It was the strangest, most ominous shade of bright green I'd ever seen and I gladly watched it flow out of me.

No visitors were allowed to enter because I was too infectious, and nobody wanted to catch what I just had, trust me. That night, despite feeling as tired as I'd ever felt, and probably ever will feel, I could not sleep. Not a wink. It was incredibly boring and also quite uncomfortable. I was in a glass prison for the foreseeable future. My ribs ached from the compressions and my body was battered from being prodded and poked – and, of course, from the poison that pumped through my veins. I had two tubes stretching my nostrils wide open that ran down my throat, another went up through my urethra and another one was stuck into my side.

I had no control of my bowels and had no option of going to the toilet anyway, even if I physically could. I was fitted with a nappy. I tried to hold on but had to give in eventually and call a nurse to help me clean up. I was mortified. It was a male nurse, which made it less embarrassing. I wish I remembered his name because he was such a lovely man and he really made my time there so much easier. He was from India and he grew up in a national nature reserve there. He knew I loved nature myself and so he'd regularly tell me stories about growing up around tigers, elephants and leopards. It triggered my imagination and took me away from it all. I'd never been to India, but the way he described it really brought me there. In turn, I told him about Roche's Point, about how I'd sit there with Dad and take in the wild Atlantic from the shadow of the towering white lighthouse, how gulls and choughs wheeled overhead and filled the skies with their iconic coastal voices, how the weird and wonderful tube-nosed fulmars cackled from their cliff-ledge abodes, and how we'd occasionally see dolphins leaping clean up out of the water, splashing back down with a glistening froth. I could tell he genuinely enjoyed his mind-journey there too. I needed this now more than ever. Although I was over the worst of it, my mind was shattered. I was deeply traumatised, although I didn't quite know it at the time. Even though I was trapped inside a glass enclosure in the hospital, my lovely new friend would bring me out of it, in a sense, every time he came to care for me.

Myself and Pops in the summer of 1990. Behind us you can see Cork Harbour, Spike Island and the railings from where we'd launch paper airplanes.

My early days of birding: posing with an ostrich at Fota Wildlife Park in Cork.

A male blackbird forages for earthworms in the lawn. During my childhood, blackbird song was the first thing I heard most mornings.

All images not credited were taken by the author or are from his own collection.

'Posing' with my parents on the day of my communion in 1995. I've never enjoyed smiling on cue, and often find it impossible. During this period of my life I would rebel and pull faces instead!

My parents and both sets of grandparents pose in front of Pops and Granny Betty's house in May 1987. L–R: David Cahill (Granda Dave), Terry Ronayne (Pops), Terry Ronayne (Dad), Sylvia Ronayne (then Cahill, Mam), Eileen Cahill (Granny Cahill), Betty Ronayne (Granny Betty).

Seeing a kingfisher up close was a moment my dad and I cherished when I was a kid. This image is of the kingfisher at UCC that I waited so long to capture, posing nicely in January 2016, just before it dove for a fish and left.

A whitethroat perches in willow scrub. Although they may not look very striking, these birds are incredible vocalists. Photo by Mark Carmody.

An overwintering chiffchaff, photographed at Delta del Llobregat ('The Delta'), Catalunya in 2019. As a young boy, I learned a lot about this bird, and many others, from my treasured *Collins Bird Guide*.

A freshly arrived migrant willow warbler, photographed in May 2021 at Mizen Head Peninsula, County Cork.

A small group of choughs feeding amongst the seaweed at Ballynamona Strand, County Cork, in 2017. Memories of seeing this bird at Roche's Point was one of the things that gave me great comfort when I was ill.

Myself and my brother Conor with our dogs Tess (left) and Bella (right) in winter 2000 at one of our regular nature walks at Cuskinny. In my hand is one of my old trusty Irish nature guides. Photo by Terry Ronayne.

A herring gull long-calling at Kennedy Quay, Cork city, in December 2018.

A fulmar photographed on the cliffs of Tory Island in June 2021.

A yellow wagtail at Low Newton-by-the-Sea, Northumberland, in September 2013.

Grey seals hauled out: this picture was taken in September 2013 when I worked as a nature guide on a boat that took people out to the Farne Islands off the coast of Northumberland.

A grey heron standing on its stick nest in early spring 2020, before the leaves have appeared, in Estany d'Ivars i Vila-sana, Catalunya.

I often saw sanderlings in Northumberland, and in Ireland, but this photo of a small group feeding at the edge of the sandy shoreline was taken at the beach at El Prat De Llobregat in Catalunya in 2019. They're running from an incoming wave, as they do with frequency.

Seabirds have always been particular favourites of mine. Here you can see a sandwich tern (named after Sandwich Bay in Kent) with a fish in its mouth, at Lady's Island Lake tern colony, County Wexford, in May 2021.

Fulmar *(Fulmarus glacialis)*
Family Procellariidae *(fulmarine petrels, gadfly petrels, diving petrels, prions and shearwaters)*
Conservation status Amber-listed (BoCCI, 2020–2026)
Vocalisations Mostly heard at the nest, where the most typical vocalisation is a hoarse series of cackling 'gah-gah-gah-gah-gah' notes.

Sometimes, I sobbed when I was alone. The reality hadn't quite sunk in, but there were flashes of understanding and it hit me in those moments. I was heavily drugged on an impressive concoction. It made me curse a lot, which is very out of character for me. I remember one evening the nurse came to change my sheets and accidentally picked up my catheter as well. He jolted the sheets and took the catheter with them, which prompted an outburst of me speaking in demonic tongues. The poor guy. The same cocktail also meant I had legitimate insomnia, and I began to hallucinate again. My parents told me they would see me in full conversation with people who weren't there. I remember these imaginary people, though. They helped me through it too. I can still picture them and hear their reassuring voices.

It was during these brief spells that a lovely old lady would appear and tell me I was going to be okay. She told me all about herself, and as odd as this may sound, she told me that she had passed away in that very ward, having had a major heart attack. You see, I was in a recovery ward for patients who had suffered serious heart ailments, because that was the organ that had been hit the hardest in me. I now had a spongy heart, which meant the muscle was thick and spongy rather than smooth and firm, so it struggled to fully contract or relax. It was also questionable as to whether it would return to normal, but thankfully it did in time.

I'm not religious nor do I believe in ghosts, but that old lady helped me hugely, regardless of where she came from. There was also an older man and a younger boy who'd appear now and then – not to console me but to make me laugh or just to have a chat. We'd often speak for hours through the night and I truly believed it was real, until my parents told me the truth. I guess my mind was creating these characters to support me and to help me through it all, and it worked.

After a few days, family and friends could finally visit, but only wearing the hazmat suits. It was so wonderful to see them all. I cried with joy when they came. My parents were regulars and my friends Walter and Kieran came with DVDs and magazines, and that meant the world to me. I had one window to my left, which also helped greatly. I'd spend my days looking out, watching for birds. I'd regularly see swallows and swifts. Although only a snippet of what I'd usually see outside, they reminded me of the world I loved so dearly and would get an opportunity to return to as soon as I recovered.

Swallows and swifts to me have always been a real sign of hope. Both are long-distance migrants that leave our shores in autumn to winter in Africa. Their departure is a sign that the wet and gloomy winter is coming. I always despaired and prepared for the wall of grey when they left. But seeing both of these aerial masters return with grace to our skies filled my world with hope and delight, knowing that better days had arrived – we'd gotten through the worst of it. I smiled with tears as they tumbled acrobatically past my window. I looked out at a world I'd almost lost. But as was always the case, my old friends were there with me, supporting me through my toughest time by far. And although I couldn't hear them through the closed windows, my head was filled with the joyous twittering of the swallows and the towering screeches of the swifts – the sound of a sunny summer's day. This was the light at the end of the tunnel I needed to get me through it all. Until then, though, I had to make do with a little snapshot of what was out there waiting for me. Like a peephole through a door. The rest was painted in with my imagination.

After five days in isolation, I was deemed safe to move out to the main ward and it was an enormous relief. I was starting to come back to my old self. They took the nose tubes out and I could finally breathe unhindered. I slept like a lamb that night at first, until I was awoken suddenly. '*Nurse! Nurse!*' The elderly man next to me was shouting at the top of his lungs. I checked my phone and it was 2 a.m. He shouted and shouted until the nurse appeared and asked him to keep it down. She asked him what was wrong, to which he replied, '*I need a haircut, nurse!*' If I was drinking a coffee, it would have hit the ceiling. I rolled in the bed in fits of laughter. This was the first time I'd properly belly-laughed in almost a week. I needed that. It was an emotion I hadn't felt in far too long: jovial happiness.

With my neighbour having been refused a 2 a.m. haircut, I picked up my iPod and started listening to music to settle back to sleep. I still remember the song: 'Synthesizer' by Electric Six, an American rock band. I'd been listening to them a lot during study month and now I broke down crying. The reality of everything that had happened came at me like a torrential downpour of emotion. I cried tears of joy,

I cried tears of sadness, I cried tears of relief, I cried tears of shock – I cried just about every flavour of tear there was. I was an emotional mess. My pillow and sheets were soaked. I was hiccuping, sniffling and shaking life a leaf. The nurse must have heard me because she came in. I tried to tell her what was happening and I just hiccuped and cried a load of gibberish. I think she knew what was going on and she just gave me a hug and spoke to me until I calmed down. I was in total shock at what had happened and I had been too out of it until then to process anything.

Jesus. I nearly died that would have devastated my parents, family and friends. I'd never again get to spend time in nature. I'd never go on to complete my course and follow my dream of studying birds. Everything could have ended. It almost did. I couldn't stop thinking about it all. My head was like a washing machine of thoughts. The nurse comforted me and made me see some sense until I eventually nodded off for the rest of the night.

I woke up the next morning with a much clearer head and a new understanding for life. I called my birder friend Harry. Since I'd connected with him on the online birding forum some years back, we'd stayed in touch regularly by phone. Our friendship had made the move from online to in-person, and we'd sometimes meet to go birdwatching together. Whenever we would find an unusual bird, we would call one another and say, 'You'll never guess what I had?', and so this is what I said to him.

He thought for a while, and replied, 'A hobby?' A hobby is a rare bird of prey that occasionally turns up in Ireland.

'No,' I said, 'meningitis!'

This made for an interesting catchup.

Hobby *(Falco subbuteo)*
Family *Falconidae (falcons and caracaras)*
Conservation status Least Concern (IUCN Red List) – does not occur on the Irish BoCCI list, as it is a rare vagrant
Vocalisations The most frequently encountered vocalisation is a high-pitched, persistent series of 'kee-kee-kee-kee-kee-kee' notes, but typically Irish vagrants are silent.

From then on, I was a different person. I understood how easily life can be taken away and I made a promise to myself: I was going to give life my all and cherish every moment. I'd grab every opportunity by the horns and I'd pour my passion into the things and people I loved. And I do this all the time now. I feel like I owe it to life for giving me another chance.

Every day, I think about this period of my life, and I sometimes still cry about it. Just now, writing this chapter, I was listening to the same song and I'm a bubbling mess. But I wouldn't change what happened to me for the world. I wouldn't recommend it either, though. This near-death experience opened my eyes and ears to the world I sometimes took for granted. It made me realise just how much nature was central to my world. I craved it when I lay there on that hospital bed. It gave me even further determination to pursue a career in ornithology – to work with the birds I loved so dearly and to one day get the chance to repay them for all that they had given me. I also think about the people who saved my life. They may not remember me, but I will remember them forever. People always want to meet their heroes and wonder how they'd be in real life. Well, I know I've already met mine and they were amazing. I just hope that they are living their best lives and that they are truly happy, because they utterly deserve it. I'll forever be indebted to those people.

I also know that nature played a huge part in my survival. Even during the peak of my crisis, I was comforted by nature. I've led a life surrounded and driven by nature. From that very moment, I was brought out as a babbling toddler in the pram, it has calmed me. Even though, in hospital, I only had a narrow rectangle of glass, it was enough to keep my head above water. My lifelong bond and enrichment with nature was so strong that I had an encyclopaedia of memories and experiences to fall back on. And I played these memories in all of their intricate details on repeat. I could recall those fun-filled innocent times with Dad, laughing and mimicking the birds of Cuskinny. The same was true of Roche's Point. I knew both of these places so intimately that I could walk myself through each in my mind's eye, as if I was really there. The smell of the sea air, the sounds of the waves and the birds, the sight of the extensive waters of Cork Harbour and the Atlantic Ocean. I could explore them all with vivid detail.

Each visit would calm and reassure my fragile body and mind more and more. My emotions were a mess. I was distraught at the trauma I'd just endured, but I was so happy and excited at the life of nature I had ahead of me. If I could take so much just from my memory, imagine what I could do in real life, now that I knew what life was *really* worth. I'd never take my freedom in nature for granted again. Right there and then, I promised myself I'd take my relationship with the natural world to the absolute limits of exploration and discovery as soon as I left the bounds of this little bed and window. And, only a week later, I was already planning my return. Summer was upon us and, after some rest, I knew that I'd be back to my adventures, and although the gull-billed tern had moved on, I promised myself that one day I'd meet it, somewhere along my travels.

Little Egret

Chapter 4

IT WAS 2009, AND TIMES WERE DIFFERENT NOW. THE RECOVERY from my illness had been slow, and I had to take care of my heart and do regular check-ups. Intensive exercise and sports were out, but after 12 months I'd been given the all-clear. I was happy to spend the summer after the meningitis episode out in nature. The vibrant mosaic of habitats at Cuskinny and the sea air at Roche's Point were a big part of my recovery, and every day I'd wake up to the dawn chorus outside my bedroom window and feel more determined than ever to do well in my college course so I could pursue my dreams. And I did do well, despite the exam nerves that never seemed to go away.

I graduated from UCC with a degree in zoology after four years, but what would I do now? There was an air of uncertainty in Ireland in terms of economic security. I was scared about entering the real world and, looking back, I wasn't ready for it either. I had been a hard worker from the get-go and this came from my parents. My mother worked tirelessly to raise myself and my brother and to keep the house running like clockwork. She was always there for us. My father would work round the clock as a mechanic in the Irish navy. He'd be up at 5.45 every morning for as long as I can remember. Although, at times, my parents struggled, they never once let it show. They'd do without so we could continue as usual, without a hiccup. I know this now and I respect them immeasurably for it.

I'd worked from the age of 16 in a local homeware store in Cobh, where I assembled flat-packed furniture for display in the shop and helped the carpet fitters pack and unpack their loads of carpet throughout the town. My boss, Morris, was a great man – very fair to work for and very easy to talk to. I was lucky that this was my first paid work experience.

The shop itself was right on the seafront of Cobh and I worked in an open space at the back of the premises. This is where the beds were set out for display, but there was also a series of very large windows that gave me a view right across Cork Harbour. Looking out straight ahead, I could see Spike Island and its eighteenth-century military fort, which served as a prison until 2004.

On the island's shoreline, I would often see a wintering flock of brent geese grazing on the algae. Small in size and with a black, grey and white colour, brent geese feed gregariously on mostly marine algae, with sea lettuce and eelgrass firm favourites. Their call makes my hairs stand on end, such is the wilderness of it, a honking, guttural 'crrronk'. A small flock of about 50 birds make this place their home each winter before they return to the high Arctic for summer to raise their young. Their worries are light here in Cork Harbour but it's hard to fathom that, when they return north, they have to be wary of polar bears and Arctic foxes. These far-flung connections of the nature on our doorstep always got my mind racing and took me out of the mundane. Although I was assembling flat-packed furniture on the concrete floor of a shop, I was, in a sense, sharing a broader space with a bird that would soon be mingling with impressive predators of the snowy north. I was just one connection away from this world as I gazed out the shop window.

Brent Goose *(Branta bernicla)*
Family *Anatidae (ducks, geese and swans)*
Conservation status *Amber-listed (BoCCI, 2020–2026)*
Vocalisations *The most frequently encountered vocalisation is a low, guttural 'crrronk'.*

To the left of Spike Island is Whitegate oil refinery, its metal chimneys and stacks protruding, graceless, from the landscape. Smoke, steam and chemicals billow into the skies where the birds soar. I didn't like this part of the view, of course. Beyond both of these, Roche's Point is visible, marking the eastern point of the mouth of Cork Harbour.

Roche's Point was a place of solace for me even at that early age, so it was wonderful to have this in my sight throughout the working day – I'd take in the boats coming and going, and look in awe at the gulls, gannets and fulmars gliding over the waves. I'd think about all nature had to offer out there and dream about my next visit over the coming weekend. Happy thoughts just a peek away.

Just in front of the windows were a series of old, tall wooden pier-supports, which marked the boundary between land and sea, jutting out from the water just beyond the concrete foundations of the shopfront. These were presumably part of a long-gone docking area, antiques of Cork Harbour's rich history in maritime trade. Those days the supports don't see any boat use, but instead are used by roosting gulls. This meant that I always had birds sitting alongside me throughout the day as I assembled the furniture.

Every weekend as I worked, I'd watch the gulls that would gather daily on the wooden beams right in front of my work station. At first, I just admired them. I found the adults easy to identify, but the various shapes and shades of the four-year stages of immature gulls had me baffled. Gulls are sometimes referred to as seagulls and the 'sea' part of this name is a real thorn in the side for birders for its redundancy, because we all know that gulls spend the majority of their lives by the sea. Some do breed on inland lakes during summer months, but they'll still return to the sea. Gulls belong to the *Laridae* family, just like our various terns do. Not surprisingly, gulls have a diet that is heavily made up of fish, crustaceans and marine invertebrates, but they do wander inland to feed on rubbish tips, ploughed fields and can occasionally even grab food from the hands of unsuspecting humans.

My curiosity was soon piqued and I decided to embark on a journey of immature gull identification – a daunting task. I had a small camera that I'd take to work with me, as well as the *Collins Bird Guide*. I had both of these behind a tall shelf by the window, where I'd peek out at the gulls on the posts. I didn't dare go out there for fear of flushing them away.

Any time an immature gull would land on a post, it spurred me into action. First I'd take a photo from behind the big shelf in case it flew off unidentified. Then, I'd open the book and begin to compare the subject to the likely possibilities. To identify juvenile large gulls, you need to understand fine plumage detail, which means looking at and understanding the differences in patterning, shades and shapes of all manner of intimidatingly named feathers. I began to immerse myself in a complex language that was alien to me, and I found myself pondering about lesser coverts, emarginations, orbital rings, mirrors, greater primary coverts, and so on. I began asking myself questions such as, 'Does the inner hand show a pale window?' and 'Has it moulted in any first-winter scapulars?' and 'Are the tertials solid dark-centred or oak-leaved?' I was no longer watching birds; I was studying their innumerable intricacies and variations. I wanted to know what I was looking at no matter what it was. I've always wanted to attach a label to things for as long as I can remember, even in my days in the pram at Cuskinny. My approach to assembling flat-packed furniture was as meticulous as my approach to gull-identification. I was efficient and always got the job done, so my boss didn't mind if I took the odd break to look at a gull more closely.

Gulls are notoriously difficult to identify well and this is because not only do we have 12 regularly occurring species – black-headed gull, common gull, Mediterranean gull, herring gull, yellow-legged gull, great black-backed gull, lesser black-backed gull, kittiwake, little gull, Sabine's gull, glaucous gull and Iceland gull – they also have several age classes, each with a different plumage. Many of the larger gulls, such as herring gull, have four age classes, with the smaller gulls, such as black-headed gull, typically having two. Calculating the age classes for each of our 12 regular gull species, we have a total of 40 possible gull variations to get our heads around if we want to be fluent in gull identification. And this does not account for aberrant plumages or hybrids, both of which occur with some frequency.

I gained a strong understanding of gull identification during these breaks, even before I got to college to study nature more formally. I enjoyed my part-time job, so when my time came to graduate I was used to working, but I had no idea how to enter or behave in the professional adult world. It was still my dream to make nature and working with birds my full-time job, but a degree no longer meant what it did in the past; they were commonplace in 2009, which meant I didn't stand out from the crowd. I needed to push a little farther and I needed to stay in my student bubble for a while longer. 'Professional procrastination' I think I'd call it. I just wasn't ready to fledge. And so, after a lifetime of living by and interacting wholeheartedly with the sea, I signed up to study a master's in marine biology, again at UCC.

My class was small, consisting of around 25 people, many of whom I already knew from my degree course. This was better for me; I've never liked large crowds. It meant that we could get to know one another on a personal level, so it really felt like a community of like-minded people. We all loved nature and wanted to follow a career path in what we adored. For me, socialisation is particularly difficult with people I don't know or in big groups – the dynamics of which just don't make sense to me, even today. But spending so much time with this little group really helped me out; it gave me more confidence to mix with people, if I had to. But I never really wanted that, it still felt forced and uncomfortable on the whole.

The course was a one-year intensive master's which would teach us everything we needed to know to start a career in marine biology, with all of us having already studied a degree in zoology or similar. We learned about marine fauna, ecology and conservation, and did plenty of fieldwork. We gained practical skills too, including survival at sea, correct VHF radio use and boat-handling.

All of this was of huge interest to me, but the highlight of the course was a week-long stay at Millport, a town on the island of Great Cumbrae in the lower Firth of Clyde in western Scotland. Here, the University Marine Biological Station Millport, established in 1897, was run by the University of London. This was the perfect place for budding marine biologists to get some hands-on experience. We took a ferry from Largs out to the island – a fitting start to our expedition. On the way out, I stood on the top deck and scanned continuously with my binoculars. A rush of excitement struck me when I came across an unfamiliar shape on the water: a bright white duck bobbing in the distance. I fixed my eyes on it, and as we drew closer, I could see lovely olive-green check panels, a black cap and sides, and an elongated yellow-orange bill. I was looking at an eider duck – a special bird that I had read so much about for years but had never managed to see – exciting!

The eider duck is a marine species that has the fastest level flight of any bird in the world, reaching speeds of up to 113 kilometres per hour! They have downy feathers, which insulate them against the cold water by trapping pockets of air, and outer feathers that have a waxy layer that repels water, preventing them from becoming waterlogged. The famous eider-down is plucked by the mother to build a warm fluffy nest for her young, and it is this same down that people harvest at the end of the breeding season for pillows and duvets. I was so excited to finally have seen one. Soon after, I started to pick out more – they were scattered all around us! I pointed them out to some of my classmates, who gushed at their beauty.

Eider *(Somateria mollissima)*
Family *Anatidae (ducks, geese and swans)*
Conservation status *Red-listed (BoCCI, 2020–2026)*
Vocalisations *The most recognisable vocalisation is that given by males in display. It sounds as if the bird had been suddenly taken by surprise: 'oww-UUUU'.*

On the island, gulls seemed to nest on every rooftop and buzzards mewed overhead. Both of these scenes were new to me – gulls did not breed in Cobh at the time and buzzards were still quite rare. The houses looked different to what I was used to back home, with a lot of red brickwork throughout. We made the short walk to our accommodation, the Marine Biological Station itself, and I just knew it was going to be a great experience.

Over the course of the week, we met and were taught by so many experts. We studied everything from seals right down to the little periwinkles in the rock pools. Life in the rock pools is something that has always interested me, ever since I was a child exploring the rough, rocky shorelines of Cuskinny Bay, overturning seaweed-strewn rocks at low tide. But here, we were taking our inspections to another level, under the guidance of some of the best marine biologists in the UK and Ireland. As is always the case, no matter what the species or habitat, the closer you look, the more you realise how much there is to learn.

Take the widely known barnacle, for example. Barnacles are small crustaceans, related to crabs, lobsters and prawns. They start out their lives floating around the ocean currents as zooplankton. Those that are not eaten by fish or filtered out by basking sharks eventually settle and anchor themselves to rocks in the shallow tidal zones of our coast, using their cement glands. These glands secrete a type of natural cement made up of various components, including calcium and polyproteins. In their adult form, they have a sharp, off-white carapace – the hard outer shell – made up of six calcareous plates, within which is an operculum, a hard opening lid, made up of an additional four plates. These plates close tightly at low tide to protect the barnacle from drying out and overheating in the sun and wind. At high tide, these plates again open up and from within flickers a feather-like filter-feeding appendage known as a cirri. These are actually modified legs. The cirri unfurls and grabs any tasty morsels that pass in the current. If there is no current, the barnacle's continued flickering motion creates a current of its own. As these cirri themselves capture zooplankton of various species, it is entirely likely that they sometimes eat their own kind: cannibals of the intertidal zone, if you will.

Barnacles occur in large colonies, which stand out from the darker tones of the rocks that become exposed at low tide. Great care must be taken when clambering these rocks at low tide, for if you happen to fall on a colony of sharp barnacles, you'll be sure to walk away with several nasty gashes. Better again, try to avoid trampling across these areas altogether for the sake of the barnacles.

Our most common barnacle in Ireland is the aptly named common barnacle (*Semibalanus balanoides*). This species has a northern distribution and occurs in the intertidal zone of northwestern Europe as well as both coasts of North America. In Millport, this was also the default barnacle, though our lecturer that morning taught us something intriguing. In the UK and Ireland, we can also look out for a stowaway, known as *Austrominius modestus* – an Australasian barnacle first seen in the UK during the Second World War, where it is believed to have been brought in on the hulls of ships. The first Irish record was detected close to Lough Hyne, County Cork, in 1957. Because of its preference for temperate conditions, this Australasian barnacle has spread rapidly throughout the UK and Ireland, where it is considered to be invasive, at times outnumbering native species. One of the key differences between this invader and our own common barnacle is the number of plates making up the carapace. The common barnacle has six plates, whereas *Austrominius modestus* has just four. It didn't take us long to get our eye in, and we were soon finding the Australasian invasive species strewn along the rocks amongst the native common barnacle. It was much more common in the more sheltered parts of the rocks. We assessed relative abundance of the two species, and whilst at times their cover was 50/50, *Austrominius modestus* never outnumbered common barnacle. Perhaps this was because of the colder waters of this northerly location, limiting its expansion.

Another species we studied in-depth was the dog whelk, a marine gastropod – in other words, a sea snail – that is a surprisingly voracious predator. They patrol along the seafloor seeking out their favourite prey: mussels. When they find a suitable victim, they begin to drill through the shell with their modified radula – like a tongue with a series of sharp, dense teeth at the tip. It repeatedly grinds the radula against the shell, whilst simultaneously secreting a shell-softening material, until it breaks through to the flesh inside. Then, it secretes a concoction of chemicals which paralyses and dissolves the mussel, turning it into a meaty soup, which the dog whelk then sucks up through its straw-like proboscis.

I sometimes saw mussels with an incomplete borehole, which leads to an interesting anecdote. Dog whelks aren't always guaranteed success or even survival. Mussels use tough byssus threads, which look and feel like sticky fishing line, to attach themselves to rocks and to any would-be predators. The proteins on the thread have an adhesive ending that can trap an attacking dog whelk, so they end up immobilised, eventually starving to death. It is a great risk, and the incomplete boreholes I saw on some mussels show who came out on top in the battle.

We learned so much at Millport and had some great times as classmates, too. We left with a thirst to learn more about the marine world and I felt that a career in marine biology, but specialising in marine birds, was something I would love to pursue. After returning back home to Cork, we fell straight into study mode, before sitting our exams and working on our theses for the summer. My thesis, 'The Breeding and Feeding Ecology of the Little Egret (*Egretta garzetta*) in South-East Ireland' was, unsurprisingly, about birds. But I focused on a bird that spends much of its time in the marine environment. No matter what path life drew me down, I always found a way to bring it back to birds. A professional life without them in it just wouldn't do, and I knew that.

Little egret is a relatively new colonist to Ireland, having first bred here in 1997. It's a regal-looking close relative of our very familiar grey heron, both of which are members of the Ardeidae family. Every feather in its body is a beautiful snow-white colour and in the summer, it develops long white plumes that flow majestically from its crown and rear. It has jet-black legs with bright lemony-yellow feet. They truly are a beautiful looking species. At the time of my master's, very little was known about its Irish ecology – what it ate, where and when it bred – so there was much to learn and I set off on a self-driven mission to discover as much as I possibly could about them. I didn't see this as a chore at all; I couldn't wait to begin. Virtually everything I wanted to know would be novel information.

Little Egret *(Egretta garzetta)*
Family *Ardeidae (herons, egrets and bitterns)*
Conservation status *Annex I (EU Birds Directive), Green-listed (BoCCI, 2020–2026)*
Vocalisations *Two vocalisations can be heard with frequency. The flight call is an explosive croaking 'kaahhhrk'. Their breeding vocalisations are perhaps one of the most bizarre bird sounds to be heard in Ireland. They sound like a cross between a turkey gobbling and a human gurgling mouthwash – 'glu-glu-glu'.*

I began my investigations in March 2010, when grey herons had taken up residences at various heronries in Cork and Waterford. I located these and got to know my way around them. Little egrets and grey herons regularly nest together in mixed heronries. On the continent, other species are in the mix, too, including great white egret, cattle egret and black-crowned night heron. As grey herons co-existed with little egrets at my sites, I decided to study their nesting habits as well.

Grey herons began nesting as early as late January in some locations, which I learned because I came across them on my regular weekend walks. They build a big stick nest close to the tops of the trees and make a lot of noise. Sometimes, they sound quite dinosaur-like. From April onwards, little egrets began to enter the heronries and build their own similar but smaller stick nests.

I wanted to learn as much as I possibly could. I started by mapping out each nest – making a blueprint of the heronry, in a sense. Then, I identified the tree species in which each nest occurred, as well as its height, girth and distance to the nearest neighbouring nest tree. A very interesting pattern began to emerge: there was a clear preference in both grey heron and little egret for coniferous tree species. Because grey herons are early nesters, when they arrive at the heronry, there are no leaves on the deciduous trees, which are therefore open to wind gusts and provide less shelter than the evergreen conifers. So, the herons settle in the more sheltered conifers, in many cases Scots pines. Little egrets come to the scene a little later but tend to nest in proximity to grey herons for safety. Grey herons are much bigger and are more aggressive, and thus the more timid little egrets are safer from predators if they nest close to their larger, more boisterous cousins.

Grey Heron *(Ardea cinerea)*
Family *Ardeidae (herons, egrets and bitterns)*
Conservation status *Green-listed (BoCCI, 2020–2026)*
Vocalisations *The most frequently encountered call is the loud and commandeering 'FRARNK!', given with a deep, husky, guttural tone; but also with a high-pitched element woven within.*

Next, I wanted to look at what they ate – but how would I study that? The idea hit me right on the head one morning whilst exploring a heronry on the Cork–Waterford border. Quite literally. As I was walking below a nest, I felt a thud. When I put my hand to my hair, I plucked off a slippery, smelly half-regurgitated mass. A little egret had regurgitated right on top of me, and the contents were still discernible. I could make out mostly prawns, but also some small crabs and fish. From then on, when I went to take measurements at my study sites, I collected falling regurgitates and preserved them in test tubes with alcohol. But I needed something more reliable – I couldn't just expect to catch projectile regurgitates to get a scientifically robust sample size. Plus, it wasn't the most pleasant of techniques.

At several of my other sites, I began to hide behind vegetative cover and wait for egrets to feed closely at the water's edge. I used a video camera with a powerful zoom function to capture the egrets fishing for several hours per visit and ended up with hundreds of hours of footage. This footage took over my life. I took so much information from it. Just when I thought I'd finished processing the hours of tape, I'd think of a new parameter I wanted to measure and I'd watch it all afresh. I'd often find myself up until 3 a.m. meticulously taking notes, asking questions and trying to find the answers.

Firstly, I had to know if I was looking at an adult or a juvenile – little egrets are sexually monomorphic, so males and females are not discernible. Adult little egrets have dark black legs with bright yellow feet; juveniles have less defined mustardy legs with varying amounts of black and duller yellow feet. Then, I could count the number of prey strikes, successes and failures for each bird filmed.

But that wasn't enough. I went back through the hundreds of hours of footage to find out the depths the birds were feeding at. To do this, I worked out the average length of a little egret's leg using available scientific literature and split the leg into different sections, which I'd use to painstakingly analyse the footage: foot on bare mud or barely submerged, water approx. halfway up the tarsometatarsus, water at the 'ankle', water halfway up the tibiotarsus, water at the 'knee' or above. Using this method, I found that adults were far more likely to fish in deeper water, with juveniles more likely to fish in the shallower water where prey was small but more abundant and easier to catch. Fewer but larger prey items lurked in the deeper water, but the rewards were richer for those who had the skills to catch the elusive larger prawns; this is why the adults hunted out there. This was when I discovered the never-ending satisfaction in asking and solving questions in nature. I found it exhilarating when theories began to fall into place.

After graduation, I was eager to embark on a career combining two of my favourite things: birds and the sea! But the reality of life after college didn't line up with my ambitions. I sent my CV to as many universities, research stations and job openings as I could find. I refreshed my inbox every day waiting for a response that never came. Every job I looked at asked for a minimum of one to two years' work experience, but how do I get this work experience? I needed to pay my way.

It was late 2010 and we were in the midst of one of the worst economic recessions the country had ever seen. Unemployment soared and masses were emigrating in search of work. I decided it might be best to work in something outside my profession until things settled down, so I applied to work in furniture shops like I had previously but none of them were hiring. I tried my hand at entering the hospitality industry and had no luck there – I had no experience and only those with previous experience were being called up. In the end, I just began handing CVs out anywhere. I printed stacks and got the train from Cobh to Cork city every day, handing them out wherever I could. It became demoralising. In the evenings, I would scour the internet for marine biology jobs and apply for anything even slightly related. Some were way above my capabilities, but I'd lost my search filter a long time back. I must have handed out hundreds of physical CVs and emailed just as many. I didn't get a single positive response.

I signed on to collect social welfare, which isn't the worst thing to happen to a person, but to me it meant rock bottom. How could I have studied for a degree and a master's and not be able to get any kind of job *at all?*

I began to party with friends to take my mind off things and I slipped into a bad place. I started to drink too much. I lost all respect for myself and had no control when I went out. Looking back, I was a pitiful mess. All I wanted to do was follow my dreams to work in nature, but I felt like the universe was doing everything in its power to stop that from happening. I became depressed. There was no nature in my life, in a professional or personal capacity, nor was there happiness or hope. I often cried to myself at home and didn't see a way out. Without nature, my one true friend and support, I had abandoned my hope in life. I wasn't myself at all. I felt eternally sad – I found it hard to find a purpose to get up in the mornings. I didn't answer my phone because I had no desire to speak to or be with anyone. I'd spend my days watching telly and feeling terrible. I just slept, woke, ate and existed. There was no light in my life.

Now and then, I'd think about what I'd survived in meningitis and I'd find some renewed hope and go on a fresh job hunt, but it always ended the same way – I'd put in a huge amount of effort for not even a reply.

This soul-breaking pattern continued for almost two years, until the morning of 7 May 2012. I got a reply to a job I'd applied for in England under the title 'Wildlife Naturalist'. The job entailed working as a nature guide on a boat that brought tourists out to the world-famous Farne Islands off the Northumberland coast. The Farne Islands are an internationally important wildlife location boasting about 5,000 grey seals and tens of thousands of seabirds, including eider ducks, fulmars, cormorants, kittiwakes, sandwich terns, common terns, Arctic terns, guillemots, razorbills and more. Coming from an island surrounded by the sea, seabirds have always been a favourite of mine. We have an impressive 24 species of seabird that regularly breed along our coastline, and have some of the most important seabird colonies in Europe, in the likes of the Saltee Islands off the coast of County Wexford, and the Skellig Islands off the Kerry coastline. Ireland plays host to internationally important breeding populations of Manx shearwater, storm petrel and roseate tern and holds 10 per cent of the world population of gannets, our largest seabird. Knowing I'd potentially be working with seabirds on a day-to-day basis was riveting to me, and I was determined not to mess this up.

The email asked me to come out for a trial in a little over a week's time. I couldn't believe it. I burst into the kitchen and announced it to my bewildered parents. When I had spat it out coherently, they understood my commotion. I wasn't the only one who was relieved; they had grown worried for me and had seen that I wasn't my usual self.

On 16 May 2012, I got on a flight to Newcastle and experienced hope for the first time in what felt like a very long time. I felt a warm buzz on that plane and couldn't wait to reconnect with nature and do what I loved doing. I was collected from the airport and brought to one of the local bars, the Links Hotel, on the way to my accommodation in Seahouses for a bit of chit-chat. My potential new boss, Andy, the pilot of the boat and an all-round nature lover, was great – he spoke about the birds, seals and dolphins he encountered at work each day with such passion that I knew I was following up the right lead. He introduced me to the locals in the bar. Seahouses is a small village, so everyone knew everyone. They were all so welcoming and immediately picked up on my Irish accent, which they jokingly tried to mimic.

I'd been without work for almost two years – the first time since I'd turned 16 – and I felt ashamed of myself. But now I felt positive. My mind was finally swirling with thoughts of birds and nature once again and all kinds of positive emotions were emerging, like plants sprouting in the desert after a long-awaited downpour. I was excited to reconnect with the friends that I'd lost, but I was even more excited at the thought that my dream of working with nature was finally a real possibility. It's amazing how quickly all of that darkness was shed with just a *chance* to prove my worth. We didn't stay long at the pub – we had arrived late in the evening, and the next morning we would be going on a dry run to take the boat out from the harbour.

I stayed overnight in a beautiful old stone house on the periphery of the village that Andy had found for me. I launched out of bed at 5.45 a.m., got ready and sat in the back garden with my coffee. All of this didn't feel real. *Something is going to scupper it all*, I thought. But then another voice told me to go for it and to look forward to a new, positive story in my life. I basked in the sounds of the resident house sparrows, which hopped and fluttered from the ivy-strewn fence by my side. A collared dove, a petite relative of our larger and more familiar woodpigeon, gently coo-ed from the ash tree at the end of the garden. It had been such a long time since I'd heard my dear old friends. I'd emerged into the light at the end of the tunnel and it beamed from a bright, blue sky.

Collared Dove *(Streptopelia decaocto)*
Family *Columbidae (pigeons and doves)*
Conservation status *Green-listed (BoCCI, 2020–2026)*
Vocalisations *Song higher-pitched and gentler than woodpigeon, with a different rhythm: 'coo-cooo-cuh, coo-cooo-cuh'.*

Andy came to collect me at 6.30 a.m. and greeted me with a smile and his loyal companion Bud, a black and white border collie that accompanied him on all of his adventures. We headed for the harbour, and it was the first time I got to see the village in daylight. I admired the chunky sandstone blocks of the old houses, with striking terracotta roof tiles. It had real character and exuded a warm, welcoming feeling. Coming to the village roundabout, the sea was visible behind the roofs. We wheeled down the hill and emerged at the harbour. A great sea wall reminded me that whilst the day was calm, the unpredictable

North Sea lay behind the wall and would surely unleash its fury on the heavily protected harbour in winter.

Dotted along the harbour's perimeter were a series of huts with pictures of boats and the wildlife of the Farne Islands, now visible a few kilometres beyond us. Andy told me that the winter just gone saw a surge so great that some of the huts were blown across the pier head with the force of the waves. But today the weather was pristine: blue skies, gulls circling and crying overhead, eider ducks paddling along and diving for crabs. It was all so inviting. It felt like the storm that brewed within me for so long had finally passed, enabling me to find peace within myself once again. This sense of calm was something I had forgotten in that dark, troubled period of my life and I welcomed it back with open arms.

Andy told me we'd just go out ourselves for today to get a feel for everything. I'm sure he wanted to see how I functioned out there. He carefully climbed down the steps to the brand-new white catamaran, and Bud nimbly jumped onto the roof before clambering down to the deck. He was clearly at home. Andy quickly showed me the engines and controls as well as a few basic but essential knots. Luckily, I was familiar with most of this because of the boat-handling course I'd done for my master's and from spending time on the water in my father's boat. Andy fired up the engines and we worked our way out of the harbour. Andy pointed out the various shallow points to avoid and explained the unwritten rules of boat-handling courtesy in the harbour. For example, we always formed an orderly queue to wait our turn to pick up our passengers from the pier. Whoever approached first went first. The rest of us circled and drifted in wait, but we all knew our place in the line. They weren't too dissimilar to those of a supermarket car park!

When we got past the walls of the harbour, the swell picked up and Andy began to motor with more determination. The sea crashed over the bow and a spray of salty foam darted through the air. We were both in the cabin, which had a clear 180-degree view of the sea in front of us. The lighthouse and gleaming white walls of the Inner Farne stood out like a beacon. From this distance you could also see great white patches on the cliffs. This was a buildup of guano, from many years of occupation by nesting seabirds. Inner Farne is the closest island to shore and is where most boats land. Behind are the Outer Farnes, separated by the Staple Sound. The Outer Farnes are made up of several islands including Staple Island and Longstone Island, on which there is another lighthouse. It was an archipelago teeming with life.

I had my binoculars around my neck and scanned the sea as I spoke to Andy. I stepped out on deck and Andy opened his window. I began to call out the different seabirds that were going by – lots of guillemots, puffins and razorbills surfaced on the sea with beaks full of sand eels. All three are collectively referred to as auks and are members of the Alcidae family. Back home in Cork, we also have black guillemot. Auks resemble penguins in their looks and in their feeding habits. Both are sleek, black-and-white seabirds that dive underwater for fish, but auks fly and penguins do not. They aren't related at all, but instead they represent a classic case of convergent evolution. That is when two totally unrelated species, or families, evolve independently to find solutions to the same problems or challenges, resulting in similar body forms or behaviours. Auks are a familiar site at many coastal cliff-faces and offshore islands in Ireland, where they nest on rocky ledges.

Eiders bobbed along close to the island shorelines – my first time seeing them since my visit to Scotland. Cormorants and shags flew past, en route to fishing grounds. Both of these members of the Phalacrocoracidae family were familiar to me from back home. I had seen both on Great Saltee Island, where they bred in rudimentary open-cupped nests on bare rock.

I listed out these facts to Andy. I knew he was familiar with these birds and probably saw hundreds of each every day, but I needed him to know that I was at home here, too.

As we neared the Inner Farne, the smell of the guano wafted towards us. It's distinctive but not unpleasant – it smells of the sea but with a strong odour of fish – the scent of a thriving seabird colony, something everyone should experience. As we inched closer again, a wall of sound enveloped us. I'd never heard anything like it. The sound of a seabird colony isn't what you'd call peaceful or melodic. It is the hustle and bustle of a hectic but thriving community. Guillemots gurgle, razorbills grunt, kittiwakes announce their names with glee. It's a lot to take in, but it's an orchestra of sounds to be cherished. Let's hope our cliffs never fall silent; if they do, we are all in deep trouble.

Increases in sea-water temperatures are a major catastrophe for the world's seabirds, and ultimately drive a series of changes through the chain, which inevitably result in a collapse in the fish and other marine organisms that hold up the great seabird colonies that are dotted around both the Irish and UK coastlines, and indeed elsewhere around the globe. Although the future is uncertain, with sea temperatures rising at twice the rate they were 20 years ago, and predicted to continue to rise, the most recent Irish seabird survey results were surprisingly positive, at least at first glance. The report summarised the fourth seabird census conducted in Britain, Ireland, the Isle of Man and the Channel Islands between 2015 and 2021.[9] Seabirds were reported to be faring well in Ireland, with 17 of 25 species increasing since the previous census from 1998 to 2002, though with kittiwake and puffin showing worrying declines. Both species rely heavily upon sand eels, which have reduced markedly in number off the Irish coastline as a result of climate change. Furthermore, looking at trends across all surveyed locations, a total of 11 species showed a decline since the previous census. Several reasons have been cited for this loss: predation by non-native predators introduced to offshore islands (for example rats and mink); climate change causing turbulent seas resulting in nest sites being swept away and providing difficult foraging conditions at sea; and overfishing resulting in a marked drop in fish stocks. All of these problems have been created by humans and only we can stop this greed-driven loss. Let's hope we can do that, before our precious seabird colonies meet a terrible demise.

Knowing the fragile situation of seabirds, it meant even more to me to be out there, with the chance to show this wonderful world to people. After all, the more people realise what beauty we stand to lose through our actions, the more people will be willing to stand up and speak out against the very actions that lead to this loss. Andy gave me the full tour that day and I had to pinch myself. When we pulled up, he asked, 'So, are you up for it?' I scoffed a yes in shock. I couldn't believe it. The proper tourist season hadn't yet started so I had to go home to Cork for a little while, but this was perfect. It gave me time to gather my belongings and thoughts and say goodbye to my family and friends. They were all happy for me. They knew how much I'd struggled.

I came back a few weeks later, and settled into a caravan that was provided with the job. It was located in a small caravan park owned by Andy's cousin. It was basic but it was ideal for me. It was a place I could retreat to after a hard day's work. Tawny owls hooted from the overhanging trees at night and the familiar 'wit-wit' flight calls of the early-rising swallows eased me into the dawn each day.

I'd cycle the 20 minutes from my caravan to the harbour each morning and back again in the evenings. I was the first person aboard to start the engines and make sure everything was in check. When that was done, I'd walk around the pier and say hello to all the familiar faces and I'd leave with a fried egg sandwich. Each day out there was pure bliss to me, no matter what the weather. I loved the tourists too. It gave me enormous pleasure to point out the wildlife to them and see their faces light up. We would slowly cruise around the cliffs at a safe distance so as not to disturb the birds. I would point up at the precarious ledges where the various auks sat on the narrowest of precipices. Razorbills looked the smartest and resembled a small human in a smart black-and-white tuxedo – the short, deep bill marked with sharp white lines. Another striking white line extends from the beak to the eye. They get their name from their razor-sharp beaks, which come in handy when gripping onto slippery fish. I would then compare the razorbills to their close relatives, guillemots. Up close you could see that their plumage is somewhere between black and dark chocolate – this isn't so easy to see from land, when birds are far out. Another obvious feature I'd point out is the bill. In guillemots, it is unmarked, long, narrow and pointed, unlike the short, stubby, white-lined bill of razorbill. When we were really lucky, we'd sometimes find a 'bridled' guillemot, which is just a variation with white patterning around the eye, resembling a pair of glasses. This variation tends to become more common the farther north you go. Puffins weren't visible from the boat because they nest in burrows in the vegetation up top, but they were easy to pick out in flight. They were much more compact compared to the other two auk species, and they also had dark underwings – both guillemot and razorbills have paler underwings.

Although the tour followed the same route each time, every trip was different, and our encounters always set their own order and schedule. Sometimes, we'd even have a few surprises thrown in: basking sharks, bottle-nosed dolphins and the occasional rare bird all popped up now and then. A huge excitement came over the radio one evening when news of a bridled tern was put out for all of the boats to keep an eye out for. Bridled tern is a striking black, white and grey tern of tropical oceans that very rarely wanders across to the UK and Ireland. And luckily, we did manage to see it!

It was a long day out there, from dawn to 6 p.m. I was so busy that I didn't get a chance to get to know many people from the village. Fortuitously, I was offered a job as a barman in the very place I landed on my first visit, which I snapped up. Because I'd been out of work for quite some time, I felt like I needed to compensate. I told them I had a wealth of bar-tending experience, which wasn't true. On my first night, I cycled to another bar where a friend worked and asked him to show me how to pull a pint so I could at least know the basics! He skilfully poured a Guinness as he laughed at the gall of me. I watched every move, thanked him and dashed out the door.

Thankfully it worked and I got the job. It felt homely, friendly and I fell into the swing of things with ease. I loved the banter there, too, and it meant I got my chance to befriend the locals. In time, I earned myself the nickname 'Irish Seán' or just 'Irish' – simple but apt. I took this as a sign of acceptance.

I worked the boats seven days a week and the bar five to six nights a week. I eventually got myself a flat in the village and had some more comfort in my life, but this was the first time I'd been properly away from home. It showed me up for how spoiled I'd been. I was 24, not a young kid by any means, and I had to learn all my life skills from scratch, and mostly the hard way. One day, I washed all of my clothes at a stupidly high temperature and shrunk the lot, but because I had a seven-day work schedule I couldn't get into the city to buy replacements, which meant I was going around in clothes several sizes too small for quite some time, much to the amusement of the locals.

Then winter came and the boats stopped running, which was a welcome relief in a sense. It meant I had some time for me, and I still had the bar job to keep me going money-wise. I began to explore the coastline by bike and foot during the day, soaking up the waders that fed along the never-ending golden sandy beaches that stretched all around. Great flocks of silver and grey sanderlings worked their way along the water's edge, pecking for invertebrates from the sand as they went, dancing with the ebb and flow.

Sanderlings are small waders that breed in the high Arctic but winter along our sandy beaches. They are members of the Scolopacidae family, which includes curlews, sandpipers, snipes and woodcocks. They live their lives on the edge, quite literally. I'd often sit down and watch their movements with a giggle. They were like jack-in-the-boxes. Every time the waves retreated, they'd run out following the exposed sands, pecking as they went. Likewise, when the waves rolled back up the shore, they darted ahead, skilfully avoiding getting swept up in the frothy crests. Bar-tailed godwits probed the wet sand with long pink-and-black beaks, intermittently pulling out massive ragworms.

Now armed with my camera, and my replenished connection with nature, I relished spending time with these waders on the beach. I'd often be there on my own, and I'd have kilometres of white sandy beach to my left and right. I'd sit somewhere above the tideline, motionless, without thought or care. This way, the birds worked their way along the shoreline, and, not seeing me as a threat, they'd eventually show themselves right in front of me. I'd observe their every move and see the intricate patterns of their feathers and appendages up close: the frosty white plumes of the zippy-legged sanderlings, the two-toned pink-and-black elongated bills of the bar-tailed godwits.

Because there was such silence, both the sanderlings and bar-tailed godwits would call amongst themselves. I'd never knowingly heard either species before, so listening to them was a real educational treat. As always, I tried my best to put the sound I heard into words – I found it easier to learn this way. As the sanderlings ran up with each crashing wave, they all began to emit a series of beautiful soft 'twick' calls to one another, as though with nervous excitement, having just missed the wave. The bar-tailed godwits were not what I expected at all! Their unique 'tu-vee' calls had a really pleasant tone that I hadn't heard in a wader before. It was an eloquent call – I liked it!

I really felt like I was back in my world again, like I'd finally recovered from that dark spell. Again, just like my meningitis episode, I think this period of no work, and what must have been depression, showed me just what nature provided me. These tough times heightened my appreciation for it all.

As the birds walked closer, oblivious to my presence, I focused on getting some shots. At this range, I'd get beautiful photos, too. I got a real kick out of capturing the elegance of these birds, and I'd spend rainy evenings editing and perfecting the photos back home. It was the gift that kept on giving.

Sanderling *(Calidris alba)*
Family *Scolopacidae (curlews, sandpipers, snipes, and woodcocks)*
Conservation status *Green-listed (BoCCI, 2020–2026)*
Vocalisations *A subtle but beautiful, soft 'twick', often given by multiple birds at once, as they run away from encroaching waves.*

I'd walk for hours on end, stopping to sit in the sand dunes from time to time. I had the best of both worlds here. I immersed myself in nature by day, doing what I loved best, and earned my keep in the bar at night. Northumberland provided me with so many new birding experiences and I just lapped them all up.

Because I was living along the North Sea coast, many species were new birds to me. During powerful easterly onshore gales in autumn, a strong passage of little auks was possible. As the name suggests, little auks are tiny! Even smaller than puffins. They share the dark underwing of puffins, but they look like small black-and-white tennis balls bombing over the water's surface. It was a thrill to see these for the first time. During these easterly blows, I'd also witness spectacular numbers of Scandinavian thrushes arriving in off the sea – mostly redwings. Redwings are closely related to blackbirds and resemble them in size and form, but have a rich brown plumage above, off-white with brown streaking below, a strong white supercilium (a stripe that passes above a bird's eye, resembling an eyebrow), as well as a flash of distinctive red on the wings. These birds were arriving from Scandinavia and were battling tough weather conditions and dealing with long-distance flights. Sadly, the unforgiving side of nature was on full show during these conditions. More than once, I witnessed redwings dropping into the sea, just short of reaching the shore. Too weak to make that final push, nature swallowed them up and provided food to its seabed inhabitants – crabs, lobsters and scavenging fish would all eventually take advantage of these pour souls.

Sticking to the northern theme, I vividly remember what is potentially one of my strangest birding encounters. I was cycling home late at night after my bar shift. There was a cloudless sky and the roads were frosting up with the cold. I cycled as fast as I could to get out of it. I was staying in a friend's house in the next village down – Beadnell, about a 15-minute cycle from Seahouses. I was cycling parallel to the big beach I'd walk at times. A long, continuous sand dune separated me from it. The beams of one of the Farne Island lighthouses clipped the side of my left eye every 30 seconds. I didn't look away from the road in my determination to get in out of the cold, but something odd made me turn. I started to see an overwhelming tinge of lime green enter my peripheral vision. I turned and was both amazed and confused at what I saw.

Firstly, there was a ghostly white barn owl flying at my same pace just above eye level, but behind it the sky was dancing with greens and reds. I'd seen this in photos, but never expected to stumble upon it like this – I was watching the Aurora Borealis. My eye changed focus between the distant sky and the barn owl, which was still keeping pace with me. What an overwhelmingly beautiful pairing, and such a bizarre situation. Somewhere between my change in focus between the two natural spectacles, I slipped off the road and fell into the side of the dune. But I was fine. In fact, I was more than fine – I was totally in awe of what was going on around me. The barn owl continued on its way, floating on silent wings, eventually disappearing into the darkness of the dunes ahead. But the sky continued to dance, with pillars of red shooting up through the shimmering greens. I sat there in absolute admiration at just how spectacular nature can be. In time, it dissipated and I continued on my way, dumfounded with glee.

After living in Seahouses for around a year, I met a man with binoculars and a wildlife camera on my travels. It turned out he lived in the next village down and, after some chatting, he invited me round to his home for a tea. His name was Gary Woodburn. His wonderful wife Olivia greeted me at their home, bubbly and full of the joys of life. I had such a lovely time there and it made me realise I missed home and the stable life with my family and friends. But I also remembered that life had been far from stable when I left.

Gary worked as a professional ornithologist, and when we got to know each other better and he heard all about my passion for birdlife, he gave me the opportunity to shadow him over the following months. He mostly conducted pre-construction surveys for proposed wind farms. This required him to pay monthly visits to these sites where he'd spend the day conducting detailed breeding bird surveys and the nights conducting similar surveys for bats. Both surveys involved walking long transects through the area, logging sightings along the way. Additional six-hour stationary surveys were conducted for birds, which also required heights and flight paths to be mapped to assess the collision risks involved after a year or two of visits were completed. I shadowed Gary on many of these surveys. I kept him company and, in return, he shared his survey skills with me. During breeding bird surveys, we came across several territorial corn buntings – their songs sounded like a bunch of jingling keys. Corn buntings were the last species to go extinct in Ireland, back in the mid- to late-1990s, and so it was a treat to see these here.

The UK population has suffered a catastrophic 86 per cent decline since 1967. This is essentially down to a marked reduction in seed and insect food sources, a general reduction in lands under cereal cultivation, a marked increase in both pesticide and herbicide use, as well as a surge in the production of silage. The traditional method of cereal harvesting, which involved stacking fully ripe cereals, has largely been replaced by harvesting grains unripe or partially ripe for use as arable silage, which is often baled and stored away to feed livestock over the winter.

Gary told me about a project he'd worked on with several farmers, whereby, under a grant scheme, they set up certain winter crops to provide the seeds the birds needed to survive through the winter. In some cases, whole fields were sown with sacrificial crops, other times buffer strips containing a mixture of grains and wildflowers were set up around field margins. Winter stubble was set up in other areas, with wildflowers left to grow in the spaces between rows. All of these enhancements saw corn buntings bounce back, and this hands-on, successful conservation really impressed me. It made me hopeful that I, too, could one day make a difference.

In relation to wind-farm surveys, the money was good but your work also had the potential to stop these behemoths popping up in the wrong place. Sure, we need to stop burning fossil fuels and we need to replace these with cleaner, less destructive forms of energy, but where turbines are placed is very important. Put them in the wrong place and they can be devastating. Take hen harriers, for example. The most recent Irish census detected just 85 confirmed pairs in all of Ireland. One of the main threats to hen harriers is the construction of wind farms in the uplands. This magnificent raptor nests on the ground in heath and bog in the mountains. These sites are no good for farming and so they are often earmarked for wind energy, which, of course, is devastating for hen harriers and other sensitive species that occur up there.

Hen Harrier (Circus cyaneus)
Family *Accipitridae (hawks, eagles, kites, harriers and old world vultures)*
Conservation status *Annex I (EU Birds Directive), Amber-listed (BoCCI, 2020–2026)*
Vocalisations *A very difficult species to hear in Ireland, in part due to their rarity, but also due to the distance they maintain from people, as well as the fact that they just do not vocalise very often. The best chance of hearing these wonderful birds is when pairs display in early spring. This call is described as a yikkering 'chuk-uck-uck-uck-uck'.*

I learned a lot from Gary, and he would become one of my greatest friends in life. He also made me realise that whilst marine biology was fascinating to me, my true calling was back on land, where the bulk of our birds are found. Up until this point, I had neither family nor many friends here, so Gary and Olivia filled a void with great love and kindness. But they had their own lives to get on with, so I didn't always get to see them.

The bar at nighttime could be a lonely place and I fell into a habit of drinking and partying with the regulars at the end of my shift. This was not a road I wanted to go down, but I missed company and there was an emptiness inside me, despite having regained my pride. That Christmas, I couldn't travel home due to work commitments and I found myself working Christmas Eve. I went home late to an empty flat and no presents. This was when it hit me. Despite the locals being so lovely to me, I realised I was here alone. I sat up late that night flicking through TV, wondering what my friends and family were doing, and what I was missing out on. I didn't sleep and my mood took a turn. I felt a deep sadness and longing for family but I didn't want to hurt them. I didn't want them to know I was suffering.

As soon as the light began to peek above the horizon on Christmas morning, I went for a stroll. I walked along the beach for an hour to reach Gary's house. It was deadly quiet out there. Everyone was at home with family, admittedly probably still in bed. My bike was in Gary's shed, having got a spin from him back to my apartment on a previous visit. I used this as an excuse and hoped I'd see them by chance. I quietly took my bike from the shed and peeked in through the kitchen window. It seemed nobody was home, the car wasn't there either.

Back home, I sat in silence and began to cry. How sad to be here all alone on Christmas Day, nothing to celebrate and nobody to celebrate with. The bar I worked in was closed for the day, so I knew I'd not see anyone there. I got thinking and remembered one of the regulars I got on well with. Rodney was a bachelor with a kind heart and a great sense of humour. I knew he was an early riser, so I called him. He answered right away. I felt embarrassed to ask him for company and I think he knew exactly what was wrong.

'What are ya doing today, son?' he said.

'I don't know really, Rodney, to be honest,' I replied.

'You're hardly sitting on your own out there, are ya?'

'I am, Rodney. I don't know what to do with myself,' I replied.

'Hold on tight, I'll be across in ten.'

My spirits lifted and before I knew it Rodney was knocking on the door with a big smile, laughing and shaking his head. 'What are ya like, man?' he joked.

It was just what I needed. Rodney took me to his house where he was preparing presents for his niece. I went with him to deliver them and he introduced me to everyone. We all sat down and had tea and, later that day, after some more present drops, we came back and had Christmas dinner together. This kind gesture saved my Christmas. I just wanted company.

This got me thinking that maybe it was time to go home. I'd already had a new niggling doubt about my career. Meeting and working with Gary showed me that there was work out there that could really make a difference. I could finally step up and help our dwindling bird populations by following in his footsteps. Even if it wasn't a hands-on job like his corn-bunting project, I could at least use my birding knowledge to prevent construction of wind farms in areas where sensitive bird populations occurred. I didn't even know such work existed until I'd met Gary and, having shadowed him out there, I knew I could do it. The bar work was great and all – I was good at it and I met some wonderful people – but it wasn't my calling. It only paid my bills.

I'd been in England for over two and a half years. I'd saved some money, had some great times and met some wonderful people, but I needed my friends and family.

Pied Flycatcher

Chapter 5

ALL WAS AS I HAD LEFT IT BUT AT THE SAME TIME THINGS were completely different. Although I was back home in the place I knew so well, the life I'd left two years previously was no more. I was a different person, mostly for the better. I felt a little out of place. My friends had all moved on and settled into their lives, and I'd grown into a new routine of hard-learned self-sufficiency. I found it difficult moving back into my childhood bedroom – like I'd taken several steps in the wrong direction. I'd also left many species of birds behind, and no longer had the wonder of the Farne Islands at my doorstep. Cuskinny felt a lot more modest to me now. My time in England had been a life-saver. I had slid into a dark hole when I couldn't find a job at home, and a job that involved being out and about in nature gave me everything I needed. It was also my first venture into the real world, without the safety net of my parents to fall back on, but I still had my support in nature throughout – my extended family. I was surrounded by wild and wonderful places and creatures there, and despite many of them being new, they were still familiar to me. When I arrived in England, I was helpless. I shrank my clothes, burned my food, and forgot to pay my bills. But then I learned how to cook, how to clean, and how to keep track of my finances. I became an independent adult.

Being back home with my parents in my late twenties felt like a step back, in a sense. In England, I had my independence, a stable job, my own money, my own apartment and my own identity. But now I found myself lying back on my childhood bed, hands behind my head and legs crossed, wondering if I'd made a mistake. I looked out my bedroom window. The bird feeder I'd gazed at throughout my childhood was still there, and I watched the great tits, starlings and robins coming and going. It brought a smile to my face, and my attention was drawn back to the gentle humming and rippling of the fish tank in my room. When I was younger, I'd watch the lush green plants waving in the current and observed the colourful, fan-tailed guppies chase one another through the ripples. It was another world in there. I did my best to recreate their tropical stream habitats with a base of stones, several old gnarled logs, a big characterful stone with crevices and tunnels, finished off with a lush mixture of live tropical plants from which the guppies would eat algae. It looked like a vibrant community. They seemed happy in there, and I would feel the same when I'd stare into their world. It was my mini-sanctuary within a sanctuary.

All of this brought me back and cancelled out my insecurities. I was here for a purpose. Inspired by the work conducting pre-construction surveys at proposed wind farms with Gary, I had enrolled for a master's in environmental impact assessment at UCC. The course wasn't due to start until September 2016, so I had several months to get into a rhythm and get some money behind me. As this was an intensive one-year master's, I needed work that would allow me some flexibility, so I decided to look for a bar job.

Back in Seahouses, I had worked five to six nights a week behind the bar and I knew the job like the back of my hand. I could pour up to four pints at a time, using hands, elbows and chin to control the pumps, and I knew everyone's orders and had them on the counter before the money touched wood. I opened and closed the bar, took stock and knew how to keep myself busy when things were quiet. I even knew how to make small talk with the customers, which was probably the biggest achievement for me. I always got along better with the older customers, though. I guess the older we get, the less bothered we are about trying to appear cool or relevant, so conversations become easier. I could chat about life in general rather than having to speak about sports. I found I really enjoyed chatting to the regulars, so we got to know one another. Sometimes, people would come to the bar for company more than for a drink. And those people seemed to find me, because I was feeling the very same – an Irishman abroad, missing family and friends.

I put together a CV and I looked down at it with pride, knowing the hole I'd pulled myself out of the get to this point. I'd regained my self-respect and I'd made it on my own. I was on a mission to use the technical bird-survey skills I'd learned while away to take the next step forward in my life.

I took the train from Cobh to Cork, the same 25-minute journey I'd taken some 11 years earlier as a naive first-year college student. I felt nostalgic as I watched the mudflats of Cork Harbour flashing by, its rich bird life feeding on the invertebrates of the silty grey estuarine muds. I passed the heronry of Fota Island where I'd conducted part of my dissertation research. All good memories.

It's incredible how our life circumstances can completely change our outlook on the world. Just under three years previously I was sitting on this very train with a folder of CVs and zero confidence, having finished college knowing that I wanted to work in nature but not quite sure in what area, how I'd get there or, indeed, if I ever would. My time in Northumberland had clarified what was important to me. Now I was sitting here feeling hopeful for the future. I stepped off the train and walked under the platform canopy that leads into the old terracotta brickwork of Kent Station. From here, it was a ten-minute walk to Cork city. My plan was to hand out CVs to every bar I could find. I figured the more I handed out, the better chance I'd have of getting lucky.

The first pub I entered, I was struck by nerves. I couldn't help but feel overwhelmed. I went to the bar and asked to speak to the manager.

'I am the manager, how can I help you?' they said.

'Hi, my name is Seán Ronayne. I'm looking for a bar job. I have a lot of experience. Would you like to take my CV?'

'Sure! We don't have anything right now, but we can keep it on file for you and give you a shout if anything comes up.'

Oh no. I remembered this response – it was a polite way of saying no. I walked back onto the street and had flashbacks to the nightmare of trying to find work before I went to England. Had I made a big mistake leaving my job in Seahouses to go back to college? I needed a part-time job to keep me going while studying, but now I was worried I'd find myself in the same loop of unemployment I'd struggled through before I left for the UK.

I persevered and called to every bar I could find. A few gave me an outright 'No' and a few more said they'd keep my CV 'on file'. I stopped for a bite to eat to muster up the energy to continue. I'd not sat down long when my phone lit up. It was a number I didn't recognise.

'Hello?' I answered sheepishly.

'Hi, is this Seán Ronayne?' said the authoritative voice at the other end.

'Yes, it's me.' Hope started to creep in.

'I'm just looking at your CV now and it's exactly what we need. Would you be available for an interview in an hour?'

'Absolutely! I'll see you then.'

This I did not expect. I called my mam straight away to tell her. She was delighted for me, and assured me not to worry.

An hour later, I was in the back room of the bar. My mind was prepared for all manner of complex questions, but it was nothing like that. I was met with a smile and a handshake, and we just began to chat. He asked about my time in England, what my goals and aspirations were. It was a warm and friendly conversation that ended with the offer of a paid trial that very night. I snapped it up.

I'd never gone into an Irish late-night bar without a bellyful of beer. It wasn't at all how I remembered it from my nights out. It was dark, crowded, noisy and chaotic. I never paid attention to this when I had drink in me. I immediately tensed up. It wasn't at all like the local bar I was so accustomed to in Seahouses. I felt totally overwhelmed – my senses were assaulted from every imaginable angle. I could feel the loud bass vibrating in my chest. The air was warm and moist and carried with it a stale-smelling cocktail of beer, sweat and farts. My head swirled with the cacophony of a thousand conversations, all shouting to be heard above the music. The dim spaces were intermittently lit up with strobe lights, revealing a sea of people with each flash. I've never liked people touching me, but here I had to wade through the crowd to make my way to the main bar. People bumped into me, stood on my toes and tipped beer on my pants as I struggled through the mayhem.

I reached the bar and stepped behind it in a sensory overload, relieved to be away from the crowd. But here there was another kind of pandemonium. There were at least eight bartenders working like lightning. I was immediately pushed to one side; no time for pleasantries here. I'd got in the way of one of the servers who was tending to an endless queue of people. Drinks were poured with speed and slid onto the counter. There was no time for finesse: beer sloshed over the tops of glasses and a sticky mess from sugary shots attached itself to anyone who touched the varnished wooden bar surface. Bartenders leaned forwards to hear orders over the noise.

This was hell on earth. I stood back in the corner of the bar at the bottom of the stairs, just hoping someone would come over to give me guidance. A voice shouted from above: 'Seán! Come upstairs a second.' I ran up and met a manager who threw me a black shirt: 'Put this on and get serving.' I did and ran down. It was pure chaos. Every bartender seemed to have their spot and were highly territorial. I tried serving at a spot but was nudged down towards the corner where a queue awaited. A hundred eyes began to follow my every move. Who did I serve first? This was my first lesson in bar politics. I served who I thought was waiting first, only to be met with hands thrown in the air with a series of frowning faces. Everyone in a busy bar wants to be served right now and I needed to learn to accept this as normal.

I began working my way through the queue, fumbling around the beer taps, fridges and glass shelves. I was very slow and my stress levels were through the roof, but I persevered because I knew all too well what it was like to be out of work. I couldn't wait for the night to end, and when the bell rang at 2 a.m. I was a physical and emotional wreck.

The bouncers came onto the floor and started escorting people outside. It would usually take a good half an hour before the floor was cleared and we could close the doors. It was only then that I could see the scale of the mess. There were beermats, broken glass and patches of vomit all over the floor. Every surface was covered in a shiny, sticky mess of half-dried shots and beer, often with vomit as well. Coats and shoes, left behind in a drunken stupor, were hanging off speakers, doors and chairs. Again, the senior staff went into autopilot and, for a moment, I was left scratching my head. Where do you begin to clean up such chaos? Then a manager gave me fast and direct orders. 'Get a cloth and surface cleaner and start wiping off tables and counters.' Other staff brushed the floors, collected glasses, stocked fridges and some cleaned toilets.

Slowly order started to come about and the atmosphere changed. The music was lowered and staff laughed and joked with each other. Some new staff members began to mingle with the others, but I dared not. What would I say? Would I tell them about birds and nature, the only things I understood? I had tried this in past situations and it hadn't worked, so I just kept to myself. This was the safest bet. I told myself I'd try to talk to people when there were fewer of them, perhaps during a day shift if I got the job. I didn't do well in groups. The dynamics of when to speak and how to keep up with all of the different personalities and conversations was something that is still difficult for me to navigate. I much prefer having a quiet chat with one or, at a push, two people.

The bar was looking like new and we were told we could either go home or stay on for a drink. I looked at the time – it was 4 a.m.! Oh my God, my poor parents. There were several missed calls on my phone. My mam was collecting me because the last train to Cobh left at midnight. I went out the side door and closed it behind me. The street was awash with the casualties of the night. People crouched in corners and vomited their guts up, others walked barefoot on the dirty street, seemingly oblivious of the broken glass, cigarette butts and vomit. I could hear some people shouting ahead. It sounded like they were fighting, so I took another turn. It was a dark, unpredictable environment out there at night, and I needed to have my wits about me as I meandered my way up the street to my mam. I could see her parked ahead of me and I made a final dash to safety. I slumped into the seat and apologised for being so late.

Then Mam asked, 'Well, how was it?'

I thought for a second, then replied, 'Yeah, good. A bit chaotic. Hopefully I'll get the job. I don't ever want to go back to my old jobless life here, even if it's just while I study my master's.'

She smiled and said, 'Good for you, Seán. Just get your head down and keep moving forward.'

We arrived home at 4.30 a.m. and I went straight to bed. My ears were ringing and my head was spinning with the madness of it all. I was hyper. No matter how hard I tried, I could not sleep. At about

6 a.m. I finally nodded off and woke again at lunchtime. I pulled myself out of bed, my head still foggy, and went straight to the shower. I got dressed and looked out the window. It was a gorgeous sunny day and I knew exactly what was needed. The previous night had me shaken and worried about the routine that lay ahead of me. But I knew how to remedy this feeling. I set out to connect with nature, as I had always done. I hadn't had the chance to wander around Cobh since moving back from England, and it was a pleasure to reconnect with my hometown. I walked down the hill from our house, the narrow street bounded by the old stone wall that I knew intimately. Having bought a wonderful Canon camera and wildlife lens in England, I never left home without it – just in case. I was always looking at the details in nature and thinking of my next shot.

Shifting my eyes upwards to the tops of the walls, I noted the familiar tall stands of red valerian. This species is an escaped garden plant but it's not invasive, in fact it's highly beneficial to many flying invertebrates. Its tall stalks are topped with dense bunches of pink, red or even white flowers. In summer, I'd walk down the wall inspecting the flowers for insects. This day was no different, and the light southerly breeze brought with it some migrant *Lepidoptera* (butterflies and moths). As Cobh is on the very south coast of Ireland, it's a gateway to migrants of all kinds – the first port of call for those departing France and heading northwest, for example.

I spotted two typical early-summer treats: painted lady and hummingbird hawkmoth fluttering along the wall-top, stopping to drink the nectar of the abundant red valerian. Painted lady is a beautiful rusty-coloured butterfly with long black wingtips and white spots. Its long wings enable it to migrate impressive distances over the sea, which is why we find this species from Europe and even Africa on our shores every summer. Our climate is too cold for them to overwinter, so when we see these rapid, zippy fliers, we can be certain that the early arrivals are migrants. The adults feed on a variety of flowering plants, but the young typically feed on a variety of thistles and mallows. They do breed in Ireland, and Irish-born painted ladies will make a southerly migration to Europe and Africa in late autumn, high up out of view. In the past, it was thought that Irish- and UK-raised individuals were doomed to die here or even drown in the sea. Radar studies have since revealed that neither of these are the case, and that butterflies on migration fly on average 500 metres above ground, reaching speeds of up to 48 kilometres per hour. So, just like birds, these fragile little creatures are incredible long-distance migrants, which is hard to fathom when you look at their paper-like wings. These are incredible feats for any species to undertake, and this was quite literally on my doorstep.

On these same southerly winds, hummingbird hawkmoth also ventured north. This species, as the name suggests, resembles a hummingbird with its extremely rapid wingbeats. They hover from flower to flower, unfurling their long, curled proboscis like a straw to suck up the nectar.

I'd only just stepped out from the house and already the pounding beats of the previous night's madness in the bar were dissipating as nature worked its magic and soothed my mind. From the top of our hill, I could see the summer sparkle of the gentle waves of the harbour below, and so, like a moth drawn to the light, I worked my way down through the town to the water's edge. At the end of the hill, a blackbird flew past with a beak full of earthworms. It darted into the cover of a garden hedgerow. From within, the innocent chirping calls of hungry mouths told me that there was a fresh new brace of young blackbirds almost ready to enter the world. The begging calls of young blackbirds are one of the most distinctive juvenile calls to be heard in Ireland, at least to my ear. They sound quite like adults, but much less structured, emitting a repeated liquid trill, 'trrp-trrp-trrp'.

Blackbird *(Turdus merula)*
Family *Turdidae (thrushes)*
Conservation status *Green-listed (BoCCI, 2020–2026)*
Vocalisations *The song of the blackbird is the most noteworthy vocalisation and is one of our most endearing avian tunes. A highly variable, low, fluty, rich and warbling song. Often interspersed with mimicry of birds from the immediate vicinity. Also capable of mimicry of non-living sound sources, such as phones and alarms.*

As I walked beneath the shade of the library arches, Cobh town opened up in front of me. First was the *Lusitania* monument, a central stone meeting point where people sat, talked and ate chips from the nearby takeaway. Behind this again was the *Titanic* museum, memorialising Cobh as the last port of call for passengers before they met their fate in 1912. Walking right would bring me along to the Deep Water Quay, where cruise ships came each summer. Memories came flooding back of a childhood spent fishing for mackerel.

Although today I am a strict vegetarian, back then I ate fish and meat. Every summer, I'd eagerly await the arrival of the great silvery shoals of European sprat to enter the shallow refuge of Cork Harbour. Sprat are a small marine fish in the herring family and are typically the size of an average adult's baby finger. In the summer months, they come inshore to breed, often in impressive numbers. Sprat are a keystone marine species that support many larger predatory fish, seabirds and cetaceans (whales, dolphins and porpoises). Sprat first gave themselves away as a shimmering of silver visible under a calm sea surface. This shimmering was a result of the adults twisting and turning as they mated in tandem.

Mackerel were never far behind the sprat and moved in great streamlined shoals, like a pack of marine wolves. Mackerel are closely related to tuna, and are built like green, black and blue bullets. Their spear-shaped elongate bodies are silver beneath and olive green to blue above, intersected with a pattern of wavy black tiger-stripes. They really are a sleek hunting machine, perfectly evolved for a life feeding in the oceans. Mackerel typically hunt in groups and herd large shoals of sprat into tight baitballs, which they then attack with vigour from below. They hit their targets with such speed and voracity that they often leap above the water. When this happens in numbers, it appears as if the sea is boiling, as the water is thrashed and sprat are flung into the air. These events are known as 'breaks' of mackerel.

I'd cast a silver lure out into the sea and reel it carefully back in, sometimes varying the speed or jigging to make it seem like an injured sprat. It worked well, especially when I could see a visible break. I always set myself a limit: I'd catch enough to feed us for dinner. But I remember clearly people using strings of up to eight feathers, taking in so-called 'full houses'. They'd remove all eight mackerel and leave them hopping about the pier, only to drop another eight some moments later. They would repeat this process for as long as they could, until they'd be left with literal mounds of mackerel. Sometimes, they'd try to sell them, but that usually wasn't very successful. After all, who would want to buy a fish they could very easily catch for themselves? It was like selling ice to an Inuit. More often than not they had their fun and just left the dead piles of fish on the pier. Why take a life for fun? Or in this case, why take a multitude of lives for fun?

Those days are long gone now, and whilst this behaviour certainly didn't help, the large-scale industrial fishing of sprat and mackerel has brought both to much lower levels than were present in my childhood. My father recalls even more impressive numbers. From his childhood home, he had a sweeping view of Cork Harbour and he recalls breaks of mackerel so large that they'd stretch for kilometres across the harbour. The collective sound of thousands of mackerel breaking – leaping out of the sea and slapping back down onto its blue surface – was so great that it often woke him on warm summer mornings. How things have changed; it's terribly sad, really.

As I walked along the seafront, I neither saw nor heard any breaks. There were no mounds of mackerel, and only a few hopeful determined fishermen. I continued along the seafront following the Five Foot Way, a narrow track that skirted the harbour front. I looked out to sea and continued to float along, reminiscing about a childhood spent along this stretch. I used to fish here at night as well, and would often see a great bull of a grey seal that would watch me in the hope I'd throw in a fish. I did at times, but was very much aware of this being a wild animal. I didn't want it to become too accustomed to coming close to humans, for I knew too well that not everyone would treat him with the respect he deserves. I think he watched me partly out of curiosity, as was the case for me. I saw him as an acquaintance, and I think that feeling was mutual. And that was enough.

My nights here were calm. I was usually alone in my thoughts, but always observing nature. Some nights, an otter would pass by, squeaking as it went. Other times, I'd witness little see-through eels swimming upstream towards the River Lee. These minute eels are the juvenile stage of the European eel, and are transparent at this point in their lives. When they meet freshwater, they take on a number of changes, most notably a transformation from transparency to an opaque grey and white. European eels have an incredible life cycle and are, in fact, born in the Sargasso Sea, south of Bermuda. From there, the glass-like eels steadily make their way some 6,000 kilometres back to Ireland following the Gulf Stream. I was seeing the arrival of these magnificent migrants having crossed the Atlantic Ocean.

Whenever I came across these phenomena, I did not always know or understand what I was seeing. But that was the beauty of it. I'd take a photo or make notes, and I'd ask myself questions. What were those little see-through eel-like fish? Why were they all moving in the same direction with such tenacity? Where were they coming from? Before the time of the internet, I'd go to the library and read books to try to answer these questions. Nature was and still is my teacher.

Later that evening, back at home, I felt mentally and physically refreshed. I received a call from the bar, a call I'd been hoping for. As the previous night was only a trial, I still didn't know if I would be offered the job. I was actually dreading the next shift, but I knew I'd take it on regardless. Anything was better than dragging my feet without financial stability. I'd never go back there. To my relief, I was asked if I'd be interested in manning the front bar for the day shift. This was right up my alley. The front bar was about the same size as the cosy local bar I was used to in Seahouses, and as it was a daytime shift

I wouldn't have to worry about the madness I'd encountered the night before. Perhaps they saw that my CV was suited to this side of the job and they wanted to put me through a test to see if I was serious about it. I was over the moon.

The next day when I arrived at the bar, it was another world. The sunlight beamed through the windows and lit up the rich mahogany browns of the walls and furniture. The lighter pine countertops shone with the green, brown and red reflections of the spirit bottles hanging from the walls. A gentle rock-playlist hummed in the background, and the place took on a whole other character. I now felt excited about my shift. I shadowed my manager as he showed me where all the switches were. He gave me a general tour of the taps, showed me how to work the till and glass washer, and left me to my devices. I made sure everything was in order, and then I opened the door to the street. A few regulars were already waiting outside. They smiled at me in surprise and I introduced myself. They were all here for teas, coffees and a chat. One or two sat at the bar to sip a beer or two. Nothing crazy.

I made sure I took care of them from the outset, and I got to know them. I pottered about and saw to everyone, kept a clean bar, and generally went about with a smile and had a bit of chat. I was on top of the world. As time went by and I got to know them a bit better, I felt I could open up more, and so I began to tell them about nature. Older people were generally more inclined to take an interest when I spoke about nature than my peers, so I felt more comfortable bringing it up. It's strange how liking nature becomes uncool at a certain point in people's lives but then becomes acceptable again later on in life.

I had a routine back in my life now, which I realised I truly needed to be happy. Some nights, I'd go out with friends. I felt so uncomfortable talking to girls, but I didn't want to be single either. Like before, I'd have a few drinks before I'd go out. Upon my realisation that alcohol gave me a temporary pass into the world of normal human socialisation, I began to use it as a crutch. And whilst I didn't drink on a regular basis, when I did, I didn't know when to stop. And this brought me trouble. I'd become a messy drunk, I'd make a fool of myself and then I'd have crippling anxiety for days. Although it gave me a short-lived release from my social fears, it wasn't worth it for all of its negatives. I knew I had an unhealthy relationship with alcohol, but I pushed away that feeling, which wasn't a good choice.

I did meet some girls but then when I'd meet them sober, things would all crumble apart. I just felt so incredibly nervous. I didn't know what to talk about and I was terrified of looking them in the eye. So much so that I'd insist on us sitting side-by-side. This gave me much more confidence to talk, because I didn't feel like they were in front of me, looking deep inside my soul. Small talk wasn't my thing, and still isn't. What's the point of it? I wanted to talk about things that mattered to me, and so I'd talk about what I knew best. I'd tell them all about my adventures and learnings, my favourite birds and animals, but it didn't go down well and I could sense it. I tried forcing myself to talk about 'other' stuff, but I didn't know much about anything else so it was even more awkward and forced. And that would be it. I'd try my best and I'd never hear from them again. It did hurt me, but deep down I knew I'd find someone in time.

I'd often lie in bed at night and think about what it would be like to be in a solid relationship, and for that person to understand my quirky ways. They weren't quirky to me, but I knew they must have been to the majority of society because, if they weren't, I'd have surely had a partner already. I'd console myself with the thought that there is somebody out there for everybody. The world is made up of so many characters, and whilst some people readily fit into and are accepted by mainstream society, others are not, and so it just takes a little longer to find a click. I'd wonder who she would be, where she may be and when I would meet her. Would she like nature like I do? I tried not to focus on that too much, as I didn't want to force it or feel too down about it.

That summer my father and I planned to take a journey together, a journey we had made many times before, but not since I'd left for England. We'd take his old sailing boat from Cobh and navigate it all the way down the coast to Cape Clear Island – an island 12 kilometres off the southwest coast of Cork. It's the most southerly inhabited part of Ireland, with a population of around 110 people. It's a Gaeltacht area, whose true name is Oileán Chléire, and most of the inhabitants speak Irish as their first language.

Its significance for us, though, was its wildlife. Cape Clear Island is a unique location from the perspective of a birder. Because it's so far out to sea, it seems like another world from an ecological perspective. It's not uncommon to see common dolphins or even minke whales from its shorelines. Some birds considered common on the mainland are considered to be rarities out there. Take rook, for example – one of the most common crow species on the mainland, but on Cape Clear it's a rarity! Also, because Cape Clear is positioned in the extreme southwest, it acts as an important last port of call for migrant birds flying south to feed up and rest before crossing out over the sea. Likewise, for birds flying north into Europe in the spring, it provides the first chance to set foot on dry land after an exhausting sea-crossing. Because trees are somewhat uncommon on the island, bar those in a few gardens, it also means that migrants are funnelled into a number of well-known establishments: the Nordy Wood, Ciarán Danny Mike's pub, the hostel and the post office are all names that would perk the ear of any birder. All of these sites are vegetated in an otherwise rather treeless island. And because large volumes of migrants become concentrated into these small areas, rarities inevitably turn up and are discovered. Cape Clear Island is a famous location for rarity hunters, and each autumn in particular it hosts strays from North America to Siberia. This adds that extra element of excitement to the place. It even has its own bird observatory, which has been used to study bird migration on the island since 1959.

When I was a teenager, Dad had bought a Dufour Arpege – a 30-foot racing yacht. Having spent a life working on the engines of the Irish navy fleet and having grown up looking over Cork Harbour, he loved spending time on the water. And as he is a trained marine mechanic, we didn't need to worry if we had engine trouble at sea. With a sail height of just under 40 feet, six beds, a cooker and a fridge, this boat was meant for adventure. And that is exactly what we'd use it for.

The boat was tied up inside the Irish naval base in a sheltered marina on Haulbowline Island – just opposite Great Island. We'd take a small ferry from Cobh to Haulbowline, the same boat my father took to work, and we'd set out on our travels from there. It would take the bones of a day to sail to Cape Clear, but we'd often break it up over a few days, stopping overnight at various ports. At first, we'd use the diesel motor, just until we were out of the narrow confines of the stone enclosures of the basin. Out into open waters, we'd unfurl the sails and cut the engine.

This was a feeling like no other. We were moving solely by harnessing the wind. There was no engine noise and the air was free from fumes. All we heard was the sound of the waves parting at the hull of the boat as it cut through the water, and the wind working its way through the sails. The salt spray would mist over our faces, and we both developed an involuntary smile. Suppressing this smile was like trying to block a sneeze: an impossibility. We were surrounded by the ocean and were being guided through it by nothing more than the wind and tides. We'd have nowhere to be, and we knew that we had days of this carefree feeling ahead of us, exploring our wild Atlantic coastline together.

From the moment we set sail, our thoughts and worries floated behind us in the tide. We'd sit on opposite sides, one taking control of the sail and tiller, the other looking out for any buoys or oncoming boats. But this was automatic; we mostly focused on absorbing what was around us. Common terns drifted overhead, like great white swallows of the sea, announcing themselves with their sharp 'kip-kip' contact calls. They dove intermittently and often came back up with a sprat or lesser sand eel in their dagger-like, black-tipped red beaks. Sometimes, they'd swallow their catch head-first; other times, they'd fly up high with it still in beak, to return to the colony where a hungry mouth awaited.

Common Tern *(Sterna hirundo)*
Family *Laridae (gulls, terns, noddies, skimmers and kittiwakes)*
Conservation status *Annex I (EU Birds Directive), Amber listed (BoCCI, 2020–2026)*
Vocalisations *Various calls, all of which have a harsh, shrill tone. The most telling call is an adamant 'kiii-uuurrrr'. The much less urgent 'kip-kip' calls are given in contact, often when foraging.*

We'd pass other boats and always smiled and waved, as is custom on the sea. I wondered why we were generally so much more courteous to one another on the water compared to back on land, where we often coexisted in a sea of anonymity. You'd never dare pass a boat and not exchange a warm greeting. Dad suggested that, because we are much more vulnerable when sailing out at sea, we all look out for one another. I think this is probably true, but I also think it's because we are also much happier out there on the open water, free from the stresses and ties of our lives back on land. Whatever the reason, it always gave me a warm glow whenever we passed other sea-goers.

We sailed on past the Spit Bank, an area of shallow water some 750 metres south of Cobh's shorelines, and a little over a kilometre northeast of Spike Island. The Spit Bank, as the name suggests, is a soft sandy bank in shallow water that poses a risk to boats of running aground during low tides. Because of this danger to passing ships, it is equipped with a red-and-white lighthouse on stilts. Cormorants hung out on the railings of the lighthouse, drying their wings out-held in the breeze. On extreme low tides, the bank was sometimes fully exposed and formed a connection back to Spike Island. My father told me of a football game he saw play out there from his bedroom window as a kid, presumably a team of prison staff from the then Spike Island prison.

We passed the bank with caution, not wanting to trap ourselves with the deep keel of the boat. Rounding the corner, we broke free from the visual obstructions of the inner islands, as we entered the outer harbour, passing over the Turbot Bank, with a view all the way out to Roche's Point at the mouth. Turbot Bank is another sandy bank that lies behind two old defensive forts, sitting on either side of the harbour. To the right is Camden Fort Meagher, to the left is Fort Davis. During the First World War, an anti-submarine net was stretched between the two forts by the British to protect the harbour from German U-boats, and some say that the abandonment of this net on the seabed resulted in the buildup of sediment, leading to the creation of the Turbot Bank. I'm note sure how true this is, but it made for an interesting story nonetheless.

As we passed the bank, we scanned for the pod of bottlenose dolphins that had taken up residence in and around the harbour. We came to expect them at this point, as they fed on the rich fish pickings that the bank offered up. A series of hooked grey dorsal fins ahead gave them away. As we neared, they turned and dashed to the front of the boat, where they rode the bow. Despite the sunny conditions, winds were high and we were moving at pace with a full sail. The dolphins took advantage of the wake produced by the boat cutting through the water. We took turns steering as the other stood at the bow and peered down at the dolphins. They moved so gracefully, pumping their tails and turning sideways in the wake. They positioned themselves behind the white crests in the clearer parts of the gushing water, where they eyeballed us from just below the surface. I'd look them right in the eye, and they would return their gaze, delicately adjusting their position to maintain eye contact. They were clearly having fun and looked at me with a sense of curiosity.

It was an intense feeling, looking at a wild, intelligent mammal like this. What were they thinking? What did they think of me? They seemed carefree and without burden, as were we. I wondered if they ever stressed about life. Surely that can't only be a human trait.

Did they have personalities? It seemed so – some were much more curious than others and appeared to nudge their way to the front of the wake to look up at us. I wondered if some found socialisation with their peers a little trickier than others. There certainly seemed to be a hierarchy. I didn't have the answers, but I felt fortunate that they gave me the opportunity to ask myself these questions as they glided through their liquid domain. In a sense, I felt like they were welcoming us as guests, as we left the calms of Cork Harbour and entered the expanse of the Atlantic Ocean.

The final familiar landmark of Roche's Point lighthouse guarded the gates of the harbour. Passing this, we were into a new territory, where anything was possible. The Atlantic can be an unforgiving place, and we were aware of this, having been caught out in a bad storm three years previously. We treated it with respect and didn't take any risks, never venturing more than a few kilometres from land as we voyaged west.

It was a long sail to Cape Clear Island, and there was no phone signal out there, which we welcomed. We took turns at the helm – and the sun beat down on us and we sat back in our bare feet and short sleeves. We chatted and took everything in, always scanning the horizon for any wildlife or, indeed, lobster pots and nets, which could very easily entangle the boat. I'd intermittently stand up at the bow and slowly sweep the horizon with my binoculars. I was looking for a cetacean blow – a sudden vertical shoot of misty whale breath – or a marker buoy signalling impressive lengths of lobster pot ropes or monofilament netting. Most scans would return nothing, and it was just run-of-the-mill procedure, but now and then I'd spot an orange or white marker buoy and direct Dad around it.

I scanned the horizon and saw an unfamiliar shape. It was round and dark but somewhat irregular. We were around 5 kilometres out to sea, so the chances of it being a net or pot were slim, but not impossible. It didn't seem to move at first, but then I noticed a slight shift. I thought it might have been a sleeping seal, which often sleep upright with their heads pointed to the sky. But something was off. As we got closer, it looked bigger and bigger, and I could see a dark mass below the water. I felt a little nervous, really. We were in deep water, looking at a very large, unknown creature. I told Dad to keep our distance so as not to disturb it. We didn't take our eyes off it, and with each metre gained, we could see more: a great ridged back, enormous black flippers and a big beaked head with eyes closed. It was an enormous leatherback turtle, the largest of all living turtles and a first for us. I'd read so much about them. They can reach a size and weight of about 8 feet and 500 kilogrammes, which is comparable to the original Mini car. We cruised by on sail and it took no notice of us. We stared at it in total awe. Never did we expect to see one of these on our journeys.

Leatherback turtles follow the Gulf Stream up to Ireland in summer, where they feed on jellyfish. They have a series of long spines pointing down their throat, which help them to swallow their prey and also prevent it from escaping once inside. Unfortunately, this system can also cause problems — problems caused by us. Our plastic bags that float on the oceans resemble jellyfish, and any unsuspecting turtle that ingests them cannot expel them as a result of their spiky oesophagus. They sometimes wash ashore here dead and post-mortem inspections reveal the bags trapped in their throats, which caused them to starve to death. This behemoth seemed to be in great shape, though. It appeared to be just taking a rest, basking in the sun at the Atlantic's surface.

These journeys with Dad were full of such surprises. On the same trip, we encountered many basking sharks cruising the coast with mouths agape, sucking up clouds of plankton as they went. Their presence was typically revealed by a pair of fins moving in tandem, the central dorsal fin peeking out like a sail, with the tip of the tail swaying like a rudder. Many more dolphins joined us on the journey, and I took every opportunity to photograph them. I'd always wanted a shot of dolphins clearing the water and, with patience, I got just that as a group of two jumped clear repeatedly. My camera was on rapid-burst mode, and perfectly captured them midair, as if they were just floating there. It is still one of my most prized wildlife photos.

We arrived at Cape Clear late in the evening, salty and weathered but full of stories. Back then there was no marina, so we tied alongside a local trawler. We spoke to the owner first, who ensured us he'd not be taking her out any day soon. Cape Clear Island is a real treasure to us for many reasons. Time has stood still here. There are few residents and some narrow minor roads. There aren't many cars on the island, and the ones that are there are often missing windows, mirrors or even doors. More than once, I had to do a double take when I saw what appeared to be a 12-year-old driving by. The vibe there is different. They aren't caught up in the hustle and bustle of our fast-paced lives. Everyone stops to say hello. It's a very personable place, where everyone is seen and acknowledged. I love this. But there's something else about it that lures me in even more: it's a famed hotspot for bird migration. In spring and autumn, the gardens are thronged with migrant birds stopping over to feed up as they enter or exit Ireland, and sometimes a rare American or Siberian stray joins them. You never know what you'll see on Oileán Chléire.

We were greeted at the pier by the friendly resident bird warden, Steve Wing, who flies the flag of nominative determinism with pride. We'd met Steve and his wonderful partner, Mary, many times before, but usually as guests in the observatory. We had such great memories of our times there with them that it was always a wonderful treat to see their welcoming faces after the long seaward journey. In years gone by, we often spent a week in the cosy shelter of the white-washed walls of the 'Obs', typically in September when migration was at a peak.

The Obs sat behind the main pier and oversaw all that passed through the harbour. We'd wander out and cover as much terrain as possible each day in search of grounded bird migrants with just our binoculars, a camera, a flask of coffee and a bag of food. We'd keep a tally of the numbers of each migrant species we'd encounter. Swallows streamed overhead on a beeline to Africa. The subtle yellows and greens of chiffchaffs and willow warblers flitted through the sycamores and hawthorns in search of juicy insects to replenish and refuel, their snapping beaks audible as sharp clacks as they captured a titbit. If we were really lucky, we'd encounter scarce, unexpected migrants, such as the wonderful blacks and whites of a pied flycatcher, flying in and out of its chosen perch with focused determination, skilfully plucking flies from the air. Pied flycatchers have occasionally bred in Ireland and may have once been more common, back when we had great stretches of mature oak woodlands – their habitat of choice. But today they are scarce gems that occasionally pop up along our coasts as irregular stopovers.

Pied Flycatcher *(Ficedula hypoleuca)*
Family *Muscicapidae (old world flycatchers)*
Conservation status *Amber-listed (BoCCI, 2020–2026)*
Vocalisations *Song seldom heard in Ireland due to the rarity of the bird, but can best be described as a series of short and highly melodic verses, with constant shifts in pitch throughout. Autumn migrants, although rare, are much more likely to be encountered on the coast. Migrants have a series of calls, the most common of which is a repeated, high-pitched 'whit'.*

On bad-weather days, we'd put on waterproofs from head to toe, double down on our hot flasks and head to the cliffs with our telescopes. On these grey, wet and windy days, onshore or southwesterly winds bring migrating seabirds much closer to shore than normal. These include species that spend much of their lives far out in the ocean, so the opportunity to see them up close from the land only happens under certain conditions. We'd hunker down in a grassy hollow and watch birds battle the powerful Atlantic winds and rain. We'd see several species of shearwaters, skuas and European storm petrels. Gulls, gannets, puffins, guillemots, razorbills, cormorants, shags and many others joined the stream of scarcer species.

Very occasionally something *really* rare turned up along this coastline. Black-browed albatrosses, a true great wanderer of our oceans, have been seen, although we were never in the right place at the right time – these are mega-rare vagrants this far north. The thought of a prize such as this egged us on to scan through each and every passing bird. These spectacles of seabird migration were enough of a sight to behold as is, but one of these oceanic vagabonds would be the cherry on top. The conditions enabled us to see pelagic migration up close and personal. All we needed to do was sit back, stay dry and warm, and watch the show.

That night, we went to the local bar where we met a roomful of familiar faces: birdwatchers, locals and regulars. There were some unfamiliar faces too, which added to the diversity of chats all around. We had a few beers and chatted to anyone who came our way. We shared stories of our adventure and they told us about theirs. We didn't overdo it as we knew we had another day on the seas ahead of us.

We spent the next night in Baltimore, a beautiful mainland town that happens to have amazing pizza at La Jolie Brise! Again, we chatted with the locals and just relaxed. The next morning we set sail for home, fully recharged and brimming with tales to bring to Mam and Conor.

On the way back, I spoke to Dad about my upcoming master's degree and my dreams to work as a full-time ornithologist. I had hopes and dreams again and I saw this as my destiny. It was early September and I would begin my course in a week. He fully supported me and told me it was meant for me, and I felt that too. To study the creatures that have given to me all of my life, and to have a chance in making a difference to their well being and persistence, was not only something I'd enjoy, but I also felt like it was a calling.

Kingfisher

Chapter 6

IT WAS AUTUMN 2016, AND HAVING HAD A SUMMER PACKED full of nature, my time to return to college had come. Six years had passed since my last graduation. And although I had finally started to find my feet, I had intermittent intrusive thoughts of being left behind – like I had wasted time in comparison to my friends.

I was two years away from turning 30 and still lived at home; I didn't drive; I didn't have a partner; I didn't work in the profession I wanted to work in. It had taken me some time to figure out exactly what type of job I could take on to work with nature. It's a much less job-rich sector. The recession didn't help my situation by any means either, but that had finally passed, and at least I was heading in the right direction with the master's in ecological impact assessment, and my understanding of what line of work I'd be looking for exactly – thanks to Gary!

I didn't have a close circle of friends to meet up with on my days off either. Although I didn't really want that, in a sense. I've always needed to spend *some* time in the company of others, but I quickly grew tired of the effort it took for me to converse and to listen. I usually needed to retreat after an hour or so. I also still did not feel socially confident, despite my years away and working in a busy bar. I thought that this was something I'd shake off upon emerging from my teenage chrysalis, but it wasn't the case. If anything, I felt more socially out of place than ever before. All of my friends were settled into their careers, they could drive, had long-established partners and some even had kids. I had none of those things, and this enabled the seeds of doubt to creep in and made me question where I was in my life.

Was I failing? Was this my fault? Had I spent too much time following what I loved instead of something that would give me stability? All my life I had grown up feeling different. I didn't like the things that everyone else liked and I found social life so difficult. Had these differences, the very things that made me stand out as an oddball growing up, now manifested themselves in another manner in adulthood, a manner that meant I wasn't hitting the life milestones that my friends were? I suspected so, but wasn't certain.

Going back to UCC after all these years added to my unhealthy twinges of inferiority. Here I was back on the same train I took at the age of 17, full of hope for a budding career working in nature. Yet, 11 years on, I still hadn't made it. I was a mature student now, my baby face swapped for a stubbly beard, and many of my course mates were several years younger than me. The innocence of a carefree life was also gone; I'd learned all too well what it is to struggle. I'd narrowly survived an early death, I had to fight tooth and nail against my struggles to find my place in the world, both in terms of a stable functioning life and a healthy social life. I'd found myself alone in a new country with no real clue how to function as a standalone adult. I had a new awareness of the unforgiving side of the world.

But these were dark, self-pitying thoughts. Nobody makes it overnight, and *everyone* who does make it has had to drag themselves through the mud in their own ways, without exception. I had to remember how far I'd come. I'd pulled myself out of a deep hole in moving to England and I'd rescued my life. *I* did that. Nobody could have saved me but me. I'd survived meningitis and I'd survived those tough jobless days, with no sign of any future on the horizon. This was nothing in comparison. I had listened to my instincts and I knew I was finally following the right path – the path that would see me becoming a professional ornithologist, working with birds as I had dreamed about since I was a teenager. I was about to start a new positive chapter in my life, and sometimes you need to take a step back before you can leap forward. This was what I was doing. I was back home with my parents, but in a year I'd be ready to embark on a new career.

A flash of lightning blue pulled me back to reality. I turned my head, and the familiar sight of a handsome blue, orange and white kingfisher shot past my eyeline. It had got up from an old constructed stone bay that cut out from the River Lee and into the then Zoology, Ecology, and Plant Science (ZEPS) department. This was the off-campus branch of UCC where I would be completing my intensive master's in ecological impact assessment. This is the course Gary recommended I pursue in order to land a job like his.

The ZEPS department was set in an old red-brick building that had made up part of an old whiskey distillery, the North Mall Distillery. In the 1920s the business, one of the most important distilleries in Ireland, was engulfed by flames and never returned, instead being used as a bottling factory until 2007, when it was acquired by UCC. They converted it to classrooms, offices and science labs. They maintained the old red-brick facade and some of the old beams inside too, but it mostly had the feel of a hospital. It was grey, blue and white and sparkling clean, almost clinical. The smell of lab chemicals wafted throughout and photographs of wildlife and scientific posters adorned the hallways. Large old wooden-and-glass units displayed a variety of stuffed animals, collected many moons ago.

Outside, it was a wonderful green campus set along the tree-lined banks of the River Lee. In spring, the early-morning starts would greet us with a vibrant dawn chorus as the tall sycamores, chestnuts and ash trees brimmed with birdlife. The kingfisher was a regular visitor to the little bay that cut out from the riverbank, and I swore I'd eventually capture a photograph of it. Like the dolphins out on the boat, it became a little mission of mine.

My classes were interesting and my classmates were all so lovely, but I had to work hard to get by. Because my days were occupied with classes Monday to Friday, I had to return to the jungle of nighttime bar shifts. I'd often get to bed at 5 a.m. and had to be up at 7 to get the train to Cork for classes. I'd try to avoid doing too many night shifts but a few were necessary so I'd have enough money to pay my way.

On weekends, I'd work days *and* nights. And the nights were tough. They were wild, messy and an assault on the senses, but as I built up speed and familiarity with the role, I developed mechanisms to get by. I wore earplugs to block out the worst of the noise, picked a set point to work from and just went into autopilot. Sunday mornings were the worst. I'd work until the early hours and then I'd have to come back in a few hours later to open up for the morning shift. Staff and whatever DJs had played the night before were often still partying when I arrived, which meant that a fresh mess was made and I'd have to shoo them away to get the doors open for morning teas and coffees. I'd sometimes have big assignments due on the Monday, too. This was the essence of my life during this period, juggling chaos, stress and a lack of sleep. But my eyes were firmly set on the light at the end of the tunnel: a career in ornithology.

Mondays' classes were tough. I tried not to sit near the front because I had a tendency to fall asleep after the weekend of bar work. The classes were fascinating, though. We learned to identify all manner of plants, how to track and detect badgers, otters and pine martens, how to conduct aquatic invertebrate samples on streams and rivers, and my favourite of all – we learned how to conduct a wide range of bird surveys. I had full confidence in my bird identification skills, but to learn proper ornithological survey techniques was of great interest to me, so I could turn my passion into a profession. No matter the weekend I'd been through, I sat up during these classes, took meticulous notes and asked lots of questions, because that is why I was there.

On our breaks or early in the mornings before class, I'd step outside and sit by the river. I'd slip away from my classmates for some time out. I'd always look out for the kingfisher when I went out there. I'd been watching it for months, ever since I first saw it flash out of view from the little bay. Over time, I built up an idea of when and where to expect it. This section of the River Lee is tidal, and at high tide it was nowhere to be seen. Likewise, at low tide, there was no water for it to dive into. It also disappeared when footfall was high. So I knew I needed to catch it when the tide was neither high nor low, and when footfall was low. So a mid-tide early in the morning would do the trick.

One morning at around 7.30 a.m., everything was lined up just right. The tide was halfway in and I knew exactly the perch the kingfisher preferred. Although I couldn't see it, I snuck out of view and assumed it was there. I made sure all of my camera settings were good. I crept up to the tree that towered over the bank. If my detective work was correct, I'd see the bird perched opposite me when I peered out from behind the tree. Still in a crouched position, I inched my head to the side, index finger on the trigger. And there it was! A male kingfisher sitting on its usual perch looking down at the water about 2 feet below it. It hardly moved. It seemed to be focusing on a fish below. I gave one last check of the camera settings and clicked the camera shutter closed. After all these years, I finally had a photo of this stunning bird, which had lived in my mind since I was a little boy. It took a dive and surfaced with what appeared to be a stickleback, then it flew out to the main channel and disappeared. I double-checked my preview screen and was elated to see a frame-filling shot of the bird. I've always loved experiencing nature, but capturing it and eternalising it like this is extra rewarding. On grey wet days when I'm stuck at home, I look back at these photos and smile. But, even better, I can share them with others, who may never have experienced the beauty of such a bird.

Kingfisher *(Alcedo atthis)*
Family *Alcedinidae (kingfishers)*
Conservation status *Annex I (EU Birds Directive), Amber-listed (BoCCI, 2020–2026)*
Vocalisations *Most commonly heard is the 'tsip-tsoooo' flight call. Kingfishers tend to be rather flighty, so learning this call will increase the number of encounters, as they are often heard before seen.*

At this point, I was very much interested in finding rare and displaced vagrant birds. We have somewhere around 200 regularly occurring bird species in Ireland (breeding, wintering and regular passage migrants), but over 500 species have been recorded here in total. Many of these birds are blown here by extreme weather events in spring and autumn. For example, in October, if we experience long-ranging, easterly winds coupled with rain, it's not unlikely that we will receive a number of far-flung Siberian or easterly vagrants. Yellow-browed warblers, Pallas' warblers and red-breasted flycatchers all breed east of us as far as the Siberian taiga but turn up here in small numbers every year after such weather events. When these birds migrate south, to their Asian wintering grounds, the strong easterlies push them west to us. If it's raining here, this then 'dumps' them down, forcing them to make landfall. The same pattern is repeated with American birds – every year, we receive a mixture of American waders, including semipalmated sandpipers and American golden plover. The most regular of the passerines is red-eyed vireo, a bizarre, exotic-looking bird with blood-red eyes, a green and white body and lead-blue legs. Strong westerly blows and rain, particularly hurricane tail-ends, bring them to us in very small numbers.

Red-breasted Flycatcher *(Ficedula parva)*
Family *Muscicapidae (old world flycatchers)*
Conservation status *Least Concern (IUCN Red List)* – does not occur on the Irish BoCCI list, as it is a rare vagrant
Vocalisations *Song not heard in Ireland, as the species does not breed. Calls from the rare autumn vagrants that do turn up sound like a dry ticking rattle 'trrrt'.*

Whilst these birds can make landfall anywhere in the country after these events, it's much more likely to find them on offshore islands or exposed coastal headlands. There are at least two reasons for this. Firstly, these birds are exhausted, having been blown well off course. So, when they see the first signs of land – be it a lighthouse or an island – they'll drop out of the sky in desperate need of rest, shelter and food. Secondly, these locations are typically windswept and, as a result, have little vegetative cover. The few gardens that do occur act as magnets, attracting these exotic vagrants.

These storm-driven waifs attract two subniches of birder. Firstly, a birder is someone who actively goes outside and seeks out birds for enjoyment. But then you have birders who are rarity-finders and twitchers. Rarity-finders are those who watch weather patterns and seek out the perfect conditions to find out-of-context vagrants. They'll look for that perfect storm: strong winds from Siberia, North America or southern Europe coupled with rain, then followed by a calm. It's usually only when the storm subsides that the rarities come out of hiding. Exhausted, hungry and cold, they'll pop out of cover and voraciously feed to regain the resources they've burned as a result of their unplanned mileage. Rarity-finders are adrenaline junkies. The rush of unexpectedly finding some really rare exotic bird that has been blown well off course is indescribable. I've been there! Your heart races at the flash of an unfamiliar shape or colour and your hands tremble. It's often difficult to nail down exactly what you're looking at in those initial moments. Usually, with some patience, the bird shows itself, and you text out the news to the various bird WhatsApp groups. Sometimes, the bird never shows again, and we refer to these as 'hoodwinks'. Every birder has a gut-wrenching hoodwink story to tell about the one that got away.

The people who receive the news of your rare bird and drive frantically to see it? Those are the twitchers. They typically keep a list and embark on a lifelong journey to see as many bird species in Ireland as possible. It doesn't take long for them to see all of our regularly occurring species – the residents, semi-residents and expected migrants. So then they need to chase accidental blow-ins to keep adding to their lists. Several people have now seen over 400 species in Ireland, which is impressive. I think I only managed to amass 300 before I stopped the chase. I did get involved in this for a little while, but, to be honest, I found it all a bit weird. It's highly competitive, political and, to me, nonsensical. I do get the thrill of the chase to an extent, but I didn't enjoy the big groups of people standing around and chatting, and the fact that it was often a tick-and-run exercise.

For me, nature has always been an immersive activity. I use it to learn and to get away from the things that stress me out in life, large social gatherings being one of them. When I go out there, I want to move slowly, to relax, to ask questions and to simply bathe in the beauty of it. I need that. Chasing birds and wondering whether or not they'll still be replenishing themselves in that one sycamore on the tip of the headland is stressful. And, sometimes, they aren't still there. At times, I travelled for hours and it was all for nothing. No, I much prefer taking my time and appreciating everything for what it is.

You can still get the thrill of the chase through rarity-finding. This has the best of both worlds: you go out with a sense of adventure and the unknown. Will a rarity have made landfall? Will I find it? I wonder what species it might be? Even if you don't find a rarity, you didn't miss anything and you still get to stroll around and take in the common species.

But rarity-finding in Ireland is hard work. We are an island on the extreme west of Europe and so we are away from the big migratory flyways of the mainland. As a result, bird migration here is much less spectacular in terms of the sheer number of birds. Even as close as the UK, the spectacle of visible migration has resulted in the formation of another subniche of birder: the vismigger. 'Vismig' is short for 'visible migration' and a 'vismigger' is a visible migration connoisseur. Vismiggers are those who position themselves at bottlenecks at dawn during spring and autumn, where birds can be seen passing in active migratory flight through small valleys, hilltops or other easy-to-follow landmarks. Here birds can be seen in their hundreds or even thousands migrating north or south. This phenomenon doesn't really happen in Ireland, at least not to the same extent. We're off the highway so to speak, an Atlantic outlier. Birds choose the most direct and safest routes, and those occur along the UK and mainland Europe.

On rare days off, I'd go with my dad to coastal headlands in west Cork, following suitable weather conditions that bring far-flung migrants. Because migration here is a trickle compared to the raging torrents of mainland Europe, these days out were often quiet. For every ten such well-timed visits, we'd strike lucky with a big one. I can recall the first time it happened with pin-sharp clarity.

It was an exceptionally balmy spring day in early April 2011. There had been a steady southerly breeze blowing from Spain, just as birds were coming back up having spent the winter in Africa. These conditions are perfect for so-called 'spring overshoots'. These are birds that, on their return north into Europe from Africa, aided by southerly winds and unusually sunny weather here in Ireland, fly too far north and make landfall, tricked by the uncharacteristic balmy conditions. We went to the Old Head of Kinsale, a peninsula that juts several kilometres out into the Atlantic. It's a well-known migrant hotspot amongst birders. We drove out to the renowned Speckled Door Bar, where we parked and continued on foot. This pub was a landmark for birders, who'd often stop there for lunch or a drink. From there, we went by foot with a pair of binoculars around each of our necks. There was very little cover on the headland for grounded migrants to hide, bar some garden shrubs and stunted sycamores. Our first house martins flew overhead with their distinctive white-rumped, short-tailed black bodies, effortlessly catching insects on the wing as they went. A very vocal species on the wing, their coarse 'prrrt-prrrt' calls alerted us to their presence before we ever saw them.

We walked out the small local road that brought us to another known hotspot, the Plantation. This is a farmer's yard, where they kindly allowed birders to enter and search the line of conifer trees he had planted around the slurry pit. This treeline offered the farmer some protection from the wind – and it offered exhausted migrants the very same help. These were also the tallest trees for several kilometres so were an obvious spot to drop down for any birds that had come in off the sea seeking a place to feed up and rest. Dad and I stretched our necks and looked up at the exposed branches of the conifers. A goldcrest flitted out and back in, snapping at a small fly that had caught its eye. This is our smallest bird and it has a fondness for conifers. Their tiny little green bodies, with white-striped wings and yellow-striped crowns, move like a jack-in-the-box. They're always on the go. Having snapped up a few flies, it flew across the yard to the other line of trees. Its delicate, thin and very high-pitched 'zee-zee-zee' calls evoked an echoed response from another nearby. Despite their cute appearance, these birds are long-distance migrants from the kinglet family. Birds from Scandinavia that jump ship in winter and come south seeking milder conditions. These birds don't breed in the yard, and so were probably migrants themselves. It was spring, so they were headed north – *But how far north?* I wondered. Would they soon be flitting about the great wild forests of Scandinavia? From an Irish slurry pit to a home shared with bears and wolves.

We peered into the slurry pit next. Believe it or not, this is a well-known spot for birds, too. There was often a thin, dry crust on top of the slurry that absolutely hopped with insects, making an easy feast for a tired migrant. We got quite a surprise when we looked over. It was full of willow warblers, members of the leaf warbler family. Another well-known Irish migrant, this one breeds here – but not in the slurry pit. They'd be destined for willow scrub around the country, where their yellow-green bodies would shimmy in song from the tops of trees proclaiming their new turf. Their song is reminiscent of a lovely spring or early-summer day. It reminds me of a ball descending down stairs – a sweet descending tune with a little flourish at the end. Beautiful.

There were clearly migrants around and so this gave us hope for something rarer amongst them. Behind the plantation was a small, looping boreen sandwiched between cow fields and bramble and gorse-based hedgerows. These hedgerows often held migrants, so we walked slowly and scanned each section meticulously. Nothing of note on the first side. We exited onto the small road at the end and walked south to enter the other boreen that ran parallel to the first, continuing the loop. We chatted and stopped intermittently, scanning every hedgerow for any bird that moved. We rounded a corner that gave view to a more mature hedgerow with some hawthorns in it. A black-and-white figure perched on top of one of the bramble bushes made me freeze. My head started to twitch and my hands began to shake furiously. It's funny how this happens. It's as if my body registers the sighting before my brain computes what I'm looking at.

'Dad, I've got something!'

'What is it, Seán?'

'It's a shrike! I think it's a woodchat.'

I took me a few seconds to stop trembling enough to confirm. Woodchat shrikes are a special kind of bird, in a rather gruesome way. They're nicknamed the butcher birds, and that really is as sinister as it sounds. They capture small songbirds, reptiles, mammals and insects, and they tear them apart with their razor-sharp bills. They then impale the prey on spikes: thorns, barbed wire, and so on. They're like small, feathered, medieval executioners. They don't breed in Ireland, but do breed as far north as France, and they winter in Africa, south of the Sahara. I'd never seen a shrike in Ireland before, but I'd read all about their vicious habits, so it was quite a thrill to see one right before me in my home county. I almost felt like I was watching an infamous villain.

Woodchat Shrike *(Lanius senator)*
Family *Laniidae (shrikes)*
Conservation status *Least Concern (IUCN Red List) – does not occur on the Irish BoCCI list, as it is a rare vagrant*
Vocalisations *Rarely, if ever, heard in Ireland, even as vagrants. On the breeding grounds in the Mediterranean, they are spectacular vocalists with an extreme talent for mimicry.*

After taking a moment to calm down, we could really look at the details through our binoculars. It sat high on top of a bare bramble branch with a gleaming white breast, a rusty red cap, and a black mask and upper body. It was actively catching bumblebees. It would watch from its high perch and swoop down on any passing victims that came to feed on the dandelions in the pasture below. Then, it would fly back to its perch where it grasped the bee by the beak and thrashed if off a branch a few times. It seemed to be immobilising the bee and removing the sting. Then, it would swallow it whole and start over again. These moments in birding were not common. Rarities are, well ... rare. We lapped it up and put the news out on the grapevine, deciding to wait until the first people arrived so we could show them where it was.

Scanning through my binoculars, I saw a birder in the Plantation, behind the shrike. He, too, was seeking out spring overshoots. I waved and waved until he finally saw us. He waved back. 'No, no,' I said to myself, and began to wave again and point. He knew I was trying to communicate something but wasn't sure what. I then changed tactics and started to beckon him up to us. He turned around and ran. About five minutes later, he appeared around the, corner of the boreen.

'What have ya got?' he said, breathless.

'Woodchat shrike!' I replied

I was proud as punch. This person was a well-established birder and rarity finder, and I felt like I finally had something to show so I could prove to them that I was a part of their gang, too. I directed him onto the bird and as he was nodding and expressing his own awe for it, a sound overhead piqued my interest. It was an explosive buzzy 'tzzeee' call from a small, incoming bird. It looked like a pipit, but this call was very different to the flatter, smoother 'sip' flight calls of the widespread meadow pipit. I knew exactly what this was. 'TREE PIPIT!' I announced in a state of excitement.

Tree pipits are another rare bird in Ireland, although a few turn up most years following their winters in Africa on their way back north to Scandinavia and the UK, and vice versa. I had never heard or seen a tree pipit before in my life, but I'd been expecting one. I'd studied it many times in my dog-eared bird guide, and I'd memorised the call through CDs my friend Harry had loaned me. These birds rarely hang around and are very vocal in flight, so I knew that its flight call would be the way I'd clinch one if I was ever in the right place one day. I was happy with that. It was coming right for us. It came closer and closer until it landed on a telegraph pole above our heads. All three of us lifted our binoculars and saw it in full view. Wow! This was such a surreal moment. We had a woodchat shrike at our backs and now, above our heads, was a tree pipit. With the sun bursting through a royal blue sky, and this duo of exotic overshoots, we felt like we were in the Mediterranean.

Tree Pipit *(Anthus trivialis)*
Family *Motacillidae (wagtails, longclaws and pipits)*
Conservation status *Amber-listed (BoCCI, 2020–2026)*
Vocalisations *Does not breed in Ireland, and thus song is not encountered. Buzzy 'tzzeee' flight calls from scarce passage migrants can be heard by those at the right place and time in spring and autumn.*

We do have other species of pipit in Ireland, the most frequently encountered being meadow pipit. Meadow and tree pipits look very alike. They are both robin-sized and have light-brown backs, sandy-brown underparts and thin vertical streaking along the breasts. But there are two features that can be learned to separate them. One is the hindclaw – the claw that protrudes from the back of the foot. In meadow pipits, the hindclaw looks freakishly long and curved to help them stand on the ground. However, as tree pipits spend the majority of their time in trees, they don't share this adaptation and have a short hindclaw. The other feature is the flank streaking. The flanks are the parts where the upper body and breast meet. The flank streaking on meadow pipit is typically thick and blotchy, whereas in tree pipit it is pencil-thin. I inspected our bird for these features, and my listening skills were confirmed – it had a short hindclaw and really fine streaking along the flanks. I took a quick photo and that was it. It took off calling and flew up high and away. As we were packing up, we met a number of birders on their way for the shrike. We wished them luck and left with a smile. This is what rarity-finding is all about. You get to be out in nature appreciating common birds, but also get the occasional buzz of finding a rarity. And when all of the stars align, you might even find two.

After moments like this, it was hard to ignore the desire to be out in nature and go to work at the bar. Although I was still shy of people, I had a longing to share my life with someone. Sometimes, on busy nights, I'd have a number passed to me across the counter. I'd blush and put it away, with no intentions of acting on it. Where would I even begin? Some nights, I'd go out with old friends and I'd drink to gain courage, but it never ended well. I didn't know when to stop and I just became silly. I knew deep down that I'd never find anyone this way, but I didn't have the social skills to even attempt to meet someone without some Dutch courage. It became an endless cycle of frustration, embarrassment and torment.

In the mornings during the week, when I'd open up the bar, I'd usually cross paths with Alison. Alison was a hardworking, down-to-earth lady who prepared the bar for openings, making it spick and span, after the chaos of the nights before. She was *so* lovely and also absolutely hilarious. With a wholesome Cork city accent and a total lack of filter, she said things as they were, calling a spade a spade, and regularly made me cry with laughter, without even intending to do so. She had this uncanny knack of telling an everyday story in a way that would have you in hysterics. She was also a very good person with a great heart. She wouldn't harm a fly and would stand up for you without hesitation. I think she knew I struggled socially.

She always told me, 'Seán, I'm going to find you a lovely lady one of these days.'

I'd laugh in embarrassment. 'Do not, Alison!' It was an ongoing joke – or so I thought.

One morning she ran down to me and said, 'Seán, I've found you the perfect girl.'

I laughed it off, as always. 'Sure, okay, Alison.'

She insisted. 'No, no, I mean it, Seán. She's a lovely Catalan lady from Barcelona. She's working today.'

'Don't you dare say a word, Alison, I mean it!'

'Too late. I told her all about you and I said you fancied her,' she said with a straight face.

'You said *what*!?'

'Yeah. She said she'd seen you around already and thought you were handsome.'

I felt a tremble of fear. 'Jesus Christ, Alison! What am I going to do now? I have to work with her.'

She paused and turned to me with a deadpan face and a raised eyebrow. 'Talk to her.'

And she walked away.

Thoughts raced around my head. Was she serious? How will I know it's her? Should I pretend nothing happened if she does appear? When will she start? My first customers came in and this took my mind off things. I fell back into my routine and had my usual chats and laughs with the same old familiar faces. At lunchtime, a lady came walking down from the back bar with a book in her hand, smiling and looking me straight in the eye. I sheepishly glanced at her and was instantly taken by her beauty. She was tall with beautiful long, blonde, wavy hair. She had these wonderful dark-brown eyes with a golden tan and a smile that melted my heart. She wore a brilliant bohemian floral green dress and a pair of brown sandals. She was gorgeous, but looked so down-to-earth at the same time.

She came to the bar and introduced herself. 'Hi, I'm Alba. I just started here. Do you mind if I sit down by the counter for my break?'

I was shaking like a leaf. 'No, of course not. Do you want a tea or coffee?'

'A green tea, if you have it.'

I knew this was the woman Alison had spoken to me about. She really hadn't been joking, then. I had my back to Alba pouring the tea, literally spilling it with the trembles. My mind was racing. I turned around, smiled and put the tea on the counter ... and then I left. I couldn't do it. I was overcome with nerves and I just shut down. I walked around the bar cleaning tables that didn't need to be cleaned. Anything to take me away from the fear of making a fool of myself in front of Alba. I didn't trust myself to have a steady, functional conversation with her. Now and then, I'd hesitantly lift my head up and look at her, and she was already looking back and smiling. I'd jerk my head back down and pretend not to see. I knew I was blowing a big chance, but I just couldn't help myself.

After her break, she stood up, smiled, and waved. 'See you later, Seán.'

'Y–yeah, see you later!' I felt like such a fool. I wanted so desperately to have someone in my life and here was this beautiful woman sitting in front of me, clearly wanting to connect and I just threw it all away.

Nature Boy

What exactly is wrong with me? Why am I so afraid to socialise? I convinced myself that she was probably just being friendly. Why would someone like her be interested in me? Nature Boy.

That night, I had a friend request on Facebook. It was Alba. I accepted and started to look at her photos. I didn't have to be afraid of making eye contact now. She really was beautiful. Way out of my league. Over the coming days, she started to like and comment on the wildlife photos I posted regularly to Facebook. Just simple little compliments like 'Wow, very cool!' or 'Beautiful shot!' I'd reply with a thank you and a smiley face.

Not long after, an instant message popped up. Just a simple, 'Hey! How are you?' We chatted and got to know one another, and this went on for days, until Alba said something that shocked me: 'Don't you know that I fancy you? Can't you see that I'm trying to flirt with you?'

I stopped and looked at the screen in shock, my mouth agape. It took me some time to process what she had written. Did she really just type what I think she did?

I replied, 'Really? I thought you were just being friendly.' How naive was I?

'Come on, man, really? Would you like to go on a date?'

I wanted to cry, I was so happy. I responded immediately. 'Oh my God, I'm such an idiot! Of course, I'd love that.'

'Great,' she replied, 'Ireland play Italy in the Six Nations on Saturday at 13.30 – are you working?'

I couldn't believe this was real. 'I'm working until 14.00, but I'm free for the weekend, then.'

'OK! I'll come to the bar to watch the game a little before kick-off and wait for you.'

I cannot describe the nerves I felt that morning, knowing Alba was coming to meet me for a date. I worked behind the counter with an extra spring in my step, and joked and laughed with anyone who came to order. Time flew and, before I knew it, the pre-game commentary was on screen and the bar was filling up. I was busy running around serving drinks as people arrived to pick their seats. I heard a familiar voice from behind me, 'Seán!' I turned around and there she was. I hadn't seen Alba in person since the first time we met, and I'd forgotten just how beautiful she really was. I was nervous, but mostly a warm, tingling sensation of butterflies in my stomach won out. Alba was wearing an Irish rugby jersey and was jumping around as the game kicked off. She looked so happy, confident and outgoing. It put me at ease, but made me wonder how she would feel with someone as socially awkward as me.

My shift ended and I made my way through the crowds. I found Alba sitting on a high stool. Before I had a chance to say hi, she grabbed me by both cheeks, pulled me in and gave me a passionate kiss on the lips. I was shocked. She let go and burst out laughing. 'Look at you, all nervous! What are you scared of? I don't bite.'

I laughed in relief. 'Wow! I did not expect that.'

She replied, 'I knew you'd be nervous, so I said I'd just skip all of that.'

I'd never met anyone like her. She didn't judge me, she didn't care what others thought and she was utterly her own person. It brought me out of my shell completely.

Nature Boy

We spoke and laughed throughout the game and had such a brilliant time. I didn't want it to end. I asked her what her plan was afterwards and she told me she was up to continue for as long as I wanted. When we found a quieter moment, I pulled out a present for her. I could see the look of surprise on her face. I'd wrapped a photo of a small tortoiseshell butterfly I'd taken by the coast the previous summer. It was one of my favourite photographs. Alba peeled back the paper and put her hand to her mouth. I saw tears welling up in her eyes. 'Oh my God, that is so sweet! Nobody has ever given me anything like this before.' She looked at it in detail, admiring the intricate colours of the delicate wings: reds, blues, yellows and blacks. Then she turned and gave me a big hug. I told her I loved nature and she started to ask me about it. I'd always been afraid to talk to girls about this, because I always bored them. But Alba wasn't like that, she really listened and I knew she was genuinely interested in whatever it was I had to say. I never once felt like I was nerding her away. I knew from the get-go that she was special.

We continued on and went from bar to bar. I guess I was afraid she'd 'find me out' for the socially awkward guy I'd always been, and I decided I'd drink to build up some courage. I ended up quite drunk, but she didn't judge me for it.

Later that night, we had some food and I slept on her couch. We spent every single free moment together for the next month. We got on like a house on fire. I became a stranger in my parents' home, much to the annoyance of Alba's housemates. And so, as crazy as it sounds, after just a few months, we discussed moving in together. We didn't need to think about it for long. And, just like that, we were an official couple and we found ourselves a little apartment to rent in Cork city. This was one of the best moments of my life. Alba would bring changes to my world in ways that I could never have imagined. If only I knew at the time what a difference she would bring. But I was so happy. It was a feeling I'd never experienced in my life, and it was only the beginning.

Hooded Crow

A male hen harrier with prey. Commercial forestry plantations, overgrazing by sheep and deer and the construction of wind farms are major threats to this species in Ireland. Photo by Mike Brown.

A great skua migrating at sea, off the West Cork coastline, in August 2015.

A migrant pied flycatcher eyeballs a passing fly from a hunting perch. My dad and I would sometimes encounter this bird during our trips to Cape Clear in the autumn.

Guillemot party photographed on the Farne Islands in July 2013. You can see a recently fledged chick or jumpling in the centre.

A robin eyes up an earthworm at Cuskinny Nature Reserve, Cobh, in December 2018.

The Old Head of Kinsale lighthouse, as photographed from our boat on a sailing trip from Cobh to Cape Clear Island in October 2016.

Woodchat shrike: this very bird is the first time I had ever stumbled upon an Irish rarity. It was a spring overshoot that I have confidence turned back when it realised its error! Photo by Laura Jones.

Small tortoiseshell butterfly photographed at Power Head, Cork. I gave a print of this very photo to Alba on our first date.

This photo, taken in December 2016, epitomises what Alba has brought to my life – utter joy.

Left: A little egret forages at Delta de l'Ebre, Catalunya. I will always have a soft spot for this species, having immersed myself in their world during my marine biology dissertation.

Below: conducting a habitat assessment at Cuskinny Nature Reserve in April 2016 in part fulfilment for my ecological impact assessment dissertation. Photo by Alba Novell Capdevila.

A hooded crow photographed at Douglas Estuary, County Cork, in March 2017. These birds, like many in the Corvidae family, are famous for their intellect.

A rock pipit on Tory Island, County Donegal in June 2021. This is one of the birds Alba and I encountered during our first trip to Cape Clear together.

A sand martin, photographed in April 2019 at Delta del Llobregat, Catalunya.

Conducting a bird survey in Wicklow in August 2011.

One of my favourite wildlife photos to date: common dolphins leaping, photographed off the West Cork coast from my father's boat in September 2015.

An otter at Mizen Head Peninsula, County Cork, in April 2022.

Putting on a brave face in our wonderful camp in the Moroccan Sahara Desert, moments before I proposed to Alba in March 2017. Photo by Alba Novell Capdevila.

Scene of the proposal: I knew in this moment that I'd come back to this very spot, later that night, under the moonlight to propose to Alba.

A teary Alba, literally seconds after accepting my proposal.

Chapter 7

LIFE WITH ALBA WAS A WHIRLWIND OF JOY AND DISCOVERY, and I just knew that I had met the person I wanted to take on the world with. We were very different people but we also shared many interests and characteristics. Our early days together were sometimes a bit of a rollercoaster, with lots of misunderstandings and clashes, but we accepted them and worked together to understand and resolve things. Alba is a social butterfly and naturally gets along with everyone she meets. She could effortlessly converse with a stranger no matter what their background or interests. I was the total opposite.

I lived a life of crossing the road when I saw someone approaching on the footpath ahead of me, just so I didn't have to go through the internal battle of when to look up and smile or think of what to say. Growing up, this always bothered me and I tried every approach under the sun, but they all felt awkward and forced. I can recall several occasions when I waved to strangers far too early, way ahead on the path, causing them to give me a wide berth. How do people know when to look up and salute? Where do you look in the lead-up? Where do you put your hands? These simple social cues weren't inherent to me, yet I could see that they were to everyone else.

I knew how to interact with nature, though. I knew how to approach a bird from a distance, without causing it to flee. Some birds are a soft touch — typically urban dwellers. Pied wagtails, for example, will let you walk right on up to them without a fuss. They're city slickers, used to heavy human footfall and seem to tolerate our noisy constructed worlds. Like me, I bet they'd prefer to be in peace, though.

Pied Wagtail *(Motacilla alba)*
Family *Motacillidae (wagtails, longclaws and pipits)*
Conservation status *Green-listed (BoCCI, 2020–2026)*
Vocalisations *The 'chiss-ick' flight call is the most commonly heard of vocalisations. Song is a joyful twittering melody, seemingly without structure or verse. To me it sounds as if the bird is practising for a final piece, which never comes.*

On the complete opposite end of the spectrum are magpies and hooded crows. Crows, famous for their intellect, maybe know better than to trust us humans, and for good reason because no other species has a track record for destruction and malevolence like our own. A study conducted on crow learning in the US found that birds learned and remembered the faces of people who had scolded or posed a threat to them, and also taught their young to avoid those same faces. This means it's entirely plausible that crows have a general awareness of the potential of threat from humans. I learned early on that crows pick up on our intentions through our body language. It's difficult not to look at a subject as you try to approach it with stealth. But this isn't enough. Crows, and indeed many species, will pick up on your gaze. Walk towards a hooded crow and stare at it and see what happens. It'll turn suddenly and look right at you, with a sense of fight-or-flight. Keep it up and it will fly off well before you get anywhere near it.

What happens when you pretend you don't see it is another story. If you approach the crow at a gentle angle and pretend to look the other way or you look at the ground, they'll be much less concerned. You have to act as if you're not interested in them. From a young age, I'd gently creep up on birds using this method, and I'd get a great kick out of it. It made me feel accepted among them, like I was just another part of nature going about its business.

In a sense, you could compare myself and Alba to the pied wagtail and the hooded crow. Alba is the easy-to-approach, sociable pied wagtail who's happy to mix with anyone and has no fear. I'm the shy and aloof hooded crow, who needs some time and understanding. But give me the time and space I need and we'll get along just fine.

Hooded Crow *(Corvus cornix)*
Family *Corvidae (crows)*
Conservation status *Green-listed (BoCCI, 2020–2026)*
Vocalisations *Call is a stereotypical 'krraahh', often repeated in threes. Hooded crows also have a rarely heard song, which consists of a series of strange, low-volume gurgling sounds, hoarse vibrations and clicks.*

Although our early days together were a combination of fireworks and flowers, we found beauty and excitement in both. Our initial dates were packed full of discoveries on both sides – like a rare meeting of two worlds, which, whilst very different, were just meant to come together to blend and support one another.

Alba had a real passion for sport, especially her beloved Barcelona football club. She had supported her home team with everything she had since she was a child, collecting every jersey and watching every game. Never in my life had I watched football, nor did I understand the passion so many people had for it. But seeing the joy and passion Alba had for the games shed some light on it for me. Just as Alba stepped into my world, open and willing to take part, I began to watch football games with her. Despite my willingness to open up to this alien world, I still did not understand it; I was just there to be by Alba's side as she sat on the edge of her seat and celebrated each goal. Barcelona didn't seem to lose, so it was rare to see her disappointed. Watching a winning side is easy. We often watched games in town, where we'd meet up with other members of the Catalan community. Everyone spoke in Catalan or Spanish, which was good for me. It enabled me to hide behind Alba and blend into the background with the excuse of not understanding, which wasn't entirely true – I'd learned Spanish in school for five years, though I wasn't very good at it.

At first, my conversations with Alba were quite one-sided. Alba would ask me lots of questions and I would answer them, usually without much detail. One day, as we were walking along the River Lee having what I thought was a fine-flowing conversation, she looked at me with sadness and told me she needed me to open up. She said that if we were to continue into the future, she needed someone who could express themselves and not be afraid of showing their emotions. This came as a bit of a surprise as well as a worry. I thought I was expressing myself, but when she spelled it out to me, I got it.

'Seán, all you talk to me about is birds and otters. We've been together for several months now, and although you are lovely to me, I feel like I don't know you. You've never told me about your childhood, your dreams or your fears. And you've never asked me the same. How can I be in a committed relationship with someone I hardly know?' At the time, all of the things she craved were small talk to me. I only wanted to talk about the one thing that made me tick. But when she said it so plainly, I realised I was in my own insular world, and that I was practically blank on the outside, even to my girlfriend.

Alba was clearly upset, and she realised that I wasn't going to open up of my own accord, so she had to intervene.

'Seán, I've had a few close relationships back home, and all of them ended for various reasons, many of which left me hurt. But all of my ex-partners were emotionally open to me, despite whatever they did to cause me pain. I could discuss problems with them and we solved them through communication. Why can't you do this? What are you afraid of? Were you hurt in the past?'

All of these were valid questions, which I mostly didn't have an answer to, although I wasn't afraid nor was I hurt. I had never been in a meaningful relationship before, so this was the first time these things were coming up. I wasn't alone anymore, but I was acting like I was. I had a beautiful partner who had spilled everything out in the open for me, yet all I wanted to do was hold her hand and feed her a running monologue on whatever nature happened before us, wherever we went. Alba went on. 'I know you love me, Seán, but I need you to show me that. I need you to tell me! I need you to make me feel it every day. Otherwise, we are just like roommates, and I don't need to invest my life in a roommate.'

This cut me deep and I started to cry. I loved Alba, despite only knowing her a few months. And to see her crying because of me really hit me. I hugged her and told her I was sorry. She hugged me back but stepped back and told me. 'I love you, but I don't need you to be sorry, I need you to be present and to make me feel like I have a partner.'

I promised her I would. We brushed ourselves off and continued on our way, but my mind was racing. *How do I express myself like that?* I'd never really opened up to anyone in that way, and I didn't know how. Was this an Irish thing? Mediterranean people are famously open, they sing and dance like nobody is watching, they kiss one another on the cheeks when they meet, and they live life with passion and zest. Irish people internalise things much more. Was it this? Or was it me? Regardless, I knew she needed me to step up so I had to figure out how.

Later that evening, when Alba was back home, I popped to the shop and bought her some flowers and a card. The flowers were her favourite: a simple and elegant blend of yellows and whites. But it was the card that held the true meaning. This is where I spilled everything. I told Alba exactly what she meant to me and how she had changed my world for the better. I felt so at ease expressing myself in the written word, even though I had never done it before. I almost felt like I was reading the words of a stranger – did I really just express myself like that? It felt liberating.

Later that evening, I came home and gave Alba the flowers and card. I watched a wave of emotions play out over her face as she read down through the card. Tears welled up in her eyes and she jumped at me with a hug. 'Thank you, this is exactly what I needed.'

From then on, we grew as a couple. Every day, I would leave her Post-it notes to remind her how I felt and, slowly but surely, I started to open up vocally, too. This was all new to me so Alba patiently helped me along and coaxed things out of me. She was so understanding.

All of these changes didn't happen overnight; we still had our misunderstandings and there were more things I needed to figure out. Although I tried, eye contact was an issue. I'd always insisted on sitting next to Alba on meal dates rather than across from her. Being put in a position with someone where I have no choice but to maintain some level of eye contact was terrifying. This might seem silly to some, but to me it was no joke.

During my years in school and college, my head and neck would literally tremble if the person sitting in front of me turned even slightly to one side so that my eyes had to intersect with their peripheral vision in order to see the board. This fear of eye contact was so bad at times that I chose not to look forwards at the board at all in case I crossed someone's gaze, so I just looked down and listened. Although I didn't know the cause of the intense discomfort I felt when looking others in the eyes, I was very much aware of it not being 'normal'. I knew people picked up on it too, and I knew it made them react in an uncomfortable or untrusting manner. I guess it made me look shifty. But, to me, it just felt so unnatural, like a chimpanzee walking upright on two legs – it was possible, but it was awkward and forced.

It eventually came up in conversation with Alba. 'Why must we always sit next to each other when we eat out? Can we not sit in front of one another and actually see each other's faces, like a normal couple?'

I'd never explained my eye contact thing to her before, and realistically I didn't fully understand it myself. I took a deep breath and began to explain. 'Alba, I have a thing about eye contact. It actually makes me really uncomfortable, and so I try to avoid it at all costs. If I'm sitting opposite someone, it shakes me so much that it essentially shuts me down. But if I sit next to them, I feel as if I can talk much more freely.'

It took her a minute to take in what I'd said. I could see her face slowly change to one of empathy and understanding. 'Ah, it's okay, love, I understand. You don't have to do it, but why don't we try? It's just me!'

I thought about it for a second, and said, 'To hell with it. You're right, there's nobody I trust in the world more than you.'

Alba slid out of her seat and sat herself in front of me. I looked at her brown eyes and her warm smile. I began to explain to her that I didn't know how long I needed to look at someone's eyes when I was speaking to them, and that I felt disrespectful if I looked away, which resulted in a battle between my brain and my eyes. I'd often hold a gaze too long and look like a crazed stalker, or not make eye contact at all and look like I was uninterested or had something to hide. She thought about it for a second. As eye contact etiquette isn't something that's taught or people think about, Alba needed to get into her own head and rationalise what she did herself. Imagine thinking about your process of breathing. What do you do? When do you do it? How long is each breath? This is how I thought about eye contact.

Alba finally had it. 'When someone is talking to you, look at their eyes, but every few seconds flick your eyes somewhere else for a break, and then bring them back again. You don't have to stare into their eyes for the entirety of the time they speak. Do the same when you're speaking.'

I replied, 'But how many seconds is a few?'

Alba giggled. 'It doesn't matter, babe. Just a few. They're not counting.'

Now, I had a rule to follow. From here on in, every time we went out for a meal, we'd sit across from one another and I'd carefully watch Alba's eye contact mannerisms when we spoke, all the while taking mental notes. It *really* helped me, and it began to boost my self-confidence *massively*. After all, eye contact with other humans is something we engage in many times, every single day. So to feel hindered in this regard is nothing short of socially debilitating. I hadn't mastered it by any means, but I was certainly much better at it.

When it came to larger meal gatherings, Alba always had my back. She was the only person who knew this quirk about me. I guess it was too embarrassing to bring up with other people because I knew it was a skill natural to almost everyone. Alba would always ask me whether I'd like to sit next to or opposite her before we'd go to big gatherings of people. My answer varied depending on the number of people and who would be sitting around me. Sitting opposite me, I could keep my head up and look to Alba. Sitting next to me, she gave me the physical comfort I needed when I was feeling vulnerable. Alba was *always* there for me, and was *always* thinking about my well being. She protected me, and this understanding and kindness solidified my love for her. I realised that Alba was my selfless soulmate. She accepted me for all of my peculiarities and was there to pick me up when I fell down or just needed some support. I loved her with every piece of me.

It wasn't just me learning from Alba, though. I had the privilege of opening her eyes to the natural beauty of the world. And although I did this at every opportunity, I now knew to take a break from it as well and instead ask her about her day or tell her what she means to me.

Over time, we were finding balance, to make our two very different ways of life meet in the middle. Otters were a thing early on in our relationship, which probably isn't something Alba expected. Ever since I was a little boy, I've always had distinct topics of interest, which I'd obsess over and take to the limit and beyond. Aside from my never-ending obsession with wildlife, I had extensive stone, coin and stamp collections. Every relative had to bring me back one of each from every foreign holiday they took.

Luckily for Alba, I'd moved on from stones, coins and stamps. Now, it was otter poo that I was specifically interested in. So, whilst most couples spent their weekends going to fancy restaurants or visiting new cities, we spent ours on our hands and knees along the water's edge sniffing poo. Otters, like many members of the Mustelidae family, have anal scent glands that emit a distinctive odour for sexual signalling and territory marking. When they poo, this scent is attached to their scat. Otter scat is, in fact, referred to as 'spraint', and it's very distinctive. Often a black or dark-grey colour, it is visibly interspersed with white fish bones. However, the scent is what truly confirms it as otter spraint. It smells wonderful (yes, you heard me), very much like a modern perfume with a strong resemblance to jasmine and a pleasant hint of fish!

Alba thought I was pulling her leg when I first told her about this legitimacy test. Was I really asking her to bend down and suck up a whiff of otter poo? I was deadly serious and gave her a demonstration.

She laughed nervously and followed suit, holding her hair back to take her olfactory senses to new and exciting places. She lifted her head back up with pleasant surprise, 'Oh my God, I thought you were joking! It actually *does* smell like jasmine.'

I've always needed a project in my life. I need an unknown, something I can work towards to find an answer or at least gain a better understanding of. When I was dating Alba, I was infatuated with otters. I read every book I could find and soaked up all that was known about them. What did they eat here in Cork city, though? Nobody knew, so this was my self-appointed project – to find out what our very own River Lee otters fed on. All I had to do was collect and analyse their poo. To do this you need to think like an otter, and to think like an otter, you need to understand them intimately, hence the devouring of literature.

Otter spraint is made up of the undigestible parts of their, mostly fishy, meals. These are waste products that their bodies expel, just like any other mammal. Otters also use their spraints as territorial markers or to advertise their sexual status, so they want this information to be easily picked up by other otters. And so they lay down these spraints in areas where other otters have the best chance of finding it. In Cork city, they regularly leave them on the upper steps that lead from the river at various points along its walled banks. Here, otters come up from the water to feed on fish and crabs and to take a rest, and so it's an obvious place for them to spraint. Their spraint is also found under bridges and culverts, where otters can temporarily leave the water.

In coastal (saltwater) areas, despite their being more open and vast, I find it just as easy to detect spraints. This is because otters need access to freshwater to wash themselves and remove the salt from their coats.

A salty coat can result in matting and general degradation, which, in turn, reduces the heat-insulating qualities of a healthy, salt-free coat. So, because coastal otters will *all* seek out freshwater sources along our coastline, these areas act as key spraínting sites, where the otters of the region exchange vital information, and give their fur a good rinsing.

Luckily for Alba, the otter spraints did not stay at home – at least not for long. They were bottled up in individual test tubes: one spraint per tube, preserved in alcohol, and labelled with the date and location. As I was still studying my master's in ecological impact assessment, I had access to the labs, which I had permission to use in my free time to analyse the spraints. The first step was to add a biological detergent to each sample and shake it up. This worked away inside the tube, breaking down the unwanted parts from the bones. After sitting for a few days, the samples were ready to assess. I'd empty a test tube into a fine mesh sieve and run it under a tap. This would wash out all of the soft biological matter and leave me with just the bones.

Using these bones, I could figure out what species were eaten, estimate how many were eaten and even estimate the size of each prey item. There were a number of specific bone types which were more useful than others. The most helpful bone, in terms of securing a sure identification, were the otoliths – the hard calcium-carbonate structure, also known as ear-bones, and, as the name suggests, enable fish to hear and to feel vibrations in the water. Different species of fish each have a different-shaped otolith, and as these shapes and variations are well studied, assessing otoliths is a highly reliable way of determining what species were eaten by the otters. Even more interesting is that fish can be aged by counting the number of growth rings on the otoliths, just like we do with trees.

Alba and I must have collected hundreds of spraints together from Cork city and from Cuskinny. It was fascinating to learn that common eels and salmon made up the bulk of the Cork city otter's diet, which is not a big surprise given the brackish nature of the waters up there, coupled with the fact that it was a regular salmon-netting haunt.

We didn't have a car – I didn't drive, but Alba did. One sunny weekend, she decided to rent a car so we could go on a *proper* date. We'd been together for months now but we still hadn't left the city. She asked for suggestions and I immediately knew where to go – Cape Clear Island. I told her all about it, how it's the southernmost inhabited part of Ireland, that they spoke Irish there and that it was also a very good place to see birds. She was in! We took the ferry out from Baltimore and that alone was spectacular. We had a choice of buying two adult returns or a couple's return. We bought the couple's return and beamed at one another – it was like a stamp of approval (and we still have this ticket, actually).

The orange and white double-decker boat fired up and off we motored. Almost immediately, I switched into nature mode and began scanning the horizon from the deck. We cruised the 12 kilometres from the pier through various islands and islets, shrouded in the glistening blues and greens of the Atlantic. The weather was balmy and the wind hardly stirred – 'Perfect conditions for spotting harbour porpoises or dolphins,' I told Alba. She had never seen either and was ecstatic at the prospect of spotting one. I told her what to look out for: common dolphins are around 6 to 8 feet long, with a grey back and golden sides. The dorsal fin is the real giveaway though. This is the fin on top of their backs that juts out of the water and curves backwards. It's difficult to miss, with a wide base that gradually tapers off at the top.

Harbour porpoises, on the other hand, are very different. They're the smallest of our cetaceans, only reaching 4 to 6 feet. They typically appear dark-grey or black and have a much smaller, even-sided-looking dorsal fin, like a little isosceles triangle. They tend to potter along close to the shore and, to me, they always seem much calmer than their hyperactive dolphin cousins.

With this information and a spare pair of binoculars, Alba was armed with the tools she needed to find and identify the most likely cetaceans along our route. It brought out her competitive streak – what else would you expect from a hardcore Barcelona football fan? We kept an eye out and admired the various seabirds as we passed, desperately looking for a fin. We had a few false alarms as we saw a little wave or a diving cormorant, but then Alba started to jump. 'I have something! I think it's a harbour porpoise. It's small, dark and has a little triangular fin.' She gave me some frantic directions and then I saw it too. We watched it for a moment before we realised there were two – it was accompanied by a tiny little calf. It was quite funny to see it pushing to keep up with the mother. For every breath the mother would take at the surface, the little one would take two or three. Alba was smitten and our weekend away was off to a great start.

The bird observatory was not available, so we decided to stay in the youth hostel located right next to the South Harbour. We woke up to a brilliant sunrise and ate breakfast together on the harbour wall, alone with just the sound of the waves lapping along the wild and rugged shoreline, strewn with all manner of entangled seaweeds and encrusted with an army of limpets and barnacles. The local rock pipits cloaked us with their melodic tumbling flight songs from above. They build up anticipation with a long series of 15 to 20 'tseep-tseep-

tseep' notes, before switching to a sharp ascending series of 'chu-chu-chu' notes, ending in a wonderful accelerating flurry, which they give as they parachute back down to the ground below. A beautiful patch of vivid-pink sea thrift sprouted from the wall alongside us and we looked out at the morning sparkle of the great Atlantic Ocean. What a serene way to begin our day.

Rock Pipit *(Anthus petrosus)*
Family *Motacillidae (wagtails, longclaws and pipits)*
Conservation status *Green-listed (BoCCI, 2020–2026)*
Vocalisations *Call a sudden, forceful 'shreep'. Song display in spring is given in flight as a long series of 15 to 20 'tseep-tseep-tseep' notes, before switching to a sharp ascending series of 'chu-chu-chu' notes, ending in a wonderful accelerating flurry, which they give as they parachute back down to the ground below.*

We took off with our hiking boots and suncream and spent the day walking through the little lanes, coastal grasslands and bogs that adorned the land, chatting and soaking up the solace of the island as we went. After some time, we lay down in the grass by the cliffs for a break and to take it all in.

We just lay there chatting. I'd never, ever met anyone like Alba and I knew wholeheartedly that she was the one. Every day out with her further confirmed how right this all was. I remembered what she'd told me about communicating things to her, and so I decided to be brave. I turned to her and told her that I loved her. Expressing my feelings is something I'd always struggled with, but being out here surrounded by nature, with wonderful birdsong that carried its way to us on a fresh sea breeze, gave me that extra comfort and confidence I needed. Alba asked for so little and gave me so much. It was the very least I owed her. I hadn't really said it in words before, and she started to cry tears of joy, as did I. We left for home stronger than ever with a camera full of photos and our heads filled with lifelong memories.

During the week, I continued to study for my master's, and I was also still working in the bar whenever I could. I had reached a point in my thesis that was super intense and stressful, so much so that I had broken out in eye styes. I had three in total and, at their peak, I peered out through red, puffy, weeping eyes and looked like I had been badly beaten. Alba was worried for me and so when my fieldwork was done, she had a surprise prepared. She told me to book some time off work and to pack my bags – she had bought some plane tickets for us.

'Where are we going?' I asked.

'You'll find out when we get there,' she replied.

It had been such a long time since I'd been abroad and I was so excited.

We went to board the flight and it was only then that I realised we were going to Barcelona. Wow! Then it hit me: *Oh my God, I'm going to meet Alba's parents.* My school Spanish was terrible and my Catalan, non-existent. Alba laughed as she witnessed my emotions go from excitement to fear. She told me she'd translate for me and that I had nothing to worry about.

And she was right. Her family were all so lovely – open, welcoming and friendly. We all did our best to communicate either through Alba or through gestures or expressions. The first Catalan phrase I learned was '*Què diu?*', which means 'What's he saying?' I heard it so many times that it stuck in my head. I was instantly made to feel part of the family.

In Barcelona, we could finally let our hair down and escape from the madness of our busy lives back home. When out for a coffee in the town square one evening, Alba sat me down under the cooling shade of a large holm oak and told me she had something to tell me. 'Seán, I never told you this, but I think it's time that you know. There's a specific reason I came to Ireland. A few years ago, a friend of mine died unexpectedly. She was far too young, and it made me realise just how fragile and unpredictable life really is. Work, belongings, the whole fast-paced nine to five grind – none of it matters, because you just don't know what's around the corner.'

I understood this all too well after my own very close call with meningitis. It's something I have thought about every day since it happened. I nearly didn't make it, and whenever I'm going through something I perceive as tough in my day-to-day life, I think about that period. That was *truly* tough, but I pushed through it and I survived. It always puts things in perspective for me and boosts me through anything that's thrown at me. If I can handle that, I can handle whatever mundane hurdle it is I'm fretting over. I leaned in closer, curious and a bit nervous as to where she was going with this.

Her friend's death had affected her in a profound way, and one evening she had been listening to music and a song had come on that changed everything. She'd decided there and then to give up the grind and do what she really wanted to do with her life. She had always enjoyed helping and caring for people, so her plan was to move to Ireland to learn English for a year so she could travel and volunteer with humanitarian NGOs in India. She gave up her apartment, her physiotherapy business and her friends – her parents thought she was crazy. But she knew it was the right thing to do. So, she moved to

Ireland with only a few phrases of English and essentially started from scratch.

And then she said it. She leaned forward and cupped her hands over mine: 'I love you, Seán, and I want you in my life, but I need to do this. I'd like to spend a year more in Ireland max. And then I need to go.'

The thought of Alba going without me gave me a heavy feeling in the pit of my stomach. Alba was everything to me.

'Will you come with me?' she asked.

I didn't need to think about my answer, not for a second: 'Absolutely!' Not only did I love an adventure, but I loved Alba too.

Alba was so relieved and she hugged me.

We went back to Ireland feeling refreshed. I completed my master's and graduated with first-class honours, but I continued to work at the bar, despite my love for wildlife and the outdoors. I felt comfortable there. It gave me structure, routine and stability. The thought of losing all of those things scared me, but Alba spurred me on. 'You need to start working in your field. Learn how to drive and move on with your life – do what you love. I'll support you while you make the transition.'

I didn't have the nerve for it at first, but Alba insisted that I take the risk. So I handed in my notice and left the bar, and I was terrified. I felt exposed – I had no routine, no income and no self-assurance. I compiled my CV and began applying to different consultancies around the country. Back in Northumberland, Gary had been conducting mandatory pre-construction bird surveys for proposed wind farms, and so this is what I aimed for too. I could make a difference, the work was plentiful, I'd be out in nature every day and it paid well.

Every day, I'd email out CVs and buff up on theoretical stuff such as survey procedures. But I was also studying driving theory. I was taking lessons every second day and driving with my father down in Cobh.

Again, that feeling of insecurity crept in. Did I quit my familiar job just to be stranded and lost like before? Alba reassured me I'd made the right move. 'It's OK, love, we have savings. I'm working and earning enough money as a physio now, and you're great at what you do. Be patient. It will work out, I promise.'

This calmed me and gave me what I needed to persevere and, to my amazement, I got an interview after just one week. It was with a consultancy that specialised in wind-energy projects and they were looking for experienced ornithologists. I looked at their job requirements, knowing I didn't yet drive, hoping I'd not see 'full clean driving licence' in the fine print. But it was there. I decided I'd go for it anyway – what did I have to lose?

The first interview was over the phone. The interviewer spoke with a cheerful and welcoming Scottish accent, which totally put me at ease. He asked me about my listed credentials and experience, and we got on really well. We were both birders and he was familiar with Seahouses and the Farne Islands. He invited me up to Galway for an interview in person, and I had a mixed feeling of elation and deceit, having not mentioned my lack of a driving licence. I took a bus up and ran over every possible scenario in my head – my usual routine of overthinking and nerves. But I had nothing to worry about. The interview went well, and the team were all wonderful. After I'd spoken to everyone and had a good meeting under my belt, I decided to come clean before it was too late. I told them I didn't drive. It came as a surprise, but I was told they may have a solution. They'd call me back with news in a few days either way.

Nature Boy

The day I was due the call, I was a nervous wreck, and Alba, just like my family, knew what was needed to calm me. Alba took some time out and we went to Ballycotton for a walk. The sounds, smells and sights of the familiar wild Atlantic brought me right back down. We talked as we took the cliff walk, with gulls and ravens gliding overhead in support. The old south-facing stone walls along the cliffs are a haven for Ireland's only native reptile: the common lizard. As they're cold-blooded, they rely on the rays of the sun to warm them up enough to move in their usual zippy manner. We slowly walked along and I pointed them out to Alba. She was bemused at first, and didn't understand the fuss – they have many species of reptiles in Catalunya. But I explained to her that this is our *only* one, and it isn't anywhere near as common as they are over there. Then she was in on the buzz as we crept along the wall boundary counting lizards as we went. Some were an earthy brown, others a vivid green, with all variations in between. They'd sit on the heat-soaked rocks, eyes closed with their heads tilted up to the sun. We had to be careful not to cast a shadow on them, as this would instantly send them to cover. We must have counted over 40 lizards along the walk, which was an Irish high count for me. My nerves had wafted off in the salty breeze until I felt a vibration coming from my pocket. It was the news I'd been so nervous about, and I looked at Alba with a face drenched in apprehension. She just smiled and nodded, as if to say 'you've got this'.

I picked up expecting the worst, and was met with that same uplifting, positive tone. 'Hey Seán, I hope you're well and enjoying the sun. I called you to tell you that we'd love to have you on board and that we have a temporary solution to your driving conundrum. We have a proposed wind-farm site in the midlands, where we could set you up in the nearest town while you work. You could cycle or walk to site while you wait for your driving test. Are you up for the challenge?'

The thoughts of a new working week out with nature, surrounded by birds and all that I love, rocketed the answer out of me. *'Yes*! I'm in!' I agreed to start the following week.

I hung up and celebrated with Alba. She was right. Finally, I was where I needed to be. I don't think I would have made this leap were it not for her. The coming months would prove to be an explosion of joy and discovery, but it wasn't without its challenges. I'd only just moved into an apartment with Alba, and I loved our routine there, but now I had to move some 250 kilometres north and live on my own for extended periods of time each month. It felt wrong, but it also felt right. My apartment in the midlands was tiny and had no TV or internet. The walls were plain and I had two windows, both of which looked at walls. That was okay, though, as I didn't plan to spend much time there.

My job was to conduct 12 six-hour bird surveys every month. To get to my new apartment from Cork, each time I took a bus to Dublin and then another from Dublin to Longford. I then had to take a taxi to the town. My bird surveys were timed to start one hour before dawn. At the peak of summer, this would mean a 4 a.m. start, and my survey points were up to two-and-a-half hours away from my Longford apartment by foot. So to arrive for dawn, I'd need to leave my apartment at around 1.15 a.m. I was perfectly happy to do this if it put me on the ladder to where I wanted to be as a professional ornithologist.

The struggle was intense at the beginning. I missed Alba terribly and I had to develop a whole new routine. I'd set multiple alarms for

12.45 a.m. and scatter them around the apartment in difficult-to-get-to places, so I had to physically get up to turn them off. The first morning, I turned off my bedside alarm in my sleep, without any recollection of doing so. I couldn't have that happen again, I *hate* being late for anything. So I'd go to bed each evening at 6 p.m., black out all the windows and wake up at the ungodly hour of 12.45 a.m. I'd have a quick shower, get my notes ready, boil some eggs, and pack a bunch of nuts and bananas as well as water and suncream. I wore a hi-vis for the two-and-a-half-hour walk along the dark, narrow country lanes. Sometimes, bars would still have people smoking outside as I set out for work. It felt so weird, but also liberating. I was on a different clock to everyone else, which meant I'd be alone in my thoughts and immersed in nature. On my nocturnal walks, I'd hear the squeaky-gate-like calls of juvenile long-eared owls begging, the goat-like drumming display of snipe as their other-tail feathers vibrated as they plummeted from the night sky. Sometimes, I'd hear foxes screaming, banshee-like, in the distance. It's another world out there at nighttime, with a whole other collection of sounds we aren't normally exposed to. I loved that. It made these long nighttime walks worth it to me.

One morning early on in the job, having just left the last lights of the village behind me, I stepped to the side of the road and turned on my flashlight. A car was approaching with headlights on. It saw my light, dimmed theirs, and slowed down to a crawl. I was out in the middle of nowhere and it was 2 a.m. I felt a bit nervous. Why were they slowing down so much? I could see they were going to stop. What did they want? Was I in for some trouble here, alone and far from help? As it neared, I could make out the white car body with highlighter yellow and royal blue stripes – it was a garda car. Ah okay, they obviously think I'm up to no good. The guard rolled down his window and looked me up and down. 'What brings you out here in the early hours with a hi-vis?'

A fair question, I thought. 'I'm going to work, garda.'

He peered over his glasses at me with a confounded look, as if I'd just spoken in gibberish. 'Where exactly do you work?'

I blurted out a cough of laughter. I totally understood his bewilderment. 'Let me explain,' I assured him. 'My name is Seán Ronayne, I'm an ornithologist. I'm new to the area but I'll be conducting surveys on the bog, commencing an hour before dawn, throughout the summer.'

His suspicion shifted and he smiled in realisation. 'Ahhh, you're a bird man! Do you want a lift out?'

My answer surprised him. 'No thanks, garda. If you drive me out, I'll only have to sit in the bog in darkness for a few hours. I'd rather walk and take in the fresh air.'

'Understood,' he said. 'Well, welcome to the village anyway, Seán. I'll keep an eye out for you on the roads in the mornings. If you ever need me, you know where I am.'

I often did bump into him on the roads and we'd stop for a 2 a.m. chat. It turned out one of his kids was living and working in Barcelona, so we had that in common. He was a fan of the birdlife in the area and he'd listen intently as I updated him with my latest findings.

Surveys on the bog were incredible. It was an old industrial turf-extraction site that was slowly winding down. Many parts were already years into a natural and unabated rewilding process, and these places were simply magical to spend time in. But to understand the beauty of the bog, you need to know what industrially extracted areas look like. They are bare, brown, straight-lined and dry, resembling a totally unnatural, almost post-apocalyptic landscape. The peat was extracted and deposited as dry, loose matter in side-by-side linear strips as far as the eye could see. Every 20 metres or so, long, deep channels ran parallel to the product lines and continually drained off the bog, bleeding it dry of life. Pumps ran on the peripheries to aid this process, and train tracks ran all around the site to extract carriages full of peat. They were mahogany-brown deserts.

Amongst the open-peat areas, gargantuan diesel-burning vehicles with tyres the size of small cars bellowed unforgivingly through the land. A land that had once held so much diverse life was now an insipid, desiccated and unrecognisable version of its former wet and verdant glory. When I was a kid, peat briquettes were sometimes burned on the fire, and we regularly used peat-based potting compost. Now, standing at the source of these seemingly benign products and seeing the impact their extractions have had on the landscape, I was truly shocked. It was capitalism epitomised. Not a thought was given to nature. It was mercilessly stripped down to a naked and embarrassed shell, all in the name of money, greed and a lack of empathy for our neighbours in nature.

In contrast, the areas that had been left to recover were bursting with life. In the parts where the peat had not been extracted down to the rocky, glacial till, bog woodland began to reappear, dominated by a mosaic of pink-tipped heather, the soft greens of scattered bilberry bushes, as well as a rich and varied tree layer, mostly consisting of various willow species and rusty-trunked downy birches. Mornings spent on the bog revealed a mellisonant roar of rich birdsong.

Blackbirds, song thrushes, robins, wrens and so many more sang in unison, each species occupying a different frequency band so as not to disrupt one another, forming an avian concert orchestra. They all had their part to play and each one complemented the other.

Some mornings, if I was lucky, I'd spot a bushy-tailed pine marten running into cover, looking like a slightly odd, rich-brown, creamy-coloured cat. Orchids were everywhere and, although I was there to record birds, I couldn't resist brushing up on my orchid ID skills. I found so many: early purple orchid, common-spotted orchid, heath-spotted orchid, marsh helleborine, common twayblade, bee orchid, and many more. Some areas that had been taken down to the glacial till layer had flooded and formed wetlands. These pools teemed with another neighbourhood of life. Here, white and fluffy cottongrass, a variety of green rushes and sedges, and an explosion of vivid purple loosestrife bordered the water, which quivered with a smorgasbord of life. The air hummed with winged insects and rare breeding waders called it home; snipe, lapwing and even curlew were scattered throughout these spots on-site. All of these species are ground nesters that need safe, dry, well-vegetated areas to nest in, with access to wetlands, where they feed on the aquatic life within. The bog had all of these characteristics in spades, especially where it had been left to regenerate. The site had a mixture of pools with vegetated margins; areas of wet, healthy, raised bog full of heather, bog asphodel and bog cotton; areas of unproved grassland; and dry heath. This mosaic of habitats was a magnet to these birds, and provided ample servings of both nesting and feeding opportunities. I asked myself the question: *Why would anyone want to spoil this with wind turbines?*

Lapwing *(Vanellus vanellus)*
Family *Charadriidae (plovers, dotterels and lapwings)*
Conservation status Red-listed (BoCCI, 2020–2026)
Vocalisations *Their call reflects an English nickname of theirs, in that is describes itself 'pee-wit'. Their display incorporates this 'pee-wit' call amongst a series of whistles and trills.*

This proliferation of thriving life was in stark contrast to the areas that we had interfered with. Comparing the two was incredibly eye-opening and showed the true scale of what was lost to our ravenous appetite for 'progress'.

My time on the bogs was a joy. I easily fell into my long walking routine, early nights and even earlier rises. I didn't care that I had neither telly nor internet. Every day out was a day immersed in nature, full of its wonders and learnings. I only went to the apartment to eat and sleep, neither of which I spent much time actually doing. I missed Alba a lot, but I called her every day and I still got to see her during non-survey periods.

I continued taking driving lessons and, when the big day came, I had high hopes. The thoughts of simplifying my life spurred me on. Saying goodbye to crazy walks and getting caught out miles away from shelter in the middle of a summer downpour sounded like a real treat. My test day came and I could just smell the freedom. I was nervous, but I felt ready. When the examiner sat in the car and told me to go, it was like my brain was hijacked by panic. I forgot how to start the car so I stalled, and this set the tone for the whole test. The entire thing felt like an episode of *Mr. Bean*. I failed miserably and went home to Alba deflated.

The waiting time for tests was through the roof. I'd blown my chance of a much easier life and maybe I'd lose my job, too. This site was a one-off and others were not doable by foot. I was on borrowed time here. But, as always, Alba picked me back up. She thought for a minute and then came up with an idea. 'Don't worry. Lots of people fail on their first go. I have some friends who are taking tests here and they said if you call the booking line first thing in the morning, you can sometimes get a last-minute cancellation that hasn't yet been refilled.' And so the ritual began. Every morning when the phone lines opened at 9 a.m. I'd call on the dot, announce myself, explain my predicament and ask for a cancellation test slot. The first few mornings were a dud, but then I had success. I was offered a slot for the following week. I was elated. But when the day came, it happened again ... this time I ran a red light.

And the process repeated. The line operators got to know me. They'd stop me as I reeled out my spiel. 'Is this the bird guy? Seán, isn't it?'

'Yep, that's me.'

'No joy yet, no? Let me see what we've got for you. How are the birds up in Longford, anyway?'

It always made me laugh and lightened the situation. I was genuinely worried. Winter was fast approaching and I knew this job would wrap up. Then what? During my days back home, I drove every chance I got and even began to memorise the lanes of the roundabouts on Google Earth. A call from work confirmed my fears. This contract would end for the winter and if I didn't have a means of driving they'd have to let me go. After going through my 9 a.m. rigmarole, I eventually landed another driving test. But this time I *passed* it!

I could finally breathe, knowing I had a secure job doing what I loved.

Siberian Blue Robin

Chapter 8

IT WAS MARCH 2017, AND I WAS FINALLY WORKING IN A JOB that I loved. Now that I could drive I was shifted to a variety of proposed wind-farm sites. I had really struggled and fought to get to this point and so I was proud of myself. But Alba was an even greater light in my life. I'd agreed to leave everything behind and go travelling with her. I knew this was highly important to her and I was willing to give everything up to follow her on her dream. I'd got this far – I'd find another job. Myself and Alba had been together for almost a year. A wet week to some but, for me, I knew that Alba was everything I ever wanted in a partner and more. She was my rock and my soulmate. I knew early on that I wanted to marry her, but I was afraid to ask her prematurely. I decided one year was a respectable length of time, so it was time to make a plan.

Nature Boy

I've always had a rather impulsive side to me – act first, think later. Sometimes, it gets me in trouble; sometimes, it brings adventure. I often can't control it, but I kind of like it. It's strange, because I also really like routine and structure. But as they so often said back in Seahouses, 'There's nowt so queer as folk.' I like that phrase – to me it's an acknowledgment, even an acceptance, that we humans can be strange and that it's okay to be so.

Alba had told me all about her long-standing plans to travel far and wide, to see the world, to experience new cultures, and to volunteer to help people, where possible. She had often mentioned to me how she'd love to travel to Morocco. She was enthralled by the culture there; it was raw, beautiful and unapologetic. Although I'd travelled quite a bit with family, scouts, and even alone, I'd never been to Morocco, nor had we travelled together (I didn't count our visit to see her family, as this was Alba's home). So, I thought it would be good for us to get away, on a trial run, before embarking on our big adventure. We got on like a house on fire in our day-to-day lives, but would we wring each other's necks on a big trip? I highly doubted it, but it would be nice to wet the feet, regardless. That night, I opened my laptop, looked at the cheapest fares by date, took Alba's passport from our room, and booked two flights there and then.

It was a liberating feeling. Zero research, zero thought to what might be on either of our agendas – just 'pim-pam-pum'. When Alba got home that evening, I skipped the hello, instead blurting, 'Hi-love-we're-going-to-Morocco-next-week.'

She shook her head in bewilderment. 'Wait, what? Morocco? What are you talking about?'

She stepped in, and I repeated it. 'I've booked two tickets to Morocco. You've always wanted to go. It'll be a warm-up for our big trip.'

She burst out laughing. 'You're really serious, aren't you?'

'Yes,' I replied. 'You haven't anything important on, have you?'

She smiled. 'Luckily not!'

So that was it – the first step of my plan was put in motion. I was going to propose to Alba in Morocco.

Through some sneaky detective work, I managed to get Alba's ring size without her suspecting what I was up to. I felt so slick. I had a fair idea what she would like. Alba is a hippy who has a disdain for consumerism, hates waste and hates spending money for no reason. With this in mind, I bought her a simple silver ring with a single little stone. Nothing too fancy, but still beautiful. It didn't break the bank and it presented her with a long-lasting token of my love and commitment.

We arrived at Marrakech late at night. But even then, the heat of the air hit me, as if I'd just opened an oven door. It was nice, though. Especially having just emerged from the grey and damp Irish winter. Alba spoke some French, which was a godsend – and it secured us our taxi to our accommodation. The first thing that struck me was the driving. I'd never seen anything like it. People zigzagged along the dusty, pot-holed roads, honking constantly. Windows remained rolled down so they could casually shout at one another, as if it were customary. Donkeys walked out in front of rocketing cabs, like nothing was coming. They had no fear, nor did the drivers.

Exhausted, we went straight to our room and straight to bed, without setting an alarm. We slept soundly, but were both gently awakened at around 4.30 a.m. There was an ethereal nasal chanting sound in Arabic, which seemed to echo from high up, through the winding streets, eventually seeping into our bedroom, where the first shafts of morning light were beginning to penetrate the blinds. Roosters sounded from all around, and I could hear people shuffling in the open living area down the hall. It took us a while to click, but we realised we were listening to the Islamic early-morning prayer chant – also known as the Fajr. This is a prayer of great importance to Muslims, and is performed first thing each day, between the break of dawn and sunrise itself. Neither of us are religious but we found this rather beautiful, and it quickly reminded us of the adventure that awaited us over the coming days.

Alba went for a shower, and I peeped into my bag to make sure the ring was still there. I felt a little like Gollum from *The Lord of the Rings* seeking out his precious. Booking the trip to Morocco might have been impulsive, but I'd planned out my proposal to Alba meticulously for weeks and I just could not mess it up. I found the box, and the ring sparkled back at me in reassurance. I snapped it shut and slid it into the side pocket, amongst my rolled-up socks. We both spent some time getting ready and, at 6 a.m., we headed onto the roof terrace where a table was already set for us for breakfast. Whilst Alba looked in awe at the medley of wonderful local foods, I took in my surroundings with scanning eyes and pricked-up ears. As always, I'd prepared for this moment, having carefully studied the expected bird species of Morocco. The unfamiliar rising 'dzwee' calls of grey-headed, rusty-red house buntings sounded all around. They're a small bird at about 14 centimetres, with a white supercilium and an angled yellow beak. An unfamiliar sight and sound to me, here they were common and fearless and seemed to occupy the niche of our house sparrows – although those were also present.

As we tucked into breakfast, the house buntings came to our feet, hoovering up our crumbs of bread as they rained down onto the warm stone floor. The jingling, exotic-sounding song of several common bulbuls drifted up to us from trees below – a series of fluid, rolled notes, pleasant to the ear, flowing in a musical harmony. A flock of little swifts darted overhead. A different species to our swifts, little swifts resemble larger, more agile house martins. They're much smaller than our swifts too, with a wingspan some 20 per cent shorter. Our swifts also lack the white rump of little swift. Best of all was their call, though. Our swifts in Ireland have a high-pitched shriek, but these little swifts sounded altogether different. They jingled! A soft, high-pitched pattering, like nothing I'd heard before. All of these new sights and sounds are my measures of a new and far-flung location. Nature is my indicator and guide always, wherever I am.

***

House Bunting *(Emberiza sahari)*
Family *Emberizidae (buntings)*
Conservation status *Least Concern (IUCN Red List) – does not occur on the BoCCI list and has not occurred as a rare vagrant*
Vocalisations *Call is a distinctive rising 'dzwee'.*

***

On the other hand, Alba is much more attuned to people and cultures, therefore we both experience places in a different way, but that also meant that we could exchange experiences and learn so much more about the places in which we found ourselves. We had a few days to spend in Marrakech before we'd head towards the Sahara Desert. This was the final step in my plan – to propose to Alba under the desert stars. I wanted this moment to be special to her, like she was to me, and I wanted it to happen surrounded by nature, not in some city or restaurant.

We spent our days wandering around the various markets and medinas, trying out the local dishes and trying our very best to communicate with local people. I religiously checked the ring was still there, and would run over the plan in my mind. And then the time came ...

We took a bus to Merzouga, the gateway to Erg Chebbi. This is the closest accessible point of the Sahara Desert. The bus journey was almost 12 hours long, and so our early departure had us arrive around dinner time. It was breathtaking, looking at the various villages and landscape changes as we took the long journey east. I was trying my best to see birds and, despite moving at speed, I could see storks, cattle egrets, shrikes and many others. I wondered how we'd know when we were nearing the desert, but it was obvious when the time came. Although the land had been sandy and arid for some time, a sudden rise in the land flickered and wobbled distantly in the heat haze. This was quite clearly the first frontier of the Sahara Desert proper.

The bus passed through a gap in the dunes that revealed a series of camp-like outhouses, and several parties of camels resting in the shade of what seemed to be the last palm trees and shrubs as far as the eye could see. Water was scarce here, and a minuscule puddle that had collected under a dripping tap attracted all manner of birds, which came from far and wide for this precious, often taken-for-granted, life-giving resource.

Upon disembarking from the cool air of the bus, the dry heat hit us like a wave. I was already sunburned from the day before so we lathered ourselves in suncream, and Alba wrapped one of her silk scarves around my neck. Two striking figures appeared from the shade of the camp behind us. I'd never seen anyone like them, in their elegance and attire. They each wore bright cotton garments that reached down to their feet. Around their heads was a wrap of the same material, with simple leather sandals on their feet. These were Bedouins and were a local tribe, well accustomed to the unforgiving Saharan conditions. Despite the sweltering heat, they seemed perfectly comfortable in their attire.

They smiled and gestured us over to their sitting camels. I'd never seen a camel up close before, and I was quite nervous. I have a very strict rule I follow when it comes to animals, wild or otherwise: don't trust anything that's bigger than I am! I had a few experiences with cows as a kid, one of which involved myself and my father running down a steep-sloped hill as newly arrived cows ran down after us, losing their footing and braking ability. It ended in my dad throwing me over a hedgerow into a field that was, as luck would have it, guarded by a ring-wearing, muscle-popping bull. It all worked out okay, thankfully, but from that moment on I've always threaded cautiously with *anything* larger than me.

The camel was huge, way bigger than a cow, and I had to *sit* on it. Alba got on without a thought, but I was hesitant. Alba and the others giggled in jest as my hesitance manifested itself physically. The camel rose from its resting position by first fully extending its hind legs, almost tipping me over the top. I let out a squirm of fright, adding to Alba's amusement. I leaned back and the camel straightened up, and we were off. We were really high up and it was a great way to take in the vastness of the Sahara ahead of us. All we could see were kilometres upon kilometres of sandy peaks and troughs, while the heavy heat of the sun beat down on us as we trundled our way through the dunes. Having got used to the heavy-footed jerking movement of my camel, I could sit back and take in this unusual experience, although this is one of those moments that I today look back at with guilt. The poor camels, although strong, had to deal with my lumbering bulk on their backs, on top of the tough desert conditions. I do feel bad about that, and it's something unethical or unfair that never even crossed my mind at the time. But we live and learn, and I think the important thing is that we acknowledge and rectify these moments when we find clarity.

After an hour or so, some shapes began to float on the horizon. They were tents of varying sizes, and the distinctively clothed Bedouins ambled around the camps, preparing for our arrival. Soon we arrived at an amazing encampment, where a series of tents enclosed a campfire. We made our way down to our little tent and settled in. I felt like Lawrence of Arabia; the whole setting was just surreal.

Our bed sat atop a simple but beautiful Berber carpet, and the tent walls were bursting with colour and intricate weavings. Inside the shade was cool compared to the desert air outside. Despite this, my palms were sweating and my mouth was dry. I knew what was coming. This was the moment I'd been building up to for so long. I told myself it would be fine, but that thought was scuppered when I looked at Alba. She was grimacing and holding her stomach. She told me she wasn't feeling too well and insisted I go out to the campfire alone. My heart sank and, despite her feeling unwell, I knew I had to coax her outside so I could eventually lead her out to the moonlit sand dunes. I begged her to follow me out for just a few minutes. She was unconvinced, but just like magic, wonderful music began to serenade us from the campfire outside. Alba's eyes lit up and she agreed to follow.

It was wonderful out there – a world I'd never experienced, so full of mysterious creatures with bizarre adaptions to cope with the extreme conditions of the desert. Somewhere in the vast expanse of undulating dunes, preposterously long-eared, sandy-coloured fennec foxes roamed. Lesser Egyptian jerboas, small sandy-coloured rodents with enormously long tails and exaggerated hind legs, hopped around the sand like miniature kangaroos. I had never experienced a location so free from light pollution. The stars twinkled, the moon shone, and the embers of the great fire sparkled and crackled. The atmosphere was electric, and the locals danced and sang. Alba held her stomach but was hanging out for the show. I knew I couldn't propose to her over the noise, and I also didn't want to make a scene in front of so many people, so I asked her if she'd like to walk outside the camp and see the dunes at night.

Her answer was instant. 'No, Seán. I feel awful and this show is amazing. I feel okay here lying down and taking it in.'

I had to think on my feet. She knew I was obsessed with wildlife, and I knew she'd believe me if I insisted she come with me to find a special animal. 'Look, love, I *really* want to see a scorpion or a scarab beetle, and the best chance is at night. Will you please, please come with me? I don't want to go alone.'

Her reply was predictable. 'Seán, come on, I really don't feel well.'

I pushed her further. 'Just five minutes, I promise!'

She sighed in response, grasping her stomach. 'Okay, Seán.'

I felt genuinely bad, genuinely terrified and genuinely ecstatic. I grabbed her hand and led her out to the dunes, tapping my pocket to make sure the ring was still there.

My hands trembled as we scrambled up to the top of one of the dunes, led by blue moonlight. I pretended to scan the ground for wildlife as I went, but instead I was dealing with a riot of nerves. We sat down at the top, taking a moment to look at the sparsely lit desert landscape. The low-pitched chugging song of a distant Egyptian nightjar broke through the silence of the desert. A curious-looking, sandy-coloured master of camouflage, Egyptian nightjars roost on the ground, their plumage perfectly matching the sand beneath. At night they take to the air and fly with their beaks wide open, where they catch night-flying insects. The sound of this nightjar brought me back to the time on Cape Clear when I first told Alba I loved her. It was almost as if it spoke up to support me. And it did. I knew this was the moment. I took Alba's hand and said I had something to tell her: 'Alba, I'm so scared, and I really don't know how to say this.'

Alba's expression quickly turned to worry.

'You know I love you so much, don't you?'

She replied, concern in her voice. 'Yeah, love, of course. Is everything okay?'

Trembling, I reached for my pocket and, in the same motion, placed the box in her hand, closing her fingers around it. Alba, still confused, looked down and darted her gaze back up at me. She opened it and I timed my next line perfectly with her realisation. 'I love you so much and I'd love to marry you – will you?'

Alba burst into tears, hugged me with a grip like no other and shuddered out her response: '*Yes!* I love you so much. Goddamn you and your scorpions and beetles.'

We burst out laughing, at that very that moment a black scarab beetle scampered past us – two birds with one stone. I had my camera and took photos of us in the dunes, tears streaming down our beaming faces, and this cheekily snapped the beetle too! This was the start of a new life with my soul partner by my side.

Back home, there was new excitement about a life to be shared. Adventures were on the horizon. We'd got on great on our trip to Morocco and we knew that a bigger trip would go down well, so it was finally time for Alba to fulfil her dream of travelling and letting life take her by the hand. As I was now on board, I also had some say in where we'd go and we would sit down and brainstorm our trip at dinner every day. We must have watched every travel vlogger there is on YouTube. India was on the cards, as was Nepal and Southeast Asia. They were all so tempting in their own way – India with its plethora of colours, innumerable subcultures, and monuments; Nepal with its towering Himalayas, vast rugged wilderness and relatively untrodden routes; and, of course, Southeast Asia – a go-to travel destination for first-time backpackers.

After many nights of humming and hawing, we settled on Southeast Asia and, if we had time, Nepal. This part was scary – we were essentially going to start a new life. We gave up our apartment, something that had taken us so long to secure in the midst of a housing crisis. We sold our car, we sold most of our belongings and we quit our jobs. This final part was the scariest for me. I'd been through so much to get to the point where I was working in a job that I loved. I briefly wondered if I was mad, if I'd given up my dream of working as an ornithologist for good by doing this. But then I thought about how much I loved Alba. She was far more important to me than any job. It was actually releasing in a major way – we'd broken free of the shackles of our capitalist-driven consumerist lives. But, this is the system our society revolves around, and so we also felt vulnerable and exposed. It's amazing how long it takes to build up a comfortable, stable life and even more amazing how quickly it can all change. Having bought one-way tickets to Bangkok, we found ourselves sitting in an empty, echo-filled room in our apartment.

We were finally on our way to a trip of a lifetime and I couldn't wait to see all that Thailand had to offer. After over 24 hours of flights and stopovers, we found ourselves on the first leg of our new journey in life.

We stepped out of our tuk-tuk into the midday sun in a busy Bangkok. Tuk-tuks are small, roofed moto-taxis perfect for the chaos of Bangkok's streets. The city was like nothing I'd ever experienced. Every sense was slapped into awakening, even more so than in Marrakech. The traffic weaved all around, occupying lanes that didn't exist. People ran across the road, dodging vehicles like they just stepped out of the Matrix. The noise of engines of all kinds, from all distances, roared through the smoggy air, which itself was thick with fumes and smoke. I wasn't prepared for this whack of anthropogenic nastiness, but I knew that this was the worst it would get – we were in a Southeast Asian mega-city, home to 10 million people. It still had its charms and attractions – it was my gateway into a whole new culture – but I couldn't wait to move on into more rural parts, where I could see more nature.

Despite the chaos, an unfamiliar but beautiful language weaved through the ruckus, and, once my senses had some time to adjust, the birds began to show themselves. I was prepared for them – I knew who to expect and where to expect them. In the weeks leading up to this trip, I had bought a number of Southeast Asian bird books and had been scouring the xeno-canto website, an online suppository of bird vocalisations uploaded by sound-recordists from around the world. I was prepared for all of the common species, and had some readiness for the more difficult species. Birds in the tropics are far more elaborate than those farther north. They tend to be much more colourful, with even greater, more complex songs. Also, female song is a lot more common in the tropics, with males and females developing an inter-woven duet.

Seeing these birds in the flesh was like seeing a celebrity. After reading up on them and gushing over their amazing colours and forms, I was starstruck. The first of the familiar faces to appear was the Oriental magpie-robin, a bizarre-looking creature resembling a cross between a magpie and a robin, sharing the colours of the former and the size and shape of the latter. Then, there were the truly exotic-looking red-whiskered bulbuls. To describe them in short, I would call them zoo-birds. Nothing at all resembles them in Ireland, with their almost ridiculous black crests, striking white throat and breast, and vivid red cheeks and vents. These birds sang their rich, tuneful 'peek-peek-awoo' song from prominent trees and shrubs all around us. It filled the air, giving it a faraway, tropical vibe.

As we meandered through the madness of the city, we eventually slipped down a quiet lane towards our accommodation. This is when my ears perked up to a sound I had anticipated more than any other. In the distance, I heard something reminiscent of a peacock, a loud and persistent 'coo-EUW, coo-EUW, COO-EUW'. This bird is the avian anthem of Southeast Asia – the Asian koel. These fruit-eating cuckoos, like our own, are brood parasites, meaning they don't raise their own young. Instead, they lay their eggs in the nests of unsuspecting crows. The males are a simplistic but striking iridescent black, with a blood-red eye. Females are dark brown with blonde speckling and stripes. With time and determination, I finally saw a red-eyed black male singing close to the top of a leafy tree. My heart pounded as I finally matched the singer to the voice. It was an impressive-looking bird, like nothing I'd ever seen before.

Asian Koel *(Eudynamys scolopaceus)*
Family *Cuculidae (cuckoos)*
Conservation status *Least Concern (IUCN Red List) – does not occur on the BoCCI list and has not occurred as a rare vagrant*
Vocalisations *Best identified by its song, which is a loud and persistent 'coo-EUW, coo-EUW, COO-EUW'.*

In a sense, I was glad to close the door of our hostel behind us. The air conditioning enveloped us and we could finally put our bags down. This was our first encounter of the famous Thai smile. The receptionist was beaming with kindness and directed us to our room. We were exhausted, but the excitement of what awaited outside was too much, and so we freshened up and hit the streets of Bangkok. I took my camera just in case any birds crossed our path, of course. Knowing how hectic the main roads were, we stayed well clear of them, and followed the narrower, cooler and less crowded side-streets. These streets are where real life plays out anyway, and that is what we were here for. To meet new people, and to see and understand new cultures.

The locals went about their business, smiling at us as they passed. A cocktail of delectable smells wafted through the air as street vendors made impressive yet simple dishes from their small but well-stocked carts. Fresh produce was in abundance, with all manner of colourful fresh fruit and veg, noodles and rice. They sold meat too, but it looked very different. It didn't look appetising to me at all. A lot of it looked highly processed, with strange colours. And then there were the birds baked on sticks, complete with heads and beaks. As most of the dishes were noodle and broth-based, they added meatballs or cuts of rubbery-looking sausage. They also had skewers filled to each end with these odd-looking meats. Alba had been a vegetarian since her early teens, but I was not, although it was something I was increasingly considering.

We selected one vendor in particular who was working all the while dishing out jovialities to her long queue of smiling customers. The smells of the spices and broth were so good that we just knew we were in for something special. I asked for some of those odd-looking meatballs in mine. The flavours and richness of the food just blew us away, but those meatballs! They tasted and felt as they looked – rubbery, and just odd. I tried a few different types of meat over the coming days, all of which left me with that same grossed-out feeling. From this moment on, I decided I would become vegetarian. It would be a good test to see if I could finally address my growing guilt over eating animals.

We were challenging ourselves to travel on a shoestring budget, living on a few euros a day. This is totally possible in Southeast Asia, but it's also possible to spend a lot. Western extravagance had reared its ugly head in the well-known tourist spots. We weren't here for that, but I guess we – especially me – had become accustomed to a life of luxury without even realising it. We had everything at our disposal at home, but now we were travelling with backpacks filled with just our very essentials. We spent one to two euros per meal, and rarely spent over five euros for a night's accommodation. We washed our clothes by hand in the shower and we mingled with the locals in the lesser-known parts of each location we visited. It was raw, gritty, honest and beautiful. I did find it tough at times, particularly in the cities because of the loudness, the chaos and the lack of peace, but it was eye-opening. I had so much 'stuff' at home and spent so much money at will, yet here I was living on very little – and I was as happy as I'd ever been.

Over the following weeks, we travelled north via train, which was simply incredible. Firstly, it was extremely cheap but, secondly, it brought us right through the heart of the country and it was possible to open the windows right down. Whilst Alba caught up on sleep, I'd stick my head out of the carriage and take in the breeze. Always on the lookout for new birds, I had my local bird book sat next to me, and I'd regularly scan the horizon as we went. Despite the speed of the train, I saw many of the larger and easier-to-detect species, such as various species of storks, herons and raptors. We'd often pass big rice paddies, filled to the brim with birds and fish. I watched in awe as the waters seemed to boil with the movement of the fish in response to the wading legs of passing waterbirds. Life abounded here, and it was an intensity of wildlife I had never experienced before.

After a few weeks of backpacking, we eventually found ourselves in the far north of Thailand, in another of its largest cities – Chiang Mai. Up here, nature was even more evident, with towering hills fully feathered in a covering of green forest. Whilst the city was full to the brim with stunning historical Buddhist temples for Alba, I just knew those hills were calling for me. At first, I didn't care for the temples, simply because I am not religious, and I had so many birds I needed to track down. I went to those for Alba because I knew she was in love with Buddhism for its peaceful, caring ways. My perception didn't take long to change, as it's impossible not to fall for the tenets of this beautiful religion. Whether you believe in a god or not, anyone who practises a religion based on humanity, compassion, giving and, most importantly to me, a kindness to all animals, is very much a person to respect, love and value. And so I began to view these temples differently.

Instead of looking at them as churches of a religion I was unfamiliar with, I viewed them as places of solace, where the practitioners of the religion were gentle, loving and compassionate. With so much badness, greed and toxicity in today's fast-paced, profit-driven world, these temples became a place of sanctuary to us both. In a way, when I visited them, I felt as I did in nature. They provided a tonic for the soul. It became a running joke of mine, that we were on one big temple-crawl on our travels in Thailand. It was true, but I had no problem with that. It also meant I was building up some brownie points for the many upcoming off-trail hikes I had in mind.

In the evenings, back at our accommodation, I'd gaze up at the hills wondering what birds I'd find up there. Alba knew exactly what was on my mind. I hadn't pushed her on it, because I knew that this trip was her dream so I didn't want to dictate our agenda. She smiled at me. 'Would you like to go up tomorrow, love?'

I turned at her and nodded with eagerness.

'Okay, why don't we rent a moped so we can get up to the hiking trails and we can spend the day up there,' she suggested.

I didn't need to think twice. 'Okay! Let's do that!'

The next morning, we were up bright and early with bags packed for a hike. We did some research and went to the nearest moped rental place. The going rate was 200 baht per day, with a 3,000 baht deposit. This worked out at roughly 5 euro and 75 euro – not bad at all! It was also required for the driver to have an international driving permit. It's a simple thing to acquire and we had both applied for them before leaving. Alba had hers but, unfortunately, mine had not arrived in time. I was waiting for my parents to receive it and send on a scan. So, we decided Alba would be the driver.

We picked out a moped and decided to rent it for three days. The guy in the shop began filling out the paperwork, then he stopped for a second and looked up. 'Have you driven a moped before?'

I panicked and blurted out, 'Yeah, I used to own a motorbike.'

Alba nudged me hard and gave me a disapproving look. I was surprised myself – it seemed to just jump out of me. Maybe the thought of not reaching those mountains was too much. Convinced by my rapid answer, he handed over the keys. He stepped back to his desk, as I tried to start it. I turned the ignition and nothing happened.

In a panic, I whispered to Alba, 'How do you start it?'

She whispered back, 'I don't have a clue! What do we do? He's staring at us!'

I looked over, nodded, and wheeled the bike outside until he couldn't see us. I quickly jumped onto YouTube and typed 'how to start a moped'. Thirty seconds later, we were helmeted and away with Alba driving. It turns out, you need to pull the brake as you turn the ignition, otherwise it won't start. But, of course, I knew this, having owned a motorbike, right?

As we took off down the lane leading to the main road, I could feel the moped wobbling. I looked in the wing mirror and saw that the owner had stepped out to see what we were at. I'm sure he was bemused by our walk-out exit. Never mind that, though. Alba was clearly feeling nervous. 'Seán, I don't like this at all! I can't find my balance. The handlebars and front wheel keep moving on me.' We exited onto the manic main road and started to build up speed, then the wheel settled. It was only at slower speeds that it seemed to wobble. We were following a GPS and trying to navigate the crazy driving as we went. I felt for Alba – it didn't look easy at all. People moved at mad speeds and zigzagged from all directions. It was all quite helter-skelter.

We came to the last big junction we needed to pass before we were on a long, straight road out of the city and up to the hills. It was absolutely bananas! Cars, mopeds, tuk-tuks, lorries and just about every other kind of vehicle were hurtling past without paying heed to road rules. Alba was afraid of the wobble, but she timed it as best she could and we made a go for it. What happened next felt like it was in slow motion.

As we thrust ourselves from the junction into the madness of the traffic, we started to lean at an angle that seemed to defy logic. I remember seeing cars and buildings sideways, then BANG! It took me a while to figure it out – but we were lying on the ground. I was to the side, but Alba's leg was under the moped. It's strange how the body and mind react to such situations. Despite the extreme danger we were in, in this exposed and vulnerable position, we just lay there in a bloodied daze, and the traffic continued to swerve around us.

I saw two people running at us through the traffic – a middle-aged man and a younger woman. They asked if we were okay. I was fine, bar some light grazing, but Alba was bleeding a lot from her elbows and ankles. The man wheeled the bike to safety, and I carried Alba behind. The woman ran to a shop and the man sat us down outside a café. Soon after, the woman came running back and patched Alba up. She was a newly graduated nurse and was delighted she could put her skills to use, as were we! Miraculously, the moped was fine.

The worst part of it all was that we still had to get out of there and back to the hostel with the moped. I knew I had to step up, despite me not having any experience of driving a moped. While Alba was gathering herself and being tended to by the lovely people who'd picked us up off the road, I wheeled the moped down a small lane behind the café. Here, I drove up and down on repeat until I built up enough confidence to take us out of this mess. The familiar sound of an Asian koel – 'coo-EUW, coo-EUW, COO-EUW' – echoed from across the street, as did the babbling of a couple of smart bulbuls.

Asian koel, a ubiquitous sound of Southeast Asia and Nepal. This one was photographed in Kathmandu, Nepal, in July 2018.

stunning Siberian blue robin that
ry briefly showed itself for me in the
lls of Pai, Thailand, in March 2018.

Photographing wildlife at
Lumbini, Nepal, in July 2018.

A swallow sits in a shop in the urban sprawl of Kathmandu, Nepal, in July 2018.

Alba and a little puppy we encountered on a cycle trip through Bardiya, Nepal, in July 2018.

Crossing into the heart of Bardiya National Park by dugout canoe at dawn in July 2018.

Walking cautiously through an area of long grass in Bardiya National Park. Tigers are known to ambush prey at this very spot.

Rhino apples at Bardiya National Park – a favourite food item of the rhinos there.

A close call at Bardiya National Park: this rhino charged us, but luckily could not get up the steep river bank!

Alba does an early morning riverside yoga session in Bardiya as she looks out at a resting marsh mugger crocodile.

Elephant footprint – from the mad bull that was running riot down by the river at Bardiya.

Part of a large group of wild Asiatic elephants coming to graze and drink by the river at Bardiya National Park.

Alba carefully scanning for tigers from a lookout tower deep inside Bardiya National Park.

Green bee-eater, Bardiya National Park.

Red-whiskered bulbul, Bardiya National Park.

Alba, Toby and I taking a rest during a hike in the Catalan Pyrenees in August 2020.

Celebrating Dad's 63rd birthday in September 2019 at Alba's family home in El Prat de Llobregat.

Alba supporting the Castellers during the festa major of El Prat de Llobregat in September 2019.

Els Diables celebrating the feste major of El Prat de Llobregat.

A lammergeier floats with grace in the Catalan Pyrenees.

A wallcreeper at last! Photographed high up in the Catalan Pyrenees in July 2020 after years of toil and failure.

Kingfisher with mosquitofish, Delta del Llobregat, Catalunya.

European bee-eater photographed in Lleida, Catalunya, in May 2020.

Watching birds migrating through Tarifa, at the very southernmost tip of Spain, and seeing them arrive to Moroccan shores in September 2020.

My mind almost drifted to my safe place for a moment, until I saw Alba grimacing and clutching at her ankles.

I drove down to her and put on my best confident face. She couldn't see my hands and legs trembling. I pulled up and grabbed our stuff, and told her to sit behind me. It goes without saying she was petrified, but I assured her it would be fine. We took off and there was that wobble again! I resisted it at first but it wasn't until I loosened up that it stopped. I then realised it was our stiffness that caused the wobble. When I got this under control, we had a fairly tense but surprisingly smooth journey back. I put Alba up to rest and I drove the moped back to the rental place. The same guy was there and he looked up at me in surprise: 'Sudden change of plan?' he asked.

'Yes. I hope I can get the deposit and other rental days back?' I replied.

He smiled and rummaged behind the counter, before handing me the cash. I thanked him and left with a sigh of relief.

The next few days were tough on Alba. Despite treatment, she developed infections in her skinned ankles and elbows, and she had to hobble about. We spent a week in the city of Chiang Mai whilst the worst of her injuries healed and she got over her painful limp. Alba enjoys spending time in cities, interacting with people and soaking up the life and culture of her surrounds – me, not so much. I found this week taxing. Often as we conversed at roadside eateries, suffocated by smog and racket, my mind would wander off and dream about the nature that awaited me up in those green hills that edged the city, away from the layers of unintelligible noise and congested air. Everything up there looked so pure, and it was calling me – each day with a more persistent, ever-demanding tone.

Towards the end of the week, even Alba grew tired of the city, and so we hatched a plan. Although her wounds were still somewhat raw, she'd passed the worst of it. She could move now without constant bursts of sharp pain. We now *both* needed an escape to nature, and so we took the steps to go to our next destination: Pai. Pai is a small hippy town some three hours to the northwest of Chiang Mai. Although we always sought out destinations on our travels that would truly allow us to connect with and experience the real people and culture of a given place, we made an exception with Pai. Once a hidden Thai gem, Pai is now a must-visit destination for western backpackers through Southeast Asia. Pai itself has a rustic small-town vibe, but seems to have more backpackers and settled westerners than Thais. But the westerners that congregate here were our kind of westerners: long-haired, baggy-clothed hippies who wanted to escape from the stresses and madness of today's hollow corporate world. These are people who simply want to connect with nature, the simple beauties of the earth, and to share kind, peaceful and educational experiences with one another. And so, this destination was a no-brainer.

We took a three-hour bus and there we were, in the heart of the Southeast Asian hippy backpacking scene. It was a sleepy town that looked like it was about to be gobbled up by the surrounding hills, which were rich with clean rivers, waterfalls, small, organically farmed rice paddies, ancient temples and dense, undisturbed forest.

We had no real itinerary here, as was often the case. We'd left our stressful, prescribed ways back in Ireland. We were not bound by time, money or place, and this was the most liberating thing I'd ever done. We wandered at ease through the town, taking in its laid-back, welcoming atmosphere. It was much calmer here – birdsong outweighed human noise. The air was purer and the people more personable. Other backpackers wandered by with baggy cotton trousers and tank tops. Many had dreadlocks, tattoos and earrings, and looked like they'd just walked off the set of *Pirates of the Caribbean*. Every street corner seemed to have a café with a little circle of hippies sitting around their buddy who was playing tunes on a guitar.

We settled into a wooden hut built along one of Pai's many rivers. It felt too good to be true. The hut itself was as if it were a part of nature – made of all-natural material, on bamboo stilts and surrounded by lush vegetation. Vivid-red dragonflies skimmed over the tumbling water's surface. Butterflies fluttered with grace from petal to petal. Our feet dangled just above the river below as we sat on colourful cushions, strewn over the bamboo decking. On our first morning, we sat here with a coffee and simply listened to and watched life go by.

A familiar sound woke me up better than any coffee ever could. I'd been expecting this one: a high-pitched 'tsee-uuu-eeet', not too dissimilar to the whistle people use to catch someone's attention from afar. I knew exactly what this was, for this colourful little sprite is a regular autumn vagrant to Irish shores. The yellow-browed warbler is a highly migratory Siberian leaf warbler that breeds in lowland and montane forests (forests that are found on the slopes of mountains). It winters in Southeast Asia and, in autumn, some birds on their travels between Siberia and Southeast Asia are intercepted by strong easterly airflows and find themselves astray on our Irish shorelines. This is where I had previously seen this species, so it was a strange treat to see this familiar face so far from home. Now *I* was the vagrant. Whereas before I was used to seeing this little bird far out of range, here the shoe was on the other foot. I myself had migrated from the colds of Ireland, and was far away from home in the tropical climate of Thailand.

Yellow-browed Warbler (*Phylloscopus inornatus*)
Family Phylloscopidae *(leaf warblers)*
Conservation status *Least Concern (IUCN Red List) – does not occur on the BoCCI list, as it is a rare vagrant*
Vocalisations *Calls from vagrants can be heard in Ireland and are given as a high-pitched 'tsee-uuu-eeet'.*

It took some waiting and persistence but, eventually, it showed itself with its tell-tale bright yellow supercilium. A supercilium is a stripe that passes above a bird's eye, and somewhat resembles an eyebrow, hence the yellow-browed part of its name. This beautiful Siberian gem also has two bright-yellow wing-bars, with a wonderful lime-green upper body plus off-white-to-yellow underparts, topped off with striking little yellow-orange legs. These birds are a joy to watch as they flit from leaf to leaf, catching little insects that are too small to detect with our naked eye. They, however, can see them with ease as they hover and flicker effortlessly, snapping their bills frequently as they snatch up their tiny-winged morsels of sustenance, calling intermittently as they go about their morning business.

With Alba happily reading and soaking up the air of calm, I asked her if she minded staying a while, to see what other birds would appear.

'Of course, love. I'm really relaxed here.'

'Me too!' I replied. And so, as is often the case, Alba's world and mine blended into a coexistence, as we both sat in peace, side-by-side, doing separate things, but together. I watched the canopy above our heads as unfamiliar birds flitted through unannounced. Some calls filtered down, but they weren't in my vocabulary, at least not yet. I did know a few though, particularly those that had the unfortunate habit of turning up as vagrants back home, as was the case with yellow-browed warbler. I had learned the calls of such birds years previously in anticipation of a chance encounter on a windswept autumn headland back in Ireland, where myself and others of my kind would scour the few desolate peninsular gardens with wind-stunted sycamores, where sodden Siberian vagrants would make landfall, desperately seeking food and shelter after their major navigational errors.

I soon heard another familiar voice amongst the unknowns above. This could only be described as a machine gun on turbo. I felt a surge of excitement, as if I had just found this mega-rare vagrant on a windy Irish headland. We have just one record to date of the Siberian superstar: taiga flycatcher. As the name suggests, this forest dweller breeds in the Siberian taiga and, again, winters in Southeast Asia. Like all flycatchers, which are small arboreal, insectivorous songbirds, it catches flies on the wing from a number of favoured perches, zipping in and out with intention and precision. It took some searching through the canopy, but then I was rewarded for my patience. It sat out on an exposed branch for all of 30 seconds, but long enough to show itself off.

At rest, I could see its distinctive orange throat amidst an otherwise non-distinct grey breast. Its brown upperparts were accentuated by a proud-cocked tail, which it frequently flicked between a relaxed and upright stance, quite like our own little wren does. As a small fly naively meandered past at range, it jolted its head and went into a state of hyperfocus. It then lived up to its name and launched itself like a rocket on a mission, with a flash of its striking black-and-white-tail and a clack of the bill as it snatched up its unsuspecting victim. It sat back on its lookout post for a moment, peered around and it was off. Wow! It was a surreal moment for me to see what would be an ultra-rare prize back home, just giving itself up for me whilst I sat in my shorts and bare feet drinking coffee at dawn. Nature in all its raw glory has the ability to knock me off my feet and bring me a sense of awe and wonderment like nothing else. I was so consumed by this magic moment that I failed to realise that Alba had put her book down and was watching me with a smile. She knew how intensely nature could woo me, and it made her happy to see me in my element.

Taiga Flycatcher (*Ficedula albicilla*)
Family Under some debate but generally considered to belong to the muscicapidae (old world flycatchers)
Conservation status Least Concern (IUCN Red List). Does not occur on the BoCCI list, as it is a rare vagrant.
Vocalisations Song not heard in Ireland, as the species does not breed. Extremely rare vagrant. Sounds like a much faster version of the 'trrrt' call of the closely related red-breasted flycatcher.

After a morning of stillness, just taking it all in, we were eager to explore, so we picked ourselves up and headed for the nearby hills. Alba was a little unsure how she'd fare as her ankles were still red, raw and oozing, and the strap of her sandals were chafing on them during longer walks. Despite this, she was eager to explore the hills – she knew they'd been calling me for some time – though I think their voices had begun to speak to her, too. So off we set, without a plan or time limit. We meandered through the peripheries of the village, as people and infrastructure became ever scarcer, giving way to small rice paddies, gentle brooks and forests. We weren't alone, though – we soon began to bump into our bohemian comrades from Pai, many of whom were barefoot. This really surprised me, and they reminded me of religious pilgrims walking arduous routes as a form of penance and atonement. But that wasn't the case here at all. These were just hippies who wanted to feel a skin-to-earth connection in nature. I took my own sandals off for a minute to try it out, and I instantly understood. It brought me back to my early childhood in the garden. To walk barefoot and feel every blade of grass, every grain of dust and every drop of water run over your skin unabated is liberating.

We humans are a sensual species who like to feel and touch to understand the world around us from the get-go, yet we spend the majority of our lives entombing this sense beneath clothes and footwear. So to let this primal instinct out of its cage feels liberating, and just *right*. Because of our modern ways, the vast majority of us have feet that are in no way prepared for wild terrain. I was reminded of this when a sharp, unexpected pain shot up through my right foot. I'd stood on a triangular, upright stone that was jutting out of the track like a miniature pyramid, waiting to remind me of my soft-touch ways. The feeling was as if I'd stepped on a piece of Lego left astray on the living-room floor. I let out a yelp and submitted to my sandals once again. Alba rolled her eyes in laughter, as a long-haired German guy shot past unshod, as if it were nothing. This guy was no newbie! His feet had seen some prolonged skin-to-earth action, with toes spread far apart like an open-palmed hand, and an underfoot that was calloused and hardened like the ground that he walked on. He was nimble and moved like a mountain goat, as if he truly belonged.

I decided to make a connection to the earth in the way I knew best – through birds. And Alba was just happy to be out in nature and getting some good physical exercise. That was her thing – keeping fit and testing her limits – and I often found it hard to keep up with her. She knew I was on a long-awaited mission, though.

As it was March, I knew these northern forests would still hold many Siberian wintering migrants, and I was all for that. Even though I was prepared for these birds, seeing one here gave me a hint of the buzz I'd feel finding one out of context back home. Above all others, I had one species in mind – the Siberian blue robin. Just typing its name now gives me the butterflies. This is a bird that has an almost mythical status in Ireland. Nobody has ever seen one there, but they do occur as vagrants now and then in the UK, so we know they're a possibility in Ireland, too. Every rarity-seeker is prepared for the unlikely event of stumbling across this dreamy beauty. Of course, for these birds, it would be very bad to be blown so far off course, so, for that reason, I hope it doesn't happen. But if it *were* to happen, and I was the one to fall upon it, I think I'd faint with excitement.

How can I describe a Siberian blue robin to you without smiling myself into silliness? I can't! These birds are *special*. And I mean that with every letter of the word. My apologies to the females, but it is the male of this species that triggers the internal fireworks. They are utter perfection. Imagine a bird slightly larger than our own robin. Now add ridiculously long legs, almost as if the bird is on stilts. Now picture two colours: above, a jaw-dropping cerulean-blue and, below, the purest pearly-white you can imagine, with both colours separated by a jet-black trim. Their elusive behaviour also feeds into their mythical status – they're proper skulkers. They hunker down low and dart through the leaf litter, with fast bouts of running and short bursts of flight. At rest, they turn their heads and flicker their tails as they seek out insects and spiders on the forest floor. They tend to stay close to dense cover alongside streams and riverbanks. As it so happened, this was the route we were taking – we were following our hobbit-like friend upstream to reach a waterfall some two hours through the forest.

Siberian Blue Robin (*Larvivora cyane*)
Family Under some debate but generally considered to belong to the muscicapidae (old world flycatchers)
Conservation status Least Concern (IUCN Red List) – does not occur on the BoCCI list, although it has occurred in the UK as a vagrant, it has yet to be documented in Ireland
Vocalisations Song a distinctive 'tsee-tsee-tsee-tsee-TSEWEE-TSEWEE'.

After some time, Alba's wounds started to shout for mercy. She had no choice but to go into hobbit-mode herself, and so off her sandals came. To my surprise, she threw herself right into it. She loved it, and I laughed at her and began to call her Frodo.

The sound of the forest was like nothing I'd ever encountered. An array of unknown, exotic songs filled the air, accompanied by a deafening roar of several cicada species. Cicadas emit a constant high-pitched drone, reminiscent of the whining of electrical cables.

And they're *loud* – really loud. In fact, the world's loudest insect is a species of African cicada, which has been recorded emitting sounds as high as 106.7 decibels at a distance of 50 centimetres! This is the equivalent of somewhere between the volume of a handheld drill and a chainsaw. Whilst these were't that particular species, they weren't far off the mark. Several hundred of them were emitting sound all at once, from all directions. We took our time, stopping to listen and look at all the natural beauty around us. Every bird that showed its face was given time. I had my little Southeast Asian bird book with me and did my best to identify unknowns as we went.

A flash of indigo blue and subtle orange overhead revealed my first ever hill blue flycatcher – it looked a bit like a flashier version of the early-morning taiga flycatcher. As we went, I had my eyes glued to the edges of riverside undergrowth, looking out for the coveted Siberian blue robin. A brief shock rippled through my stomach when I caught a glimpse of snowy-white underparts and a darker upperpart by the river. I stopped and raised my binoculars and gushed with awe. I'd never seen a bird look so dapper.

On a rock amongst the fast-flowing river was a jet-black and snow-white bird, with a bobbing tail almost longer than the bird itself. The black upperparts were intersected with various patches of gleaming white to accompany its white breast. Then the tail had smart white intersections along its length. It was utterly beautiful. I had to look it up and discovered it was a black-backed forktail, described as a shy bird that forages along watercourses, mainly feeding on aquatic insects and crustaceans.

After feasting on this cosmic eye-candy, we continued on our trek. Alba's wounds were feeling much better, free in the air and the cooling water we often passed through. Now and then, she'd step in something icky, and I'd cheekily laugh at her from the comfort of my fancy sandals. My high-horsed position didn't last long before karma took me down a peg. I lost my footing and twisted my ankle, which resulted in a loud snap. Thankfully it wasn't my foot that snapped, but the strap that held one of my sandals together. I tried walking with one sandal but it had my balance playing all kinds of tricks on me, and so, after all of my laughing and calling Alba a hobbit, here I was barefoot, several kilometres into the dense and unpredictable Thai jungle. I wish I hadn't made so much fun of the Pai hippies or Alba, because it turns out I was a proper baby about walking barefoot. And Alba had *zero* sympathy for me. Rightly so, too. I tried to persuade her to turn back, but she was having none of it.

'Let's find that Siberian blue robin, shall we, Seán!?' She spoke with loving sarcasm. Not wanting to broadcast my embarrassing defeat, I kept my little screams to myself and carried on with my metaphoric tail tucked in.

I spent a lot of time looking down for fear of standing on something spiky, and I think this is what brought it to my attention. Through a gap in the undergrowth between my throbbing feet and the flowing river was a flash of movement. I stopped and peered through and my heart went into overdrive. A bird hunkered down low, bobbing its tail – it looked long-legged. My nerves took grip and I worried I'd not see it again. I looked ahead at a larger opening in the bush and waited. And then the most majestic cerulean blue appeared with a gleaming white chin and a big beady black eye. I heard myself making a sound I didn't know it was possible to make as a human – pure incoherent gobbledygook. Perhaps I was embracing my inner hobbit. The bird took another step into the open, as if testing the waters. Its long, gangly legs came into view. Alba was in on the act, too, and there it was in all of its immeasurable glory – a male Siberian blue robin. If I had died there on the forest floor in my bare feet, I would have died a complete man. I took a trophy photo and got one last glimpse before it melted back into obscurity. I waited until we'd walked uphill a bit before I screamed just like Alba did when Barcelona scored. We're not so different after all. My brief but magical glimpse of this otherworldly 'Sibe' was akin to her beloved Suárez scoring the winning goal against Madrid. I never once thought or complained about my feet for the rest of that day, powered by the memory of a bird that would forever live in my mind.

We continued on our travels for three months, traversing Laos, Cambodia and back down as far as southern Thailand. We experienced a whole new world, taking in every temple under the sun, deep-diving off-track into every village and culture who'd have us and, of course, there was the wildlife. We did everything in our power not to miss a thing: from rare freshwater Irrawaddy dolphins to 6-foot Asian water monitors; from offshore-island-roosting large fruit bats with a one-and-a-half-metre wingspan to gentle spectacled langurs. And I'll never forget the birds: stupendous Oriental pied hornbills, enormous white-bellied sea eagles, and so many more. This journey opened our eyes to the mystery and wonder beyond our own doorstep; especially me – the green-eared traveller. After three months, we hummed and hawed about what to do. Do we go back to our lives as cogs in the broken machine, or do we throw caution to the wind and live in the moment, just for another while?

We still had savings and didn't have jobs waiting on us in Ireland, so, a week later, we were in Nepal, ready to go again. Southeast Asia was a great introduction to long-distance backpacking, as it was tried and tested by many before us. Nepal was another beast. People do travel there, but it is in no way as prepared for commercial tourism as Thailand, and that is the charm of it.

The Mahendra Highway traverses Nepal from east to west, covering over 1,000 kilometres, as it runs along the southern boundary of the Himalayas. Either side of this the roads are rather simple and often unusable without a heavy-duty four-wheel drive. As in Southeast Asia, life here was cheap for a backpacker, but it was tough on the people. We saw a lot more poverty than we had in Thailand and, for me, it was a real eye-opener. Over a period of two months, we covered the length and breadth of the country, mostly residing in homestays – homes of local families where we got into the thick of real Nepalese life – working on farms and cooking on open fires. The work was tough and unforgiving, and the food, although simple and repetitive, was wholesome, filling and tasty.

My standout homestead was a rather special adventure. It was a small farmstead high up in the eastern hills of Illam, almost on the border with Darjeeling in India. These hills were famous for growing tea and, apart from these plantations, they were wild and rugged. We took an overnight bus from west of Katmandu and it took us a gruelling 28 hours to reach Illam, but it was worth the trip. The farm, run by Dika and Bibek, was part-nature, part-sustenance. They had everything they needed: egg-laying chickens, a single cow, and various herbs and vegetables, and a modest tea plantation to provide income. Dika greeted us with a delicious cup of masala tea, made with ingredients from their farm: milk from their cow, tea from their plantation. And from the local market she added cloves, cinnamon, cardamom and *a lot* of sugar. What struck me most about their farm was that there wasn't even a hint of industrialisation or disdain for 'pesky' nature, as is practically the norm in Ireland. I walked around looking at the beautiful wilderness that enveloped the farm. I counted at least five species of orchid. Orchids are very sensitive to changes in their environment. Back home, they are only found in the rare places that are untouched by heavy hands. But here, they were growing in abundance.

As Alba and I meandered through the tea plantation, highly migratory olive-backed pipits flushed and gave their classic metallic 'shreep' calls from around my feet, momentarily disturbed as they crept amongst the vegetation where they sought out invertebrates to fuel their continued journey northwards to Siberia.

Olive-backed Pipit *(Anthus hodgsoni)*
Family *Motacillidae (wagtails, longclaws and pipits)*
Conservation status *Least Concern (IUCN Red List) – does not occur on the BoCCI list, as it is a rare vagrant*
Vocalisations *Flight calls impossible to tell apart by ear from the 'tzzeee' calls of the closely related tree pipit. However, detailed analysis of sonograms can resolve identification confusions.*

We continued up to the back of the farm where we met a smiling Bibek, the man of the house. He stood up from a bending position where he was picking wildflowers. He pointed out different species with love and admiration as he told us their medicinal purposes. There wasn't a machine in sight, and I'm sure 'weedkiller' isn't in his vocabulary. Here was Bibek picking wildflowers intimately by hand, wildflowers he knows by name and that he respects. In Ireland, we treat the equivalent species as a pest that needs to be 'controlled' or replaced with aesthetically pleasing non-native plants that are usually little to no use to our native invertebrates and other fauna. How sad. We really have become lost, and I feel like we have totally deviated from a harmonious path through nature – the very thing that keeps the world in a healthy state of balance and being.

In Illam, the people not only tolerated nature, they understood it, they were a part of it and they lived with it in symbiosis. Every morning, we would wake at dawn to collect firewood, start the fires, tend to the farm animals and pick many baskets of tea leaves. Dika and Bibek led a hard-working life, but they were also happy. They lived in a nature-filled glade full of eclectic, melodic birdsong, with a far-reaching splash of colourful wildflowers – tended to by a sea of floating butterflies and bees. This place opened my eyes to how far we have deviated from nature in our daily lives back home. Until you see or become aware of what we have lost, you don't even realise it. But when you have seen it, it will forever remain in your memory – I gained a new baseline of healthy, happy living. It gave me further drive to make a difference to nature back home, somehow, one day.

We spent a full week at the farm, detoxing from city life, but our time had come to visit one more location before we had to leave.

After some thought and discussion on our travels, we made the choice to move back to Barcelona rather than Ireland. Alba really found the weather in Ireland tough, and she missed her home and her family. For me, I just love an adventure. The thoughts of moving to a new country, with a new set of birds to engross myself in, excited me. I was used to trials and tribulations and I knew it would be tough. I'd have to face the prospect of finding work in my field again and, this time, I'd have the additional obstacle of language. But, as always, I thought back to my meningitis episode. I can't be afraid! I'm lucky to still be here, and I have to take on new opportunities with passion and courage. You never know what may come of them.

But we still had some time left in Nepal before we moved to Catalunya. Although we'd travelled throughout Nepal and seen lots of it, we still hadn't seen any of the larger mammals: Bengal tigers, leopards, Asian elephants, one-horned rhinoceroses and marsh muggers, to name but a few. Alba made contact with a lodge in Bardiya National Park that was offering free board and guided jungle walks on weekends for anyone who was willing to come and proofread the English on their webpage, socials and leaflets. This was an offer too good to turn down, so off we set to the western end of the country, not far from the Indian border.

Bardiya National Park is a lush, largely undisturbed protected area spanning a total of 968 square kilometres – that's over 8,000 Cuskinny Nature Reserves! I found it difficult to even imagine that scale of wilderness. The majority of the park, some 70 per cent, is made up of dense forest, with the remaining 30 per cent comprising a mixture of riverine habitats, grasslands and savannah. No people live inside the bounds of the park, having been resettled elsewhere following its establishment.

Our bus dropped us off at a large wooden gate on the side of a main road, bounded by forest on either side. At this gate was parked an open-back 4x4, with two men wearing khaki-green cottons and peak caps. We were the only ones getting out, and so both parties knew we had found the other. Their English was excellent and so we got stuck straight into a bit of chat. They started to tell us all about the park, what animals they'd been seeing, and about all of the current goings-on in the village – some 30 minutes' drive beyond the gates. We sat sideways in the open-back, and Dharma, the front passenger, was the main one keeping up the chat. He was a local ornithologist and wildlife guide who worked in the national park, bringing tourists in to see the wildlife.

The farther we drove, the less human influence there was. We arrived at the colourful pillared gates of our lodge and parked up inside – Dharma closing the great big gates behind him. I couldn't help but notice that the walls were wide and tall – almost fort-like. The gate too was a solid lump of towering spiked metal. I asked Dharma why the lodge was so heavily fortified. He looked at me and smiled. 'Elephants!'

Of course!

He continued. 'Actually that reminds me. Be very careful if you go down to the river for a walk. There is a mad bull in musth that's knocking down walls and chasing anything that moves. He's very dangerous. You need to be careful out here – a few people die from unfortunate interactions with wild animals almost every year.'

I felt a surge of nervous energy; I'd never been in a wild place where I wasn't the most dangerous mammal. Domestic cows and bulls don't count! I felt a sense of excitement, almost as if I was a daredevil risking life and death out here. In a sense I would be, but the risks would be very low as long as I used some common sense and followed the guidance of Dharma and others.

The following morning, we were to be brought out on our first walking safari into the depths of the Bardiya wilderness. Dharma told us to get some sleep because we had an arduous journey ahead of us and we'd need to have our wits about us.

That night, we lay in our cabin and I listened to the calming nocturnal soundscape that blanketed us in our wooden cabin. Crickets, frogs and owls delicately wove their soothing tunes through the tranquil village air. I always like to be prepared and so I began googling everything I could find about Bardiya. What kinds of animals were there? What habitats are there?

And then I googled something I wished I hadn't: 'Bardiya AND wildlife AND killed'. Oh God! Lots of news stories popped up in my feed: people killed by tigers, rhinos, elephants and bears. A title from 2016 caught my eye: 'Dutch tourist says he's lucky to survive Nepal tiger attack'. Why was I reading these!? It was as if some morbid curiosity urged me to delve into the gory details of the risks that lay ahead of us. I also read that the one-horned rhinoceros is considered to be one of the most dangerous animals in the park, again with several deaths recorded every year or two – lovely! At least they can't climb trees though, which cannot be said for the sloth bears that also roam the park. Despite their relatively small size, they take on tigers much larger than they are. Apparently they are relentless berserkers once they are triggered. Even better, they run faster than us and they're excellent swimmers. Oh, and it's also said that they tend to go for the eyes and genitals when they launch an attack. I was reading these stories aloud to Alba with gasps of shock.

She warned me, 'Seán, you're really not persuading me into doing this. One more of these and I'm definitely out. I'm already thinking it's a bad idea!'

'Oh no, no! I'll stop,' I replied. 'Pretty scary though, isn't it?'

She glared at me. 'Seán ...'

We awoke to our alarms at 6 a.m. We had a long day ahead and so we had breakfast on the go as we climbed into the 4x4 with our guides Dharma and Krishna, who took us to the main entrance of the park. It was standard for tourists to be guided by two people, so one could watch ahead and one behind. These guides also ensure that visitors do not engage in any behaviour that would disturb the wildlife.

Many of the species within the park, including tigers, rhinos and elephants, are endangered and protected. The World Wildlife Fund have even stated that Bardiya National Park has played a major role in the conservation of the Bengal tiger population, which doubled the Nepalese population by the year 2022. But this not only benefits Bardiya; tigers from the park have also repopulated the previously tiger-deprived Banke National Park with more than 20 tigers, from a low of zero in 2010. However, it is also home to the endangered gharial crocodile, the Gangetic dolphin and several rare birds, including Bengal florican, lesser florican, the silver-eared mesia and sarus crane. Army personnel patrol the park to prevent poachers from hunting elephants and rhinos for their tusks, or from killing any other animals for whatever reason. The park entrance was guarded by these heavily armed soldiers, which added to the growing sense of adventure and danger.

Alba looked at their guns and then looked back at me. 'Seán, are you sure about this?'

I smiled and continued to rattle my head in every direction, taking it all in. This was the most exhilarating excursion of my life.

We stepped down from the vehicle and showed our ID. A quick inspection and a nod from the guards and we were ushered in on foot. We walked through some trees and down to a little bay in the river. Here we met another armed guard who brought us towards a tiny hand-carved dugout canoe that was tied to a tree on the bank. Our guides knew the guard well. They clapped hands in a familiar, informal greeting and started speaking in Nepalese. I saw a glint of excitement come over their faces. They finished up and approached us.

'They've seen a tiger here this morning. Right opposite the bank here – on the other side. Only about an hour ago.'

A shudder of fear shot up my spine. Am I walking myself into something I can't turn back from here? I was led by Dharma to the little canoe, which was so small that he could only bring one person across at a time. I stepped on first and nearly rocked it over. Dharma laughed and told me to crouch down. He then stepped in and paddled across. A morning mist floated over the river, adding to the sense of ominous mystery about the place. I jumped out and instantly felt the need to watch my back. Behind me was a dense, dark thicket of jungle that was home to the large mammals I'd been reading about all night. I felt a real sense of vulnerability – of being in their world now. We humans are used to being the boss wherever we go, and here I felt like an ant.

Alba came next – I knew by her face that she was scared. We looked at one another and then looked at the far bank where Dharma and Krishna were saying a few words to their friend. 'God, will they ever hurry up,' I said, looking over my shoulder into the darkness of the jungle. I watched as they approached – every paddle stroke appeared to me in slow motion as I repeatedly checked over my shoulder.

They landed and began giving us a pep-talk. 'Okay, guys, before we go, we'd like to set a few boundaries. Just remember, this is a totally wild area and, of course, it's full of wild animals. We do not carry guns, as we have no intentions of bringing harm. We have a stick each, and you will walk between us. Animal attacks do happen, but they are rare. They don't want to harm you, but very occasionally we can startle them or they may have young. If we do find ourselves in danger, we need to respond differently depending on the animal. If we face a tiger, don't panic! This is very important. Maintain eye contact and slowly back away. If you face a rhino, climb or hide behind a tree, or run in a zigzag pattern – they aren't really agile. For elephants, run as fast as you can and hide behind a strong tree. If you come across a sloth bear, especially one with young, then you pray. They are faster than us, they can swim really well and they can climb trees. All we can do is use our sticks and hope to scare it away.'

My heart was palpitating. I looked at Alba and she was as white as a ghost.

Dharma smiled at us. 'Okay, let's go, guys. I will lead, and Krishna will stay behind you.'

I felt like we were entering another world. The sounds, the smells, the beauty – it was all so intense. The wall of eclectic bird sound was immediate. The familiar 'coo-EUW, coo-EUW, COO-EUW' calls of the Asian koel jumped out at me right away, remembering it from Thailand. I called it out to Dharma, who nodded in agreement. I didn't have the ear I had back home in Ireland. Although I could clearly hear distinct and different songs, I wasn't sure what they all were. Dharma's ear was totally tuned in to it all, though. He pointed everything out to me. We'd wait until a new bird was singing clearly, standing out from the crowd. A rich, fluty melodic song with short verses floated down from above. It sounded familiar to me, so I looked at Dharma. 'Golden oriole?'

'Almost! It's a black-hooded oriole.'

Ah-ha! This made me feel better. Golden oriole is a bird I had heard in continental Europe many times, so at least I was in the right family. Dharma stopped me again, 'Shh, listen!' It sounded like a pigeon or a dove – a hoarse, rising 'whoo-ooOO-whooo'.

I turned to Dharma. 'A dove of some kind?'

He replied with enthusiasm. '*Yes!* A spotted dove.'

We stopped again, and he beckoned me to listen, somewhere low down. Behind the trees, I heard a simple three-note song, 'too-chee-deeer'.

I looked back at Dharma and laughed. 'Not a clue!'

'Puff-throated babbler,' he responded enthusiastically.

We moved fast, as did the birds. I had to rely on Dharma's ear for confirmation for now.

We walked through a tiny trail that opened out into a grassy area. Monkeys sat feeding on fruit at the periphery of the treeline. Dharma stopped and turned to us. 'Guys, the long grass here is very dangerous. This is where the tigers hide to ambush deer and monkeys. Please follow us and be aware of your surroundings.'

I never felt so scared yet so alive in all my life. My heart pounded and my senses had truly awakened.

Dharma stopped and gasped in excitement. Looking down, he pointed and exclaimed, 'Tiger print! We need to move. It's very fresh.'

I was going to do whatever Dharma told me to do. I clung to his shadow, not saying a word. Weirdly, I got a sudden, overpowering smell of popcorn as we continued through the chest-height, serrated grass. Even the grass was edgy here! We held our arms up high to avoid a length of paper-cuts. We reached a clearing as we entered back into the forest. The thought of that popcorn came back into my mind. How weird was that! Dharma stopped and had a rather worried expression on his face. Now in the safety of the clearing, he took a wide-eyed sigh of relief. Rather shaken, he looked at myself and Alba.

'Guys, I didn't want to say it to you before, but we were very close just now. I think we may have been under the eye of a hiding tiger. Did you smell it? Their pee smells like popcorn. It was very strong, very fresh. We were close just there.'

This hit me like a punch to the chest. The danger is here – it's rare but it's very real.

We trekked through the shaded paths of the jungle, remarkably feeling a lot safer, having run the gauntlet of the tiger's grassy ambush spot. The jungle bubbled with wild sound. I didn't know what the vast majority was, but it was utterly beautiful. I'd never heard such a rich and varied soundscape – it was incredibly uplifting. I had my camera over my shoulder and I was photographing everything that caught my eye. A wild peacock sang from the top of a tall tree, its call echoing through the jungle. How strange to see them in their true wild context – I'd forgotten that they actually exist outside of zoos and elaborate old estate houses. Following that theme, a chicken ran across the trail. Taken aback for a second, I wondered what it was doing out there, and then it clicked. This was no chicken, it was a red junglefowl – the original ancestor of today's domestic chicken.

It looked like a more showy version of the latter, with the familiar fleshy red crest flopping about its head, a rusty-brown shawl and wings set amongst a bottle-green and black body with a frock-like, elaborate black tail.

I'm lucky in that I've always had very sharp senses. I see patterns and details that speak to me, and my eyes are always scanning in every direction. Looking at the leaf litter as I passed between a gap in two trees, a pattern jumped out from the sombre brown tones of the rotting leaves. A straw-yellow pattern amidst a chocolate brown. It caught my eye and I crouched closer for a look. I instantly jumped back in surprise. It was a very large Burmese python, looking right at me and flicking its tongue. Our first close encounter with one of Bardiya's powerful hunters. This one seemed mellow enough, though.

We continued following Dharma's all-seeing, cautious lead. We were next to the river now, which we could hear and see through some of the gaps in the jungle. Eagle-eyed and informative as ever, Dharma stopped and pointed to the ground. 'Rhino apples! Rhinos love these.'

Then, he turned to point at a pile of steaming poop. I saw his expression turn to one of slight concern. 'This is fresh – we are close. Be careful here.' We moved on and, some five minutes later, a big open bend in the river enabled us to step out and look back along the stretch of water we'd just walked. Dharma started to jump in excitement as he looked through his binoculars. 'Rhino! Rhino! A BIG one. It's feeding by the bank.' Again there was that expression of slight concern. He pondered for a second and then looked at us: 'We *were* close. We walked right past it.' Then in a hushed tone he asked us, 'Do you want to go back?'

The thought of it seemed like a suicide mission to me. I'd read all about an angry rhino the night before. I gulped and looked to Alba.

'Okay!' she said.

I was in shock. 'What! Are you serious?'

She looked at me, surprisingly mellow. 'Yeah, why not?'

Dharma and Krishna were keen to give it a go, too. Krishna looked at me. 'Don't worry, Seán. I grew up with rhinos. They have very bad eyesight – we just need to sneak up and look from the trees. It will be fine.'

So that was it.

We took a mental note of roughly how far down this rhino was from the bend, and we trekked back, taking care not to step on any twigs. The tension in the air was palpable. We came to those rhino apples and Dharma suggested we try from there.

We slowly crept in towards the riverbank, crawling through a gap in a bush. We stood up and were thrown into a state of panic. It was right there – now it was just feet from the bank, and we'd startled it. It grunted and turned towards us. Dharma climbed up the nearest tree and pulled Alba up behind him. I followed and scrambled up the tree but fell backwards onto the ground. I screamed in terror and tried to climb again – I couldn't. I could hear heavy thudding, splashes and grunts. I turned in fear, expecting to meet my fate. Krishna was crouched down looking to the rhino ... and he was laughing. What the hell?! He beckoned me over and I replied with a bewildered shrug. Was he crazy?

'Seán, it's okay! The bank is too steep. He's trying but he can't get up. We are safe!'

I looked up at Alba, who was in absolute hysterics. I was too shaken to react. I turned back and looked to the rhino. It was true. The banks were steep and muddy. Although it did try to charge us, it just couldn't manage it. I looked at my hands. They were trembling, as were my legs, my butt and just about every other part of my body. I inched closer to Krishna.

'It's okay! Come on, Seán. Now, he is calm.'

I sat next to Krishna and looked at the rhino. It was maybe 12 feet away. I looked it right in the eye and it looked into mine. We'd come to an understanding – we both knew there was no threat. We maintained a mutual gaze for a few seconds before it gently snorted and began to wade across to the other side of the river. Alba and Dharma climbed back down the tree. We settled here for our lunch and hardly spoke a word, the experience of it all still sinking in. It was both the scariest, most exhilarating, yet most humbling wildlife encounter I've ever had. I will never, ever forget that moment. And, in a way, I hope I never have another like it. I was lucky that bank was as steep as it was.

Not long after, we decided to call it a day. A new adventure awaited, and we were about to begin our new chapter, starting our lives afresh in Catalunya. I was torn about our return to Europe. On one hand, I'd be giving up this life of freedom and adventure, this lack of external control in our day. We did as we pleased and had no ties to anyone or any place. On the other hand, I knew that it couldn't go on forever. We live in a society driven by money, money we need to earn. But at least I could earn it doing something I loved.

The way I saw the world had changed so much after my travels and experiences in general in the past few years. I'd seen nature at levels of abundance and variety I didn't know existed. I thought that one day, I could do something in Ireland to bring about the changes so desperately needed, to bring nature back to levels comparable to Nepal. I also knew that Catalunya still had meaningful wild spaces. The Pyrenees were crying out for me. I'd always wanted to go there, to explore its vast peaks and wildflower meadows, its lush forests and its cold, clean rivers. I could still immerse myself in true nature upon my return.

My plan was to go back, study Catalan and Spanish, teach English to get a start, and eventually break into ornithological conservation work there. I felt confident and excited about it. Alba, of course, was delighted to be returning to her homeland, and I was also feeling a sense of calm and purpose about it. It would be a challenge, but I was all for it.

Alpine Swift

Chapter 9

IT WAS LATE SUMMER 2018, AND I HAD A COCKTAIL OF emotions moving to our new home in Catalunya. Fear and excitement led the way as we walked into a life with no home, no work and, for me, a whole new culture and languages to navigate. Spanish is widely spoken on the streets and in the cafés, but Catalan is the mother tongue of Alba, her family and her people. I had some experience with Spanish from school and so that would be easier to learn, but her family all only spoke Catalan at home, so that was equally important to learn. I wanted to learn it regardless, though, because I knew and respected how important their Catalan identity was to them and to their people.

Despite so many unknowns, the excitement overshadowed the fear. I was excited for so many things, and it was these things that took up the most swinging room in my brain.

I was excited for the new birds, and for the amazing wild spaces I had to explore. I was excited for the sun and the food. And I was excited about embracing the rich Catalan culture that I had heard so much about from Alba as we sat inside our Cork city flat on grey, dreary winter days – thinking of our future ahead.

We first moved into Alba's parents' home in El Prat de Llobregat – a town on the outskirts of Barcelona. We had a spare room to ourselves. It was spacious and charming. A large bed sat atop a cool marble floor, and a large window looking onto the sunny street outside, where excited chittering sounds of alpine swifts, like a group of chatty mice, bubbled in from up above the high-rise flats that dominated the town.

Alpine swifts are giants of the swift world, and far exceed the slim proportions of our own common swifts back home. Though their form is much the same – like jet-black boomerangs or zippy stealth bombers – their white breast and chin give them an extra flare. An echoing of pleasant house sparrow chirps emanated from the eaves of the street where irregularities in the stonework provided them with homes along each row of apartments.

Alpine Swift (Tachymarptis melba)
Family *Apodidae (swifts)*
Conservation status *Least Concern (IUCN Red List) – does not occur on the BoCCI list, as it is a rare vagrant*
Vocalisations *Flight calls very different to the screeches of our own common swift, instead a series of high-pitched twitterings that accelerate and decelerate with speed.*

Alba's family home stood out from the rest of the street: an old stone farmhouse, lost amongst a street of modern giants. This farmhouse once stood amidst a mosaic of agriculture and wild space, but was now enveloped by sky-reaching tower blocks where much of the birdsong had been swapped for the rattling of air-con units and the bass beat of reggaeton tunes. It was okay, though, because I had known that we were just a stone's throw away from nature. And even in the city, everything was still that little bit wilder compared to what I had known in Ireland. Wildflowers were allowed to reach their colourful glory. There were no sickly brown scorch marks, the tell-tale sign of weedkiller I was so accustomed to from home. More insects buzzed through the air: butterflies and dragonflies were common sights drifting down the streets, availing of that fringe of urban wildness.

Just outside the city, a small-scale, more nature-friendly form of agriculture existed. There were no cows and their associated ryegrass deserts, nor was the scent of the air tainted with their slurry. Instead, the land was dotted with smallholdings that grew artichokes, grapes, carrots, lemons, broccoli, and just about every other type of fruit and veg that can grow under the ever-glowing Mediterranean sun. These plots were what some would consider 'messy' but, to nature, this is the essence of life. The beautiful entanglement of wildflowers and trees scattered amongst the holdings gave life to a complex web of insects, birds and an ecosystem that harmonises with our need to grow food. This balance between nature and agriculture is something that has become increasingly rare in the world, particularly so in my home county of Cork, where the intensive dairy industry – that has sucked so much life out of the Irish landscape – is at its most extreme. I do not say this with a desire to finger-point and blame. I say this out of the sadness I suffer for the wildlife we have lost. I have met many farmers who care very much about nature and their lands that they know so intimately, but for them to get by and make a living in Ireland, they often need to operate in a way that is inharmonious with nature. Of course, there are also farmers out there who simply don't care about nature.

Our desire for tidiness in the world around us also has a lot to answer for. Tidiness in nature is not transmissive to a thriving, vibrant ecosystem, yet it is something we as humans crave and seem to inflict on every plot of land we lay our feet upon. Weedkiller, chainsaws, hedge-trimmers and leaf-blowers are some of the tools of our never-ending quest for straight lines and sterility in Ireland. But in Catalunya, I didn't see that same level of desire for 'tidiness'. It was a breath of fresh air to walk through the streets here – with wildflower-filled verges and unruly nature in cracks and crevices amidst the concrete and tarmac. Beyond the city limits, the agricultural zone of El Prat was far removed from the industrial cow-grazed landscape that was all-too-familiar to me from home.

Life with Alba's parents was a little awkward for me. They spoke no English, and I was too embarrassed to speak the little Spanish I had. Catalan was just a pipe dream. We communicated through pointing, facial expressions and gestures. It made me feel a little bit like a caveman. I knew I had to learn a functional language if I were to get by in any capacity and so I chose to work on my Spanish, because at least I had a basic level that I could expand upon. But I also had another language to learn, one which to me was far more important than any human language. This was the language of the land – that of the birds, the trees and all else that made up the wilder parts of the terrain. To address this meant an immersion in nature that came naturally to me. And because we had savings, and because Alba knew I needed to work on my Catalan fieldcraft skills to get work in ornithology, this time spent in nature was an allowable investment. To me, it was a green card to let myself loose in nature, free from the worries of the world – but it was also a necessary education to get me up to speed with my new surroundings.

Alba found work very quickly – she was on her home turf and could converse in all of the relevant languages, now including English, which was a great asset to her. English is a highly sought-after language in Catalunya, where many, especially the younger citizens, speak it to some extent, and thus English-language classes and schools are highly regarded.

Each morning, we would rise at dawn together. Alba would prepare to teach health and safety classes, sometimes in English, and I would prepare for an education in nature. We'd eat breakfast together, often with Alba's parents. A variety of olives were a given, as was freshly squeezed orange juice, with the fruit sourced directly from a towering tree that drooped over their dry earthen yard, laden with the weight of its jumbo-sized loads. This tree provided welcome shade to the back garden, and was also home to a resident blackbird, which sang proudly from its peak every morning. The olives and juice were accompanied by rustic, locally sourced bread. Free-range eggs from the local market were whipped into an omelette, sometimes set with local artichokes. The diet here was much better than what I'd given myself back home – usually a bowl of sugary cereal and milk, with some highly processed bread.

After this nourishing start, I would walk Alba to her workplace. Her parents' heavy front door opened out to a bright blue sky – the cool shade of the marble-floored hallway would be flooded with an intense light that my squinting Irish eyes were not accustomed to. The power of the light always surprised me. This wonderful sun combined with the comforting warm air put an instant smile on my face – Alba's too. A kiss and a hug, and we would go our separate ways for the day.

Not yet driving for fear of a shift of sides in steering wheels and lanes, I'd walk to my new learning grounds – Delta del Llobregat. This is a wonderful urban nature reserve, built in mitigation for the construction of Barcelona airport. This nature-filled oasis lies between the hectic airport to one side, and the equally busy sprawl of the Barcelona port to the other. It is separated by the Llobregat River, to which it owes its name. To me, this was the only delta, and so this is what I affectionately called it: The Delta. These words were spoken from my mouth many times every day, and still are. The Delta is home to almost 20 natural habitats, including but not limited to coastal lagoons, Mediterranean salt meadows, wooded dunes with pine and Mediterranean tall humid grasslands. It is designated as a Special Protection Area, a Site of Community Importance and a Special Area of Conservation under the combined Birds and Habitats Directives (Nature Directives). An impressive total of 113 bird species protected under the Nature Directives are found in the Delta.

With this impressive resumé, the Delta was a no-brainer for me – to update my crafts and become familiar with the flora and fauna of Catalunya. Each morning, I would arrive at the gates to the reserve just as they opened – donned in shorts and a T-shirt, with my camera over my shoulder and my binoculars around my neck. But most importantly, I was lathered in suncream like any pale, freckle-skinned Irishman should be, if he knows what's good for him. Alba told me of a nickname locals gave us sun-naive holiday-makers: Gambes! This translates as 'prawns', and the meaning is self-explanatory.

Just like I have always done, I formed a methodical routine I would follow every day, built around my essential visits to the Delta. Each morning began with a sun-blushed dawn chorus that contained many new voices unfamiliar to my Irish-trained ear. I knew these were the voices of my new neighbours and I was desperate to become acquainted with them. I was electrified by the challenges of my new surroundings. I didn't go anywhere without my camera. Anything that moved was snapped. But what about the unknown melodies? How could I have a chance to figure out the many mystery sounds that occurred all around me? I found a second-hand Olympus LS-12 on eBay for €90, a rather basic, entry-level sound-recorder that was about the size of the old Nokia 3210 and comfortably sat into my pocket. I took it everywhere with me but it frustrated me greatly. Anything I recorded sounded crackly and unclear – sometimes the bird was barely audible amidst the noise. Disappointed with my new tool, I ditched it on the top of my wardrobe to gather dust. It didn't stop my daily ventures out to the Delta, though.

I was adamant to learn in whatever way worked. I'd slowly weave through the dusty tracks, senses heightened and reserved for nature alone. At the peak of summer, a plane bellowed overhead every sixty seconds, but, with time, I learned to block them out. I did not see or hear them, despite them rocketing feet above me, leaving a trail of swirling dust and a violent swishing of foliage as they rudely cut through the Delta airspace. I moved slowly – chameleon-like, turning my eyes from a static head. I frequently encountered Sardinian warblers. Although ubiquitous throughout Catalunya, they had a certain charm about them, and they made you work to see them in full glory. This only made me appreciate them all the more. Broken glimpses of slate-grey bodies skulking through the undergrowth were often all they'd reveal.

To those willing to give time and patience, they'd eventually give up their secrets. But not for long. A striking black-as-night hooded face with a blood-red eye-ring sent my pulse racing. Exquisite, simplistic beauty – the best kind of beauty. They proclaim their place with authority and confidence: a deafening burst of fast, piercing rattles, enough to make you jump if caught by surprise. Often this sound was the only indication of their presence, but it was enough to let me know I was in good company.

The trails would lead me slowly down to the wooden bird huts that overlooked the marshes, where I'd sit for hours and just allow nature to unfurl around me.

One morning during the peak of spring migration, I was sitting looking out over one of the marshes, having a break and taking some shelter from the sweltering heat outside. I wasn't focusing too much on anything in particular. I was just looking out through the opening of the wooden hide, watching birds come and go, often with raised eyebrows, and a fixed, wide-eyed, half-focused gaze. Thoughts floated through my mind, just like the birds who were feeding vigorously over the water, fuelling up for their continued northbound migrations.

An unfamiliar sound began to drift through to my ears. I snapped into life, taking a sudden sharp inhalation of breath and focusing my eyes. My curiosity was piqued. It seemed to come from above. It drifted closer and closer – a swift and quirky 'kah-wek'. It repeated itself, again and again. I looked up and saw what was either a small gull or a tern. I locked eyes on it just as it circled a few times and began to descend, having seen the water below.

It was clearly another migrant taking a moment for some opportunistic feeding. I followed it down to water level with the naked eye and lifted my binoculars. I was overcome with emotion. It *was* a tern, but not just *any* tern. I saw this as a blessing. Life had turned around and Catalunya was meant to be. I was looking at a gull-billed tern. I didn't get to see it with the nurse at Womanagh Bridge, but my time had finally come. I sat there beaming as I watched its white wings with stunning black cap and bill float with grace over the water. I almost never saw this bird. In fact, I almost never saw any bird again. It made me realise how lucky I was to be here. Over a period of months, I was soon fluent in Catalan birdlife, but regular life needed some work.

Sardinian Warbler (*Curruca melanocephala*)
Family *Sylviidae ('typical warblers' and a number of babblers)*
Conservation status *Least Concern (IUCN Red List) – does not occur on the BoCCI list, as it is a rare vagrant*
Vocalisations *A very loud, slowed-down rattle 'TCHE-TCHE-TCHE-TCHE-TCHE'.*

When I wasn't wandering in nature, I was in the local library studying Spanish, brushing up on what little I remembered from my school days. Languages were never my forte, at least not the human kind. Several months into my stay, I felt like I had enough basic Spanish .to start applying for jobs. I'd never get by in a job that required conversational Spanish, and so I decided the most sensible thing to do would be to teach English, though the thought of doing that terrified me.

Throughout school, my biggest fear was having to stand up in front of the class to read out passages. I'd sweat profusely, shaking from head to toe with nerves. Even my larynx would tremor, resulting in an output not too unlike a deranged sheep. The nerves had the additional unfortunate effect of making me erupt into nervous, even hysterical, laughter. This unintentional spectacle meant that my classmates enjoyed my stand-up scenes, which made me even more nervous.

I tackled this fear head-on when I started teaching. It wasn't easy, not by any means. Those unfortunate symptoms were still present, bar the maniacal laughing, thankfully. But we humans are very adaptable – we're survivors. I needed to do this – to earn money, to have a routine and to maintain my self-respect. The first weeks were tough; not only did my highly introverted self have to perform and make the classes fun, but I also had to lead and gain the trust and respect of my students. I began to make slideshows and I imagined how I'd feel if I were in the seat looking and listening to me. I get bored and distracted so easily, and so I designed my classes for who would undoubtedly be my toughest student – Seán Ronayne! My slideshows changed from plain, text-filled images of rules, examples and general boredom to humorous, demonstrative, photo-filled screens with fun animations, bright colours and simplified summary texts. I added in role-play games, online quizzes, and had the students teach one another. Amazingly I began to enjoy my classes to some degree, or at least I learned to survive and do things to the best of my abilities.

Kids were much tougher students than adults and, at times, they really broke my spirit. On my worst days, I would curse myself in my mind as I looked out at the class, asking myself what I was doing with my life. On those bad days, I perceived them as mischievous little imps who set out to make my day as bad as they possibly could. I felt like a washed-up loser. Why wasn't I out in nature finding a way to work with what I loved so dearly, instead of sitting in front of a class of kids whose sole intention seemed to be to ignore and torment me? This, in turn, would spur me on to go to the library to try to improve my Spanish and Catalan – I knew this would be key to my escape back into a career in nature.

As has always been the case, I shared every shred of my nature learnings with Alba, but Alba opened up my eyes to her wonderful Catalan culture, and I truly fell in love with that, too. Catalan folk, in my eyes, are a highly admirable, liberal, peaceful, community-based and grounded people. They're warm and open, and are there to make the best of and share life together in unison. They're also extremely inviting and caring – I was never once made to feel like an outsider there. My people, the ornithologists, took me right in under their wings. They shared their great knowledge with me, revealing locations of birds that had taken them many years to find. They switched languages and spoke to me in English, no matter what their level. They invited me to their events and took me to various training sessions. This is just who they are – and what a great way to move through the world that is.

When I first met Alba, embarrassingly, I didn't even know that Catalan was a distinct language in its own right. In fact, in my ignorance, I thought it was a dialect of Spanish. I wasn't long being corrected. Whilst Catalan shares many words and verbs with Spanish, it is most closely related to Occitan – an ancient Romance language found in the south of France and southern Italy. Catalan also has direct ties to Portuguese and Romanian. Compared to Spanish, Catalan has a much greater and more complex verbal conjugation system, and has also retained more of its links to Latin. The first giveaway of a Catalan approaching is the greeting '*Bon dia*'. The Spanish equivalent is '*Buenos días*', and is, to my ear at least, said in a sharper tone.

Catalan people are also still very much connected to nature and have a kind and compassionate outlook on the other species we share the world with. As a standout example, Catalunya became one of few communities in Spain to ban the horrendously cruel tradition of bullfighting, by vote in the Catalan Parliament in July 2010. Catalan people are also very attuned to the land and what it has to offer based on its seasons. Mushroom and asparagus picking, chestnut and pine-nut gathering, hiking, cycling and so many more activities requiring an understanding of the land are carried out by the Catalan people year-round, which demonstrates a strong, widespread connection to nature that I find really beautiful. Even more warming is the fact that these activities are both family- and community-oriented.

I had the joy of collecting and roasting chestnuts with Alba and her niece in the forested foothills of the Pyrenees during my first autumn there. It was pure, unadulterated joy. The shaded woodland floor was strewn in a carpet of chestnuts, with scattered groups of friends and families crouched, gathering, chatting, singing and laughing. This simple activity provides a true connection to nature and temporarily brings us back to a time when we read the land as well as we did the watches on our wrists or, indeed, the phones in our pockets. Collecting chestnuts is raw, rewarding and honest, and awakens all of our dormant senses – dulled and dampened by the modern comforts of the Anthropocene.

Kneeling down in the humus, the cool, wet leaves and soil envelop the hands and the skin is gently prickled by the chestnut's spiky, protective, outer shell. Dirt gathers under the nails and stands as a reminder of this direct hand-to-soil interaction – a long-lost pairing for most. The air carries the scent of the soil beneath us, a comforting earthy, loamy, musty cocktail of organic riches that nurtured the very sweet chestnuts it gifted us. Above in the autumnal canopy, wizened leaves just about hold on for one last dance. A dappled orange-red light, like that which shines through a great stained-glass window, throws a mellow, ripened shade upon our hands, as jays chat and screech from the treetops high above. In my mind, they represent the choir singing from the chancel. This here is *my* church – nature in all of its serendipitous glory. Up there, they too are taking advantage of and caching the chestnuts, and in this time and place I felt no different to these jays – we were both there as bonding family units, interacting and gathering food provided by Mother Nature. We have chestnuts on our forest floors in Ireland, too, but there they lie unknown and forgotten, rotting and unattended – too many for the jays to take.

Nature Boy

Aside from a change of scenery and a new adventure, another reason we moved back to Catalunya was for Alba to return to education. Although she already had a collection of degrees and master's and over 13 years' experience as a physiotherapist, she decided she'd love to pursue a career in education, and for this she'd need another master's. So, whilst I learned all about the flora and fauna of Catalunya, Alba was working hard on her own studies. Towards the end of the course, she and her classmates undertook internships, where they were placed in a school to teach for one month.

One morning, Alba's class received a visit from a representative of L'Associació Asperger Catalunya – the Asperger's Society of Catalunya – and Alba's jaw hit the floor. All of the traits they described were familiar to her. That evening the hall door swung open and Alba rushed in, beckoning me to sit down.

'Seán, I need you to listen to me. Today, we had a visit from the Asperger's Society of Catalunya. It was so interesting, but almost everything they said described *you!* Seán, I think you are autistic.'

I was shocked, but quickly became fully alert. 'What did you say?'

Alba, again with an unbroken gaze and a reassuring smile said, 'Babe, I think you're on the spectrum.'

I heard it correctly, but I still couldn't quite take in what she was saying. 'Are you sure? Why do you think that I was described?'

She rattled off a list of traits they quoted to her. 'Okay, tell me this isn't you: an obsession with distinct topics, a necessity for routine, extreme sensitivity to noise and touch, an eye for intricate detail, a literal interpretation of almost everything, a deep disdain for eye contact ...'

I stopped her there, taken aback, shook, even. 'Wow! That really does sound like me, doesn't it?'

Wide-eyed and a bit overwhelmed, I sat down in front of my laptop. I pulled up an online Autism Spectrum Disorder (ASD) test, and had Alba sit next to me. I had to shake myself into focus, and I took the test as honestly as I could. I asked Alba not to answer for me just so I could be sure of the results. If anything, I subconsciously softened the answers that sounded like they may have pointed to ASD. I answered fifty specific questions, each with five answer options that went on a scale from strongly agree to strongly disagree. My heart raced as I read each question, each reminding me of a quirk in my life that, until now, I had found so difficult to put into words. All of the questions resonated with me. I scanned through them carefully and really thought about my answers.

- 'I prefer to do things on my own rather than with others.' – strongly agree!
- 'I notice patterns in things all the time.' – strongly agree!
- 'When I become interested in something, my interest is often intense, strong and deep.' – strongly agree!
- 'I often notice small sounds when others do not.' – strongly agree!
- 'I like to collect information about categories of things (e.g. types of cars, birds, trains, plants).' – strongly agree!
- 'I find it challenging to make small talk or engage in casual conversations.' – strongly agree!
- 'I tend to take things literally and have difficulty understanding sarcasm or humour.' – strongly agree!

- 'I have a strong attention to detail and notice things that others often miss.' – strongly agree!
- 'I find it challenging to navigate and understand social dynamics in groups.' – strongly agree!
- 'I have a tendency to hyperfocus on specific tasks or activities.' – strongly agree!
- 'I tend to have difficulty understanding social cues and norms.' – strongly agree!

As I went through the test, tears began to well up and blur my vision. Not one to typically show or express emotion, I tried to hide it, but I knew Alba was watching me. She gently placed her hand on my back to give me reassurance and support. I couldn't hold it in any longer. The tears broke through and began to stream down my cheeks. I wasn't sad at all, though. I finally felt both understood and enlightened. This really *was* me.

Everything made so much sense and I suddenly felt like I belonged in the world. I broke down into an uncontrollable sobbing mess, collapsing into Alba's embrace. I cried myself dry and sat up – red-eyed and dazed. I just stared at the wall in a trance, until Alba beckoned me.

'Come on, babe – it's okay, just finish the test. You're almost there.'

A few more questions and I hit 'submit'. After what seemed like an eternity of virtual processing, there it was in black and white: 'High probability of ASD – it is advisory that you seek professional medical advice.'

Right there and then, Alba sent an email to L'Associació Asperger Catalunya asking them to start the process of a professional diagnosis, but in English. The whole process was made so easy by a wonderful, caring specialist by the name of Dani. I paid him several visits, each time conducting a number of highly detailed tests, activities and interviews. He never gave anything away, despite me asking if he thought I was autistic. He told me he thought he knew the answer, but would prefer to see the process through to completion before he gave me his opinion.

I remember the day I received my result. I was away with Alba visiting a beautiful rustic village in the foothills of the Pyrenees. I saw the email notification appear from Dani, and I asked Alba to read it. I was so scared. What if the result is negative? Does that mean I am just a weird guy who doesn't fit in? To read all of these familiar traits and knowing that there is a reason behind it really comforted me – it gave me answers, it enabled me to 'forgive' myself, in a sense. So the thought of not having that logic, that clarity behind it all, it terrified me. Who would I be then? Where would those answers be?

Alba began to read snippets aloud.

- 'He shows socially unmodulated eye contact.'
- 'Social initiations with a certain degree of inadequacy, not so much in the speech content, but rather due to a lack of coordination between his speech, gaze and gestures. Difficulties are detected to spontaneously offer information about his thoughts, feelings or experiences.'

- 'Responds appropriately to examiner comments but he's not always consistent in spontaneously asking for information about them. Limited reciprocity. It does not allow the conversation to continue smoothly.'
- 'Low social interest is detected.'
- 'Theory of mind impairments are observed (a struggle to see phenomena from any perspective other than your own).'
- 'Repetitive behaviour patterns and restricted interests are observed.'

Alba took a long pause, followed by a deep breath. She looked up and finished her reading. 'The diagnostic conclusion, having administered appropriate tests and based on clinical observation, points to an Autism Spectrum Disorder.'

Wow. I simply cannot describe how comforting those words were. I instantly felt a huge weight lift off my shoulders – a weight that I had carried for so long, but didn't know existed until the moment it was gone. I floated in its absence having learned to bow under its mass, all these years. The following months were a journey of understanding, of forgiving, and of embracing. I was proud of who I was – I didn't shy away from the diagnosis. Not one bit. Nothing in me had changed – I just understood myself more now.

I began to recall moments from my past that now made sense. I could make my peace with them and move on. When I was very young, I had a military routine that began each night and prepared me for the morning ahead. I remember it so vividly because I carried out those same steps thousands of times. I would first lay down a small towel on the ground, just outside the shower. The large towel lay there next to it. My school uniform, socks and jocks lay on the corner of the bath. My deodorant, hairbrush and hairdryer were laid out on my side cabinet. My cereal was poured into a bowl in the kitchen and aligned on a placemat. The spoon was sat inside the bowl, ready to get to work at the point of milk being poured in the morning. My bag was packed and sat at the front door. Everything *had* to be put in its place, and if someone interfered with it, I'd hit the roof. This structure and routine has been present throughout my life and still is to this day. I also still get very upset or anxious if someone or something breaks my rituals. This is a very common trait of us with ASD.

I thought back to my difficulties making and maintaining friendships throughout my life – I now understood why. All of that acting the clown in school was my reaction to a world where I didn't feel I belonged. I was bored and out of place, and so I tried to entertain myself and to make others laugh. Animals, wild and domesticated, are well recognised for their ability to calm people. And for people with ASD, they are widely used as a therapeutic tool, and for good reason. Animals are far less complex and don't judge us like people do. They don't hold grudges if we mess up either. I think that those of us with ASD seek animals out due to this lack of complexity.

I'd feel so uncomfortable at dinner events, even well into adulthood. (I still do.) I didn't know where to direct my gaze or how to engage in small talk. I'd put on a brave face until I was totally numbed, no longer able to pretend. I'd eventually have to make an excuse to leave and take a gasp of air, and if the hosts had a cat or a dog I'd go rub them. This is what resulted in me being called Nature Boy. I sought out the company of my animal friends where and whenever I could. I knew and understood them with ease compared to my complex human conspecifics.

But then I thought about my sensitivity to sound. Yes, the noise of our modern world pained me, but my sensitive ear was also highly attuned to the intricate complexities of the many sounds of nature. My extremes of hyperfocus and prolonged attention to detail – both common interconnected traits of ASD – meant I could take on a topic of interest and give it my all. This was a positive for me; I love the passion and excitement I get for the topics I'm interested in.

Looking back at the stories of my life in this context was an enlightening and self-forgiving process. I wasn't the odd, unlikeable guy I had sadly accepted I must have been. I just wasn't as good at socialising as others were. And now that I knew this, I also knew that I could work on it. It doesn't come naturally, but I could still figure it out. I smiled and gave myself an internal hug.

Then, there was the eye contact – something that bothers me to this day. I laughed at my awkward encounters with dates over the years, and Alba reminded me of her own experience of it on the receiving end. 'Well, Seán, I thought it was a bit strange for sure. But I knew that you were a kind and loving man, and so I just accepted it as a quirk of yours.'

Again, I thought of my sensitivity to loud or unwanted noises, and my fight-or-flight reactions. How I would black out with anger when my neighbour persistently blared his bass through his home cinema system mounted on our shared dividing wall. While it's certainly true that this guy was an inconsiderate narcissist, my extreme anxiety and stress caused by this was now much more explainable. It really annoyed Alba too, a neurotypical, so my neighbour isn't off the hook because of my sensitivity. But my experience was one of *extreme* distress. It made my life a living hell. On the other hand, though, this aural sensitivity combined with an attention to intricate details also made sense for another reason! I now knew why I was drawn to the sounds of the birds from my days in the pram, and why, once again, I found myself mesmerised and immersed in the world of bird sound and all of its finite details.

My life and my being all began to make sense now, and although there are many everyday challenges associated with ASD, I understood that there were also many positives: hyperfocus, extreme awareness of fine details and, in my case, my sensitivity to sound would stand to me in a way that would alter my life path in an inexplicably great way. It would lead to a career I lived for and truly loved.

Some weeks down the line, I began to share my diagnosis with friends, family, acquaintances and even non-acquaintances. The reactions were largely supportive, but some really stuck it to me in a totally unintentional way, and all for the same reason, more or less. Many people said something to me that really bothered me, most likely in an effort to relate to me or to make me feel less bad about the diagnosis. What they said seems benign at first, but to people like us, it isn't at all. They simply said, 'Ah sure look, we're all a bit on the spectrum, I wouldn't worry about it.' This would be followed by a one-off experience like: 'Sure I hate people eating loudly myself' or 'Sure, I have to have a routine or structure in everything I do myself'. All this actually does is denounce us autists and dilutes our experiences of this condition to a little thing that we all suffer from to some degree. And this is not the case at all. Autism can be extremely debilitating to those farther along on the spectrum. To those of us lower down on it, our lives are still very difficult, living in a world made for 'normal' people.

I thought about a metaphor for this outlook on Asperger's and it goes as follows. If you wake up in the morning and you have nausea, are you a little bit pregnant? If you find yourself with swollen ankles, would you put yourself on the pregnancy spectrum? Of course not. Likewise, having one, or even multiple autistic-like behaviours does not put you on the autism spectrum. It takes more than a few quirks to warrant a diagnosis. Those with a medical diagnosis have *many* recognised ASD traits that, together, interfere with an ability to lead a 'normal' life. So please, although I'm sure you mean well, the next time you speak to someone with an ASD diagnosis, do not try to relate to them by saying, 'We are all a little bit autistic.' Because we aren't. The spectrum does not begin at zero, and we are not all on that spectrum. Telling us that we are all a little bit on the spectrum is just (unintentionally) dismissive and belittles us as people.

Not long after this great revelation, something happened that symbolised it all, at least in my mind. I was driving up the Pyrenees with Alba for a mixed day of hiking and birding. As Alba's trusty Peugeot 206 chugged along the dirt tracks that wound through the evergreen forests and into the open rocky peaks, a shadow was cast upon our faces. Unsure of the source, we both turned to see one of the most majestic raptors of all – the mythical lammergeier. Lammergeiers are the most flamboyant and strangest of the Catalan vultures, with their diet of bones with jelly-like marrow interiors. Boasting a nine-foot wingspan, they have a black and rusty-tinged plumage, complete with two black plumes that hang above the beak, making them look like something from another world. I watched it as it soared effortlessly alongside us, looking confident and at home in nature. It was where it was meant to be. I smiled and knew I was at home too. I *was* Nature Boy and I had no shame in it.

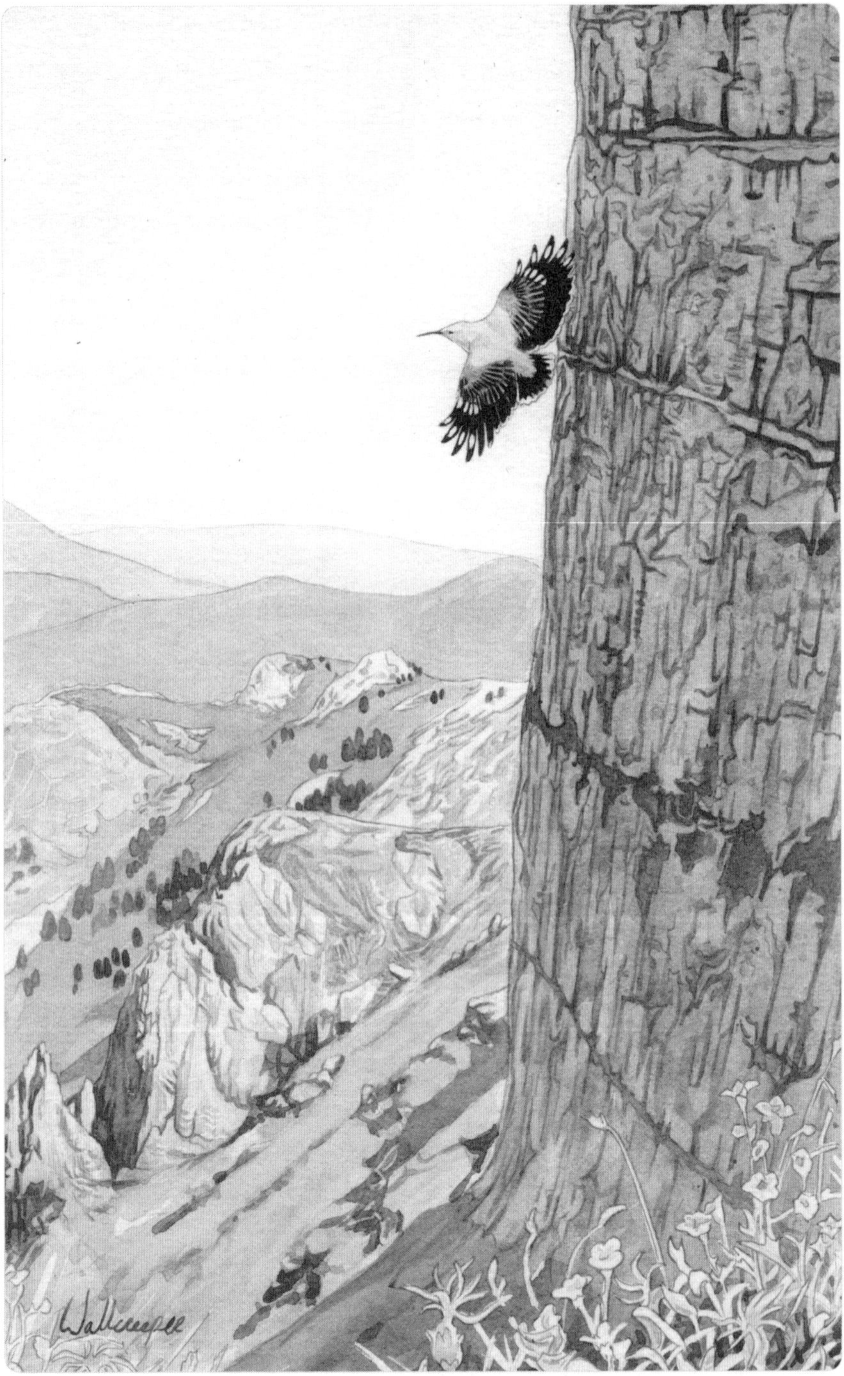
Wallcreeper

Chapter 10

THE NEXT TALE FROM MY NEW LIFE WAS ONE OF THE MOST pivotal moments so far. I got wind of a very interesting talk to be given in September 2019 by Magnus Robb, the wildlife sound-recordist and composer, at the Ebro Delta Birding Festival. This national park, some two hours south of Barcelona, is famed for its paella rice, which is grown in a vast expanse of freshwater lagoons. This is complemented by a large share of wild spaces, ranging from wetlands to salt pans to estuaries. I'd been there once before during the day, and was blown away by the sheer variety and number of birds.

Of equal importance to this story is Magnus himself. I'd heard a lot about him but never had the chance to encounter him, so it was only now that I really began to look into who he was and what he did. Magnus is a classically trained musician by vocation and has composed several works based around birds. But Magnus also had a brilliant ear for birds. Today, he works for The Sound Approach, a small team set up by Mark Constantine – one of the co-founders and CEO of the cosmetics firm Lush – to sound record the birds of the Western Palearctic as completely as possible. His scheduled talk captivated my imagination – it was going to be about the autonomous capturing of birds calling in the dark of night as they pass overhead on their nocturnal migrations. I attended his presentation amongst a packed audience in the largest marquee at the festival – and, as ever, I dragged Alba along.

Magnus had amassed a large following through his work with The Sound Approach. He had an encyclopaedic knowledge of birds and unique tales of adventure full of details and insights into bird sound, often unique or never before heard. Magnus described in almost mystical detail how he captured the sounds of masses of incredible birds in the dead of night, passing over his home in Portugal, while he himself slept soundly in his bed. He described documenting habitat-specific birds – birds he'd never expect to encounter in the region by day, which were flying and vocalising at close range at all hours of the night.

The concept that it was possible to encounter any bird from any place or habitat blew my mind. I hung on his every word and was enchanted by his tales. His reputation preceded him, and so, after the talk I approached him – a little starstruck. I needn't have been so nervous, though – he was lovely and very willing to answer my long list of questions. I asked him if he thought I could apply this technique from my land-locked balcony, surrounded by a sea of high-rise flats. Would I intercept birds in this human-made world devoid of the greenery or complex mosaic of wild habitats I'd normally seek out to go birding?

He smiled and gave me the simple answer I was hoping for, 'Oh absolutely!'

I continued, 'I only have a little Olympus LS-12 recorder – do you think this would suffice to capture birds high up in the sky?'

Again, he replied confidently, 'Oh I'm sure it would do just fine! It's certainly worth a shot. Just remember to protect it from the wind and rain.'

I could see I had interrupted him and a friend, and so I smiled and thanked him, to which he reciprocated. And the seed was set. I gave Alba a wide-eyed vacant look. She smiled and rolled her eyes. She knew that look. This was the start of a new, relentless obsession that I'd eat, sleep and dream.

Upon our return to El Prat, I wasted no time. The thought of intercepting this nocturnal world over our very own flat was burning in my brain for the entire journey home. I opened the car door, ran upstairs and went straight to the kitchen. Alba left me to it – she knew I was in another universe.

And so, with my trusty Olympus LS-12 sealed inside a Pyrex jug using clingfilm and an elastic band, I took my first steps on my sound-recording journey. After the first few months living with Alba's parents, we had moved into our own apartment on a busy street in a densely populated area of El Prat de Llobregat. I set up my 'high-tech' recording system outside that evening at sunset, on our tiny little concrete-locked balcony. I pointed it to the sky, pressed record, closed the door behind me and hoped for the best.

The next morning, I had to dive deeper, but listening to a ten-hour recording would be impossible, so I used sound-editing software called Audacity and taught myself how to identify the *shapes* of bird calls by looking at spectrograms. A visual representation of the calls that I could scan quickly was much more efficient, and I could stop and listen to the recordings when I saw a shape of interest.

Each bird species has a unique shape or series of shapes that represent their calls. Often birds flying at night have vocalisations associated with these nocturnal flights. This is what I was seeking out. These calls are usually renditions of calls they give during the day but, heard out of context, they can throw the listener. Some calls can be given rarely during the day but used widely at night, meaning most people will not be familiar with them.

The nocturnal confusion pair of whimbrel and little grebe are a classic case in point. Whimbrel is a large wader of the Scolopacidae family, closely related to the curlew. Its typical flight call, and indeed its nocturnal flight call, is a series of whistles given in quick succession at the same frequency: 'pi-pi-pi-pi-pi'. Now take little grebe, it is in no way closely related to whimbrel at all. It's a small member of the Podicipedidae family and spends its life on lakes and ponds where it dives underwater for fish and aquatic invertebrates. Nobody would ever mistake these two by day but, by night, they fool many. Little grebe uses a nocturnal flight call very similar to whimbrel, only that it begins with a few isolated 'pip' notes, followed by a flurry of slightly descending 'pi-pi-pi-pi-pi' notes. When you really break it down, it's clear which of the two you are listening to. But starting out, before you become accustomed to listening to and seeing the fine details, they can easily catch you out.

It was when viewing these spectrograms that the world of sound changed for me: I identified two black-crowned night herons uttering their dog-like explosive 'kwark' calls as they navigated their way over the city lights, migrating south to spend their winters in the wetlands of Africa.

Black-crowned Night Heron *(Nycticorax nycticorax)*
Family *Ardeidae (herons, egrets and bitterns)*
Conservation status *Least Concern (IUCN Red List) – does not occur on the BoCCI list, as it is a rare vagrant*
Vocalisations *Flight call a husky, terrier like 'kwark'.*

After telling Alba the good news, I went to my fellow birders in the 'Nocmig Catalunya' WhatsApp group – 'nocmig' is the term used for the study of nocturnal migration of birds. What our group lacked in size it made up for in enthusiasm – they all went wild. Every morning, we would update each other on the bizarre and unexpected birds that revealed themselves over our roofs each night – purple herons, great spotted cuckoos, black-winged stilts and, amazingly, a crazy recording of a vagrant yellow-browed warbler pushed west from Siberia. My claustrophobic balcony had turned into a window into the incredible world of nocturnal migration, where birds streamed overhead at night, sometimes in their thousands.

I'd caught the bug, so I upgraded my second-hand recorder and Pyrex jug for a Dodotronic parabolic reflector. With my parabola, I could reach farther into the night sky and capture the vocalisations of even more nocturnal migrants. The surprises kept coming – curlew sandpipers, little bitterns, purple swamphens, all wetland species so out of context in the urban jungle. The seed of obsession was firmly planted.

European Bee-eater *(Merops apiaster)*
Family *Meropidae (bee-eaters)*
Conservation status Least Concern (IUCN Red List) – does not occur on the BoCCI list, as it is a rare vagrant
Vocalisations *Flight call a charming, fluttering 'prrioop', often given in quick succession.*

I threw myself into hours upon hours of analysis, scanning the spectrograms and learning to identify each new sound by sight. Having come to a point of understanding of my ASD, as well as venturing on a new path to deal with and better manage its negatives, I was also wholly embracing its positives. Mainly my hyperfocus, my deep obsession with specific topics, my sensitivity to sound and my mind for intricate details. All of these could be combined to provide me with a genuine superpower. If I could harness these to work on something I truly loved, I felt I could be unstoppable. And so my journey into bird sounds really began.

Having now become unreservedly hooked on capturing the sounds of the mysterious world of nocturnal migration, I decided to take a more hands-on approach in seeking out the sounds of Catalan birds in the flesh. This would thankfully extend my adventures beyond my little balcony and bring me to the truly magnificent, unspoiled wild spaces of Catalunya. I began to record as many species as I could find, but I set myself the ultimate challenge – to sound record one of the most elusive and sought-after birds of all in Catalunya: the mythical wallcreeper.

Wallcreepers are best searched for in the winter. During the breeding season, they spend their time at the very tops of the

Pyrenees in steep, rocky, often inaccessible terrain, where they are like a needle in a haystack. No right-minded person seeks them out up there – it's a virtually impossible task. During the winter, however, they descend to lower ground and seek out habitats that reflect the towering peaks of their breeding grounds. During the months of October through to April, they are best searched for in low-lying cliffs, cathedrals, monasteries, large bridges, dams and just about anything else that resembles their steep, rocky summering grounds. Because these locations are much more confined in space compared to the peaks of the Pyrenees, you stand a better chance of intercepting them. They're still a very rare bird, though, and nothing is ever guaranteed with them.

Wallcreepers are visually unmistakable: they look like a striking red, black, white and grey butterfly, with vividly intricate patterns of all four colours, especially when they spread their wings in flight. They almost look too beautiful to be true, such is the richness of their plumage. Likewise, their bills take on a very strange form for a delicate little songbird. It's unique in that it's a long, drawn-out, down-curved work of art. Its form acts as a specific tool: they use their beaks to pick out spiders and other insects from crevices in the rocky gullies and precipices of their high-altitude abodes. Their English name also describes their mannerisms to a tee – wallcreepers spend their time walking up the sheer cliff-faces upon which they feed and nest, appearing to defy the laws of physics as they ascend vertically at dizzying heights, as if it were nothing.

When creeping along these sheer rocky walls, they blend right in, lost in a sea of stone. However, when they take flight, their presence is announced by a sudden burst of red, grey, black and white – the jewels of the high Catalan Pyrenees. This image was the prize that drove me to seek them out, and so the quest to sound record this elusive phantom of the clouds began.

Wallcreeper *(Tichodroma muraria)*
Family *Tichodromidae (wallcreeper)*
Conservation status *Least Concern (IUCN Red List) – does not occur on the BoCCI list, has never occurred as a vagrant*
Vocalisations *Song is a high-pitched, plaintiff whistling that rises and falls throughout.*

Since my arrival in Catalunya, I had visited nine different wintering sites for wallcreeper, each time spending a full day searching, but to no avail. I also had my sound-recording hat on for some of those final failed visits. These failures hurt even more, but I was adamant to persist. I don't give up too easily on my obsessions. But, sometimes, things happen that are out of my control – the sudden arrival of Covid-19 was one of those moments. In fact, I was out and about on the day of the first national lockdown – 15 March 2020. I was looking for wallcreeper at a known wintering site in Huesca. I failed, of course.

Restrictions during Covid were tough in Catalunya. During lockdown, we had no right to leave our homes for exercise, except for distinct reasons – a doctor's appointment, to buy essentials or similarly pressing matters. If stopped on the street, you'd be required to prove your intention and, if you were found to be flouting the restrictions, you'd be fined on the spot. Luckily for me, I had my Nocmig to bring nature to me. I'd record from my balcony every night and escape into the nocturnal migratory flyway that crossed right over our heads.

The noise of the neighbours was a real problem for me. They were bored senseless and often partied through the night. During the day, people shouted from window to window in an effort to maintain social contact with other humans. To me, my living space became a noisy hell-hole and I struggled with it immensely. Each evening at 8 p.m., people clapped for the carers on the frontline, inspired by Clap for Our Carers in the UK. But this did not end there. What started out each evening as a nice gesture transcended into a continuous blaring of horrendous music through open windows, accompanied by relentless drinking, screaming and a general racket, often through to the early hours of the morning. Earplugs were no match for the chaos, and I was denied the only thing that healed me of my stresses and anxieties – access to nature. Thank goodness for Nocmig. Although it's no match for direct immersion in nature, it still enabled me to interact with the natural world in a limited but fascinating way. It's what kept me going. I'm not sure how I'd have coped with lockdown at all if it weren't for my nightly recordings.

One evening Alba approached me with an interesting proposal: 'Babe, I have an idea. I know you love to help animals in need, as do I. And I think we have an opportunity to make a real difference.'

Intrigued, I nodded, eager for her to continue. She smiled and carried on. 'So, there's this dog shelter in Barcelona. They have a *lot* of dogs, and because of lockdown restrictions the volunteers cannot get in. Only a small handful are permitted to travel. They're struggling, and they're looking for people to temporarily adopt until the lockdown blows—'

I interjected, 'I'm in! Let's do it!'

Alba smiled. 'I thought you'd be on board. Okay! So I was thinking, why don't we ask for the one that needs it the most. Let's ask for the oldest or sickest dog. The one that nobody wants. Let's give him or her the love they deserve.' This melted my heart. Alba is such a good person, and this idea was so beautiful. I replied with damp eyes, 'I love this idea! Let's do it!'

Fast forward several hours and there's a knock on our door. We're met with two masked volunteers and a very nervous-looking short-haired, sandy-brown, curly-tailed dog. They informed us that he was very nervous and that it would be best just to let him come to us. They gave us a quick back story. Toby had been confiscated from a squat with six other dogs, all of them much larger than him. They had been there for four years and had been beaten and starved. They'd fought for food scraps from the bin. He'd spent another four years at the shelter, stuck in a concrete, caged cell. Nobody wanted to adopt him because of his peculiar habit of tilting and wobbling his head, the result of a long-untreated ear infection – a final gift left to him by his abuser.

Toby had scars on his face and limbs, and he stood there shaking with his tail between his legs. The volunteers coaxed him in and closed the door behind him. We let him be. He stood out in the dark hallway staring in at us in the living room. He stood there shaking for one hour before he very nervously inched himself into the room. We had Dori's spare bed laid out for him, and he totally ignored it. Dori was Alba's sister's dog who we often minded during the week. Judging by the patches of concrete-worn, hairless skin on Toby's legs, we concluded he did not know what a bed was or what function it served. He eventually settled onto the cold hard tiles and slept with one eye open.

I tried my best not to interfere, but I just couldn't help myself. I lifted him onto the bed. He looked at me in shock. I very gently rubbed his head and let him be. This slow game of trust-building went on for several days until, one week in, he finally caved. It was beautiful. He just blossomed into this all-giving, sweet, loving little guy, and he became our hairy son! One of the exemptions of the lockdown was dog-walking; those with a dog were permitted to walk within 150 metres of their homes twice a day. Although this is not why we adopted him (I swear!), it was a relief to get out there, and this really helped get us through it all, too.

By the time lockdown restrictions eased, we were into summer 2020. Now that I had my freedom back, the world was my oyster. I could have gone anywhere, done anything, but the wallcreeper was still on my mind. I had unfinished business. Finding a wallcreeper in the winter had been tough – in fact, it proved to be a total failure. Now it was summer, the task was several times more difficult, but I had to try and I was up for the challenge. There are approximately 300 pairs of wallcreeper in Catalunya, and the Catalan Pyrenees, where they breed in summer, stretch over 9,430 square kilometres! Furthermore, because they seek out the highest, most inaccessible rocky cliffs, finding them in summer is enormously difficult. But the idea of taking this on actually excited me.

I didn't waste any time, and Alba, knowing how important this was to me, gave me the all-clear to head for the Pyrenees in her trusty old Peugeot 206 for the weekend. At this point, I had been driving for a while – having got used to travelling on the other side of the road with my bicycle at first. And so off I went, looking a little like Mr. Bean in my unfit-for-purpose vehicle. It did the job though – just about.

A few Catalan friends tipped me off as to where I could start my unlikely-to-end-well quest. Because of the sensitivity of the species, I will not allude to any specific locations. On the first day, I didn't head directly to those suggested places but instead just took in the fresh air and the magical nature of the Pyrenees – it being my first real venture outdoors since lockdown began. I just soaked up all of the familiar birds and spent some time with them.

I climbed to the peak with parabola in hand and recorded many interesting sounds. A big surprise were a series of mimetic skylarks, a member of the lark family that also occurs in Ireland. Because skylarks nest on open ground, they don't typically have tall trees to sing from, so instead they fly high in the sky and spread their song far and wide. I knew they were capable of mimicry, but these birds were imitating the sounds of something quite unexpected to me – marmots! This whole little subpopulation all included marmot mimicry in their song, I guess it shouldn't be such a surprise, as they're widespread up there themselves, and very vocal, too. Their call is a piercing, repetitive chirp, which sounds like it's coming from a monstrous bird!

In hindsight, my decision to walk to the peak on my first day wasn't a great one. Especially seeing as I continued to a second peak right after, and did so off-track for the entirety of the journey. Hours later, I found myself back at the car, totally exhausted and limping from the overzealous hiking of the day. To top that off I took a wrong turn en route to my overnight parking location. My intention was to park at the base of the route I would take up to my potential wallcreeper spot the following morning. I had planned to arrive there at 5 p.m., but ended up four hours behind schedule!

When I arrived, I was jaded and desperate for sleep, especially knowing the climb I had ahead of me in the morning. And trying to sleep in a Peugeot 206 as a 6 foot 2 inch human was not at all pleasant. I tried my best to get some kind of sleep, but it was near impossible. I had a crick in my neck and just about every muscle in my body was screaming out in discomfort. I watched the clock and got up as soon as the light would allow. So at 5.30 a.m., I rose from the car – shattered.

I set off right away and, instead of following any tracks or routes, pointed myself in the direction I needed to go and just started walking up. This was a bad idea. The terrain was relentless, and I was often met with impassable barriers – large gullies or dense thickets that I needed to go around and re-route. This was my mistake for going Rambo. My next big error was not bringing any water with me. Although the day started out fresh, the sun soon picked up and it began to swelter. On previous hikes, I'd always find streams or pools to drink from, and I assumed this would be the case here too. It turned out it wasn't. So I ended up becoming genuinely dehydrated. And to make things worse, after climbing up approximately 2,000 metres, I realised I had, somewhere along the line, taken a massive detour in the wrong direction, downhill, into a forest. This added about two to three unnecessary hours onto my already exhausting climb.

I ended up becoming so dehydrated and thirsty that, for the first time in my life, I feared for my safety as a result of a lack of water in my system. I began to become very dizzy, at times feeling like I was on the point of blacking out. I eventually found a tiny little muddy puddle, and in my desperation I knelt down and licked it entirely dry, taking some sloppy muck in too. It didn't taste good, nor did it quench my thirst. In fact, I think it made me feel worse.

This was the point where I really thought to myself, *If I don't find some water somehow, I could be in real trouble here.*

I continued weakly along the path until I saw the cables and buildings of a ski resort ahead. Now that the snow had melted, it was closed for business, but I pushed on up there anyway. I was so lucky that there were workers there doing some routine maintenance. I made a beeline for them, and I'm sure they thought I was some kind of crazed idiot. (And, on reflection, maybe I was.) I was absolutely battered from my misadventure – covered in bloody scratches, hair drenched in sweat and my face as red as a tomato. I ran towards them limping and waving my arms like a dishevelled madman who had crawled out of a bush.

When I finally got close enough to speak, my oral cavity was so dry that my tongue stuck to the roof of my mouth, and I just couldn't get any coherent words out, and so I just submitted to whispering out 'Aiguaaa' ('Waterrr'). They all looked at each other without speaking, but their faces said it all – they couldn't quite believe what they were seeing and hearing. I honestly think they didn't know whether I was playing a prank or on the verge of keeling over. Without saying a word, and with a look of concern, one of the men disappeared to a back room. He returned with a two-litre bottle of ice-cool water and told me to take it away, probably fearing for their safety!

I was so thirsty I grabbed it out of his hands and immediately began to chug from it like a maniac, spilling it all over my face and neck in the process. They looked at me once more with utmost concern, and slipped back into the building. I drank almost the entirety of the bottle in twenty seconds, and then tried to ration the last cupful for the journey downhill to the car, limping all the way. Towards the final leg of the trek down, my mouth began to dry once again and my dizziness returned, this time accompanied by nausea. I did make it, thankfully, and I submitted to going back home defeated, a day early. But I went home a wiser man – for the next trip I knew where *not* to go and I knew what *not* to do!

The following weekend, I returned with some better route-planning and several bottles of water. This time, I took a different route. It was tough, but I knew where I was going and I kept myself well hydrated.

An hour or so in, I reached a suitable wallcreeper habitat within the zone that was recommended to me. I sat and began to watch this sheer cliff-face. It was vast and I just knew the odds were stacked against me. I sat there for about three hours, scanning the immense walls of rocky wallcreeper habitat, and I saw nothing. At this point, I was feeling like my wallcreeper mission was just not meant to be, and so I decided to return to the car, but using a different route to the one that I had taken up. I found myself looking down a very steep scree slope that ran down a gulley between two sheer cliff-faces. This route really scared me – it was incredibly precarious. There were no tracks and no people, probably for good reason. I was some 8,500 feet up, which amounts to two-and-a-half times the height of Ireland's highest mountain, Carrauntoohil.

I knew this was the only way down if I wanted to take an alternate route to get a different angle on the cliffs I had been watching. I decided to go for it, and I quickly came to the realisation that this was the most dangerous route I had ever been on in my life. The scree was extremely loose and, if I took a wrong step, I knew I'd slide down pretty fast and pretty far, too. It probably wouldn't end well either. It was frighteningly steep and, at some point, it ended in a sheer drop-off which would certainly have killed me. I crawled my way down to a grassy bank that allowed me to access the scree-strewn gully proper. From here, I half-crawled with extreme caution in a zigzagging manner.

I ended up deep down into this valley when I saw some movement on the ground in front of me, maybe just 12 to 15 feet ahead. It was a bird. I saw flashes of red and black. I knew what I *thought* it was but, in a state of disbelief, I lifted my binoculars. My head and neck instantly became twitchy – it was a male wallcreeper! The whole situation felt like a dream. I reached for my trusty Olympus, which I had wedged in my right-hand pants-pocket, and discovered it was already actively recording. In fact, it had actually recorded the moment I stumbled upon the wallcreeper itself. In this recording, you can hear me cautiously scrambling down through the loose scree, stones shooting downhill underfoot, followed by a pause, then several 'Oh my God!' exclamations and a few expletives. I then pointed the parabola at the wallcreeper and I was so lucky – it sang out a burst of song at extremely close range, then got up and flew away into the distance. My hands were shaking with nerves, and I genuinely asked myself, 'Is this real? Did that really just happen?' I really mean that – I was so exhausted that I thought I might have hallucinated the whole thing.

I listened to my recordings and heard that sweet, sweet song playing back at me from the Olympus: a plaintiff, ascending series of whistling notes, the second note with a purposeful tremble to it. Zero anthropogenic noise, too. It was the perfect recording of a dream bird. I fell back down to the scree, overwhelmed with emotion. I had just made one of the first ever sound-recordings of a wallcreeper in Catalunya and I'd fulfilled my first major sound-recording challenge, despite all of the hurdles it had thrown at me.

After I'd taken some time to come to my senses, I continued down the scree slope and eventually found some solid vegetated ground and turned a corner and there again, at my feet, was the wallcreeper!

I now focused on getting photographs to pair with the beautiful sound-recordings, to immortalise this bird forever. I couldn't believe what was happening: it came closer and closer and closer, until it walked right up to my feet. This bird had given me the runaround for years, and now it was just giving itself up, acting as if it wasn't even aware of my presence. I actually felt invisible. It felt all wrong, but then it dawned on me. This bird was in such an inaccessible location that it had probably never seen a human before nor did it see me as a threat. I took as many photos of the bird as I could, and even ended up with some shots of its long probing beak, light shining through its nostrils, with a layer of fine spider webs lining the tip. I felt like I was in the presence of a god.

This is the moment I knew I wanted to pursue wildlife sound-recording in a much more meaningful way. And with talks of Covid lockdowns coming back, my hopes of gaining full-time employment as an ornithologist in Catalunya were scuppered. The English-teaching kept me going and I had started to pick up my first bird-survey contracts. I'd also begun to pick up work as a bird guide, bringing English-speaking tourists who didn't know the lay of the land to specific bird targets. But none of these jobs would be possible if another wave of Covid struck, which seemed likely.

So, as we would both be able to find work back in Ireland, we decided to call our Catalan adventures a day, at least for a time. We returned home to Ireland, bringing Toby with us, just in time for Christmas 2020, and a new life-altering project began for us both. I sat at my parents' table on New Year's Eve and launched Irish Wildlife Sounds. The journey that was about to unfold was something I could never have predicted.

Great Spotted Woodpecker

Chapter 11

WE HAD TO LIVE WITH MY PARENTS FOR A WHILE WHEN WE first moved back from Catalunya. I had a job to come back to, surveying proposed wind farms, and because Alba was now fluent in English, we knew she'd find work easily, too.

So, here I was on New Year's Eve sitting at my parents' kitchen table. The very table I'd sat at and looked out to their bird feeder as a little boy. I had so many happy memories from this very spot, but now I saw things differently. I felt different, and I was. That week, I'd decided I was going to sound record every regularly occurring bird species in Ireland. I wanted to embrace and follow my new-found love for the art of wildlife sound-recording, but I also wanted to take my mind away from negativity. I felt like I had downgraded massively in moving back to Ireland, where true wilderness does not exist, at least not in any meaningful way. But I had to stop thinking like this. I needed to be positive and to bring back that thirst for knowledge and sense of awe and wonder in nature that I've always had in my home country. And that was the summary of my project – it was a personal, even selfish, mission. I created a website and a rudimentary logo, as well as a Twitter account –I did intend to share my work, but for no reason other than to get a virtual pat on the back for my efforts.

The early days of the project were a lot of fun. I consulted xeno-canto, to give me an outline of what species had been captured here already. I filtered the search bar for Ireland, and was surprised and equally delighted to learn that so many birds were missing from the list. Species as common and omnipresent as mallard and house sparrow were yet to be represented. I knew I had a fun and fulfilling challenge ahead of me.

I spent the first few days confined to the house. I was starting from scratch, so everything was new to me. I focused on my parents' bird feeder to start. It was snowing at the time and so birds flocked to it. I placed my parabola on a tripod and left it pointing towards the peanuts for the day. It recorded all day long and, each night, I'd collect it and save the best sound clips. Because I wasn't present, and because the birds took no notice of the equipment after a while, I got some really beautiful, intimate recordings of all of the regular garden birds: blue tits, jackdaws, chaffinches, house sparrows, and so on. I probably recorded around 25 species just in this one little spot.

Knowing my prospects of continued work in Catalunya were very poor, towards the end of my stay there I had applied for a position in my old company in Cork and, thankfully, they were glad to have me back. Shortly after arriving back home, I began my new job, and this required me to conduct daily bird surveys that would come with a pass to travel freely to survey sites amidst the new set of lockdown restrictions. These surveys were to inform potential wind-farm projects of the birds that were present on a given site, as is required by law before planning permission is granted. It can be a frustrating job to work in, at times. People generally hate the sight of wind turbines and, in a way, I get that; I'm not sure how I'd feel about them appearing in my vista. I've also been accosted, far too many times to count, by members of the public who see me, a bird surveyor, as a face of the potential development threat that looms over their neighbourhood. Sometimes, they really lose all logic – one person demanded that I leave, and then threatened and proceeded to call the guards, describing me as a suspicious-looking male wandering around the neighbourhood with binoculars. They fail to realise that we bird surveyors do not have any commercial interests, and to get to the point of bird-identification fluency takes many, many years of constant practice and, of course, an absolute love for birds. We are not there to push the construction of any project, nor are we there to stop it. We are there to conduct a lengthy series of robust surveys to transparently assess the avian sensitivities on-site.

People do, however, need to stop and think about where we are with energy harnessing in today's world. We know that we cannot continue burning fossil fuels – this is a fact. Fossil fuels are finite, and the burning of these is also one of the main drivers of climate breakdown. Turbines can cause bird collisions and cast flickering shadows, they are an eyesore and they make a frequent whooshing noise, which too can interfere with birds that rely heavily on acoustics as a vital means of communication in their world.

Some argue that solar panels require more energy and fossil-fuel-dependent equipment to mine, build and transport than the energy they ultimately produce. Toxic chemicals used in the manufacturing process can also case much harm. Furthermore, there have been several studies published that report incidences of water-dwelling bird species mistaking the shiny surfaces of solar panels for water, resulting in mass crash-landings and deaths. No alternative energy solution will ever be completely flawless but we need to spend more time and investment on our renewable sources of energy to make them less harmful to wildlife and, indeed, less of a thorn in the side to humans because, like it or not, alternatives to our current addiction to fossil fuels were needed yesterday.

For me, I feel there is an enormous conflict of interest in the Irish Environmental Impact Assessment arena. The current system whereby bird-assessment reports are visible to developers for review, before submission, is highly flawed. Why? Well, the answer is simple – developers want to develop. And developers do not want bird surveyors who find and report lots of problems – these 'problems' being the presence of rare or protected birds. I've worked in this industry for many years, and have been employed by several companies and as a freelancer, and I have developed a true sense of disgust the more I delved into things. It's true that not everyone lets the money lead the way in this game, but many do.

Over the years, I've submitted numerous bird reports to developers for review, and I've lost count of the number of times my language was dumbed-down to make the results sound less serious. Language in these reports is very important. A slight change of wording can mean the difference between a pass or a fail. I was once even told that my report was 'alarmist', and it came back with a sea of corrections, all language-based. The numbers in the report didn't lie, nor could they be changed. The site in question was grossly unsuitable for wind-turbine development. A catastrophic loss of bird life over the thirty-year lifespan of the wind farm was predicted. They couldn't change these numbers, but they could try to change the language surrounding them. Often when high loss of a given species is predicted, this loss is compared against the total national, or even European, population in an attempt to make the loss seem insignificant. Again, it's all a game of perception and language.

Take a look around our country. Look at where the wind farms are cropping up and ask yourself: Do these belong here at this location? The answer will often be a simple no. How many of our rare raised bogs and sensitive uplands are earmarked for turbines? How many already have turbines? Lots. Whilst some do get stopped in their tracks, many do not. In my opinion, the first step in tackling the issues that are rife within this industry is to prevent developers' freedom to choose who surveys and produces reports. What's stopping developers from only choosing surveyors who are more likely to roll over? Also, I strongly believe that developers should have *zero* say on language or results submitted in ornithological reports.

Despite all of these doubts rattling around in my head, I decided to continue with the surveys and to do them to the very best of my ability. I thought to myself that it's better someone who knows and cares about accurate bird identification does the job rather than someone who does not.

During my bird surveys, I'd always have a recorder by my side. Any opportunity that arose to capture sound, I was on it. I also ran a separate recorder far enough away from me so it didn't pick up my rustling. I'd set it up hidden in a hedgerow or tree and allow it to record passively for six hours or more. I soon began to build a large collection of 'countryside' birds: treecreepers, siskin, redpoll, raven and other species – non-generalist species that you typically wouldn't expect to come to bird feeders or to a garden with just a scattering of trees and wild cover. Each evening, I'd edit my sounds at home, and I became extremely sensitive to interferences in my tracks. I soon became aware of just how common road noise was, aeroplane passes too. I came to detest both – I felt like they tainted the precious melodies of the wonderful birds that I set out to represent. And so, this led to me seek out areas with a combination of healthy habitat and an absence of road noise to make my recordings – a frighteningly difficult task here in Ireland, the second most car-dependent country in Europe, after Cyprus!

Over time, I found myself being assigned fewer bird surveys and more reports: Appropriate Assessments, two-year summary reports, and Environmental Impact Assessments. I detested them and often felt like I had words put into my mouth. I felt like a used pawn, at times. To cope with my entrapment while writing reports at home, I knew I had to find a way to escape to nature, and so I searched for long-form soundtracks of Irish nature to listen to so I could pretend I was out there. But it turned out they didn't exist, and so this started a new sub-project for me – to sound record long-form tracks in the best remaining *fragments* of wild habitat in Ireland, but only if they lacked any anthropogenic noise interference.

I began collecting dawn choruses and seascapes from all over the country – I'd leave my recorders out for hours, even weeks, to capture what I wanted. These collections would eventually lead to me releasing a digital album in 2024, entitled *Wild Silence*, consisting of 13 long-form tracks, three hours in total, with 25 per cent of proceeds being donated to BirdWatch Ireland, an environmental NGO that champions bird conservation in the country.

The next element of the project was to set up two permanent 'listening stations' at prominent coastal bird-migration locations. The intention was to have these record from dusk to dawn every night of the year and so I purchased two Wildlife Acoustics SM4 minis. These amazing units can run for approximately six weeks on this schedule. They are also waterproof, with microphones that are highly wind-resistant, which is ideal for long-term deployments in Irish weather.

I set up my first listening station in the extreme southwest of Ireland – on the very precipice of the rugged Mizen Head peninsula, some 150 kilometres from Cobh. This far-flung peninsula, not far from County Kerry, has long been a favourite place of mine. Here the hedgerows are that little bit more dense, the fields that little bit wilder, the cows that little bit scarcer.

The Atlantic Ocean calls the shots down there. The smells and sounds of the sea are never far. Barleycove beach – to me the closest thing to the Bahamas in Ireland, with its white sands and towering dunes – sits in a sheltered nook, taking refuge from the vigour of the wild Atlantic just beyond. Soft, gentle and welcoming, it lies nestled safely amongst the sharp, black, jagged rocks that surround it – protecting it from the frequent storm surges. Several gardens dotted along the Lighthouse Road each have tales to tell of exotic wind-driven waifs from Arctic Canada to Siberia.

When bird migration is in full flow, just about anything is possible at these sweet spots – you never know who you'll meet. For us birders, this adds an additional air of excitement and charm to the place. I remember seeing a North American yellow warbler flitting around some wind-stunted, salt-burned willows near the tip of the peninsula in late August 2008. It stood out like a sore thumb – a small ball of highlighter yellow that fluttered and gleaned insects from the leaves. It was far more colourful than any native songbird you'd expect to see at this location. It made landfall after a big low-pressure system crossed the Atlantic and hit our southwest coast. This whipped up birds that were migrating down the eastern US seaboard, en route to South America, dragging them way off route to Ireland and the UK. A few such birds were found that time, actually. There was another yellow warbler on Cape Clear Island, in fact. I remember this one well, though, because it was the first time I'd ever seen a North American songbird blown across to Ireland. I'd seen this species in Florida a year previously (2007) and it brought back a flood of memories – mainly of where I'd last encountered them – a mangrove filled with alligators and swarming with mosquitoes. It was bizarre seeing it out on the wet and windy Mizen Peninsula, knowing how far it had come.

Mizen Head was the perfect place to monitor bird migration acoustically. Because it's in the extreme southwest, birds filtering down from north to south naturally funnel out through the peninsula here. This extreme southwesterly position means North American vagrants, like the 2008 yellow warbler, although rare, are a fairly regular occurrence on Mizen in the autumn. As mentioned, these birds are migrating from Canada or northern US states, southward to South America, they get caught up in hurricane tail-ends and are pushed across to Ireland. The majority don't make it, eventually drowning at sea, but some do – maybe having taken a lucky break on a passing ship. Upon seeing the first sight of land, such as the jutting peninsula of Mizen, they make landfall.

Other famous North American rarities that have turned up there include buff-bellied pipits, red-eyed vireos, blackpoll warbler, hermit thrush, ovenbird and American golden plovers. And this is to name but a few. Knowing that lighthouses attract migrants at night, I thought that this would be the best place to set up my listening station. And so, in June 2021, I placed it at the base of the lighthouse. Here, I hoped to intercept waders coming in from the sea – common sandpipers, whimbrel and whatever else was on the move. I expected out-of-context common species – wetland specialists arriving in over the waves, such as little grebes, moorhens, water rails and coot. I also assumed I'd catch songbirds – tree pipits, spotted flycatchers, yellow wagtails. I was expecting big things.

A month later, I collected it and analysed some results there and then. I had to make a decision: is it worth continuing here or will I move the listening station? Expecting wall-to-wall calls of birds migrating through the night, I was highly disappointed when I skimmed through the recordings. The majority of the nights were too windy to decipher, which made sense – it was right at the tip of the peninsula, facing into our volatile Atlantic. Secondly there were hardly any birds! In the mornings, there were the expected voices of herring gulls and rock pipits but, at night, I didn't have a single migrant. I had decided to move it, so I began zooming in and out of Google Maps looking for a suitable spot. And then the answer came – the sheltered estuary of Lissagriffin!

Wind here is always very low, it was full of resident and stop-over estuarine birds, whose voices I would capture during the quiet spells, between flyover nocturnal migrants. It was a win-win situation.

I thought very carefully about the recorder's placement. I stood on the shoreline of the estuary and slowly took in my surroundings – simultaneously thinking like a bird, like a thief, and like the many elements that posed a threat to my expensive device. It was low tide. I looked around at the muddy shoreline and observed waders – black-tailed godwits, curlews, dunlin, redshank and greenshank, all in numbers, wandering around, probing through the mud for buried marine invertebrates. I observed flight-lines of birds travelling from the beach to the inner estuary. These lines and pockets of feeding activity pointed me to where I needed to place the unit in order to intercept the most action. I let the birds lead the way.

Next, I had to think about the tide – I needed to make sure the unit was safe from big waves on windy days, and I also needed to keep it hidden from any sticky fingers. I found some bushes a few feet above the estuary, well off the beaten track, and so this would become the home of the Lissagriffin Listening Station for the next three years. Having set the unit to record from dusk to dawn, I concealed it away from prying eyes, and just sat in position to become accustomed to any indigenous non-avian sounds my ear would need to be aware of. After all, I would be listening to this location for the next 1,000-plus nights in their entirety, so it was important that I established that baseline of familiarity with the soundscape.

I sat on the grassy bank of the estuary and closed my eyes. The sound of the sea had many voices: the flow of the water as it ebbed through the various channels, the sound of the wavelets slipping over the muddy shorelines, the splashes of birds as they fed and preened, and the sound of the surf pounding on the sandy shores behind, which was muffled by the towering sand dunes that protect the inner estuary. The hum of a milking machine in the distance kicked in, momentarily breaking my tranquillity and summoning an involuntary grimace. Occasional passing cars could be heard several hundred metres away on the small causeway road that dissected the estuary. Gulls echoed their seaside shanties overhead – my hairs stood on end. I love this sound *so* much.

So as not to potentially waste recording time at another unfavourable site for a month, I decided to pop back a week later just to see if this spot really was worth settling into for three years. I nervously approached the mark I'd left it at. What if it was damaged or stolen? I climbed up the bank and peered into the bushes – there it was, exactly where I'd left it. I took out the SD card, replacing it with another. It was a weekend and so Alba and I decided we'd camp out in our Peugeot Rifter and make the most of the sun. It's not a camper van as such but the back seats fold down and we can fit in a foldable, memory-foam, double mattress. That night, I went through the data. I set up a camping chair and a little table outside our bed-fitted boot, where Alba and Toby lay resting. Here, I processed my sounds in the warm summer air, under a calm moonlit sky, lulled into a sense of comfort and belonging, amidst the rhythmic sound of crashing waves – the heartbeat of our Atlantic Ocean.

I'd long planned for this process and so was well prepared. Each night was broken down into several recordings of one hour, spanning from civil dusk to civil dawn. Civil dusk and dawn occur approximately

45 minutes after and before sunset and sunrise, respectively. The time is considered to cover the true nocturnal window, according to Magnus Robb as well as the British Trust for Ornithology. Every bird call was registered manually by me and assigned to species level, with a time stamp within the hour assigned. For busy periods with lots of calls going over, I used several clickers to count calls.

At first, the process was slow as I became familiar with the shapes of the different calls on the sonogram – the visual representation of the captured sounds. I stayed up processing and perfecting my analytical technique well into the early hours, at which point I was flying. Then, towards the end of the batch, on 2 July at 4.42 a.m., a totally unfamiliar shape appeared. Its sonogram form was very different to the Lough Ness monster-style shape I'd identified as a calling redshank or the upside-down U of an oystercatcher. Instead, it resembled a Nike tick. I highlighted the call and pressed play. It sounded vaguely familiar but out of context – a short, high-pitched 'chew-eet'. I'd heard this somewhere before, but I knew it wasn't something I'd encountered in Ireland. It did sound a little bit like a spotted redshank – a scarce migrant and wintering species. It wasn't right, though. It sounded higher-pitched and slower – the sonogram shape was also different.

Scratching my head for some time, a vague memory came to mind. I recalled someone once describing the call of semipalmated plover as somewhat reminiscent of spotted redshank. Semipalmated plover is an extremely rare vagrant to Ireland, so I didn't believe that this would match, but it was worth ruling out at least. At this point in time, there had been just six verified records of semipalmated plover in Ireland, with none from Cork. It is the North American close relative of our own ringed plover. Although both species look very similar, a number of useful but subtle physical features separate the two. Semipalmated plover is ever so slightly smaller than ringed plover; it also, as the name suggests, has little webbings between its toes. With very close views, you can make out that semipalmated plover has a yellow orbital ring, whereas ringed plover has an orange one. Vocalisations are another reliable method of separating the species. On the sonogram, this is particularly easy: ringed plover calls look like a shallow letter M, whereas semipalmated plover look like ... a Nike tick.

I went to xeno-canto to search through a sample of semipalmated plover calls from the US and found an example recorded at Cape Canaveral Seashore in Florida. I switched to sonogram mode and I was amazed. It was a perfect Nike tick – it even appeared to be around the same duration and frequency as the Mizen mystery bird. It sounded the same, too. I opened another example – it looked and sounded the same. I opened many more, each the same. I downloaded one of the Floridian examples, then cut and pasted it into my audio file of the mystery bird. They looked like two peas sitting in a pod – visually inseparable. Again, they sounded identical, too. Panicking and bursting with excitement, I sent a few premature texts to a few close friends: 'I think I have something *huge* here. Mizen. Rare.' I received back a few bewildered responses along the lines of 'What are you talking about, Seán?' I had an idea. There's a great AI-based bird sound identification app online: BirdNET. It's a very accurate and reliable tool. I first fed it the downloaded semipalmated plover call from Florida. It returned with – semipalmated plover, 100 per cent certainty. I then fed it my mystery bird, and the answer rocketed me off my little camping chair as I shouted in both shock and delight. I woke up Alba.

'What the hell is wrong with you, Seán!?'

I apologised and saved her the nerdy details for the morning.

Semipalmated Plover *(Charadrius semipalmatus)*
Family *Charadriidae (plovers, dotterels and lapwings)*
Conservation status Least Concern (IUCN Red List) – does not occur on the BoCCI list, as it is a rare vagrant
Vocalisations *Call is a high-pitched, disyllabic 'chew-eet'.*

Some hours later, after a restless sleep, I texted out the news to a number of national WhatsApp groups. The responses were varied – some replied with celebratory emojis, others questioned the process, and how I came to this conclusion. And rightly so. I was claiming a species new to County Cork, but I hadn't seen it, nor had I heard it! I put together a long-winded, annotated description of my identification criteria, and people mostly accepted it. It was still a highly unusual, even bizarre, situation. A new species for Ireland's largest county must now be potentially added to the records, but it hadn't been encountered by a soul, not even me.

This bugged me so, that day, I searched for it, but to no avail. Others did too. I detected it again on the sound files a few days later, and so that gave me hope. These kinds of far-lost vagrant waders often stay for long periods of time, though. A record of the same species from Achill Island, County Mayo, from 2016 stayed on for several months over a number of winters.

Then, on 1 October, I received a call out of the blue from a well-known Cork birder, Paul Moore: 'Seán, I think I have your plover! It looks good, I just need to see a few more features to be certain.' He hung up, telling me he'd text again when he was certain. I'd forgotten about this bird, to be honest, but now I was fully invested. Over the coming minutes, I didn't take my eye off the phone. Then a message flashed up: 'It's a semi-p plover!' I was elated. This was the first record for Cork, and now my unusual manner of detecting this rarity was also awarded some legitimacy.

Around the same time as setting up the Mizen listening station, I also wanted to set up a second in the southeast or east coast. Again, I looked at Google Maps one evening, thinking about a suitable location. I looked at the east coast – the closest point to the UK and mainland Europe. This is where the main flyways lie, but surely some of those birds must cut across from Scotland and fly down the east coast, I thought. The southeast corner of Wexford and Wicklow theoretically looked ideal. It already had a reputation as a hotspot for migrant birds by day and so, by night, it would surely be the same. I was working on a survey site one week per month anyway and so this gave me time to explore and toy around with sites after surveys.

There are a number of well-known ornithological spots amongst the birding community in the southeast: Lady's Island Lake, Tacumshin and Cahore Marsh in County Wexford, as well as Buckroney Marsh in County Wicklow. I dabbled at all of these sites, leaving recorders out for a night or two at a time. I assessed nocturnal movements and sound quality back in my bed and breakfast at night. I had a lot of experience with the Wexford sites through years of birding, but Buckroney was new to me and so I was keen to test that out with a longer trial window. I knew the Wexford sites were well covered by birders during the day, but Buckroney was much less watched, and this drew me to it like a moth to a flame. I'd have a chance to discover.

I left one test unit out in late June of 2021 and collected it on my next survey period in July, still on a high from my semipalmated plover. The marsh itself is inaccessible, which is great. We humans cannot get at it. But the lush peripheries are just about in reach. I parked alongside the boundary of the marsh and wandered in through the rather wild field that bounded it. The closer I got to the marsh, the wetter it became underfoot. I navigated a sea of highlighter-yellow flag irises and vivid purple loosestrifes until I was met with a dense thicket of reeds and willows. A sense of relief calmed my nerves upon sighting my unit still snuggled down and listening. I took it out with the intention of setting it up permanently at Tacumshin later in the week. I'd been there quite a lot on recent visits and it just screamed at me for attention. That place is special, and I just knew it would deliver.

That night I began the process of analysing my recordings from Buckroney. Scanning along, I first came across a very close great spotted woodpecker, which worked its way up to and, eventually, began tapping the device itself! When it stopped doing this, my best recordings so far of this species' call followed! The deployment was already worth it. Continuing to scan through the audio, darkness fell and, some time later, the first of several curlew sonograms appeared, along with some bleating sheep and mooing cows, breaking the silence of the previous hours. I was feeling quite chilled, in autopilot, scanning and 'eagle-eyeing' every shape as it whizzed past on my computer screen, when I saw an interesting form jump out. I went back a little and paused. This looked familiar ... and rare!

It took me a second or two to register where I recognised it from, and then it hit me – I had seen this very sonogram shape in the spring of 2020, back in Catalunya. It looked a perfect match for a Baillon's crake, but it couldn't be: Baillon's crake is another 'mega' rarity in Ireland, with just three previous accepted records on the Irish list (1845, County Cork; 1858, County Waterford; and 2012, County Wexford).

***

Bailon's Crake *(Zapornia pusilla)*
Family Rallidae *(rails)*
Conservation status *Least Concern (IUCN Red List) – does not occur on the BoCCI list, as it is a rare vagrant*
Vocalisations *Flight call an explosive, sharp 'krrr-eeuk'. Display, given from cover, usually at night, is a drawn-out rattling that sounds frog-like.*

***

I hadn't actually listened to the recording yet, and I went to do so, fully expecting to hear something other than a Baillon's crake, but what I heard sounded exactly like the Baillon's crake call I had captured autonomously in Catalunya the previous year. The call is what can only be described as an explosive 'krrr-eeuk' and it is given in flight, both during nocturnal migration and in regular short flight in-habitat.

A cocktail of panic and déjà-vu set in. I'd only been through this scenario the previous week. I rushed to xeno-canto to search for other nocturnal flight calls of the species and, no matter how hard I tried to calm and convince myself that I must be mistaken, it just wasn't happening. This was potentially huge! As it turned out, it was a possible fifth Irish record, not fourth – news later emerged of another recorded singing in the spring at an undisclosed location elsewhere in the country.

I sent my recording for second opinions to Killian Mullarney, Magnus Robb and Stanislas Wroza – all highly regarded sound specialists. To my delight, one by one, each filtered back with the words I so desperately wanted to hear – they all agreed. Wow! The fifth Irish record of a mega-rarity, and it was detected by an autonomous recording device – what a strange record ... *again*!

Times are changing and technology is really carving out a new niche in ornithology. Records like this shine a light on just how much we miss when the sun goes down and, in many cases, birds that would hardly ever have been detected by day will now be brought to light. This nocturnal flight call has been captured by enthusiastic nocturnal recordists in recent years in numerous countries where they are rare, including Spain, France, the Netherlands, England and now, finally, in Ireland too!

I later set up the second listening station at Tacumshin and, over the three years of the project, both it and the Lissagriffin station collected a tremendous amount of data relating to the nocturnal migration of birds in Ireland. And these rare finds turned up every few months. Such unknown but expected surprises helped me push through the quieter periods, because I knew a firework was only ever a click away.

At this point, bird sound was the entirety of my world, alongside Alba and Toby. Having lived with my parents for the first few months after our return from Catalunya, we eventually found a place of our own to rent, only a ten-minute drive from Cobh. During the day, I surveyed and sound-recorded birds. At night, I sat in our spare room and analysed the sounds from my listening stations. At weekends, I sought out species I needed to document. And in the moments I found in-between all of this, I was devouring bird sound books, as well as any other source that would inspire me or update my knowledge. I was all in, and some more. This is part of who I am. It's always been this way. Some obsessive topics come and go – otter poo, fishing, antique bottle-collecting. I never forget what I learned, though. Birds and bird sound, however, have always been present, and always will be.

At nighttime, just before civil dusk, I'd put my parabola outside in the garden and point it up to the sky to intercept whatever birds passed overhead on their starry journeys north or south. I pointed the parabola strategically so that it also pointed to the gable of our roof. This was because a pair of starlings were nesting in there. I love starlings for so many reasons. Their smart black iridescent plumage dotted with shiny little sequins reminds me of a dress one would wear to a fancy cocktail bar. Their spectacular winter murmurations, like a shoal of fish in the sky, are one of nature's must-see wonders. And their song! Their song is what draws me the most.

I think most people will know that starlings are great mimics. That is, they soak up and imitate the sounds of other birds, mammals or even inanimate objects they encounter in their homestead. During one of my deep-dives of this period, I discovered that starlings are lifelong learners, and that many birds are not. Most songbirds have a critical learning window, often just the first few months of their lives, after which their song is set for life. But because starlings can learn indefinitely, they can continue adding to and updating their song for as long as they don those shiny sequins in style. So, I was curious – would 'my' starling update its mimetic repertoire and, if so, would these updates reflect seasonal natural history events that I, too, witnessed?

In early spring 2022, the starling began to sing with spirit from the gable peak each morning. The song was already packed with mimicry: mallard, hooded crow, rook, jackdaw, chaffinch and some kind of unknown mechanical noise were all in there. The starling followed a series of predictable verses, with phrases and notes in a repeated order each time. In this sense, the song structure was no different to a popular song of our own. Now that I had a baseline to compare against, I could monitor any would-be changes or updates to the mimetic repertoire of this bird over time.

In February, the resident foxes began to vocalise nightly. The most commonly heard sound was the so-called vixen's scream. It is believed that this is a vocalisation given by the female to advertise her availability for mating, although some contest that males also use this vocalisation for the same purpose. Whatever the case, the starling learned this call too! And, in late February, it incorporated a 'vixen's scream' into its song.

From March onwards, birds began their nocturnal migrations north, and the most frequent of these also made it into the new rendition of the starling's song. Moorhen, golden plover and snipe were all added to the starling's ever-growing repertoire. This blew me away and really put mimicry on my radar. Listening back to the starling's song became my evening ritual – I was excited to see and hear any updates. He was learning and updating with everything he had, for this was the time of year to impress and to woo his female. The song seemed to settle for a while, but I still checked it just in case. One morning, I heard what sounded like *me*, interrupting its song. I tutted to myself for spoiling the track. But something didn't really sound right. I went back and listened to the part in question again. It definitely sounded like me, but a little odd. Perhaps I was distant and muffled. It sounded like I was saying 'c'mere' (come here) in my Cork accent. Shrugging it off, I continued. A few verses later, and there it was again, in the very same position in the verse. It was the starling! It had added *me* to its repertoire. And then it dawned on me. With the change in the weather, we'd been letting Toby out in the garden a lot more and I called him back in from the door, right under the starling's nest hole: 'C'mere! C'mere, Toby.' I had no idea that starlings mimicked to this extent or that they updated their songs in this way. I *needed* to learn more. I needed to find more mimics!

I started to read about mimetic birds, and the species that kept popping up was marsh warbler. In Europe, this is considered to be the ultimate mimic. Some say its song is almost wholly composed of mimicry of other species. And, as it's a lifelong learner that winters in Africa, it also brings African mimicry back to Europe in the summer. The idea of this left me spellbound. To hear my own roof-nesting starling repeat the stories of our own little world fascinated me, so imagine hearing what a seasonal transcontinental wanderer would have to say!

Marsh warbler is a very rare vagrant in Ireland, though, and so I knew I couldn't bank on that species. I began to list off other options in my head. There must be another migratory mimic. I wracked my brain, thinking of options, and then there was that jolt of excitement!

Back in 2019, when I was living in Catalunya, my good friend Harry Hussey shared a sound-recording of a common whitethroat he'd made at Spurn Point in England. All it took was sixty seconds for this bird to knock my socks off. In that time, it mimicked up to ten species with great accuracy, including common redshank, herring gull, common ringed plover, dunlin, yellow wagtail, Sandwich tern and curlew. As this bird was breeding on a coastal headland, it was likely mirroring the species of its chosen territory. I found this incredibly endearing. I did some research on whitethroat mimicry but I didn't find any reference to African mimicry in the repertoire or whether it's a lifelong learner or has a critical learning window. Harry's snippet also didn't allude to either. It seemed to me like there was a huge gap in our understanding of whitethroat mimicry, and so I decided that I would take on the task of recording every singing male I found from here on in. I was a little bit early though. It was April, and the first migrants typically didn't set up territories until early May. I thought back to my first discovery of whitethroats, having watched that wonderful episode of *Amuigh Faoin Spéir* by Éamon de Buitléar. I remembered that excitement and felt it afresh. I couldn't wait for my friends to return. I was older now and could have a more adult conversation with them. What would they have to tell me?

I'd been posting my most beautiful and unusual recordings to Twitter as I recorded them, and I started to slowly build up some followers. The snippet I posted of my roof-nesting starling blew up. It was the human mimicry that got people. Later that evening, I noticed an email notification from Kathleen Harris of *The Irish Times*. They were looking to interview people who had interesting jobs and spotted my recordings on Twitter. They asked me if I'd be interested in doing a short video profile with them. The thought of this nearly made my heart jump out of my chest. *Me?* I could hardly say 'hello' to a stranger. How could I possibly talk to a stranger *with a camera*, which would inevitably share my face with thousands of people? I mentioned it to Alba and her response did something that would change the course of my life: 'Babe, this is your topic! It's *your* story. Nobody knows it better than you do. It's your own very personal take on things. Just talk to them like you talk to me. I love your stories about birds. They're so different and I learn a lot from you. They must be asking you for a reason – just go and be you!'

I trust Alba with all of my core, and so, as nervous as I was, I replied with a yes. I closed my eyes, hit enter and asked myself what had I done. I had plans to go to Killarney National Park over the weekend to sound record a drumming great spotted woodpecker and so I suggested we meet there.

Great Spotted Woodpecker *(Dendrocopos major)*
Family *Picidae (woodpeckers)*
Conservation status *Green-listed (BoCCI, 2020–2026)*
Vocalisations *Contact call a sharp 'PIK'. The most iconic sound however is not a vocalisation but instead comes from the bill hammering a favoured tree in drumming display. This sound is surprisingly loud and happens at speed, with between 10 and 20 strikes occurring in a one-to-two second window.*

I found myself parking opposite the park entrance on a calm spring morning. Still groggy, I tugged my wellies into fit, saddled myself with my cumbersome bag of electronics and set out with my curious-looking parabola in hand. It was still dark but the sun was peeping up and I could see the expansive treeline a few hundred metres ahead. Kathleen wasn't here yet – I was much earlier than planned. I get really stressed about time – early is on time, on time is late. Most 'normal folk' are still in bed this early, which is great for me. It means fewer cars for my ears and mics to contest with.

The closer I got to the wood, the more worried I became about what I'd asked Kathleen to navigate through. The ground underfoot became wetter, muddier and less forgiving the closer I got to the trees. I'd never really met a journalist before and I had ideas of her arriving in corporate attire with wholly unsuitable footwear. Journalists, please forgive my judgement!

The wood here looked familiar. It was a wonderful wet woodland, dominated by a tangle of alder, willows and birches, and was partially shrouded in a blanket of white mist. The familiarity of this place suddenly clicked – the little wet woodland at Cuskinny was just like it. A home away from home. These wet woodlands both shared something in common – they were close to bodies of water. In the case of Cuskinny, the Ballyleary Stream ran right through its heart. Here, the wood bordered Lough Leane and also provided a crossing for the River Deenagh to enter the lough. There's something primal about these wet woodlands. They feel sacred. Too wet to tame, they remain largely untouched by human influence. They look as if they may host some mythical creatures from the annals of Irish mythology. Dead and decaying wood are scattered amongst the beautiful chaos of the woodland floor. From these grow all manner of water-laden mosses and ferns. Beetles scampered from the hole-ridden, water-sodden woody fibres, where birds pried protein-packed larvae from within. From the wet, unperturbed soils grew a wealth of sedges and rushes with splashes of vivid yellows and greens provided by carpets of opposite-leaved golden-saxifrage, an ancient woodland indicator species, and a sign that this wonderful natural assembly has been this way for many years, its wetness keeping it out of touch from the hand of 'progress'.

I looked up – the leafless trees towered overhead, at all manner of angles. Many grew straight but some had fallen. Refusing to die, they simply grew upwards from their leaning positions. Some trees *were* dead but continued to stand tall and provide life. Then I thought of the woodpeckers. Another eureka moment. *This* is what brought them here – the first record for Kerry. These wonderful ecosystem engineers *need* dead standing wood, as do many other creatures. Here, they carve out their nest holes in wood that's softer and easier to hollow out. And just like the fallen, rotting logs, these standing soldiers also provide homes for invertebrates that feed on the soft wood, in turn providing food for woodpeckers and more. It pains me to see dead standing wood cut down and removed from recreational woodlands, as if we know better. In fact, we only reveal our lack of understanding of this wonderfully complex ecosystem. A tandem of relationships that have co-evolved over eons.

The light was beginning to brighten my way and the first birds began to sing. The birds with the largest eyes led the way. Their greater light-gathering abilities mean they can see predators before smaller-eyed birds. As soon as they sing, they reveal their locations, not only to rival males, but to the sharp ears and prying eyes of any nearby predators, so they need to be ready to perceive threats and to flee. Large-eyed song thrushes and blackbirds first carolled their tuneful melodies, which carried far and wide. Some minutes later a woodpigeon joined in, followed by a robin. I had my parabola set up to record. I crouched down, hands on my headphones with closed eyes – focusing on the sound. But I heard some interference in the distance. Footsteps? I looked up and turned my head to face down the long track I'd approached from. Someone was coming. A gush of nerves flooded my belly at the sudden thought of speaking on camera. I lifted my binoculars and was surprised to see a woman dressed in hiking gear carrying a large tripod and a camera. It must be Kathleen, but this was not at all the corporate fancy-pants my mind had conjured up. She looked like one of *my* kind – someone who was prepared for a day in nature, not afraid to get dirty. She looked very much at home as she squelched through the mud in the twilight.

She waved and smiled. 'Hey! You must be Seán?'

'And you must be Kathleen!'

We shook hands and I immediately felt at ease. There was an air of normalcy around her, a lack of ego. I knew she was cool from the get-go, and this totally calmed my nerves. I apologised to her for dragging her through the muddy tracks at dawn, and she laughed it off – 'Oh no, I love this. I go hiking all the time. It's a joy to be out of the office, especially with all of this birdsong all around us!'

Kathleen asked me to go about my business as if she wasn't there. She began to set up her equipment, and I did the same, placing a few mics around the site. I became lost in my little world and routine and was half chatting to her, half taking care of my work.

I glanced at her briefly, before turning my head back in surprise. 'You're filming!'

'Yeah!' she said with an amused giggle, 'just keep doing what you do and pretend I'm not here. You're doing great.'

Semipalmated plover in the flesh! Having discovered this bird via autonomous recording in July 2021, it was a big relief that the record was eventually confirmed in person by Paul Moore, very close to my recorder. Photo by Brian McCloskey at Mizen Head, County Cork.

Sound recording with my trusty Dodotronic parabola at Rossleague, County Cork in March 2021. Photo by Alba Novell Capdevila.

Audacity spectrogram showing the initial call detection of the Mizen Head semipalmated plover (left), followed by a semipalmated plover from Florida (middle) and finally a spotted redshank (right) for comparison.

Photographing seabirds from Mizen Head in May 2021, on one of our many weekend camping trips during the duration of the sound recording project. Photo by Alba Novell Capdevila.

A Mediterranean gull, one of my favourite birds, at Cork Harbour.

Part of a flock of quarter of a million starlings murmurating over Lough Ennell, County Westmeath. This was the first shoot for our documentary *Birdsong* in March 2023.

A starling poses in beautiful iridescence.

The last known pair of Irish ring ouzels, photographed by Robert Vaughan in the Donegal mountains in May 2022.

An Irish ring ouzel carries food to bring back to a nest of hungry mouths. It's inexplicably sad to think that this scene may very well fizzle out in our lifetime. Photo by Robert Vaughan in May 2002.

Camping out on Tory Island, County Donegal, in search of corncrakes. Photo by Alba Novell Capdevila.

Corn bunting – the last species to have gone extinct in Ireland, here photographed in Catalunya in May 2019.

Listening to a rock pool with childish curiosity as limpets noisily graze algae from the rocks. Photo by Alba Novell Capdevila.

Sound recording and shooting scenes in June 2023 for *Birdsong*.
Photo by Kathleen Harris.

A puffin looks at us head-on on Skellig Michael. Photo by Alba Novell Capdevila.

Part of the *Birdsong* team after a successful weekend shooting on Skellig Michael in June 2023. L–R: Ross Bartley (cinematographer), Kathleen Harris (director), me, Alba and Aideen O' Sullivan (co-producer alongside Ross Whitaker [not in shot]).

Birdsong premiere at the Lighthouse Cinema, as part of the 2024 Dublin International Film Festival. Photo by Alba Novell Capdevila.

Birdsong poster. Courtesy of True Films. Photo by Chris Maddaloni, design by Steve O Connell.

Chatting to Tommy Tiernan about my project and journey on stage at the *Tommy Tiernan Show* in November 2023. Photo by Melissa Mannion.

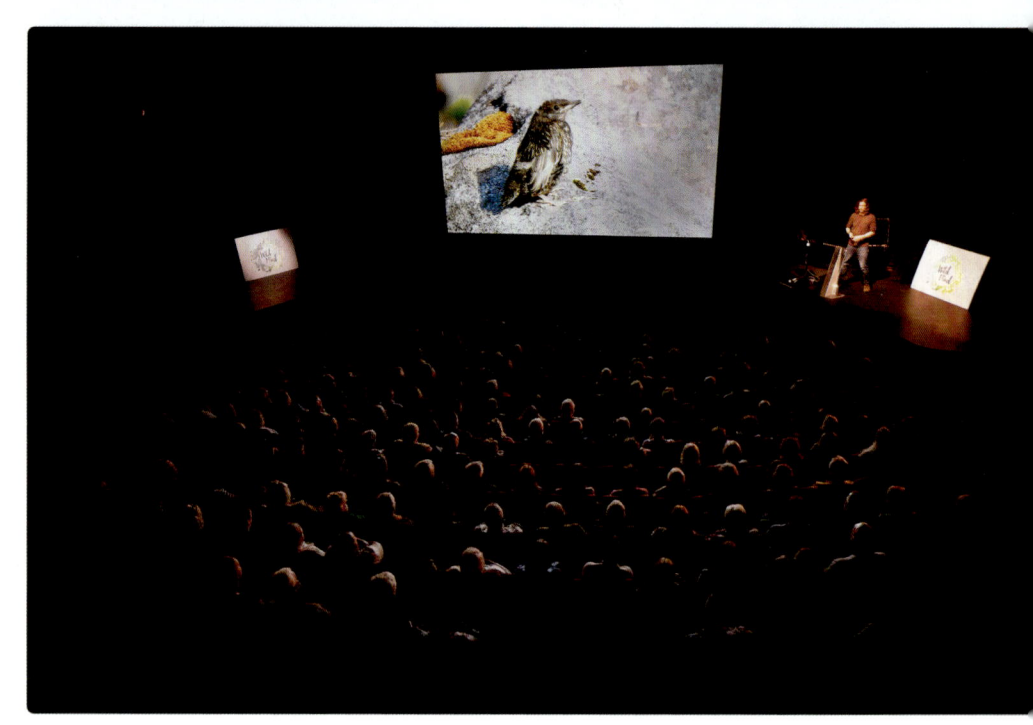

Speaking to a full house at Siamsa Tíre, The National Folk Theatre of Ireland, County Kerry, in June 2024. Photo by Emi Laguna, Roxy Media. Stage photo is of a juvenile ring ouzel, and is taken by Robert Vaughan.

A family photo taken in West Cork in February 2024 before three become four.

Out for a misty walk in West Cork in August 2024. Alba is now carrying our little Laia. Photo by Terry Ronayne.

I followed her advice and I found it surprisingly comfortable. If it had been in some studio or formal setting somewhere, I'm sure it would have been different, but here I felt at home and Kathleen looked the same. She asked me various questions about what I was doing and told me not to look directly into the camera. This was easy for me – I'd spent a lifetime dodging direct eye contact when talking to people. The camera just felt like a giant eye to me, and so not making direct eye-to-lens contact came naturally.

Kathleen sat me down for what she labelled the 'master interview'. All of this technical jargon was new to me. I was just happy to talk to someone about my love for birds and the natural world. The master interview is the core shot of the piece and is central to the published work. Any documentary about an individual or group of individuals has a story that travels through time and place, but always comes back to a familiar, often seated, shot of the interviewee. I got into a seated position by a large oak and Kathleen started rolling. She asked me what birds I had left to sound record, how the project started, what I thought of the state of Ireland's natural spaces, etc. I answered freely and without nerves, which surprised me greatly. I remember answering a question when I involuntarily jumped to a standing position, leaving half of my body out of frame. A rare but familiar sound took precedence over all else. My brain is always only half in tune with human conversation; my attention is only partly yours. Birds and natural sound take precedence.

It was a brambling – a rare Scandinavian finch that winters in Ireland in very small numbers. I gave this very description aloud as I ran away from a bemused Kathleen, camera still running. She ran after me and we both captured the moment – my first ever brambling call, and Kathleen captured me switching between worlds. After the job was done, I dusted myself off and apologised, only then realising that I had run off without warning in the middle of Kathleen's piece.

Brambling *(Fringilla montifringilla)*
Family *Fringillidae (true finches)*
Conservation status *Amber-listed (BoCCI, 2020–2026)*
Vocalisations *Call is a very distinctive, nasal, shrill 'kwehhEEHH'.*

I settled back down and we picked up from where we left off. It was going well too, until I heard a loud drumming sound coming from behind me: WOODPECKER! I got up and ran away from Kathleen again. She was more prepared for my sudden departure this time, and so she ran after me again, trying not to laugh at the madness of it all. I was shaking with excitement. I'd never sound-recorded a woodpecker drumming in Ireland before. Woodpeckers did not exist here when I was growing up, so to hear this powerful sound in an Irish wood made my hairs stand on end.

Woodpeckers made it to Ireland for the first time around 2008. It's not known why this happened, but it's presumed the British population was doing really well, and that so many territories were occupied there that birds needed to expand out in search of new places to live. From their initial arrival in 2008, they had gone from strength to strength, spreading throughout the country as an established breeding Irish bird. Woodpeckers are wonderful ecosystem-engineers that excavate cavities in trees that can later be used by many other species of birds. So, not only do they bring visual and aural beauty, they bring ecological function, too.

With the woodpecker finally under my belt, Kathleen gave me the thumbs-up. 'That's great, Seán. We've got more than enough.'

Walking back, I felt a real genuineness in Kathleen and I started to open up to her. I told her about my ASD, about my love for nature and also that I was vegetarian (we vegetarians and vegans seem to like announcing that, it's true). It turned out that Kathleen was vegetarian too and loved animals, and so we just clicked as people. I think this helped me with the whole filming process.

Some weeks later, the film went out online for *The Irish Times*. It was just over six minutes in length, and it was beautiful. Kathleen was a master of her craft and I was so proud to share it with my friends and family. Later, Kathleen told me that it had amazing feedback and proved to be one of the most popular videos they did all year. This really surprised me. I felt that my topic was so niche, and I was used to doing my thing alone, without the verification or wider interest of other people. This was a pivotal moment in how I perceived my work; it hinted at my project potentially standing for something much greater than my desire to capture the sound of every regularly occurring bird species. Maybe I *could* make a difference?

Peregrine Falcon *(Falco peregrinus)*
Family *Falconidae (falcons and caracaras)*
Conservation status *Annex I (EU Birds Directive), Green-listed (BoCCI, 2020–2026)*
Vocalisations *The incessant husky, yet slightly high-pitched 'kehk-kehk-kehk-kehk' alarm calls are the easiest of vocalisations to encounter.*

Nature Boy

Some weeks passed and I found myself back doing my bird surveys in County Wicklow. I was watching a peregrine falcon flying through a deafeningly busy quarry. Peregrine falcons are mightily impressive birds. The fastest animal on the planet, they can reach diving speeds of over 320 kilometres per hour! These dives end in the peregrine pummelling its unsuspecting prey with its feet – an instant death. Peregrine falcons are protected under Annex I of the EU Birds Directive.[10] Now green-listed in Ireland, they were once much rarer, suffering greatly at the hands of a number of since-banned pesticides.

Large dumper trucks with wheels the size of garden sheds trundled up and down dusty tracks, sending a curtain of white dust into the air. All kinds of bangs and explosions emanated from seemingly every direction – industrial Kango-hammers, mechanised stone drills, stone-grinders – and I was impressed by the peregrine falcon's resilience in the face of such imposing anthropogenic destruction. I felt my phone vibrating in my pocket. I was surprised to see that it was Kathleen calling. I didn't expect to hear from her again now that the piece was long since published.

I answered in a surprised, almost questioning tone: 'Hi Kathleen, how are you?'

Hey, Seán, how is everything?' I sensed a nervousness in her voice, a slight quiver.

'Is everything okay?' I asked.

She replied, 'Yeah, I just wanted to ask you ...'

Kathleen went on to nervously ask me if I'd be interested in doing a longer piece on my work – a documentary for TV. She was explaining the process in great detail, really quickly. I stopped her in her tracks – 'I'm in!'

There was a pause on the line for a second, before Kathleen responded, 'Really?'

'Yes! It sounds amazing. I'm sure I'll be nervous in the beginning but I'd love to have the platform to share the thing I love so dearly with the nation.'

Although the idea of it all excited me, I had to contain myself. Nothing was certain yet, and Kathleen explained to me that she would need to apply for several rounds of funding, find a producer and have a broadcaster agree to host the film. She told me it would take some time and not to think about it too much for now.

As I tried to put the conversation with Kathleen out of my mind, an old friend of mine arrived back and we had a lot of catching up to do.

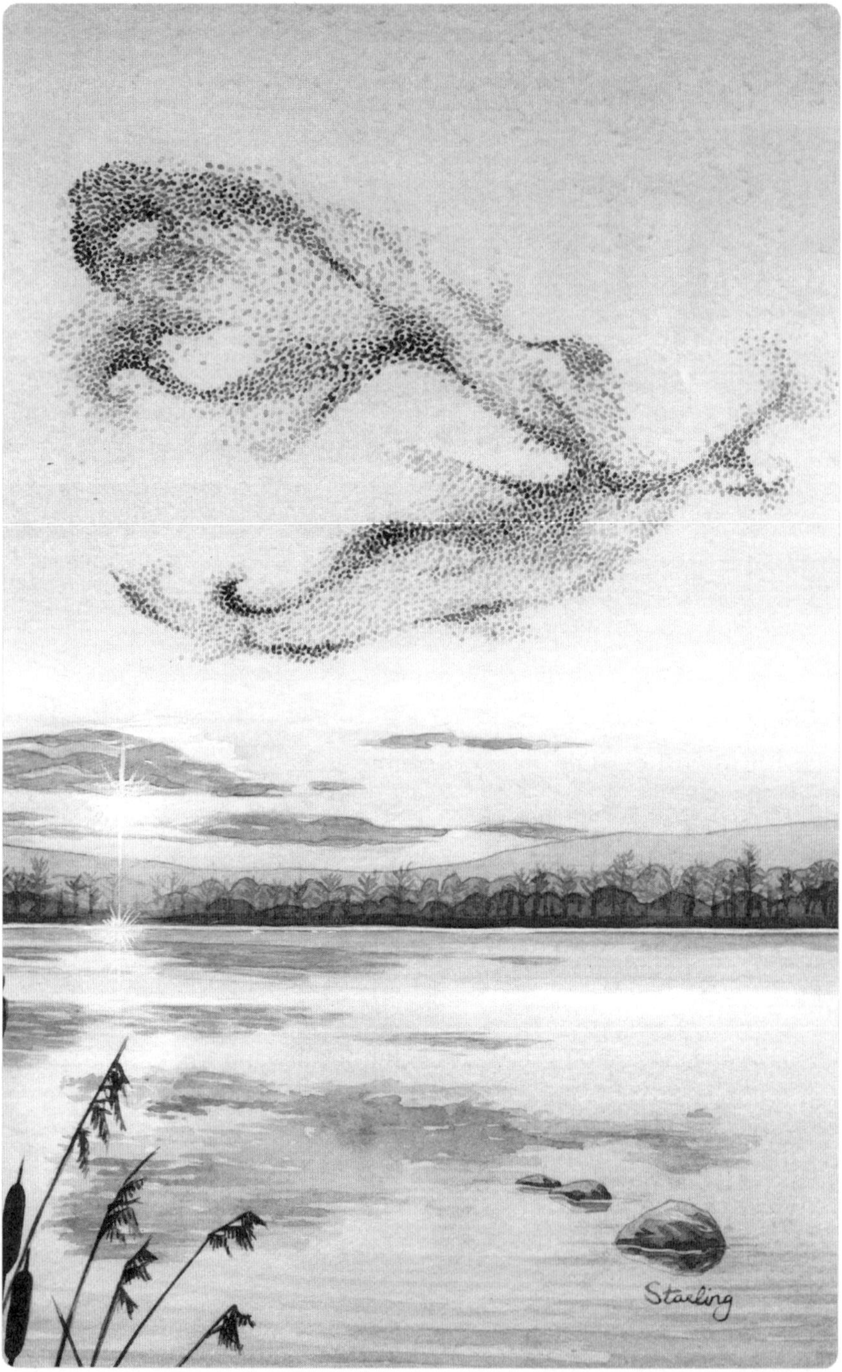
Starling

Chapter 12

BEFORE I KNEW IT, IT WAS MAY 2022 AND THE WHITETHROATS had returned home to Ireland in force. Having spent the winter in the balmy Senegalese subtropics, they were now back in their dense scrubby fortresses. They seek out spiky thickets of canary-yellow gorse, impenetrable thorny bramble bushes and thick patches of wicked stinging nettles. Here, they build a nest close to the ground in the safety of nature's plant guardians. My aim was to capture the songs of as many singing males throughout the country as time would permit. In September, they'd leave for Senegal once again.

Harry's recording told me there were stories in there, but just how far would those stories span? That magical encounter with my first ever whitethroat when I was a child has lived with me throughout my life. From seeing it in Éamon de Buitléar's *Amuigh Faoin Spéir* to going with my dad to see it in the flesh at Roche's Point – probably my first experience of species detective work. It was one of those rare special moments: pure, joy-filled, simple and honest. And now I felt like I had a chance to really get to know this bird and to show the world just how special it really is. It was almost as if the whitethroat had a burning desire to tell me something – like our worlds were meant to collide in some way. And now, some twenty years later, I was ready and willing. My old friend had my full attention.

Common whitethroats have many vocalisations, but there are two standout song-types. The first is the typical song they give from the tops of their favourite song perches – whatever is tall and available to them in their chosen territories: the tops of trees, gorse, even phone wires work. This song is a series of short, gravelly, predictable verses with a few seconds' pause between one and the next. Typically, there is little to no mimicry in this song-type. However, when a rival male or a prospecting female appears, this is when the magic happens. The singing male needs to pull his pants up and show them what he's made of. He can't let a rival male take his spot, so he needs to show him who's boss. As for the female, he needs to do everything in his power to impress her. So, up he gets, flying high into the air above his territory. Here, he hovers over his dominion, kept afloat with a burst of rapid wingbeats, as he belts out a whole new song, composed almost entirely of mimicry. Instead of his short, predictable, gravelly verses, he is now lashing out the long strings of notes and phrases he's soaked up from the environment around him.

It has long been theorised that such displays of mimicry in birds is a reflection of the genetic fitness of an individual. Birds with good genetics have a greater ability to learn and retain complex songs. This is attractive to a potential mate because she knows that these good genetics will be passed onto her offspring. To a rival male, this mimetic prowess is off-putting, as it signals this bird is strong and healthy, and that it may lose against this bird if a physical conflict were to arise. This was also the song that was most attractive to me.

Everywhere I went over the course of the summer, I was always looking out for whitethroat habitat. Alba was used to the routine. If we visited a friend or went to check out a new town or city, the deal was that we needed to look for whitethroat habitat nearby so we were both happy. I looked at Google Maps for any scrubby-looking spots and bookmarked them for a recording session later that same day or early the next morning. When I was out surveying during the week, I'd do the same. I'd find some territories and leave recorders running there passively until I'd collect them after my surveys were done, some hours later. I wanted to sample as many habitat mosaics as possible, too. Whilst scrub is key, the habitats that surrounded the territories would, in theory, dictate the voices in the mimicry. And so, I recorded in dense willow stands in raised bogs, along woodland edges and openings, in the thicket-like hedgerows of farmers' fields, and in scrubby gorse and bramble patches amongst coastal dunes. Anywhere that held a singing whitethroat that intersected my path or reached my ever-listening ears, I was on it.

When a bird was in full mimetic flow, it was a joy to listen to – like a manic jazz musician lost in the bliss of the music. The bird would let rip, giving it all it had in an unhinged yet beautiful disarray. It always happened so fast, out of the blue, as if it were suddenly transformed to another creature that just had to spit something out. One minute, it was calm and collected; the next, it was up there belting out its big, beautiful musical mess. I'd listen live and try to pick out the mimicry. It was tough, like trying to interpret a language I was just starting out in – by the time I had translated the first few words in my head, I'd missed so much of the rest of the sentence that none of it made sense any more. Despite this, I tried anyway, but I knew the real stories wouldn't come to me until I paid it the attention it truly deserved, back home at my desk. I continuously collected these songs until the whitethroats said farewell for the year. Some weeks later, nestled in my office, I sat at my desk all wrapped up and looking out at the autumnal leaves. I thought of my friends, en route to Senegal. What would they see? Who would they encounter? Would they make it? And would their captured songs tell me about these journeys?

   I gathered all of my recordings together in one folder and began the long and arduous process of listening to each in great detail – each one many times. Upon seeing or hearing mimicry, I would add a digital label to the sonogram. That way, I could label the mimicked species under the corresponding shape in the sonogram. When a song was fully annotated, I would have a snapshot or a roadmap of this bird's experiences in life. I did not know if whitethroats, like starlings, were lifelong learners, but I strongly suspected they would be.

   I kept it simple at first. It was a big task, and so I picked out all of the Irish mimicry and saved each piece: swallow and house martin mimicry were most frequent, followed by house sparrow, goldfinch and great tit. This made sense – they were all widespread, common breeding birds that whitethroats would encounter. Coastal birds reflected their sea-faring neighbours in their ballads: sandwich tern was common, as was oystercatcher. Redshank, chough, common sandpiper, curlew, dunlin, herring gull, ringed plover, little tern, green sandpiper, Arctic tern, grey heron, black-headed gull, golden plover, rock pipit, roseate tern and whimbrel also made appearances! Once it was within their physical capabilities, the whitethroats absorbed and imitated the sounds of any bird they heard with frequency.

Starling *(Sturnus vulgaris)*
Family *Sturnidae (starlings)*
Conservation status *Amber-listed (BoCCI, 2020-2026)*
Vocalisations *An incredible vocalist and lifelong song-learner, meaning it can continually work on and improve upon its technique and repertoire. Song is a mixture of scratchy sounds, pops and clicks, mixed with a high degree of vocal mimicry – the imitations of birds, mammals and even non-living components of the surrounding area.*

My first surprises came when I started to pick out yellow wagtails and tree pipits. Both of these birds are notable migrants in Ireland. Neither breeds here, and they pass through in only very small numbers – far too irregular to have been learned here. I thought back to Catalunya where both were very common and vocal on migration. They moved by day and night, and were a staple of my birding in spring and autumn. Perhaps these whitethroats heard them there. Regardless, I had a strong inkling they heard them somewhere in Iberia. But I needed something more – I needed a species that placed the whitethroat in Iberia with more confidence. More familiar voices stated to reach out to me, again bringing me back to my happy times in Catalunya: Thekla's lark, zitting cisticola, tawny pipit, serin and western Bonelli's warbler – all common birds back at my old Catalan haunts. I now knew that these whitethroats were at least learning into October, several months after the first Irish juveniles fledge, typically around July.

I was so close to getting the full picture, and now I really wanted to detect some African mimicry in the repertoire of our Irish whitethroats. But how would I do this?

I already knew that whitethroats tended to winter in and around Senegal, but I'd never been anywhere near there, nor did I have any experience of Senegalese avifauna. I knew whitethroats liked to mimic birds that spent a lot of time calling in flight, as demonstrated by their propensity to imitate both barn swallow and house martin. I also spoke to my friend Magnus, who told me that he was detecting a lot of mimicry of various bee-eater species in common redstarts in Portugal. Bee-eaters spend the majority of their lives calling on the wing, and common redstarts are *outstanding* mimics, so to hear this came as no surprise to me.

I opened up xeno-canto and filtered search results for Senegal. Reams of results came back – 47 pages worth, and almost 1,500 recordings. I switched results to sonogram view, then I scrolled through each and every recording, taking mental notes of sonogram shapes and looking at species names. This process took me several weeks. I then went back over my whitethroat recordings and began to label interesting-looking notes as 'African?'

I didn't hit any matches. I became disheartened and took a break from it for a week. Then, I came back and decided to focus on those bee-eaters. I found mimicry of European bee-eater right away, but it could have heard those in Iberia *or* Africa. I kept pushing and, with perseverance, it paid off. *Bingo!* I found a perfect example of blue-cheeked bee-eater mimicry! This species does *not* occur in Iberia, but breeds in northwest Africa (mostly Morocco), as well as the Sahel region (that incudes Senegal), where it also winters.

So, this placed our whitethroats in a broad but strictly African geographical region, ranging from Morocco to Senegal, more or less. This wasn't good enough – I needed something more refined, something that placed it in the wintering region with certainty. For nights on end, fuelled by multiple servings of double espressos, I kept pushing and hoping, until I did that thing again … I went from total silence and focus to shouting at full volume, jumping off my chair like a madman. Alba banged on the wall. I ran into the pitch-black bedroom and started shouting to her in maniacal gibberish.

'Go away, Seán. It's two in the morning! What is wrong with you? Why do you keep doing this?!'

I had no idea it was as late as that. I apologised and crept back to my lair, where I proceeded to fist-pump and whisper-shout to myself around the room. I'd only come across a *gorgeous* match for white-throated bee-eater. This species breeds along the southern edge of the Sahara Desert and winters in the rainforests of Senegal to Uganda. This places our Irish whitethroats *right there*, in their wintering grounds.

I sat in silence for several minutes, thinking about the implications of this. I now had 'our' whitethroats singing their roadmap in life. They were telling me who they spent their time with on the Irish breeding grounds, who they met on their travels through Iberia and, most amazingly, who they heard way down in subtropical Senegal on their winter vacations. These birds were singing their life stories to me. These tales from their epic migratory routes were like stamps on a passport. It gave me chills just thinking about it. What a beautiful, intimate representation of these birds' lives. I felt privileged to have this amazing journey communicated and shared with me.

It also made me think – these birds are also a poignant symbol of our interconnectedness in the world. We are all brothers and sisters in life. We share this planet as one, and these delicate little wonders are the webs that join the dots. I wish we humans could be more like these whitethroats, who come and go in song and peace, vagabonds and beings of the world who see neither colour nor creed. It also made me think of the world in a novel (to me) ecological perspective – what we do to the land here in Ireland has implications around the globe, like ripples in a great big pond. If we, through our actions, impede the breeding success of these Irish whitethroats, this loss is felt way down in Senegal, too. I'd never thought about things in this way. On our insular little island, we feel like our actions are contained, the results localised, but they are not.

That year I recorded 79 clear whitethroat songs, from which I detected mimicry of a whopping 72 species. This project is still a work in progress and I am certain that there are many more voices to come forward. I don't think I'll ever tire of our brilliant little whitethroat. People have asked me many times what my favourite bird is and I can now say with absolute certainty that it is the whitethroat. It's a relatively under-praised little bird, generally speaking. But I hope I've shone a light on this wonderful creature, and that the next time you pass an area of scrub, you'll think of the whitethroat. Better yet, I hope you experience one. And please, say hello from me.

With the identification of African bird vocalisations in the whitethroat's vocabulary and doing a job I loved, even if it was flawed, I didn't think things could get any better. Then, towards the end of 2022, I received another call from Kathleen. I answered hesitantly, fearing the worst, but I knew by her tone it was good. She told me that we'd been awarded funding for a one-hour documentary and that RTÉ would broadcast it! The amazing Ross Whitaker and Aideen O'Sullivan would produce, the iconic Irish wildlife cinematographer Ross Bartley would film, and the incredible Iseult Howlett would edit.

It was also around this time that I started to get quite a few talk requests. The idea terrified me. I felt like I had nothing to offer and thought of my schooldays quivering in front of my peers. Thankfully, my experiences in teaching English had knocked some of the fear out of me and, deep down, I wanted to share my sound-recordings and to tell the many stories that lay behind them.

Alba loves giving talks, and she was excited for me. As always, she had my back. 'You can do this! I've told you before, I love your bird stories – they're really different, and you turn into another person when you speak about your birds. People will love it and I'll help you with everything.'

I thought about it, feeling unsure of myself.

Every moment spent outside in Ireland hurt me greatly. I would look at all the wrongs being done to nature and complain to Alba incessantly. I wasn't saying these things to be pedantic, I was saying them because it was all too much for me. I was overwhelmed with sadness and frustration because most of the damage was totally avoidable and unnecessary. I'd often confront people (council workers, farmers and contractors mostly) cutting hedgerows for no good reason during the closed season. They'd usually scoff at me and I'd be left feeling even sadder and more deflated. I was so frustrated that the messaging on this topic wasn't bigger and backed properly by the government. Our general disconnection from the land was plain for all to see, even more so for people with a background in ecology, like myself. And it filled me with deep, often tearful sorrow, every day. Complaining about it all was a way for me to let off some steam – the angst and hurt were just unbearable at times.

But Alba could only take so much before she snapped me into reality, as she so often does. 'Seán, can you please stop complaining about the land like that? It's getting tiring. I'm sick of it, actually. Instead of moaning about it to me, why don't you actually do something about it?'

I apologised and bit my tongue, but she got me thinking. She was right. Me moaning about the wrongs day-in, day-out would never make a difference. I was looping in a never-ending cycle of loathing and sadness. I was poisoning myself, becoming bitter. But what if I were to try to address these issues in these talks and in the film? That *could* make a difference.

At this point in the project, I had seen a lot. I saw the land differently now. I saw it for what it really was: a broken shell of its former glory, a mosaic of intensively managed farm plots, with bald, overgrazed mountains, polluted waterways, drained bogs and a smothering of commercial conifer plantations. But there was still beauty out there and this was worth celebrating.

I began to realise that this project was not about me any more; it had become something much more important. It was a showcase of the wonderful avian voices of the land we call home, a testament to the beauty of what clings on for life, a world worth cherishing and preserving. I felt as though sharing the voices of these birds was a way to awaken something in people – to move them into caring more. I decided that focusing on the negatives wasn't the way to make a change, at least not for me. Although I understood that it would be important to alert people to the problems, I decided not to dwell on them *too* much – I didn't want to get stuck in the mud and sadden people. Instead, I wanted to woo people into action. Beauty brings love and hope, and love and hope fuel change.

This is the moment I truly realised that my work could act as a tool to fight for positive ecological change in Ireland. At this point the purpose and meaning of the project completely shifted in my mind. Instead of serving me, it could serve Irish nature as well as the people. All along, I was too shy and unsure to see it like this, but people responded to the sounds in such a beautiful way. People would thank me, but they'd also share back their own memories and experiences with birds. There was something about bird sound that seemed to capture people in a way that I'd not experienced before. And so I agreed to the talks. I created a slideshow that told my journey of discovery through sound. I addressed the issues that blight our landscape, but I didn't dwell on them. Instead, I focused on the beauty and the mystery of what we had left – what could be saved and expanded upon.

My first talk was terrifying. I *did* shake like a leaf, but I felt like another person. That bleating sheep from my schooldays wasn't up there on stage. The talk was very well received and I realised that I could do this! These talks went from strength to strength and they became a vital tool to spread my messages of awareness and of love for our natural world.

Nature Boy

In late February 2023, I received the call from Kathleen I'd been waiting so eagerly for – we were ready to begin. At this point in time, I was well into the project. I only had around 25 species left to sound record. These birds were the rarest, the most silent, the most elusive – and sometimes all three of those combined. Filming was set to capture the biggest adventures and challenges of the project. They would be there for the most exciting moments. Kathleen told me they'd like to record in the first week of March until September or October, but what she proposed was not what I'd expected. She'd heard about an epic starling murmuration at Lough Ennell in County Westmeath, and asked if I'd like to sound record it. It would be the first scene of filming if I agreed to it. Things were tight – I had a list of really difficult species to record that year and, frankly, the idea of this diversion made me nervous. I wondered if it was necessary. She told me that she'd already been in touch with farmers, and the wonderful photographer James Crombie.

As well as being an award-winning press photographer, for the past three years James had been following this starling murmuration with his camera. It was his passion project. I could relate to that. At its peak, the murmuration reaches up to a quarter of a million birds. This gigantic flock is made up partly of locally bred Irish birds, but the bulk are winter visitors escaping the colds of Scandinavia and eastern Europe. Come the spring, they'll head back to those places again in order to breed and raise a family. The conditions there in winter are simply too harsh for them to survive and so they seek out milder climes. During the day, these birds spread out, feeding within a 30-kilometre radius of their chosen roosting sites.

Leading up to dusk, they all begin to make a beeline for the roost. The roost at Lough Ennell is the largest of its kind in Ireland, and for good reason. It is situated in the centre of the country, making it a natural point of convergence and, more importantly, it has an extensive reed-fringed periphery within which the starlings huddle together each night. The lake and its marshy edges prevent land-based predators from accessing the starlings. Here in the dark, wintry nights, they huddle close together in their thousands, their combined body heat raising the temperature enough to sleep in comfort. But before they hunker down, they meet in the sky above the lake in their thousands, moving in unison, like a winged, chirping shoal of fish. Studies have revealed that each individual starling keeps in check with its six to seven closest neighbours in order for the flock to move in tandem. They move as if they were a single organism, wheeling, outstretching, condensing and shapeshifting in a visually spectacular feat of coordinated flight. But they don't just do this for fun. Because they gather in such numbers, they attract the attention of aerial predators – sparrowhawks and peregrine falcons mostly. These birds do their very best to pick a life out of the sky before bed, but the starlings' erratic, coordinated movements make it as difficult as possible for these skilled hunters.

At first I thought, *I already have so many recordings of starlings. And we are really up against it this year. I have around 25 extremely difficult species to sound record. Is it really wise to pursue this audio capture?* I thought about it for some time, and then I agreed. I'd never seen an Irish murmuration of this proportion before, and I certainly hadn't ever sound-recorded birds in this manner before. I'd only ever focused on their vocalisations, really. I kind of felt embarrassed that I had to be asked to do this. *Of course I want to sound record the collective wingbeats of quarter of a million starlings*, I thought. This project was more than just collecting the call of every bird, right? It was about sharing the beauty of our natural world and inspiring change. I was fully invested and was thinking about how this recording might sound and how people might perceive it.

We pulled up to a small car park on the shoreline of Lough Ennell. Kathleen was already there, greeting us both with a smile. Alba had not met her yet and so they were happy to finally link up.

Ross Bartley appeared from the boot of his four-wheel drive with his enthusiastic, welcoming smile. 'Hi guys, I'm Ross. I'll be working the camera for the next few months. Lovely to meet you both.'

Just like Kathleen, there was an instant sense of genuineness, but also one of determination and focus. Ross and Kathleen spoke to one side for a minute. Myself and Alba stood back and left them to it. We were both very nervous – this was so new to us. Then they called us over, and I could tell they had a plan. Kathleen, our director, led the way.

'Okay, guys, so we need to get some shots of you both walking out the track to get to our spot. We don't have a lot of time though. We need to be there at least 45 minutes before dusk so we can get in place before the starlings do. We don't want to disturb them. So you two just walk ahead of us and do your thing. Pretend we aren't there.'

I'd done this before, but I could see that Alba was a little unsure. Just like she's always done for me, I did my best to calm her. I gently took hold of her hand and off we walked – I pointed out all of the birds we passed to take her mind off the camera. Ross was, at times, running ahead to get us head-on and, other times, shooting from behind. Alba soon fell into the swing of things and, before we knew it, we were at our spot.

We looked up to see a dense stand of straw-like reeds, about 7 feet tall, stretching as far as the eye could see. We could only see part of the lake behind them, but were impressed by its size – an area of approximately 12 square kilometres. We set our bags down in a spot of solid ground next to a gnarled hawthorn tree, an aged character of the land that had probably watched starlings murmurate at that spot for over a hundred years. Beyond this point, heading towards the reedbed, the ground became highly irregular and wet. Deep circular puddles were dotted all around, amidst rounded, vegetated tussocks of sedges and grasses, like a series of hardly navigable stepping stones. This was the safety perimeter that protected the starlings' roosting spot in the reeds from any landward threats, and I could see how they'd do the job.

I was feeling a little stressed now, time was approaching and I still needed to set up my kit and get it into position. I knelt down to get ready and felt a strange nibbling sensation in my hair. I looked up and got such a fright. Two horses had come to say hello, one taking a keen interest in my mop of curls. As I've said, I'm very wary of any animal that's larger than me, even more so since my run-in with that Nepalese rhino, and, as much as I love all of these big animals, the horses were flustering me. Alba, always watchful, could see my hesitancy and so she coaxed them away and began to plait their hair into little braids, taking it out of their eyes. They didn't move a muscle – in fact, they seemed to enjoy it!

My settings were just right, so I slowly and carefully bunny-hopped from tussock to tussock, to get my mic set up next to the edge of the reedbed. I splayed out the legs of the tripod just to make sure nothing fell into the water that surrounded me, double-checked my settings, popped on headphones for a quick sound check and I was done. I turned to Ross and gave him the thumbs-up, before cautiously hopping back to the solid ground beneath the hawthorn. Alba came back to join me and we waited in nervous anticipation. The friendly farmer who owned the land had arrived. I turned to him and whispered, 'How will I know it's time and where do they come from?'

He whispered back, 'Oh you'll know when it's time – they'll come from all around you and they'll converge right over your mic.'

I thought for a second before asking, 'Do you think they'll come?'

He smiled, looking out to the fading sky. 'They'll come.'

Not long after, my ears began to pick up a dull but growing rumbling sound. *Please, tell me that's not road noise again?* But it grew and grew until I saw a dark cloud converging over the lake. It was the starlings!

My eyes perked up and, silently, I looked at Alba and excitedly pointed out the nearing black mass. It looked like a plague of locusts were approaching. Within tens of seconds they were over our heads, shimmying and dancing in unison. I'd seen a murmuration before but I knew Alba hadn't. I looked over at her and her mouth was wide open as she gazed up at the sky. There was no wind at all that night, yet it sounded like a hurricane was ripping through the airspace above us. It was quite like the sound of an angry ocean, like the surf pounding and retreating in waves.

I was mightily impressed as it was, but then I noticed the flock growing. Group after group flew into sight, joining the dancing bulk of birds. Each second it grew in size, sound and impressiveness, until finally one enormous flock of tens of thousands of birds appeared almost out of nowhere. The sound of the collective wingbeats of a quarter of a million starlings was now ROARING through the air. This mega-flock WHOOSHED like a fighter jet as it passed low over our heads. The sound was truly deafening. The automatic reaction was to duck – it sounded as if we were about to be hit by a truck. During these close passes, what sounded like falling drops of heavy rain pitter-pattered all around us. It was starling poop bucketing down, splashing in the puddles in amongst the vegetated tussocks and slapping off our coats and exposed skin. I giggled to myself – every one of us was dotted in splodges of white starling excrement, as were our bags, electronics and just about every inch of the ground beneath us.

The flock was at its peak now. We counted three sparrowhawks and a peregrine trying to pluck birds out of the sky. This really sent the murmuration into full defence, which meant that their aerial displays became a work of fine art. They twisted, turned and shimmied at great speed – stopping, turning and changing direction like nobody's business. The sound was like nothing I'd ever experienced in my life. My ears and all of my senses were completely immersed in this astonishing spectacle of nature. Every hair on my body stood on end and I felt a gush of warm emotion flowing through my veins. I looked back at Alba with a smile and she just couldn't contain her expression. I'd never seen someone's jaw open to the extent hers did. I looked back at Ross and his eye was glued to the camera with a laser-like focus. I shifted my gaze across to Kathleen, who looked like she was about to burst into tears with excitement.

Right there and then, I knew we were all witnesses to something really special – a moment we would cherish for the rest of our lives – and it gave me huge hope and inspiration for the final leg of this journey.

Soon after, the flock coordinated one last dance before descending into the reedbed en mass, tumbling out of the sky with one last display of grace and unison. The sudden silence was bizarre. It felt like stepping out of a nightclub onto an empty street at 4 a.m. It was only then that I realised just how powerful the sound of this spectacle had been. We all took a breath, looked around at one another and began to laugh! It was a laughter I'd never experienced before – one of shock, awe and relief. We were all deeply moved by what we'd just experienced, and knew that we'd captured something incredibly special.

'Anyone for dinner?' Kathleen exclaimed. We were off to an amazing start and so we agreed to sit down, have a bite to eat and to formulate a filming plan. What birds were next? When and where would we shoot next? What licences would we need? We picked a rather swanky-looking Italian restaurant, and were met with some odd looks. It took me a moment to realise why – we were still covered in starling poop! But man, it was worth it.

Next up on our list of shoots was Donegal. Donegal was a special site which held many crucial pieces of the puzzle. It was my best bet for corncrake, red-throated diver, golden eagle and ring ouzel. All of these would pose significant challenges and I'd need to be granted separate licences from the National Parks and Wildlife Service (NPWS) to sound record each. I'd also need to be accompanied to locations by an NPWS ranger. At the time, I was still working full-time for a company doing bird surveys, so I took a week off especially for this adventure. I lined everything up with the film crew and we aimed for mid-May.

We started out with the easiest of the lot – the corncrake. Although these are rare on a national level, where they do occur, they are *loud* and persistent callers. Granda Dave, my mother's father, used to tell me how they kept him awake at night in 1940s rural Limerick – he used to bemoan them! Back in the heyday of the Irish corncrake, it wasn't only Granda Dave who complained about them, in fact their nocturnal racket inspired a curse aimed at those who entered a person's bad books: codladh an traonach chugat (the sleep of the corncrake to you).

Corncrake *(Crex crex)*
Family *Rallidae (rails)*
Conservation status *Annex I (EU Birds Directive), Red-listed (BoCCI, 2020–2026)*
Vocalisations *Call a harsh and resonant 'crex-crex-crex-crex', after which its Latin name is derived.*

I was reading all that I could on corncrakes in Ireland, between Google and an amazing book of Irish avian mythology and folklore: *Birds of Ireland: Myths, Legends and Folklore*,[11] lent to me by Ross Bartley, as I made the ferry journey out to Tory Island, Ireland's most northwesterly point and one of the last bastions for corncrakes in the country. We were full of excitement as we rocked and bounced over the crashing white horses of an animated Atlantic. An apt journey for the wild rock that lay out there on the horizon. I excitedly pointed out a small group of puffins on the water, shortly before a minke whale surfaced a hundred metres in front of the bow, puffing out through its blowhole as it surfaced and letting go of its breath after a dive.

Tory appeared closer on the horizon and, before long, we were setting foot again on dry land. We'd be staying overnight in the Harbour View Hotel. The plan was to rest up and rise an hour before dawn to get into position to film, sound-record and, hopefully, see some corncrakes.

It sounded like a sensible plan and so, naturally, I decided to do the opposite. I dropped off my bags, picked up my recording equipment and headed for the eastern end of the island.

Tory is a strange place, with hardly a tree to be seen throughout. Many common bird species are absent from the island because of this lack of trees, coupled with the island's exposed offshore location, but parts of it are specifically managed under the EU-funded Corncrake LIFE project, setting out early and late cover plots (ELCs), areas of dense hogweed and nettle, for example, that stand out from shorter vegetated areas that surround these plots and provide tall areas of hiding throughout the breeding season. These ELCs are highly beneficial to corncrake populations. Delayed hay or silage crops as well as conservation-friendly mowing techniques are also adopted.

As soon as I began my descent of the hill towards the lake, I could already hear a number of corncrakes calling from cover. I didn't see them, but that didn't matter this time. I made my way to the edge of the lake itself and set up my equipment, where I ran a headset extension cable back to the earthen track. I sat in some soft grass next to an old lichen-encrusted stone wall and began to listen to my recording live. I was glad I'd come out here, despite my exhaustion from the long journey up from

Cork in the early hours of that same morning. I sat there listening to the crexing calls of the corncrakes – like a finger running down a comb with force. This crexing description not only refers to the sound of their calls, but also lends to its Latin name of *Crex crex*.

Closing my eyes and opening my ears, I thought of Granda Dave with a smile, and laughed at the thought of him cursing the corncrakes behind his house as a boy. I also thought of the loss – both my loss of Granda and of Ireland's loss of the corncrake. How hard to believe that the corncrake was once widespread and common throughout the country. The intensification of our agricultural systems has a lot to answer for. So many species would have nested in the hay meadows of old, hidden in the lush mixture of grasses and wildflowers, which only met their end in the autumn through the empathetic arcs of a hand-swung scythe. In this manner, farmers felt every blade of grass run past, the scythe acting as an extension of their very own touch. They felt and understood the land deeply. We held a mutual respect for one another and we lived together in harmony. The ground-dwelling birds had ample time to raise a number of broods in the safety of the tall foliage, with bees and insects aplenty – pollinating and providing a rich protein source for hungry chicks.

Today, we've swapped that way of life for sterile fields of ryegrass, where fountains of cow excrement are sprayed multiple times a year, and grass is cut for silage as early as May and as many as six times per year. With improved agricultural grassland now the single most dominant land cover type in Ireland, what chance did our ground-nesting birds have?

This same scenario has affected so many – skylark, meadow pipit, curlew, lapwing and more – all friends of our ancestors. Today, they're barely acquaintances. Many don't even know they exist at all. These are sad and negative thoughts, but they're the truth. An internal battle played out in my mind. I'd told myself I wouldn't dwell on the negatives. I needed to be thankful that I was here in the moment and listening to those corncrakes that Granda cursed in his rascal-like way. They're still here. And, better yet, the EU LIFE project was working, with a 35 per cent increase in the corncrake population in the past five years, as reported in 2023.[12]

Accompanying the multiple crexing corncrakes were several skylarks, singing their rambling melodies from a hovering height above. These were also faring well as a result of the corncrake habitat management, ground-nesters as they are. As the light faded, a familiar sound launched up into the sky from multiple points. The sound of displaying snipe actually comes from the vibrating outer tail feathers of the birds as they plummet from great heights. After each dive, they climb back up again and repeat. How wonderful. Displaying snipe sound like a bleating young goat. Snipe have several names in Irish, many of which nod to their goat-like sounds. Gabhairín deorach translates to 'wandering little goat'; gabhairín reo to 'little goat of the frost'; and meannán aeir to 'kid (young goat) of the air'. Their goat-like sound was clearly not lost on our ancestors. Snipe too have suffered a drastic decline in Ireland, a country that has lost 90 per cent of its wetlands in the past 300 years – more than any other country in the world. Snipe, a wetland specialist, has suffered greatly as a result.

Snipe *(Gallinago gallinago)*
Family *Scolopacidae (curlews, sandpipers, snipes and woodcocks)*
Conservation status Red-listed (BoCCI, 2020–2026)

Seán Ronayne

Vocalisations *Flight call a sharp, nasal 'pshhh'. The most commonly heard display is in fact not a vocalisation at all. In spring and summer, males climb tens of metres above their chosen territories at night, before plummeting back down to the ground. During this free-fall, the outer-tail feathers vibrate and make a sound a little like a young goat!*

I remember a bog in my hometown of Cobh where I first heard these as a boy. I was frightfully stressed in the build-up to my Junior Certificate exams, and I cycled out to the bog at dusk on many an evening. I didn't go there to see or hear anything in particular, but I was met with several 'sky goats' displaying with vigour over the bog. I didn't know what they were at first, but stood there in awe of the sound. The weight of my pending exams dissipated into thin air and I sat there into the dark of the night before cycling home, replenished and ready to take on the world. Sadly, that same bog is now drained, and the sky goats are no more, only living on as a happy childhood memory. Nevertheless, it was great to hear them once again, especially with the collaboration of the corncrakes and skylarks.

I sat there and realised that I was listening to a remnant of a lost soundscape – this trio of magical creatures would have been a common encounter throughout the lands of Ireland at one point. Again, I reminded myself, it's still here and it can come back, seeding from this fragment of hope. I sat with closed eyes and really focused on the sound. I felt myself drifting into a state of total calm, the sound slowly fading out, until there was nothing.

Slumped over in the grass, I woke up some time later, groggy and confused. I looked at the time – it was 1 a.m.! I'd fallen asleep, although my experience of 'the sleep of the corncrake' was very different to the

Irish curse of old. Mine was healing, blissful and … special. Coming to my senses, I realised I didn't have a key to the hotel. I picked up my stuff and ran. Everything was in darkness, bar a small lobby light. I peeked in – the reception was empty. Uh oh! Maybe I'd be sleeping with the corncrakes for *real*. I knocked a few times and got no response. I put my head to the front window and jumped with fright – someone else was doing the same. They jumped back, too, equally startled. It was Kathleen – she'd been up working in the lobby, setting out the plan for the week. We laughed and both told each other off for being up so late. The following morning we just about managed to get out the door on time, and boy did those corncrakes perform!

Our trip to Donegal was all go, but everything went to plan. We met all of our targets but left the most difficult and the most pressing until last.

Ring ouzel is a species that had become so rare by the time I entered the world, I didn't even realise it was an Irish breeding species until my late twenties. Ring ouzel is a very close relative of our very familiar blackbird. In fact, ouzels look almost identical only for a crescent-shaped white bib on the chest. Whilst 'our' blackbirds are mostly resident, ring ouzel is only partly so. They spend the winter in the Atlas Mountains of Morocco, where they primarily feed on juniper berries.

Ring Ouzel *(Turdus torquatus)*
Family *Turdidae (thrushes)*
Conservation status *Red-listed (BoCCI, 2020–2026)*
Vocalisations *Song is a slow-paced, melancholic series of simple notes, repeated two to three times. The most common form is 'tyew-tyew-tyew'.*

In Ireland, they seek out our mountain peaks where they take up residence in the summer months in rocky gullies, scree slopes, and cliffs with varying degrees of heather and bilberry cover. Once this species bred in almost every Irish county, bar the lowest-lying in the midlands.

I knew ring ouzel was in dire straits in Ireland, but it wasn't until I did my research that I realised just how bad things really were. I spoke to Allan Mee and Robert Vaughan, who had been surveying the species in Ireland for some years. They were among the few people who truly witnessed the final stages of demise of this old character of the hills. Shockingly, they told me that in 2022, just one single pair were detected in Ireland, despite extensive surveying. This was extinction in its final decaying stages and nobody really knew about it.

I was both saddened and appalled all at once. How could we have let this happen? It's true that some external factors are at play (climate change and the chopping of their precious winter juniper resources for firewood), but we are largely to blame here in Ireland. Our uplands are bald and sickly and have been for many, many years. They may look normal to most, but this is a direct symptom of shifting baseline syndrome. If nobody remembers our uplands when they looked *truly* healthy, then their current state of barrenness is what we know – *this* is normal. But it's not.

Our uplands are treated like one big open grazing-field, eaten down to nothing. They're burned each year to encourage fresh grass growth, destroying habitats, plants, invertebrates, lizards and active nests. Non-native, profit-driven conifer plantations also have their role in the degradation of our hills, where they are planted in rare and sensitive habitats, driving out the inhabitants in the name of money and greed.

My mind drifted back to the Catalan Pyrenees where ring ouzels still abound. Here, a rich tapestry of habitats co-exist, and visitors are attracted from far and wide to hike and bask in the glorious nature-filled slopes. These places are not by any means cloaked from foot to tip in forest – not at all. The lower reaches have the densest covering, but higher up, a bountiful mosaic of habitats occurs – large expanses of wildflower meadows, crystal-clear streams, scattered patches of native woodland, craggy areas of jagged rock, and so on.

In Ireland, we would have had a similar mosaic – scattered copses of birch and rowan, large tracts of rugged heather and bilberry, healthy wet blanket bog, dry and wet heath, 'unimproved' grassland and more. But now these places are trashed, treated as a commodity for a few at the expense of many. Unsustainable densities of sheep, goat and deer now roam these lands, where they graze the place lifeless. Imagine an Ireland where the mountains were not used as a gargantuan animal pasture, swarmed with such densities of bleating mowers, and, instead, landowners were incentivised to replenish the nature that had been lost here.

Sheep farming is more often than not highly subsidised. So why can't we instead subsidise farmers *not* to have hordes of sheep wreak havoc on the lands through this over-intensive grazing? How about a land that is still farmed but in a way that is more sympathetic with nature or, where possible, not farmed at all?

Of course, our native flora and fauna would benefit hugely from this, but so would people! Our uplands would be dealt a huge boost in flora and fauna, and our own experiences up there would be much more nature-filled, educational and inspiring. So many of the mountains in Catalunya are owned by the state and are used widely by members of the public seeking out peace and beauty in nature. They are just *bursting* with eclectic, untamed nature – true wild spaces. Why then are *our* state-owned uplands largely treated as open farms? If these sites could be prioritised for nature, it would be a good start, at least. Another big issue up there is the carpets of conifer plantations. Again, we have a semi-state body that is responsible for planting and taking profit from these. It beggars belief.

The case of the ring ouzel in Ireland truly *is* sad, and as much as I want to look at the positive side of this story, it just isn't possible. There were no publicly available records of the voice of an Irish ring ouzel when I began planning to record the species. Perhaps they existed somewhere in an archive, waiting to be found, but find them I could not, so I could only assume that they hadn't been documented by sound.

I was certain that ring ouzel was on the cusp of extinction in Ireland. Even if this last pair raises young, when a population of birds falls below a certain threshold they become genetically unviable. The exact threshold is uncertain – I've seen 50 birds given as a loose figure. Whatever the case, one pair is *undoubtedly* below the threshold. Thus, based on our understanding of just one confirmed national breeding pair, the Irish ring ouzel could be said to be functionally extinct. And soon it would be fully erased from the landscape for good, but I refused to let it die voiceless. Whilst it's almost certainly too late for our ring ouzel, perhaps its haunting melancholic song could symbolise the loss we are experiencing in Ireland, a reminder of the beauty we are erasing from the landscape – a beauty that doesn't need to go, a beauty we can save if we put our minds to it.

Look at the corncrake, after all. Reversal and recovery *are* possible. But we need to get to these birds before they are too far gone. And rather than scrambling to pick up the pieces at the last minute, we need to take a long, hard look at ourselves and make large landscape-level changes. We need our government to take things seriously. Whilst it's true that some of those in power care greatly, our general lack of nature protection shows that many do not. Please, clamp down on the senseless hedgerow, treeline and verge cutting during the nesting season, and remove the many loopholes that make this law utterly meaningless. Put a halt to the burning of our uplands each spring – the same places go up year-in, year-out. Stop the planting of conifers in our uplands. Stop allowing wind-energy projects to go ahead in places they shouldn't. Improve our public-transport systems and get cars off the road. Ban weedkiller, and ban the sale of harmful invasive plant species – amazingly it's still possible to buy *Rhododendron ponticum* in garden centres. I find this astounding, given that this species is probably the single most harmful non-native plant in the country, choking out the last remnants of native woodlands and said to cost €2,457 per hectare to remove when it becomes established!

Take the management of our national parks seriously. More often than not, they are indistinguishable from any other parcel of land on the island. Invest money in them – employ *more* rangers, work to eradicate invasive plant species in an impactful manner, reduce or remove grazing pressure, restore degraded habitats. Prioritise them not for people, but for nature. I could list more, but even if these measures were taken, biodiversity would be given a huge boost overnight.

But all of this aside, I believe the first step to achieving positive change is to look at the land as a place we are only temporarily loaned.

We don't own it, nor are we the sole occupants. It is not our blank canvas to do with it whatever we please. We need to stop and think about our actions.

If I do this, what will it affect?

Is it necessary?

If we stopped and thought about these things, I believe it would heal the land in a thousand ways.

We as individuals can make huge positive changes, too. We can focus on allowing wilderness back into our gardens, we can cut out weedkillers and reduce our meat consumption and plastic use. We can keep our cats indoors. We can join a conservation body, such as BirdWatch Ireland, and help fund real on-the-ground conservation work. And we can also pressure our politicians and government to make the big changes.

On the day of our ring ouzel visit, we were all nervous. Capturing the sounds of this dying bird – the last of its kind – was probably the single most important task in this project. I wanted to immortalise this bird, record a sound that our ancestors were so familiar with, a sound that was almost certainly about to die out forever.

We met with Robert Vaughan, a Dublin born, Donegal based ornithologist and wildlife artist, in the uplands of Glenveagh National Park on a barren, empty, windswept hill – a classically overgrazed Irish mountain site. All around us, the vegetation was grazed bare, and both sheep and deer droppings littered every foot of the land. We passed many deer, as well as some roving sheep. Sheep aren't allowed here, but the fences are in a state of disrepair and so nothing is stopping them – they don't know they're not allowed.

We were accompanied by an understandably nervous and rightly protective NPWS ranger by the name of Martin Toye. This was the last known pair of Irish ring ouzels – the last thing we wanted to do was disturb them. He gave us 30 minutes max – in and out. Rob pointed us in the direction where he had heard the male the previous year. The wind was gusting and whistled into my ears. I didn't stand a hope of hearing or recording one today, but I had my long-term recorder, which I could drop off for six weeks. This was the plan. Guided by Martin, we trekked up a gulley where the male had sung. I dropped off my rig and we left.

We walked out of there in silence. This could be my one shot to record an Irish ring ouzel and it didn't look promising. Rob called me a few days later and said the ring ouzel was back. It was around the corner, singing from another gulley. I had a bittersweet feeling about that. It was back but my recorder was in the wrong spot. Rob was licensed to study this pair, and he needed to set up a trail camera in the territory to monitor progress. Thankfully, he moved my recorder when he did this. He visited the spot daily, and he made my day when he sent a long-distance photo showing the male singing on a rock just above my recorder!

Several weeks later, he collected the unit and I met him in Dublin, where we analysed the contents of the SD card. We breathed a sigh of relief when we discovered the first recording, but they only got better and better. We managed to capture their melancholic three-note song, alarm calls, flight calls, contact calls and, amazingly, begging calls from freshly fledged juveniles. I believe these are the most important recordings I will ever make as an Irish wildlife sound-recordist, and I sincerely hope I do not find myself in a similar position in the future – desperate to record another beautiful species on the brink of extinction.

Luckily, our next target was a total contrast to that of the ring ouzel. It was a shining example of hope. Some weeks later, we found ourselves back in the northwest, this time in County Mayo. Our target was an extraordinary little bird, only discovered in Ireland in the early 1900s that then went extinct and was inevitably brought back through direct, hands-on conservation measures. The red-necked phalarope is an extremely interesting bird. Robert Lloyd Praeger, an Irish naturalist and writer, born in the 19th century, described them as fairy-like when he stumbled across them at their sole Irish breeding territory, a year after their initial discovery.

Red-necked phalaropes are dainty waders with long narrow beaks; and white, black and grey plumage, with striking red necks. They breed on shallow vegetated pools where they spin in circles on the water, picking little invertebrates from the surface. Amazingly, the roles of the sexes are reversed. It is the females that are brightly coloured, and they also do the wooing, with several females often chasing a single male in courtship. When the female lays the eggs, her job is done. She ups and leaves, heading west, where she spends the winter on the sea off Peru. The male incubates the eggs and tends to the young when they hatch, before they, too, all get up and join the females.

Red-necked Phalarope *(Phalaropus lobatus)*
Family *Scolopacidae (curlews, sandpipers, snipes and woodcocks)*
Conservation status *Annex I (EU Birds Directive), Red-listed (BoCCI, 2020–2026)*
Vocalisations *Call is a loud, strident 'CHIK'. But the most distinctive of their vocalisations is a soft duetted chittering given by both sexes during the courtship display.*

The phalaropes of Mayo fizzled out some time in the late 1900s. By the time BirdWatch Ireland bought Annagh Marsh, their one-time most southerly breeding site, it had become heavily silted and vegetated, which is largely unsuitable for phalaropes and, indeed, other waders such as lapwing, redshank and snipe that all bred here in former times.

Across the water in the Shetland Islands, off the northeastern coast of Scotland, a man by the name of Dave Suddaby had a wealth of experience in successfully restoring red-necked phalaropes to their former breeding sites there. Dave was sought out and eventually employed by BirdWatch Ireland to work his magic here. He got straight to work, firstly by removing silt build-up in the pools with a mechanical digger, as well as removing rank vegetation from the interiors. Whilst rather brute-looking at first, the pools, in time, began to look a lot like their former selves.

A regime of light winter grazing was also brought back to maintain a diverse and healthy plant sward surrounding the pools. Whilst the phalaropes feed on the pools themselves, it is in the surrounding vegetation that they nest, so it was important to address the species-poor, grassy mess that had developed around the peripheries of the pools. The whole marsh was also fenced off with both electric and barbed-wire fences. It surprised me when I saw it for the first time – it looked like a heavily fortified prison. Though these heavy-handed measures prevented foxes, mink and otter from predating nests (raiding and eating chicks or eggs) and, with this, all that was needed was a cocktail of time, patience and luck.

We met Dave at the famed marsh, and I was taken aback by the beauty of it. It brimmed with plant life in the short, eclectic sward:

a variety of stunning orchids, striking yellows and purples of flag iris and purple loosestrife, and lovely shallow pools that were packed to the brim with clouds of low-flying midges and gnats – the ideal larder for any hungry phalaropes. Dave was brimming with pride, you could see this place had been nurtured into being with love and passion. He explained how several years had passed after the restoration process with no sign of recovery. Encouragingly, other species bounced back in impressive densities. Redshanks, the sentinels of the marsh; snipe, the sky goats; and lapwing, the national bird of Ireland. But the cherry on top was yet to come.

One misty spring morning, some ten years into the restoration project, as Dave was walking the site with his son, a sharp high-pitched 'plip' called from the mist behind. Dave turned his head to the source and saw a stunning female phalarope land on the water. Hardly believing his eyes, he sat and watched for several hours – and discovered that there was in fact a pair, a male and three females. The phalaropes of Mayo were back! From this moment on, they went from strength to strength, and now there are several pairs that call Annagh Marsh home once again. Birds have even begun to turn up at other sites, perhaps spillovers from the success at Annagh.

Just as Dave wrapped up his story, he froze and pointed – 'Two females and a male right ahead!' He reassured me not to worry, they're really tame. Just crouch down by the water's edge and they'll eventually work their way down to you. I did exactly that, and just like that wallcreeper back in the tops of the wild Pyrenees, a stunning male red-necked phalarope spun its way along the periphery, stopping right in front of me and my running mic.

A female got up in flight and crash-landed next to the male with a splash. They began to call, flutter and fly. I held my breath and pointed the mic in silence. That beaming smile of old crept up on me – I just knew I'd nailed it.

I left the place feeling positive and hopeful. I needed that after those poor ring ouzels. Sometimes, I get overwhelmed in the sadness of it all, but then these wonderful people and their stories pick me right up. We need to remember that there are amazing people like Dave out there doing incredible work and all they ask for is our support. Indeed, joining a conservation body like BirdWatch Ireland is a direct positive action any one of us can take right now. In doing so, you are directly funding this type of invaluable conservation work, and you, too, make your mark in the fight to restore and support nature.

As my project went on, I began to get more and more talk invites, mainly through my updates of the project on social media, where I'd always share or describe the sounds. People really wanted to hear our birds! I improved my speaking technique and I grew in confidence. The nerves were always there before each one, but I welcomed them.

My dad rightly warned me, 'The day they're gone, you're in trouble, Seán. Embrace them.' He was right. Those nerves made sure I was ready. They gave me the edge I needed.

As well as the talks, I also began to receive a lot of different media requests – various radio chat shows and newspaper interviews. I gave them my all and I grew as a person – I became more outgoing and forthcoming. I'd finally found my purpose in life. But I also felt privileged to have this platform to speak out for the thing I loved most – nature. And I felt like I owed it. It needed me now and I felt I had to step up. I wanted to. It had always been there for me, after all.

It was there for me on my deathbed when I had meningitis, there for me in my darkest times of unemployment and depression, and it was there for me when I needed the courage to express my most tender, most vulnerable feelings to Alba, the love of my life.

My phone flashed with an email preview one evening in mid-September 2023 and my heart fluttered. I had to do a second take. The subject of the email said 'The Tommy Tiernan Show'. Tommy Tiernan is an Irish comedy legend, and his television chat show is *huge* – way bigger than anything I had ever been involved in to date. I'm not one for telly, but I'd seen an episode or two in my parents' house. The format is unique in that Tommy doesn't know who his guests will be; they walk out and this is the first he knows of them. Sometimes, he recognises the more famous ones, but the beauty of this show is that it gives normal people with interesting stories the time of day, and this is where the magic happens. I opened the email and was stunned to see that I was invited to join a Zoom chat with the senior guest booker, with a view to them pitching me to their team. I know this would be a huge stage for me and my story, and, if successful, I'd have a massive opportunity to spread my message and to share the unique sounds and stories of our vulnerable birds. I couldn't mess this up. I prepped for this chat like my life depended on it and, when the time came, I felt ready. Over the video call, I told them all about my tales of recording our most endangered birds, about jays imitating barking dogs, about starlings speaking in Cork accents and about cod communicating through muscle stridulations. I was in my element and enjoyed every minute of it, and I thought they did too. A few days later, and I was asked on! I was over the moon.

Fast forward to 3 December 2023. Myself, Alba and my dad were in the green room backstage with the cameras rolling out front. The first guest was on and my father and Alba were on the couch watching a big telly mounted on the wall. Snacks and drinks were brought to the table. In the meantime, I was pacing up and down like a man possessed. Alba beckoned me to sit but I just couldn't. I'd never in my life been this apprehensive about anything. I was scheduled as the last guest so I still had time. I continued to pace and read my little notes. Only I didn't read anything at all. My eyes glazed over the same few words on repeat, not taking in a thing. I'd never met someone as renowned as Tommy Tiernan before, nor had I spoken on national TV. All the what-ifs and potential catastrophes swirled around my head on repeat. A call of my name sent a shockwave through my body. False alarm – they needed me in the make-up room. I laughed at myself in the mirror as I was padded down with an orangey-pink powder. It looked quite extreme compared to my usual bare-skinned appearance. I gazed at myself, wide-eyed. *Now I look like an Oompa Loompa, to top things off*, I thought to myself.

The lovely make-up artist laughed at my expression. 'Don't worry, love, the camera won't pick it up as your eyes do. This will just dampen the shine of the lights is all.'

'Okay, thanks,' I replied, lost in the worries of what lay ahead.

I returned to the room and smiled in embarrassment at my dad and Alba. They erupted into apologetic fits of laughter – not because of the extreme orangey facial tones I had convinced myself of, but in response to the awkward Father Dougal-esque look of discomfort I wore in response to the facial paints I now donned.

I said nothing and returned to my pacing – muttering the words on the sheet without purpose or meaning.

Alba walked over to me and put her hands on my shoulders. 'Babe, look at me. Calm down, please. You've got this. I've told you a hundred times before. You were meant to do this. From the day I met you, I've loved your weird and wonderful tales of nature. They're uniquely you and you tell them in a lovely way that only you can do. Just be you. Forget that sheet. Go out there and talk to him like you talk to me when we're out in the woods. This is your world!'

I never believed in myself as a kid, and even today I still struggle to. Throughout my life I have been a misfit – an awkward oddball who struggled to fit in. But I believed in Alba. This pep talk grounded me, and just at the right time, too. Within moments, my name was called and I was walked to the curtain. I blew Alba a kiss and she winked at me with confidence. And that confidence was contagious to me. I was set. My nerves were replaced with a clarity of mind and an air of excitement. I was counted down from ten and told to walk out. I just went for it. I exploded from behind the curtains with pace, smiling eyes fixed on Tommy as I approached.

We shook hands before taking our seats, where I exclaimed. 'I bet you don't have a clue who I am anyway?'

He smiled in curious confusion and replied with an inquisitive 'No' that beckoned an explanation.

'My name is Seán Ronayne – I'm an ornithologist and, for the last three years, I've been on a mission to sound record every bird in Ireland.'

It rolled right out, and that lack of error or vocal tremble was the last reassurance I needed to be me. I was at home now. I was totally chilled and ready to flow with whatever came back at me. I was excited to share my world with Tommy. I felt like I had full control over what I said out there. It was strange, almost as if things moved in a kind of slow motion. I could think with clarity before my words came out. We covered everything from the aims and goals of the project to fun snippets of mimicry, to my ASD diagnosis. But best of all was the story of the common whitethroat and how it imitated and brought with it the sounds of Senegal to my doorstep in Cork.

In the moment, I was delighted with how it all went. I stepped off and went back to the green room, where it was all a blur. This happens to me frequently. I think my brain kicks in and protects me during really stressful events. I started to doubt myself. What did I say? Did I mess it up? I began to catastrophise. Alba and Dad reassured me all was well, but there was no speaking over my doubting mind. I stopped talking about it and was disappointed. In my mind, I had messed up a huge opportunity to woo people over and to try to make a difference, in my way.

The airing date was 6 January 2024. I was dreading watching the moment I had made a fool of myself on national TV. As we don't have TV channels at home, we went to my parents' house to watch it. I didn't say a word to anyone.

My family all sat down and chatted, and I began pacing around again. They knew I was stressed and so they let me be. My moment came and I could hardly watch. But my apprehension turned to a smile. I was happy on there! I was saying things as I'd hoped I had. Tommy was smiling too, he seemed to be genuinely interested. My mother loved it – she hadn't seen it from the green room. All of a sudden, I felt better about it. Feeling tired after the stress of it all, I took out my phone to check the time. It was vibrating and flashing as if it was glitching. I unlocked it and looked closer, trying to figure out what was wrong. They were notifications – my phone was absolutely blowing up with emails, texts, WhatsApp messages, Twitter and Instagram notifications. What? Why? I opened the messages, fearful for any negatives, but they weren't negative at all. I started to scan through them one-by-one.

'Loved this guy. Fascinating.'

'Gosh, what a lovely interview! Seán's enthusiasm coupled with his professional expertise was breathtaking.'

'Please give him his own show, could listen to this guy all day.'

The phone kept on flashing. I had never even considered this side of things. I thought the piece would go out and that would be that. But it wasn't – the phone went on like this for over a week. I found it hard not to look at it. I was just totally overwhelmed by it all, but in the best of ways. Soon after, the offers came in – more radio and newspaper, TV appearances, and three different book offers. I had to take some time out to process it all.

I went up to Cork city just to walk and stop for a coffee, and I was approached by people on the street. Again, I didn't expect this and thankfully everyone was lovely. I found a quiet little café and sat in a corner to get some headspace. Although I was blushed with the kind words and compliments, a touch of anxiety was starting to creep in. I asked myself the question – what was happening? Why were people responding like this? I know I'm not some kind of special, wonderful being. It was something more than *me*. And then it dawned on me – people must have a thirst for a renewed state of Irish nature. They want to hear it in all its beautiful forms, and they want to hear its stories in this new format.

That must be it, right?

I still don't know, to be honest, but regardless of the reason, this wonderful response has given me an even greater confidence and purpose to stand up and speak for our natural world.

Not long after this, filming with Kathleen wrapped up. It was now over to the edit, and all I had to do were media interviews and a few photo shoots. I had only three of my target birds left to sound record – grey partridge, red-breasted merganser and great skua. I'd captured the sounds of 195 species, amassing a library of over 12,000 recordings.

Since *The Tommy Tiernan Show* aired, I'd been inundated with talk requests and I was now touring the country sharing the sounds of our birds and telling their stories. The poster was created for the documentary and it utterly blew me away. I adored it. The documentary was also finally named and very aptly so as *Birdsong*.

I signed a book deal with Hachette Ireland in February – the same publishers behind Eoghan Daltun's incredibly successful *An Irish Atlantic Rainforest*. Life was just off the walls. We were caught up in a surreal whirlwind. I had so many talks on that I devoted my time to them completely.

A few weeks later, Alba and I went out for breakfast one Saturday morning – it was nice to get out, but little did I know things were about to become even crazier. Back home, Alba came into the kitchen and tapped me on the shoulder.

'Look, babe.'

I turned around and Alba was holding out a white plastic stick with two blue lines. Surprised, I replied, 'What? Do you have Covid?'

'No, Seán!'

Confused, I looked at her and asked again, 'What is it then? I don't understand.'

She looked a bit disappointed. 'Seán! I'm pregnant!'

'WHAT!? Are you for real?' I was with her now. In a state of shock, I asked her again. 'Seriously? It's not Covid?'

Alba glared at me. 'Seán! I'm pregnant. I've taken eight tests in two days.'

I had to sit down. I was so happy, yet so scared. I was in a state of disbelief. Alba felt the same. She'd had a traumatising miscarriage the previous year and, despite us trying again, it seemed like it wasn't meant to be. We had given up. We hugged and cried happy tears. What a crazy, crazy year.

Next up was the premiere of *Birdsong*. It would air at the Lighthouse Cinema as part of the Dublin Film Festival on 1 March. All of my family came, all of the crew and several friends. It was a huge moment, and one we'd been counting down to for months. The place was sold out and there was a real buzz on the night.

Myself, Alba and my parents were all very nervous about it. This would be the first time any of us had laid eyes on the finished piece, and behind us was a sea of people. But, from the moment it started, all the way through to the credits, we were moved, enthralled, entertained, humoured and filled with pride. Kathleen and team really put their all into it and we were incredibly touched. We had a Q&A at the end and I burst into tears giving the initial speech. The audience stood up and gave a standing ovation while I recovered. It was a profoundly beautiful touch.

We had several other screenings over the next few weeks, but one in particular will remain in my memory forever. You may remember Professor Mary Horgan – the woman who saved my life when I had meningitis. I'd already thanked the other doctors from that period of my life, but I'd never seen Professor Horgan again, not since the day she saved me. I'd already thanked the other doctors from that period of my life, but I'd never seen Professor Horgan again, not since the day she saved me. I wanted to reach out to her to express my thanks and to show her what her actions had enabled me to achieve. I managed to find her email address and sent her a note with the subject line: 'You saved my life'.

Hello Mary,

My name is Seán Ronayne. You may not remember me, but I will always remember you and will forever be indebted to you.

In 2006, I was admitted to the CUH at death's door, having just turned 18. All of my vital organs were shutting down and I was on the cusp of passing. We didn't know what was happening and it was all so sudden.

You came in on your day off and found a diagnosis just in time. I had meningitis (Type Y – I think?).

I'm currently writing a book about my life, for other reasons, but this is an important part of who I am, and I am writing this story up as one of the chapters. It's brought back so many buried emotions and even now I am crying intensely writing this to you. I don't know why I didn't write sooner, actually.

Surviving this changed me as a person and I have dedicated my life to studying and capturing the beauty of nature.

For the last year and a half, I have been working with a documentary crew capturing my journey to sound record every bird species in Ireland, as well as sharing the issues they face in today's world. It has many strong messages within and we recently screened it in the Dáil.

It will air on RTÉ One in time, but it screens at the Irish Film Institute on 25 March at 20:30. Would you be interested in going? I'll buy you a ticket (or tickets) if so.

Regardless, none of this would have been possible if it wasn't for you. People like you are true heroes and make the ultimate contribution to society.

Thank you with all of my heart,
Seán

Some days passed and I feared that my email would not reach her. Professor Horgan is a busy woman – as well as a practising physician, she is also president of the Royal College of Physicians of Ireland, a consultant at Cork University Hospital and the dean of the University College Cork School of Medicine. I came to an understanding that she didn't have time to reply or that my email slipped under the radar, but then came a response. In it, Professor Horgan was so gentle and humble. She thanked me for my email and told me that she remembered me. She also took me up on my offer but she insisted she'd pay for the tickets. I was overcome with emotion. This woman saved my life. Without her, none of this would have happened. To have her come along and see this beautiful piece that I was so proud of meant the absolute world to me.

Before the screening, people gathered in the foyer of the IFI. I was doing my best to mix and mingle when I saw a face coming towards me through the crowd. It was her! I felt so nervous. I approached her right away – ambushed her, even. 'Mary! It's me! I'm Seán!'

I swallowed a lump in my throat. I didn't want to descend into a mess in front of her. But she was lovely. Despite her incredible achievements, she was very down-to-earth, which made me appreciate her even more. There were two screenings that day, and this was the second, but myself and Alba didn't have the time to hang on for it because we had our first baby scan the next morning. So the plan was for me to introduce the show rather than sit through it again and do a Q&A.

I had a talk prepared in my head. I wanted everyone to know what Mary had done for me. I wanted them to know the hero that she is. I told Alba my plan to pay tribute to Mary but I also told her what I wanted to say. I had a strong hunch that I wouldn't make it all the way through the speech.

The moment came and I introduced *Birdsong*. I told everyone about the journey and what it meant to me and then I paused. I took a deep breath and glanced at Mary in the crowd.

'There's someone very special in the audience today, someone I would like you all to know. When I was 18, I contracted meningitis and it very nearly killed me.' My eyes welled up and I paused, once again, taking a deep breath before continuing.

Alba half stepped forward, not knowing if she should take control or not. I looked at her in tears and then back to Mary.

'That night a specialist by the name of Mary Horgan came in on her day off and she save—'

I broke down crying. But it *really* came out of me. My shoulders bounced and my head dropped to my hands. Alba ran up on stage and took the mic.

'She saved Seán's life and he wants everyone to know what she did for him. He wanted to say that, without her, none of this would have been possible and that he will forever be thankful for what she did.'

I was crouched down just off-stage, still crying, hiding myself in embarrassment. The whole audience stood up and gave a roaring applause. They applauded for Mary and they applauded to help pick me up. I never really understood all of the technicalities of smooth human interactions but, in moments like these, I didn't need to. This was all of the goodness of humanity coming out to show love and support for two people they didn't even know.

I waved and left, flooded with all kinds of emotions. I'll never forget that night and I'm so grateful I finally had the chance to meet with one of my heroes, Professor Mary Horgan.

Birdsong aired on RTÉ One on 26 May 2024. Again, Alba and myself went to my parents' so we could all watch it together, but this time I was prepared for the response. I knew what to expect, and I was also appointed a duty-of-care psychologist by RTÉ, Dr Malie Coyne. She was lovely – highly professional but deeply personable. At this point, we'd seen the film over twenty times, but it was still a joy to watch.

Afterwards, the phone started again – the same as before. I ignored it this time – I had to, at least until things settled. The last time I was overcome with a sense of obligation to reply to everyone and I suffered quite a bit with anxiety. I knew this time I could not. I did my best and hoped people would get it.

This time I expected some backlash – this was a much longer piece than the Tommy Tiernan appearance and so, by law of averages, I reasoned that I must have upset someone. I covered a lot of sensitive topics. I write with such surprise and gratitude that I didn't get a single negative comment.

This time, however, the reaction on the street was much greater. People stopped myself and Alba everywhere we went – again, everyone was so nice. I got several beautiful emails from parents of kids diagnosed with ASD, thanking me for reassuring them that their kids will be okay. I was inundated with emails just thanking me in general for speaking up for nature. You have no idea how much this meant to me. This project has thrown me on a life-changing trajectory and given me a true purpose in life. I am so privileged to be able to stand up for my beloved nature, and I will continue to do so in my way for as long as I live. I promise that.

Conclusion

TO THE KIDS, OR INDEED ADULTS, WHO ARE READING THIS and feel like they too don't quite fit in, in this world: I see you and I say, don't be afraid – don't be afraid to be yourself, don't be afraid to be different. And remember that it's okay not to fit in; in fact, sometimes, it's fun not to fit in! Just follow what feels right and do your best to be kind to people, to nature and to yourself, and you can't lose.

And, whilst it's certain that nature in Ireland is on its knees like never before, we also know that it doesn't have to be this way, and I believe that, even now, it isn't yet too late. Positive changes are happening amidst the gloom, and we know that these changes can be amplified. We just need to speak up and put pressure on those who don't want to act, to make sure they do. There are multiple conservation programmes running in Ireland that have shown strong results: programmes that have set out to increase populations of corncrake, curlew and red-necked phalarope, to name but a few.

We know that farming constitutes one of the major land uses in the country; in fact it occupies more land than any other activity in Ireland. Whilst we know that many flout the rules that inevitably lead to habitat degradation and species decline and loss, many also really care, and want to do the right thing. I think it's very important that we make this distinction. Farmers are often vilified and tarred with the same brush, and this is extremely damaging and unfair. I have visited many farms in recent months (and learned a lot – as a townie!), and I have seen first hand the love for the land and the nature within that many have. I have also heard and seen things from their perspective, which is important too.

To work together and make positive changes we need to understand the desires and needs of both sides. This is their job – it's how they earn their money. For them to lay aside sections of land or to harvest or manage things in a way that deviates from the mainstream, often harmful, methods costs money. It comes from their pockets. So, not only do we need as many famers as possible to come on board with methods that are as sympathetic as possible to nature, we also need the funding to enable and reward these methods. There are schemes in place, but these need to become commonplace as soon as possible, and they need to truly benefit nature and compensate the farmer.

We also need stronger, more direct, government action. Our national parks are in a major state of 'disrepair', for want of a better word. This is not down to our NPWS rangers and staff. Again, I have met and worked with many over the past few years and each and every one was in the job because they *love* Irish nature and want to make a positive difference. But they are working with an unfit-for-purpose budget and are understaffed. These are the people on the ground, fighting against invasive species, fighting to impose wildlife laws (as weak or strong as they may be) and fighting to hold onto, and improve, Irish wildlife. But they're spread far too thinly and are limited to the funds they are allocated each year. To those in power who can improve upon this situation, I implore you to do so. Our national parks have the capacity to become places of *true* magic and wonder. We do not have any meaningful sites with these characteristics. Our people and wildlife both deserve and need this to change. Invest more, please. Be serious about it – don't beat around the bush. The benefits would be untold for all, human and otherwise.

Again, to the Irish government and those with the power to make change, I also ask you to take on the many low-hanging fruits. Tighten up the hedge-cutting laws – there are far too many loopholes and more often than not these lifelines that run through the landscape like a network of green refuges are cut for no other reason than an inexplicable obsession with aesthetics, much to the detriment of our dwindling wildlife.

Ban weedkillers outright. It's a no-brainer that any chemical requiring a mask to deploy, and that is classified as a probable human carcinogen by the World Health Organization, is going to have detrimental effects on wildlife and humans. There are numerous studies that verify this.

We also need you to crack down on the spreading of slurry right before major rainfall events, as well as the spreading of same right up to the waterline. As previously mentioned, agriculture has the largest land share in Ireland, and is also the greatest polluter of waterbodies.

I see this disputed all the time, but the facts are there for all to see. Again, we know that many *do not* flout these rules, and we thank and respect you for that. But many *do*, and they need to stop, because these actions are not only affecting Irish wildlife – they also affect our right to clean and safe water. This is not okay.

With all of this in mind, you may be wondering what *you*, the reader, can do to help bring about the positive changes nature needs. Firstly, know that nobody is perfect and that everyone can make changes, big or small, to improve the situation for Irish nature. Before I give any specific suggestions, here is one simple way of thinking that can help us all to improve things. Try not to view the land around you as *your* property and yours alone. That we do so is purely a human concept. Such an idea of territory and possession is anathema to the plants and other creatures we share the land with. If we all respected the land around us as a shared space with our wild neighbours in mind, I think we would naturally treat the land in a way that would benefit their well being – just through this way of thinking alone. If I maintain this lawn, what species am I depriving of life? And if we maintain this mindset before and during our actions outdoors, I think the right thing to do will always slap us in the face.

That aside, here are some simple actions you can take today.

Make space for nature. Every inch counts. If you have a garden, consider ditching the lawn and replacing it with a wildflower meadow. But do please be careful when you source your 'wild' flowers, though, as many companies sell non-native colourful flowers that they claim are wild but that are, in fact, just another fancy garden-centre plant. Irish nature does best with what it evolved with. I can highly recommend Mr Sandro Cafolla's wildflowers.ie.

In many cases, wildflowers will appear of their own accord, but if a garden has been managed for a long time, then often it will need a little help. To learn more about the steps required to establish a wildflower meadow, I highly recommend https://biodiversityireland.ie/practical-advice-on-managing-wildflower-meadows/. I understand that kids like to play football and that you too like to sit in the short grass – that's okay! Even part of your lawn as a wildflower meadow would be a huge benefit, especially if we all took the steps to add one.

For those of you who don't have much space, don't worry. Let me tell you a story. At the time of writing, I live in a small rented house. When myself and Alba moved in a few years ago, all we had was a stone-slabbed terrace that led to a communal lawn, shared by the houses of our estate. Each garden is dotted with non-native, waxy plants, useless to wildlife. Worse yet, the groundskeepers cut the grass every three days in summer, and spray edges and verges with weedkiller a few times per year. I need a space to step out into to escape to nature, and here it did not exist.

I can't take credit for what happened next – it was all Alba. Alba bought several large pots, some 5 feet in length, filled them with soil and stepped back. Along the very edge of our stone-slabbed terrace we opened things up, simply removing a few feet of the grass along the border, exposing the soil.

In just a year, the transformation was incredible. In these small spaces, relieved from the smothering grip of the extensive lawn, cut-leaved cranesbill, prickly sow-thistle, birds-foot trefoil, dandelions, common daisies, willowherbs, common buttercups, wood avens and many, many more wildflowers appeared of their own volition. They've been there ever since. In summer, the great willowherbs and prickly sow-thistle in particular gave our little terrace some privacy – each reaching heights of 5 to 6 feet. Better still, they both burst forth with flowers and attracted a wide variety of bees, hoverflies, butterflies, ladybirds and more. The prickly sow-thistle flowers and goes to seed for several months, and each evening it attracts a pair of bullfinches that hide in its towering entanglement of cover, delicately feeding on the white seeds it churns out throughout the summer months. Every day I go out there to take a breath and to sit and watch nature come and go amongst the leaves, stems and flowers of our tiny little patch of wilderness. It makes me smile, and it fills my head with curiosity. And I need that. These wild spaces are essential not only for nature, but for us, too.

I kindly ask all of you to please ditch weedkiller. It's *so* toxic and such an enemy to nature. Please. Look at weeds for what they *really* are – native plants that belong and serve a true function in Irish nature. The *true* weeds are those that are bought in garden centres and supermarkets. Whilst they are okay in small numbers, if that floats your boat, maybe try to explore some of our native colourful wildflowers. There are *many*! They're free, beautiful and they'll benefit nature more. People often claim that their non-native flowers are great for bees. And often they're right. But they're not great for the many species that have co-evolved with our wildflowers. Many of our wild plants host very specific invertebrates, often larval stages, that specifically seek these plants out to see out their life cycle. For example, the larval stages of the holly blue butterfly feed largely on native holly and ivy, and red-clover case-bearer, a moth, only lays its young on red-clover, where their larval forms feed on the seeds of the plant. A whole book could be written on the very specific relationships that exist between both native wildflowers and invertebrates.

If we have *these* plants, the bees can feed and the other species which are dependent on them can *also* benefit.

We also need to urgently address all of the poisons that are sold on shelves in bright and wonderful colours, like treats in a candy shop – ant killers, slug killers, wasp nest killers, and so on. All horrendous stuff, each with a long list of secondary impacts to us and wildlife. We cannot just pour these products at will, whenever a wild neighbour dares to live alongside us. Embrace your neighbouring wildlife. They have just as much right to be here as we do. And to the shops that sell this kind of stuff – I suggest you have a good think about what it is you are profiting from and what implications it has on the land around us.

I think I also need to mention domestic cats – real bird-killers. There are few studies on Irish bird fatalities as a result of cat predation, but many have been published elsewhere, including from the UK. Based on extrapolations from these studies, it is estimated that somewhere in the region of 16 million birds are killed by cats every year in Ireland. Think about the implications of that. Now imagine if we were to remove this statistic from the table. What a difference it would make!

So, although I understand and fully accept that cats are cherished members of our families, we need to realise that they are detrimental to wild birds, but they don't need to be. We either need to keep our cats indoors, at least during the bird-breeding season or we need to find a way to prevent them from killing birds when they are outside. Several studies have shown that cat collars with bells are largely ineffective in preventing bird deaths – mainly because the cats learn to move in ways that prevent the bell from sounding. Cats are stealthy, sleek movers, after all. However, other studies have shown that mentally and physically stimulating cats through playtime can greatly reduce their hunting urges! I think a combination of these methods, with a supplement of common sense, is the answer.

Most important of all, reader, we need to have hope and not to focus on the negatives. Yes, 63 per cent of our birds are at risk of extinction, but we can change that.

How?

By reconnecting with nature, and by pulling your friends and family along. Teach your kids! Kids, teach your parents and grandparents! Get out there and explore. Ireland is still full of beauty and wonder, and often in the most unexpected of places – even right on your own doorstep. Embrace it, befriend it, get to know it, learn from it, and it will change your world in ways you could never have imagined.

Remember to listen with an open mind to the world around you. Listen to nature and all that it has to say. There are many hidden messages just waiting for us to stop and take notice. We just need to be willing to listen to them. Nature needs our ears, it needs our understanding, and it needs our voices. We need to stand up and fight for nature, for it gives us so much and asks for so little in return. Don't ever think that your one little voice doesn't count, because it absolutely does. Your one little voice can create a revolution. And together all of our little voices can create *real* positive changes. So let's listen to nature, speak on its behalf, and make the changes we all need and deserve.

Endnotes

1. George Griffiths, *Chronicles of the County Wexford* published in 1887, quotes Solomon Richards' first-hand record, written in 1682, of the arrival of a small flock of magpies to the barony of Forth in the far south of County Wexford: 'One remarque more is, there came with a stronge blacke Easterly wind, a flight of Magpies, under a dozen as I remember, out of England, or Wales, as 'tis verily believed, none having ever been seen in Ireland before. They lighted in the Barony of Forthe, where they have bredd ...'

    Robert Leigh of Rosegarland, writing in 1684 states: 'About eight years ago there appeared in these parts ... a parcel of Magpies, which now breed.' His account pins the arrival date of the colonisation to about 1676.

    Both quoted in Herbert F. Hore (ed.), 'A Chorographic Account of the Southern Part of the County of Wexford, written Anno 1684,

by Robert Leigh. Esq., of Rosegarland, in that County', *The Journal of the Kilkenny and South-East of Ireland Archaeological Society (1859)*, p.467.
2. species.biodiversityireland.ie.
3. Gilbert, G., Stanbury, A. and Lewis, L., 'Birds of Conservation Concern in Ireland 4: 2020–2026', *Irish Birds*, 43, 2021, pp.1–22.
4. Shephard, T.V., Lea, S.E. and Hempel de Ibarra, N., '"The Thieving Magpie"? No Evidence for Attraction to Shiny Objects', *Animal Cognition*, 18, 2015, pp.393–397.
5. Swift, Kaeli N. 'Wild American Crows Use Funerals to Learn About Danger'. Dissertation, 2015.
6. Wilkins, M.R., Odom, K.J., Benedict, L. and Safran, R.J., 'Analysis of Female Song Provides Insight into the Evolution of Sex Differences in a Widely Studied Songbird', *Animal Behaviour*, 168, 2020, pp.69–82.
7. Birkhead, T.R., *The Magpies: The Ecology and Behaviour of Black-billed and Yellow-billed Magpies*, T. & A. D. Poyser, 1991.
8. Mullarney, K., Svensson, L., Zetterstrom, D. and Grant, P., *Collins Bird Guide*, Collins, 1999.
9. Burnell, D., *Seabirds Count: A Census of Breeding Seabirds in Britain and Ireland (2015–2021)*, Lynx Nature Books, 2023.
10. For information on the directive, see: www.npws.ie/legislation/eu-directives/birds-directive.
11. Anderson, G., *Birds of Ireland: Facts, Folklore and History*, Gill Books, 2017.
12. For information on the report, see: www.npws.ie/news/minister-noonan-welcomes-survey-data-showing-positive-soundings-return-corncrake.

Appendix

Invasive bird species in Ireland

Red-vented bulbul (Pycnonotus cafer) A high-impact invasive, native to Asia with no Irish records to date (species.biodiversityireland.ie). There are also no UK records to date, although there have been six records in Belgium and 900 in Spain.

Indian house crow (Corvus splendens) A high-impact invasive, native to Asia with two records noted (species.biodiversityireland.ie). The most common entry path is as stowaways on ships. The primary impacts are direct competition with native species, predation upon the same and disease transmission. As it happens, the most recent Irish record (2010) of this species turned up in Cobh and even paid a visit to my parents' garden!

Ruddy duck (Oxyura jamaicensis) A high-impact invasive, native to North America, first reported in the wild in Ireland in 1973 with 830 records noted to date (species.biodiversityireland.ie). All European birds are derived from a single-source population of seven individuals that were introduced to the UK in 1948. From here, they spread across many European countries with great success. The biggest threat they pose is hybridisation with the closely related, native and very rare white-headed duck in Spain. Bizarrely, ruddy duck is protected in Ireland during the breeding season, but has an open hunting season during the winter months.

Canada goose (Branta canadensis) A high-impact invasive, native to North America, first reported in the wild in Ireland pre-1900 with 343 records noted to date (species.biodiversityireland.ie). The primary impacts are direct competition with native species, disease transmission, as well as crop damage on agricultural lands.

Egyptian goose (Alopochen aegyptiaca) A medium-impact invasive, native to Africa. There are just two records to date (species.biodiversityireland.ie). Introduction is usually through escapes from zoo collections. Populations in the UK and elsewhere are established and expanding, and so birds may come to Ireland from these sites. The primary impacts are direct competition with native species, habitat degradation through trampling and water-fouling, hybridisation and disease transmission.

Sacred ibis (Threskiornis aethiopicus) A high-impact invasive, native to Africa, which is omnivorous, highly adaptive and long-lived. There are no Irish records to date logged on species.biodiversityireland.ie, but they are earmarked because of the close proximity to the western France population. Populations can establish and expand quickly, and they impact through direct competition, predation of ground-nesting birds, and trampling of vegetation at communal roosting sites.

Common myna (Acridotheres tristis) A low-impact invasive, native to Asia, with no Irish records to date. Earmarked because of its success as an invasive species in many countries outside of its natural range. Impacts include competition with natives and as a pest to agriculture.

Rose-ringed parakeet (Psittacula krameri) A high-impact invasive, native to Asia and Africa, first reported in the wild in Ireland in 1998 with 72 records noted to date (species.biodiversityireland.ie). These birds are commonly kept as pets, leading to their escape, where they can quickly establish free-ranging populations. They compete with a range of cavity-nesting bird species, resulting in reduced nesting sites.

Resources

- One of the most amazing experiences of my life was recording the *Birdsong* documentary. Details available at: www.birdsongfilm.com
- BirdWatch Ireland – https://birdwatchireland.ie/
- BirdNet – https://birdnet.cornell.edu/
- NPWS – https://www.npws.ie/
- Irish Birding – https://www.irishbirding.com/birds/web
- The National Biodiversity Data Centre –https://biodiversityireland.ie/
- The Sound Approach – https://soundapproach.co.uk
- Merlin – https://merlin.allaboutbirds.org/
- Earth FM – https://earth.fm/
- Xeno-canto – https://xeno-canto.org/

- Macaulay Library – https://www.macaulaylibrary.org/
- Wildlife Sound Recording Society – https://www.wildlife-sound.org/
- Audacity – https://www.audacityteam.org/
- Raven – https://www.ravensoundsoftware.com/
- Wildlife Acoustics – https://www.wildlifeacoustics.com/
- Irish Wildlife Trust – https://iwt.ie/
- Irish Whale and Dolphin Group – https://iwdg.ie
- Kildare Wildlife Rescue – https://www.kwr.ie/
- Wildlife Rescue Cork – https://wildliferescuecork.com/
- Seal Rescue Ireland – https://www.sealrescueireland.org/
- Reporting a wildlife crime – https://www.npws.ie/wildlife-crime
- Native Irish Wildflower Seeds – https://wildflowers.ie/
- Wildflowers of Ireland – https://www.wildflowersofireland.net/
- A Guide to Habitats in Ireland – https://tinyurl.com/y3r79b9w

Irish Bird Sounds

These tables show birds I've sound recorded in Ireland, listed in chronological order. Note that some locations have been withheld in order to protect the species.

No.	Date	Location	Common Name
1	25/12/20	Cobh, Co. Cork	Blue tit
2	25/12/20	Cobh, Co. Cork	Rook
3	25/12/20	Saleen Creek, Co. Cork	Song thrush
4	26/12/20	Cobh, Co. Cork	Mute swan
5	29/12/20	Saleen Creek, Co. Cork	Curlew
6	29/12/20	Saleen Creek, Co. Cork	Dunlin
7	29/12/20	Cobh, Co. Cork	Dunnock
8	29/12/20	Saleen Creek, Co. Cork	Redshank
9	29/12/20	Saleen Creek, Co. Cork	Teal
10	30/12/20	Cobh, Co. Cork	Black-headed gull
11	30/12/20	Cobh, Co. Cork	Grey wagtail
12	30/12/20	Cobh, Co. Cork	Jackdaw
13	30/12/20	Cuskinny, Co. Cork	Mallard
14	30/12/20	Cobh, Co. Cork	Pied/White wagtail
15	30/12/20	Cuskinny, Co. Cork	Reed bunting
16	30/12/20	Cobh, Co. Cork	Rock pipit
17	31/12/20	Cobh, Co. Cork	Common gull
18	31/12/20	Cobh, Co. Cork	Herring gull
19	31/12/20	Cobh, Co. Cork	Oystercatcher
20	04/01/21	Cobh, Co. Cork	Hooded crow
21	08/01/21	Cobh, Co. Cork	Barn owl
22	08/01/21	Cuskinny, Co. Cork	Pheasant
23	08/01/21	Cobh, Co. Cork	Redwing
24	08/01/21	Cobh, Co. Cork	Snipe
25	09/01/21	Cobh, Co. Cork	Blackcap
26	09/01/21	Cobh, Co. Cork	Collared dove
27	09/01/21	Cuskinny, Co. Cork	Jay

Latin Name	BoCCI	Annex I
Cyanistes caeruleus	Green	No
Corvus frugilegus	Green	No
Turdus philomelos	Green	No
Cygnus olor	Amber	No
Numenius arquata	Red	No
Calidris alpina	Red	No
Prunella modularis	Green	No
Tringa totanus	Red	No
Anas crecca	Amber	No
Chroicocephalus ridibundus	Amber	No
Motacilla cinerea	Red	No
Corvus monedula	Green	No
Anas platyrhynchos	Amber	No
Motacilla alba	Green	No
Emberiza schoeniclus	Green	No
Anthus petrosus	Green	No
Larus canus	Amber	No
Larus argentatus	Amber	No
Haematopus ostralegus	Red	No
Corvus cornix	Green	No
Tyto alba	Red	No
Phasianus colchicus	Green	No
Turdus iliacus	Red	No
Gallinago gallinago	Red	No
Sylvia atricapilla	Green	No
Streptopelia decaocto	Green	No
Garrulus glandarius	Green	No

No.	Date	Location	Common Name
28	09/01/21	Cuskinny, Co. Cork	Kingfisher
29	09/01/21	Cuskinny, Co. Cork	Long-eared owl
30	09/01/21	Cuskinny, Co. Cork	Long-eared tit
31	09/01/21	Cuskinny, Co. Cork	Moorhen
32	18/01/21	Annagh, Co. Cork	Robin
33	18/01/21	Cobh, Co. Cork	Starling
34	18/01/21	Annagh, Co. Cork	Wren
35	19/01/21	Annagh, Co. Cork	Blackbird
36	19/01/21	Annagh, Co. Cork	Mistle thrush
37	21/01/21	Ballingeary, Co. Cork	Raven
38	22/01/21	Marlogue, Co. Cork	Greenshank
39	23/01/21	Cobh, Co. Cork	Bullfinch
40	23/01/21	Marlogue, Co. Cork	Great northern diver
41	23/01/21	Cobh, Co. Cork	Great tit
42	23/01/21	Cuskinny, Co. Cork	Grey heron
43	31/01/21	Cobh, Co. Cork	Chaffinch
44	31/01/21	Cobh, Co. Cork	Magpie
45	01/02/21	Saleen Creek, Co. Cork	Black-tailed godwit
46	01/02/21	Barnadivane, Co. Cork	Fieldfare
47	02/02/21	Cobh, Co. Cork	Peregrine
48	04/02/21	Cobh, Co. Cork	Coal tit
49	04/02/21	Cobh, Co. Cork	Goldfinch
50	05/02/21	Cobh, Co. Cork	Brent goose
51	05/02/21	Cobh, Co. Cork	Greenfinch
52	06/02/21	Cobh, Co. Cork	House sparrow
53	06/02/21	Cobh, Co. Cork	Siskin
54	06/02/21	Cobh, Co. Cork	Woodpigeon
55	26/02/21	Cuskinny, Co. Cork	Little grebe
56	27/02/21	Cuskinny, Co. Cork	Gadwall
57	28/02/21	Cobh, Co. Cork	Buzzard
58	28/02/21	Cuskinny, Co. Cork	Chiffchaff
59	01/03/21	Inchigeelagh, Co. Cork	Goldcrest

Latin Name	BoCCI	Annex I
Alcedo atthis	Amber	Yes
Asio otus	Green	No
Aegithalos caudatus	Green	No
Gallinula chloropus	Green	No
Erithacus rubecula	Green	No
Sturnus vulgaris	Amber	No
Troglodytes troglodytes	Green	No
Turdus merula	Green	No
Turdus viscivorus	Green	No
Corvus corax	Green	No
Tringa nebularia	Green	No
Pyrrhula pyrrhula	Green	No
Gavia immer	Amber	Yes
Parus major	Green	No
Ardea cinerea	Green	No
Fringilla coelebs	Green	No
Pica pica	Green	No
Limosa limosa	Red	No
Turdus pilaris	Green	No
Falco peregrinus	Green	Yes
Periparus ater	Green	No
Carduelis carduelis	Green	No
Branta bernicla	Amber	No
Carduelis chloris	Amber	No
Passer domesticus	Amber	No
Carduelis spinus	Green	No
Columba palumbus	Green	No
Tachybaptus ruficollis	Green	No
Anas strepera	Amber	No
Buteo buteo	Green	No
Phylloscopus collybita	Green	No
Regulus regulus	Amber	No

No.	Date	Location	Common Name
60	01/03/21	Inchigeelagh, Co. Cork	Meadow pipit
61	03/03/21	The Gearagh, Co. Cork	Golden plover
62	03/03/21	Toonsbridge, Co. Cork	Greylag goose
63	03/03/21	The Gearagh, Co. Cork	Little egret
64	03/03/21	The Gearagh, Co. Cork	Treecreeper
65	03/03/21	The Gearagh, Co. Cork	Wigeon
66	04/03/21	The Gearagh, Co. Cork	Great white egret
67	04/03/21	The Gearagh, Co. Cork	Whooper swan
68	06/03/21	Cobh, Co. Cork	Lesser black-backed gull
69	07/03/21	Cobh, Co. Cork	Knot
70	14/03/21	Cuskinny, Co. Cork	Great black-backed gull
71	15/03/21	Cobh, Co. Cork	Ringed plover
72	18/03/21	Goulacullin, Co. Cork	Skylark
73	19/03/21	Cobh, Co. Cork	Coot
74	31/03/21	Annagh, Co. Cork	Willow warbler
75	02/04/21	Curraghglass, Co. Cork	Linnet
76	14/04/21	Ballyhouras, Co. Cork	Common crossbill
77	17/04/21	Mizen Head, Co. Cork	Chough
78	17/04/21	Cork (Near Mizen Head)	Grasshopper warbler
79	18/04/21	Curraghglass, Co. Cork	Whimbrel
80	22/04/21	Knockdown Head, Co. Cork	Sardinian warbler
81	24/04/21	Toor Pier, Co. Cork	Common sandpiper
82	24/04/21	Toor Pier, Co. Cork	Sandwich tern
83	24/04/21	Toor Pier, Co. Cork	Sedge warbler
84	27/04/21	Cahore, Co. Wexford	Reed warbler
85	27/04/21	Cahore, Co. Wexford	Stonechat
86	27/04/21	Cahore, Co. Wexford	Whitethroat
87	28/04/21	Cahore, Co. Wexford	Little ringed plover
88	28/04/21	Cahore, Co. Wexford	Yellow wagtail
89	30/04/21	Mizen Head, Co. Cork	Lesser redpoll
90	30/04/21	Mizen Head, Co. Cork	Quail

Latin Name	BoCCI	Annex I
Anthus pratensis	Red	No
Pluvialis apricaria	Red	Yes
Anser anser	Amber	No
Egretta garzetta	Green	Yes
Certhia familiaris	Green	No
Anas penelope	Amber	No
Ardea alba	Green	No
Cygnus cygnus	Amber	Yes
Larus fuscus	Amber	No
Calidris canutus	Red	No
Larus marinus	Green	No
Charadrius hiaticula	Amber	No
Alauda arvensis	Amber	No
Fulica atra	Amber	No
Phylloscopus trochilus	Amber	No
Carduelis cannabina	Amber	No
Loxia curvirostra	Green	No
Pyrrhocorax pyrrhocorax	Amber	Yes
Locustella naevia	Green	No
Numenius phaeopus	Green	No
Sylvia melanocephala	N/A	N/A
Actitis hypoleucos	Amber	No
Sterna sandvicensis	Amber	Yes
Acrocephalus schoenobaenus	Green	No
Acrocephalus scirpaceus	Green	No
Saxicola rubicola	Green	No
Sylvia communis	Green	No
Charadrius dubius	Amber	No
Motacilla flava	Amber	No
Carduelis cabaret	Green	No
Coturnix coturnix	Red	No

No.	Date	Location	Common Name
91	01/05/21	Toor Pier, Co. Cork	Shag
92	01/05/21	Cahore, Co. Wexford	Swallow
93	05/05/21	Kilcoole, Co. Wicklow	Little tern
94	07/05/21	Ballyhouras, Co. Cork	Cuckoo
95	08/05/21	Mizen Head, Co. Cork	Tree sparrow
96	09/05/21	Mizen Head, Co. Cork	Manx shearwater
97	18/05/21	Doneraille, Co. Cork	Great spotted woodpecker
98	22/05/21	St. John's Wood, Co. Westmeath	Garden warbler
99	22/05/21	St. John's Wood, Co. Westmeath	Great crested grebe
100	22/05/21	Boora Bog, Co. Offaly	Lapwing
101	22/05/21	Co. Monaghan	Wood warbler
102	23/05/21	Cahore, Co. Wexford	Sand martin
103	24/05/21	Cahore, Co. Wexford	House martin
104	24/05/21	Arklow, Co. Wicklow	Lesser whitethroat
105	25/05/21	Lady's Island Lake, Co. Wexford	Arctic tern
106	25/05/21	Tacumshin, Co. Wexford	Bearded tit
107	25/05/21	Lady's Island Lake, Co. Wexford	Common tern
108	25/05/21	Lady's Island Lake, Co. Wexford	Mediterranean gull
109	25/05/21	Tacumshin, Co. Wexford	Shelduck
110	25/05/21	Lady's Island Lake, Co. Wexford	Turnstone
111	26/05/21	Wicklow Mountains, Co. Wicklow	Spotted flycatcher
112	26/05/21	Wicklow Mountains, Co. Wicklow	Whinchat
113	28/05/21	Ballyhouras, Co. Cork	Woodcock
114	02/06/21	Mizen Head, Co. Cork	Hawfinch

Latin Name	BoCCI	Annex I
Phalacrocorax aristotelis	Amber	No
Hirundo rustica	Amber	No
Sternula albifrons	Amber	Yes
Cuculus canorus	Green	No
Passer montanus	Amber	No
Puffinus puffinus	Amber	No
Dendrocopos major	Green	No
Sylvia borin	Green	No
Podiceps cristatus	Amber	No
Vanellus vanellus	Red	No
Phylloscopus sibilatrix	Red	No
Riparia riparia	Amber	No
Delichon urbicum	Amber	No
Sylvia curruca	Amber	No
Sterna paradisaea	Amber	Yes
Panurus biarmicus	Green	No
Sterna hirundo	Amber	Yes
Larus melanocephalus	Amber	Yes
Tadorna tadorna	Amber	No
Arenaria interpres	Amber	No
Muscicapa striata	Amber	No
Saxicola rubetra	Red	No
Scolopax rusticola	Red	No
Coccothraustes coccothraustes	Green	No

No.	Date	Location	Common Name
115	05/06/21	Tory Island, Co. Donegal	Corncrake
116	05/06/21	Tory Island, Co. Donegal	Fulmar
117	05/06/21	Tory Island, Co. Donegal	Wheatear
118	11/06/21	Tacumshin, Co. Wexford	Baillon's crake
119	17/06/21	Avoca, Co. Wicklow	Red kite
120	20/06/21	Buttevant, Co. Cork	Swift
121	02/07/21	Lissagriffin, Co. Cork	Semipalmated plover
122	06/07/21	Lissagriffin, Co. Cork	Short-eared owl
123	18/07/21	Mallow, Co. Cork	Stock dove
124	18/07/21	Mallow, Co. Cork	Yellowhammer
125	26/07/21	Lissagriffin, Co. Cork	Wood sandpiper
126	28/07/21	Skellig Michael, Co. Kerry	Leach's petrel
127	28/07/21	Skellig Michael, Co. Kerry	Storm petrel
128	31/07/21	Skellig Michael, Co. Kerry	Cory's shearwater
129	03/08/21	Lissagriffin, Co. Cork	Green sandpiper
130	10/08/21	Tory Island, Co. Donegal	Sanderling
131	23/08/21	Lissagriffin, Co. Cork	Tree pipit
132	26/08/21	Skellig Michael, Co. Kerry	Puffin
133	27/08/21	Skellig Michael, Co. Kerry	Guillemot
134	30/08/21	Tacumshin, Co. Wexford	Pectoral sandpiper
135	13/09/21	Tacumshin, Co. Wexford	Bar-tailed godwit
136	14/09/21	Tacumshin, Co. Wexford	Grey plover
137	15/09/21	Tacumshin, Co. Wexford	Little stint
138	19/09/21	Tory Island, Co. Donegal	Lapland bunting
139	25/09/21	Tory Island, Co. Donegal	Pink-footed goose
140	25/09/21	Tory Island, Co. Donegal	Snow bunting

Latin Name	BoCCI	Annex I
Crex crex	Red	Yes
Fulmarus glacialis	Amber	No
Oenanthe oenanthe	Amber	No
Zapornia pusilla	N/A	N/A
Milvus milvus	Red	Yes
Apus apus	Red	No
Charadrius semipalmatus	N/A	N/A
Asio flammeus	Amber	Yes
Columba oenas	Red	No
Emberiza citrinella	Red	No
Tringa glareola	Amber	Yes
Oceanodroma leucorhoa	Red	Yes
Hydrobates pelagicus	Amber	Yes
Calonectris diomedea	Amber	Yes
Tringa ochropus	Green	No
Calidris alba	Green	No
Anthus trivialis	Green	No
Fratercula arctica	Red	No
Uria aalge	Amber	No
Calidris melanotos	Green	No
Limosa lapponica	Red	Yes
Pluvialis squatarola	Red	No
Calidris minuta	Green	No
Calcarius lapponicus	Green	No
Anser brachyrhynchus	Green	No
Plectrophenax nivalis	Green	No

No.	Date	Location	Common Name
141	11/10/21	Lissagriffin, Co. Cork	American golden plover
142	12/10/21	Power Head, Co. Cork	Kestrel
143	20/10/21	Lissagriffin, Co. Cork	Spotted redshank
144	29/10/21	Gorey, Co. Wexford	Brambling
145	15/11/21	South Slobs, Co. Wexford	White-fronted goose (Greenland)
146	19/12/21	Ring Marsh, Co. Wexford	Jack snipe
147	25/12/21	Ring Marsh, Co. Wexford	Common scoter
148	26/12/21	Cobh, Co. Cork	Feral pigeon
149	27/12/21	Bull Island, Co. Dublin	Pintail
150	27/12/21	Blackrock, Co. Louth	Twite
151	30/12/21	Cuskinny, Co. Cork	Water rail
152	05/01/22	Ring Marsh, Co. Wexford	Dotterel
153	16/01/22	The Lough, Co. Cork	Shoveler
154	30/01/22	Blarney, Co. Cork	Dipper
155	30/01/22	The Lough, Co. Cork	Tufted duck
156	22/03/22	Arklow, Co. Wicklow	Carrion crow
157	22/03/22	Cahore, Co. Wexford	Cetti's warbler
158	25/03/22	Ring Marsh, Co. Wexford	Garganey
159	10/04/22	Dingle, Co. Kerry	Iceland gull
160	16/04/22	Tacumshin, Co. Wexford	Lesser yellowlegs
161	25/04/22	Tacumshin, Co. Wexford	Little gull
162	02/05/22	Wicklow Head, Co. Wicklow	Kittiwake
163	02/05/22	Wicklow Head, Co. Wicklow	Razorbill
164	03/05/22	Wicklow Town, Co. Wicklow	Black guillemot
165	05/05/22	Ring Marsh, Co. Wexford	Roseate tern
166	07/05/22	Wicklow Mountains, Co. Wicklow	Merlin

Latin Name	BoCCI	Annex I
Pluvialis dominica	Green	No
Falco tinnunculus	Red	No
Tringa erythropus	Amber	No
Fringilla montifringilla	Amber	No
Anser albifrons flavirostris	Amber	Yes
Lymnocryptes minimus	Green	No
Melanitta nigra	Red	No
Columba livia	Green	No
Anas acuta	Amber	No
Carduelis flavirostris	Red	No
Rallus aquaticus	Green	No
Charadrius morinellus	Green	No
Anas clypeata	Red	No
Cinclus cinclus	Green	No
Aythya fuligula	Amber	No
Corvus corone	Green	No
Cettia cetti	Green	No
Anas querquedula	Amber	No
Larus glaucoides	Green	No
Tringa flavipes	Green	No
Hydrocoloeus minutus	Amber	Yes
Rissa tridactyla	Red	No
Alca torda	Red	No
Cepphus grylle	Amber	No
Sterna dougallii	Amber	Yes
Falco columbarius	Amber	Yes

No.	Date	Location	Common Name
167	06/06/22	Bellmullet, Co. Mayo	Red-necked phalarope
168	23/06/22	Lissagriffin, Co. Cork	Night-heron
169	07/07/22	Ring Marsh, Co. Wexford	Curlew sandpiper
170	10/07/22	Great Saltee, Co. Wexford	Cormorant
171	10/07/22	Great Saltee, Co. Wexford	Gannet
172	10/07/22	Ring Marsh, Co. Wexford	Glossy ibis
173	25/07/22	Rostellan, Co. Cork	Sparrowhawk
174	26/08/22	Ring Marsh, Co. Wexford	Citrine wagtail
175	15/12/22	Tacumshin, Co. Wexford	Bittern
176	28/01/23	Howth, Co. Dublin	Purple sandpiper
177	05/02/23	Tacumshin, Co. Wexford	Water pipit
178	18/03/23	Rathlin Island, Co. Antrim	Eider
179	26/03/23	Wicklow Mountains, Co. Wicklow	Red grouse
180	21/04/23	Tacumshin, Co. Wexford	Black-winged stilt
181	05/05/23	Glenveagh, Co. Donegal	Golden eagle
182	13/05/23	Glenveagh, Co. Donegal	Red-throated diver
183	28/05/23	Donegal	Pied flycatcher
184	28/05/23	Donegal	White-tailed eagle
185	01/06/23	Glenveagh, Co. Donegal	Ring ouzel
186	23/07/23	North Cork	Hen harrier
187	06/09/23	West Cork	Melodious warbler
188	21/09/23	West Cork	American wood warbler sp
189	01/10/23	West Cork	Red-breasted flycatcher
190	06/10/23	West Cork	Redstart
191	12/10/23	Toor Pier, Co. Cork	Yellow-browed warbler
192	28/10/23	West Cork	Waxwing

Latin Name	BoCCI	Annex I
Phalaropus lobatus	Red	Yes
Nycticorax nycticorax	Green	No
Calidris ferruginea	Red	No
Phalacrocorax carbo	Amber	No
Morus bassanus	Amber	No
Plegadis falcinellus	Green	No
Accipiter nisus	Amber	No
Motacilla citreola	N/A	N/A
Botaurus stellaris	Green	No
Calidris maritima	Red	No
Anthus spinoletta	Green	No
Somateria mollissima	Red	No
Lagopus lagopus scotica	Red	No
Himantopus himantopus	Green	No
Aquila chrysaetos	Red	Yes
Gavia stellata	Amber	Yes
Ficedula hypoleuca	Amber	No
Haliaeetus albicilla	Red	Yes
Turdus torquatus	Red	No
Circus cyaneus	Amber	Yes
Hippolais polyglotta	Green	No
N/A	N/A	N/A
Ficedula parva	Green	No
Phoenicurus phoenicurus	Red	No
Phylloscopus inornatus	Green	No
Bombycilla garrulus	Green	No

No.	Date	Location	Common Name
193	01/12/23	West Cork	Firecrest
194	08/02/24	South Slobs, Co. Wexford	Bewick's swan
195	10/05/24	West Cork	Black Redstart
196	24/07/24	Wexford	Nightjar
197	Yet to be recorded	N/A	Red-breasted merganser
198	Yet to be recorded	N/A	Great skua
199	Yet to be recorded	N/A	Grey partridge

Latin Name	BoCCI	Annex I
Regulus ignicapilla	Green	No
Cygnus columbianus	Red	Yes
Phoenicurus ochruros	Green	No
Caprimulgus europaeus	Red	Yes
Mergus serrator	Amber	No
Stercorarius skua	Amber	No
Perdix perdix	Red	No

Acknowledgements

THERE ARE SO MANY PEOPLE I OWE FOR THIS BOOK BECOMING a reality. Firstly, I need to thank those who never got to chance to read this. Pops, Granny Betty and Granda Dave, I love you all so much and your memories and legacies will live on in this book forever. Thanks for the support and inspiration. Granny Cahill, I love you and I hope I can show you this in person, soon.

To my parents – thank you for always being there for me, and for your constant sacrifice, love and support. I wasn't an easy kid, I know that. I was hyper, restless, always on the go. Thanks for putting up with me and sticking it out! I'm so lucky that you didn't diss my obsessive passions and instead, not only accepted them, but paved a way for them to blossom.

To my brother Conor – thanks for being my sidekick growing up. Although we had slightly different interests I have great memories of our childhood together, and it wouldn't have been half as fun or interesting without you in it.

To my soulmate Alba – you are my best friend and the love of my life. You saved me from my own self and made me into the person I am. I'm far from perfect, but you've made me a much better version of myself. I am so lucky to have you in my life, and I look up to you in so many ways, even if I don't express that too well, please know it. You are going to be the best mother to our little Laia, and I can't wait to see you both flourish together.

To everyone at Hachette Ireland – thanks for bringing this to life. Ciara Doorley, Joanna Smyth, Stephen Riordan, Elaine Egan, it's been such a joy to work with you all, and you made the whole process so smooth and enjoyable. I really felt like I was in safe hands, and that people were very much willing to listen to what I had to say.

I am hugely grateful to Robert Vaughan who complemented the book highly with his incredible illustrations. I have long admired Robert's work and to have him put his mark on the piece is a true honour. The same goes to Steve O Connell – your graphic design is simply epic. It has really made this book, but also the film and my album. I really appreciate you!

To Catherine Gough – you helped me an untold amount during this process. Your editing style was such a joy to me. Not only did you point out my errors in the kindest way possible, you also complimented my work throughout. This was really important to me. As a first time writer, I often lack belief in my work, and your empathetic and encouraging comments were exactly what I needed. You brought the best out of me – thank you!

To Aonghus Meaney and Claire Rourke – thank you so much for

your eagle-eyed approaches to proofing the text. You picked up so many little fine details that I know I would have missed and helped to really tighten things up.

I haven't kept a big circle of friends in my life, and that is just down to who I am. But there are a few I'd like to mention, and please don't be offended if your name doesn't appear here, it's really tough to remember and fit everyone in!

Walter Mahoney and Olly Hegarty – you were always there from the very beginning. We made some great memories throughout our childhood. Gary Mahoney, my sidekick in class – thanks for the giggles throughout secondary school. In UCC I made a lifelong friend in Trevor Dinan – a great guy that I'm fortunate to have befriended. And of course, Kieran Foley, a valued part of my little group of friends in UCC, who brought me a *Kerrang!* magazine when I was seriously ill, scared and quite broken in hospital recovering from meningitis. You have no idea how much that perked me up. Walter, your DVD collection did the very same – thank you both so much. During my years in England, I met so many great people who made me feel right at home: Stuart, Jordan, Connor – thanks for sticking by me. Gary and Olivia – thanks for giving me a second home, and essentially becoming an extension of my family. Ben – thanks for being you, we had some moments that to this day I still erupt into laughter thinking about. Rodney – thank you for saving me on Christmas Day. I was in a really dark place and you helped me so much. And to Dave and Sheila – again you helped me an untold amount and I'll be forever grateful to you.

A special shoutout goes to Harry Hussey, Graham Clarke and Brian Lynch – thanks for always having my back and for putting up with my constant sharing of bird sounds and stories, and for 'getting' my odd sense of humour. You've all been in my life ever since I started birding on a more serious level, and I am so thankful to have maintained a friendship with you all.

If it wasn't for Kathleen Harris and Chris Maddaloni, I don't think this book would have come to light, either. Thank you both for giving me a voice. Chris – your photos are just wonderful, and you're such a gentleman. Kathleen, you are such a joy to work with and to have as a friend. Your kindness, understanding and willingness to listen have really helped me get my story out. Your film *Birdsong* blew us all away. And, of course, a huge thank you also goes out to Ross Whitaker, Aideen O'Sullivan, Ross Bartley, Iseult Howlett, Paul Finan and everyone else who worked on the film.

A hearty thank you to Tommy and Yvonne Tiernan who have been so kind in not only giving me a platform on national television, but also in supporting me and helping me promote ever since. I really appreciate you both.

A big thanks to Eric Dempsey and Jane Powers, friends of mine and both great authors, who gave me invaluable advice at the beginning of my writing journey. You made it seem a lot less daunting!

There have been several people who took the time to read over this book, giving me their thoughts and some their quotes. This feedback has been invaluable to me, and again it has really given me the confidence I was lacking. Thank you Niall Hatch, Anja Murray, Magnus Robb, Manchán Magan, Eoghan Daltun, Graham Clarke, Killian Mullarney, Una Mullaly, Ken O'Sullivan, Katherine and Bernie Krause, Ella McSweeney and Padraic Fogarty.

And a huge thanks to all of the photographers who kindly gave permission for their photos to be used in the book.

I have another group of very special people to thank in Professor Mary Horgan, Dr. Peter Morehan, Dr. Harry Kelleher, Professor Carl Vaughan and everyone who came to my aid on my darkest days – you saved my life, and I will be eternally indebted to you. I genuinely think about you all every week. You're all heroes of the highest regard and I respect you dearly. Thank you.

And finally, I want to thank you, the readers, and to everyone who has supported my work and just been so kind to me. I'm a shy introvert, and it's my love of nature that pushes me to step out onto the stage. It takes a lot out of me to do that, even though I love it at the same time. I just want all of you to know that your kind words and comments all reach me, and they fuel me to continue doing what I do. I appreciate you all very dearly!

Index

Bold entries indicate illustrations

A

African cicadas 233–234
albatrosses 150
algal blooms 28–29
alpine swifts **252**, 254–255
American birds 159
Amuigh Faoin Spéir (Out Under the Sky) 48, 316, 327
Animal Behaviour 382
Animal Cognition 382
An Irish Atlantic Rainforest 366
Annagh Marsh 358, 358–360
Asian koels 218, 245–246
Asian water monitors 236
Audacity 279, 387
Australasian barnacles 98
autism 266–275

B

Bailon's crakes 311
Barcelona ix–xv, 279–293
  environment 255–256
Bardiya National Park 240–250
barn swallows 10
Bartley, Ross 335, 340
basking sharks 148
bee-eaters xiii
bird migration 29, 163–167, 302–312, 327–334
BirdNET 307
Birds of Ireland: Facts, Folklore and History 382
Birds of Ireland: Myths, Legends and Folklore 345
Birdsong 366–372, 386
bird species (Catalan) 258–262

409

bird species (Ireland) 159, 299, 304
bird species (Thailand) 245–248
bird surveys 297–299
    Seahouses 120–122
BirdWatch Ireland 25, 301, 355, 358, 386
black-backed gulls 30
blackbirds 21, 135
black-crowned night herons xii, 280–281
black-hooded orioles 246
bogs 199–202
bramblings 322
brent geese 91

C
Canada geese 6, 384
Cape Clear Island 6, 141–152, 189, 302
Catalunya 253–254
    Catalan identity 253–254, 264
chiffchaffs 46, 149
choughs 65
Chronicles of the County Wexford 381
Cobh 1–3, 25–27, 135–136, 295–296
collared doves 107
Collins Bird Guide 50–52, 92, 382
common barnacles 97–98
common dolphins 52
common myna 6, 385
common terns 143
conservation 354, 358–360, 374–380
cormorants 63–64, 64, 144
corncrakes 345–347, 349
corvids, *see* magpies

Covid-19 xv, 284–286, 293
crabs 35–36
Crombie, James 338
curlews 33
Cuskinny Marsh Nature Reserve 25–31, 43–44, 51, 52–53
    algal blooms 28-29

D
Daltun, Eoghan 366
dawn chorus 42
de Buitléar, Éamon 48, 316, 327
Delta del Llobrega 258–259
dog whelks 98–99
dolphins 148

E
Ebro Delta Birding Festival ix, 277
eels 138
Egyptian geese 6, 384
eider ducks 95–96
El Prat de Llobregat xii, xiv, *see* Barcelona
EU Birds Directive 65
European bee-eaters 282

F
farming methods 255–257, 335–336, 374–380, *see also* conservation
Farne Islands 105–123
fin whales 52
Florida 32, 34
foxes 314
fulmars 81

G

Galley Head 51–52
Glenveagh National Park 355
goldcrests 164
golden saxifrages 34
Great Island 1–3, 27, 62
Great Saltee Island 6
great spotted woodpecker **294**, 310–311, 317–318, 319
grey herons 30, 101
Griffiths, George 381
gull-billed terns **58**, 76
gulls 92–94
    types of 93

H

harbour porpoises 190
Harris, Kathleen 316, 320–323, 335, 366
hen harriers 120
herring gulls 63–64
hobbies 85
hooded crows 30, **176**, 178–179
Horgan, Professor Mary 368–371
house buntings 209
house martins 29
Howlett, Iseult 335
hummingbird hawkmoths 134
Hussey, Harry 54

I

Indian house crow 6, 383
invasive bird species 6–7, 383–385
invasive species 354, *see also* conservation
Irish Birds 382
Irish bird sounds 388–403

K

kingfishers 31–32, **152**, 155–156, 158–159
Kinsale 163–167

L

lammergeiers 275
land management 336–337
lapwings 202
L'Associació Asperger Catalunya 266
leatherback turtles 147–148
little egrets **88**, 99–103
Lloyd Praeger, Robert 357
long-tailed tits 33–34

M

mackerel 136
magpies **xvi**, 3–10, 22–23, 178–179
master's in ecological impact assessment 153–155, 188–190, 194
master's in environmental impact assessment 127, 153–157
meadowsweet 34
Mee, Allan 351
meningitis 68–87
migrant birds blown off course 159–161
migration xii–xv, 314–315
Millport 95–99
Mizen Head 302–303
Moore, Paul 309
Morocco 206–215
Morris, Kathleen 324–325, 337–338, 338
moths 38, 133–134
Mullarney, Killian 51
mute swans 29–30, 31

N

National Parks and Wildlife Service 344
Nepal 237–250
Nocmig (nocturnal migration of birds) xiv, 281, 285
North American rarities 303
Novell Capdevila, Alba xii, 177–185, *see also* Ronayne, Seán
    ambition 193
    Barcelona FC 190
    Buddhism 221
    family 192–194, 253–259
    meeting 169–175
    Nepal 237–250
    pregnancy 367–368
    Thailand 216–236

O

open-peat areas, *see* bogs
orcas 55–56
oriental magpie-robins 217–218
O'Sullivan, Aideen 335
otters 186–189
oystercatchers 41, 63–64

P

parabolas xiii
peacocks 218
peregrine falcons 323
pied flycatchers **124**, 149, 150
pied wagtails 178
puff-throated babblers 246
pygmy shrew 52
Pyrenees 264–266, 287–293

R

rarity-finders 160–163
red-breasted flycatchers 159, 160
red-necked phalaropes 357–358
red-vented bulbuls 6, 383
resources 377, 386
rhinoceroses 248–249
ring ouzels 350-353
Robb, Magnus ix–x, 277–278, 312
Roche's Point 48–49, 62–64, 91
rock pipits 190–191
Ronan, Mrs Wanda 27
Ronayne, Seán
    ambitions 151
    autism diagnosis 266–275
    Barcelona ix-xv, 192–194, 253–259, 279–293
    bar job 129–132, 139–141, 156–157
    bird surveys job 194–203, 296–300, 324
    bird watching 258–262
    Cobh 295–296
    college 59–62, 66–67, 89–90, 94–95, 125–129
    conservation 336–337
    driving 202–203
    early childhood 1–23, 25–33
    effects of unemployment 103–105
    grandparents 1–5, 11–18, 22–23, 345, 348
    master's in ecological impact assessment 153–155, 188–190, 194
    master's in environmental impact assessment 127, 153–157
    meningitis 68–87

meningitis recovery 88–90
Nepal 237–250
parents 32–38, 141–152
Pyrenees 287–293
relationship with Alba 177–185, 191–197, 205–215, 284–287, 312–313, 362–364, 367–368
school 39–47
Seahouses 104–123
sound-recordist x–xii, 279–282, 295–296, 302–312, 334–337, 338–344, 388–403
teaching 262–264
Thailand 216–236
thesis 99–103
rose ringed parakeet 6, 385
Roynane, Conor 51
RTÉ 335
ruddy ducks 6, 384

S

sacred ibis 6, 384–385
sanderlings 116
sand martins 29
Sardinian warblers 260–262
seabirds 105, 107–112, 151
Seabirds Count: A Census of Breeding Seabirds in Britain and Ireland (2015–2021) 382
Seahouses 104–123
semipalmated plovers 306–310
Senegal 49, 327–329, 332–334, 364
Siberian blue robins **204**, 232–234, 235–236
skylarks 349
snipes 348–349
songbirds 46

sonograms 330
sound-recordings x–xii, 279–282, 295–296, 302–312, 334–337, 338–344, 388–403
sparrowhawks 7
spectrograms xi–xii, 280, 282
starlings 313–316, **326**, 338–344
Suddaby, Dave 358
swallows 9–10, 29, 149
swifts 29

T

taiga flycatchers 229–230, 234
Thailand 216–236
The Irish Times 316, 323
The Magpies: The Ecology and Behaviour of Black-billed and Yellow-billed Magpies 382
The Sound Approach 278–279
The Tommy Tiernan Show 361–365, 366
thrushes 319–320
Tiernan, Tommy 361, 372
tigers 243
tree pipits 167–169, 331
tree population 20–21
twitchers 161

U

UCC 56, 59–62, 89, 94, 125–128
University College Cork (UCC) xiv

V

Vaughan, Robert 351, 355
vismig (visible migration) 162

W

wallcreepers **276**, 282–284, 292–293
water mint 34
waxwings 52–54
whimbrels 280
Whitaker, Ross 335
white-bellied sea eagles 236
whitethroats **24**, 49, 327–334
Wild Silence 301
willow warblers 50–51
Woodburn, Gary 118–121
woodchat shrikes 165–167
woodland 318–320
woodpeckers 322–323
World Wildlife Fund 243
Wroza, Stanislas 312

X

xeno-canto 217, 296, 307, 311, 332, 386

Y

yellow-browed warblers 227–228
yellow-legged gulls xii
yellow wagtails 331

meningitis recovery 88–90
Nepal 237–250
parents 32–38, 141–152
Pyrenees 287–293
relationship with Alba 177–185, 191–197, 205–215, 284–287, 312–313, 362–364, 367–368
school 39–47
Seahouses 104–123
sound-recordist x–xii, 279–282, 295–296, 302–312, 334–337, 338–344, 388–403
teaching 262–264
Thailand 216–236
thesis 99–103
rose-ringed parakeet 6, 385
Roynane, Conor 51
RTÉ 335
ruddy ducks 6, 384

S

sacred ibis 6, 384–385
sanderlings 116
sand martins 29
Sardinian warblers 260–262
seabirds 105, 107–112, 151
Seabirds Count: A Census of Breeding Seabirds in Britain and Ireland (2015–2021) 382
Seahouses 104–123
semipalmated plovers 306–310
Senegal 49, 327–329, 332–334, 364
Siberian blue robins **204**, 232–234, 235–236
skylarks 349
snipes 348–349
songbirds 46

sonograms 330
sound-recordings x–xii, 279–282, 295–296, 302–312, 334–337, 338–344, 388–403
sparrowhawks 7
spectrograms xi–xii, 280, 282
starlings 313–316, **326**, 338–344
Suddaby, Dave 358
swallows 9–10, 29, 149
swifts 29

T

taiga flycatchers 229–230, 234
Thailand 216–236
The Irish Times 316, 323
The Magpies: The Ecology and Behaviour of Black-billed and Yellow-billed Magpies 382
The Sound Approach 278–279
The Tommy Tiernan Show 361–365, 366
thrushes 319–320
Tiernan, Tommy 361, 372
tigers 243
tree pipits 167–169, 331
tree population 20–21
twitchers 161

U

UCC 56, 59–62, 89, 94, 125–128
University College Cork (UCC) xiv

V

Vaughan, Robert 351, 355
vismig (visible migration) 162

W

wallcreepers **276**, 282–284, 292–293
water mint 34
waxwings 52–54
whimbrels 280
Whitaker, Ross 335
white-bellied sea eagles 236
whitethroats **24**, 49, 327–334
Wild Silence 301
willow warblers 50–51
Woodburn, Gary 118–121
woodchat shrikes 165–167
woodland 318–320
woodpeckers 322–323
World Wildlife Fund 243
Wroza, Stanislas 312

X

xeno-canto 217, 296, 307, 311, 332, 386

Y

yellow-browed warblers 227–228
yellow-legged gulls xii
yellow wagtails 331